THE STORY OF
MAYO

YO

eehan

Mayo County Library

First published in 2003 by Mayo County Council
Aras an Chontae, Castlebar, Co. Mayo

A CIP catalogue record for this book is available from the British Library.

ISBN 0 95196 244 2

Design by Sally O'Leary
Index by Carole Devaney
Printed and bound by Cashin Print, Castlebar, Co. Mayo

Contents

Foreword

Is mór an onóir domsa, mar Chathaoirleach Chomhairle Chontae Mhaigh Eo, an réamhrá a scríobh don leabhar iontach seo a léirionn gnéithe éagsula de Chontae Mhaigh Eo. Tá an t-ádh orainn go bhfuil daoine inár measc a d'oibrigh go dúthrachtach chun an leabhar seo a chur i gcló.

As Cathaoirleach of Mayo County Council, it is a great pleasure for me to introduce this outstanding publication, *The Story of Mayo*, which celebrates Mayo in all its aspects – its landscape, its archaeology, its history and its people. The book is a beautifully presented, comprehensive record of daily life in Mayo from earliest times to the present. In its pages, the unique character of the people of Mayo is revealed through their work on and off the land, their cultural and artistic expression, their educational and sporting achievements, their spiritual endeavours and their political struggles. The book presents gems of new information, with stunning visual records of life in Mayo, in a fresh and accessible way. Whether it is the exploits of Seán Lavan and Martin Sheridan in the sporting arena or of Granuaile and Mary Robinson in their respective political spheres, the achievements of Mayo's men and women are celebrated in this book. Through its pages, the essence of Mayo is unveiled and the debt owed to past generations is recalled. It reminds us of our struggles, our heartbreaks and our successes, as well as the spirit that has brought us to the third millennium. Today, this spirit is being channeled into creating a county that is thriving economically and culturally while also preserving the best of our past.

The maritime county of Mayo is Ireland's third largest county. It is a place of spectacular beauty, boasting a breathtaking Atlantic coastline, rivers and lakes, mountain ranges and unique preserved boglands. The islands off Mayo are numerous, rich in archaeological remains and support a great diversity of wildlife. Mayo is today home to over 117,000 people and is a thriving centre of economic and cultural activity. It is also an historic homeland to descendants of many Mayo emigrants and we are proud to remember them among our sons and daughters.

This innovative project was enthusiastically managed by Austin Vaughan, County Librarian. The staff of the County Library Service undertook the mammoth task of compiling the publication, using the rich resources of the library. Rosa Meehan, the author, expertly developed the concept and researched and compiled both the text and illustrations, resulting in this superb production. We dedicate the book to all the people of Mayo, at home and abroad, and to our predecessors who helped to make us the people we are today. It is a wonderful resource, which inspires us to remember and be proud of our past, to learn more about who we are, appreciate our unique heritage and give us confidence to forge a bright future in Mayo.

In the words of the great Charlestown author, John Healy, 'and so, to the men and women who produced us, the living and the dead, the mentioned and the unmentioned, we acknowledge the indebtedness. It, too, is mighty for they were in their day, a mighty people . . .'

It is my sincere hope that every household in Mayo will own, and derive great enjoyment from, a copy of this publication. Tá súil agam go mbeidh cóip den leabhar faisnéiseach seo i ngach teaghlach ar eagla go ndéanfaimid dearmad ar oidhreacht uaibhreach ár gContae dúchais. Maigh Eo Abú!

Frank Chambers
Cathaoirleach, Mayo County Council

Introduction

Ba mhaith liom mar bhainisteoir Chontae Mhaigh Eo fáilte a chur
roimh an leabhar breá seo. Is fíor-tráthúil an foilseachán é agus
muid ag tús na mílaoise, am an-oiriúnach dúinn chun breathnú
siar ar gach gné de stair an chontae ó thús. Is saothar mór é tabhairt faoi
leabhar den chineál seo a scríobh agus is léir dom gur éirigh go hiontach
le Rosa Meehan san obair sin.

As we prepared to celebrate the start of the third millennium, there
was much reflection on the passing of time. Mayo County Council
considered how best to commemorate this most significant of milestones.
Michael Mullen, the distinguished Mayo author, must be credited with
first proposing the idea of 'the great book of Mayo'. The idea took hold
and it was decided to commission a publication that would provide an
innovative and imaginative chronicle of Mayo's history and heritage. The
objective of the project was to narrate the 'story' of Mayo: the influences
and events that have shaped our environment and our history, and the
people who have formed our opinions by their actions and ideas. The
result is *The Story of Mayo*.

The book is organised into eleven chapters, all of which can be read
independently. Collectively, the book brings to life the pivotal moments
in our county's history – moments of triumph and failure, of hope and
despair, of joy and sorrow. It provides insights into all aspects of life in
Mayo – landscape, culture and heritage; social, political and economic
development; educational, musical and sporting achievements; and
forms of religious expression. *The Story of Mayo* is not a seamless
narrative, but there is a continuity of themes that becomes clear
throughout the book – those of survival, adaptation, toil, creativity and
hope. The people of Mayo reacted to challenges in a variety of ways,
adopting or rejecting change, borrowing new ideas and applying them to
their own needs while affirming and shaping their own unique identity.

The text of the book is wonderfully enhanced by the inclusion of
hundreds of carefully selected images, which provide us with a greater
appreciation and understanding of Mayo past and present. The historic
images, selected from the resources of Mayo County Library and from
national photographic collections, provide an insight not only into the

subject matter they depict, but the interests of the photographers and those who commissioned them in the late 19th and early 20th centuries. In a similar vein, the inclusion of visual records of our local monuments, public sculptures and more ancient churches, castles, monasteries, trade and administrative buildings not only collectively reveals our architectural heritage but also the skills, aspirations and values of the people who designed and built them. These images are now recorded for posterity, as well as being made available to a wide audience through this book.

The narrative begins by introducing the evolution of the physical place we call Mayo and the elements that suggest its unique character. The earth was already very old when 5,000 years ago the first of Mayo's farmers began to cultivate the land at Céide Fields on Mayo's north coast. Much later, in the 5th century AD, St. Patrick came to Mayo and found a people with an inherent mystical tradition, which adapted to Christian spiritual expression. The Anglo-Normans arrived in the 13th century, beginning the era of military and political conquests of Mayo that was to continue through the Tudor period, the dark days of Cromwell and the Penal Laws of the 18th century. The agricultural landscape, shaped during the period of landlordism and the Ascendancy, was significantly changed after the Great Famine of the mid-19th century – a cataclysmic moment in Irish social history. The Famine had a particularly devastating effect on the people of Mayo – a fact acknowledged by the siting of the National Famine Monument on the shores of Clew Bay at Murrisk.

After the Famine, many families in Mayo survived on remittances faithfully sent home by far-flung economic migrants and the great figure of Mayo-born Michael Davitt emerged. Davitt, a vociferous supporter of democratic change, was a founder of the Land League movement that brought about the dismantlement of the landlord system. In the 20th century, Mayo County Council made an outstanding contribution to advancing the social, economic and cultural life of the county through the provision of a comprehensive health system, water and sewage, the building of houses and roads, the creation of a comprehensive library service and the facilitation of vocational education. Today, the people of Mayo have achieved a greater measure of prosperity: we are better housed, we have better education and work opportunities, and our communities work in partnership towards enhancing the quality of life in the county.

This book draws upon the many and varied sources that contain Mayo's history – visual, manuscript and printed. Indeed, most of these sources are available in the extensive Local History collection in the Central Library in Castlebar. The results of the scholarship of the great Mayo historians, past and present, is held there. The list includes H.T. Knox, Dean D'Alton, J.F. Quinn, Áine Ní Cheannain, Bernard O'Hara, Nollaig O'Muraile and Gerard Moran. We also acknowledge the work of dedicated local archaeologists and historians, as well as the commitment and enthusiasm of local museums and community organisations that commemorate local events and customs, confirming the value we place on our heritage. It is hoped that this book, while illuminating the past, will also be a catalyst for further research and interpretation of our multi-faceted history.

The world of the Céide Fields is radically different from our own. The Great Famine and its aftermath is searingly painful to our modern sensibilities. Yet those times influence who we are today. This book is not an exercise in nostalgia for the mythical 'long-ago'. Rather, it provides an appreciation of the process of continuity, adaptation and change. In reading it, we acquire an understanding of the unique character of the county and the possibilities for its future. To know that our people survived and that their work and struggles, courage and successes laid the foundation for our own sense of identity is an inspiring thought. In this new millennium, we will face our own struggles and there will be new successes and new chapters of Mayo history to be recorded.

In his drama *The Playboy of the Western World*, J.M. Synge's character Pegeen Mike says at the end of the play, 'Well, the heart's a wonder: and I'm thinking there won't be our like in Mayo, for gallant lovers, from this hour to-day'. We can recognise and sympathise with her feelings of pride, but we can also believe that Mayo and its people, its gallant lovers and its actors on the world stage will continue to achieve and survive in this magnificent county.

Comhghairdeachas le Rosa Meehan agus le gach duine a raibh baint aige leis an bhfoilseachán seo agus táim cinnte go mbeidh se léite ag na milte a bhfuil ceangal acu le Chontae Mhaigh Eo, anseo agus ar fud an domhain.

Des Mahon
County Manager, Mayo County Council

Acknowledgements

This book would not have been possible without the contributions of many people. Mayo County Council wishes to place on record its thanks to all who assisted in the book's production, whether by providing information, sourcing records, checking dates or locating old photographs and documents. Our apologies to any person who has been inadvertently omitted.

A special debt is due to all the staff of Mayo County Library whose research and support made this publication a reality. In particular, we wish to thank Ivor Hamrock for sharing his vast knowledge of Mayo history sources. Thanks also to Richard Hickey and Tom Murtagh who generously shared their expertise, to Mary Gannon for administering all the financial aspects of the project, to Noreen Hoban and Pat Ryan who provided much professional and personal support, and to Deirdre Lavelle for her superb administrative skills. A special thanks is due to Claire Ryan for sharing her knowledge of sport in the county and to Mary Murphy and Marquerite Foy for reading the manuscript and making useful suggestions. Thanks also to Christy Lawless for sharing his in-depth knowledge of Turlough, to Eleanor O'Toole for her expertise in equestrian sports, to Breege Lavelle for her research on the Belmullet area and to Barbara Varley for her research on all aspects of Ballina's history. Thanks also to students Sandra Cunningham and Lisa Moore for their vital input in the summers of 2000 and 2001 respectively.

We also extend our gratitude to historians Bernard O'Hara, Professor Gearoid O'Tuathaigh and Dr. Kevin Whelan, who read the manuscript at various stages and contributed valuable suggestions that helped to make the book more comprehensive.

We are also indebted to all those members of the public who generously gave of their time and whose valuable inputs have contributed greatly to the project: Mark Adams, Simon Berrow, Gerry Bracken, Mark Brennock, Joe Byrne, Angela Campbell, James Campbell, Deirdre Canavan, John D. Clark, Aiden Clarke, John Coll, Michael Commins, Fr. Patrick Conlan, Gerry Cribbin, Eamon De Burca, Sr. Teresa Delaney, Clodagh Doyle, Lorna Elms, Eugene Field, Noel Filan, Fergus Gillespie, Joe Gilmartin, Noreen Hennigan, Cathal Henry, Robert Heslip,

Noreen Holland, Bronach Joyce, Carmel Joyce, Tom Kelly, Michael Kenny, Michael Livings, Margaret MacCurtain, Seamas Mac Philib, Fiachra Magowan, Hugh Mannion, Sylvia Meehan, Padraig McDermott, Patria McWalter, Amy Pierce Miller, Grace Mulqueen, Johnny Mulvey, Micheal Murphy, Micheal Nallen, John O'Connor, OSA, Seán Ó hÉalaí, Cormac O'Malley, Noel O'Neill, Terry Reilly, Mike Robinson, John Ruane, Neil Sheridan, Betty Solan, Declan Turnbull, Kitty Turnbull, Gerry Walsh, Seán Walsh and Alex Ward.

Thanks are also due to all who supplied photographs, including the staff of Bord Fáilte, Anthony Roche of Dúchas, Davison and Associates (Fr. Browne Collection), Anthony Leonard (copyright holder of J.J. Leonard's photographs), Mayo Naturally and Gary Wynne (copyright holder of the Wynne Photographic Collection). To Mayo's fine professional photographers who contributed to the publication, we are indebted – Angela Campbell, Tom Campbell, Frank Dolan, Tommy Eibrand, Patrica Forde, Liam Lyons and Eamon O'Boyle. We are grateful also to the many other individuals and organisations that supplied photographs and gave permission for their reproduction. In particular, we wish to thank the various national cultural institutions who supplied photographic prints, information and assistance with copyright: the Ulster Museum, the Manuscript Department of Trinity College Dublin, the Library of the Royal Irish Academy and the Ordnance Survey Office, Dublin. Indeed, we extend our appreciation to all those, past and present, who have helped ensure an historical record of the lives of the people of Mayo.

Finally, our gratitude is due to Sally O'Leary, whose patient hard work is evident in the inspiring design of the book, to Carole Devaney for her editing and indexing and to Cashin Print of Castlebar, for their efficiency and flexibility.

Dr. Johnson once remarked that a person 'will turn over half a library to make one book'. Mayo County Library's collection has been turned over to produce this remarkable book. It is comprised of hundreds of carefully selected photographs, paintings, maps and letters from our collection, all linked by a narrative that takes the reader on a journey through the history of our county from earliest times to the new millennium. The milestones of Mayo history are brought to life in a stunning collection of images that reveal the magnificence of the county whose beauty and spirit move all who set foot in it. Rosa Meehan with the staff of Mayo County Library have produced a visual and historical treasury that is as fascinating and varied as the county it portrays.

Austin Vaughan
County Librarian

Chapter 1

A People and a Place

A landscape of immense beauty, a simple rural lifestyle, a rich culture lost to most of Ireland – Mayo conjures up a vast array of images and impressions. But among those born and bred there, Mayo evokes a fierce attachment, loyalty and pride. For the many thousands of emigrants who left Mayo, the county remains 'home'. For those who live in Co. Mayo, it is a dynamic county with burgeoning possibilities in a time of change, while remaining a place of enduring beauty imprinted with the marks of many generations.

Irish counties have become synonymous with expressions such as 'the Banner county' or 'The Kingdom', or with particular songs such as 'Boolavogue'. The somewhat resigned phrase 'Mayo, God help us' has become associated with the county. Its origins remain obscure. When asked where they came from, it was the answer given by the many generations of seasonal workers travelling to the east of the country or to England and seems to predate the Great Famine of 1846-50. John McCormack, the celebrated Irish tenor, offered one interpretation when he wrote, 'I now understand the expression "Mayo, God help us". It must mean "God help us to appreciate the beauties Thou hast laid before our eyes".'

With a land area of 5,398 sq km (2,084 sq ml), the maritime county of Mayo is situated on the western seaboard of Ireland. It is the island's third largest county, making up about 8% of the landmass and containing some 558,605 hectares (1,380,369 acres). The Atlantic Ocean borders the north and west of the county, while it is land-locked to the east by the counties of Sligo and Roscommon, and Galway to the south.

The making of a territory

Long before the geographical area became unified under the name of Co. Mayo, various smaller territorial divisions were recognised for different religious or political purposes. Gaelic chieftains divided the country into *tuatha*, delineating their local kingdoms. Over these was the 'Overking', who ruled over several petty kingdoms. Finally, the 'King over

Fáilte go Chontae Mhaigh Eo

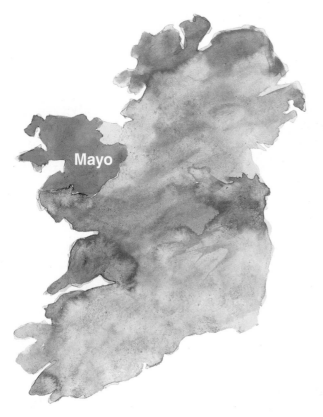

Mayo

Overkings' reigned over the Province, made up of all the kingdoms in the area. Townlands were the smallest administrative divisions and became standardised from the 17th century.

The spread of Christianity, from the 5th century onwards, saw many monasteries established throughout Ireland. These religious houses became spheres of political and economic influence and power. They gave way to medieval parishes, which were later co-opted as Civil parishes and, after the Reformation, as Church of Ireland parishes. Subsequently, new Roman Catholic parishes were established.

The Anglo-Norman invasion of the 12th century saw the introduction of the baronial system into Connaught as part of the attempt to conquer, administer and tax the province. Initially, there were ten baronies in the area that became Co. Mayo – Burrishule, Carra, Clanmorris, Costello, Erris, Gallen, Kilmaine, Murrisk, Tirawley and Ross (though the latter was soon removed). Tirawley was the largest barony, with 1,316 sq km (508 sq ml). With the reorganisation of local government in 1898, baronies lost their administrative importance and their individual identities, with the notable exception of the Barony of Erris which retains to this day a sense of place.

Mayo is one of five counties carved out of the province of Connaught. The ancient land of Connaught traces its origins back to the literary texts of the 2nd century, taking its name from a mythical ancestor of Niall of the Nine Hostages called Conn Céadchathach (Conn of the Hundred Battles). The area known as Co. Mayo was born as an administrative entity in the troublesome 16th century when the Gaelic-held lands in Connaught came under the rule of the English Crown by legalistic and violent means. The county was named after the Abbey founded by St. Colman in the 7th century known as Maigh Eo, which means 'plain of the yew tree'. Co. Mayo, established for political purposes, has long since become a major element of identity for a people and a place.

The mapping of Mayo in the 16th century reinforced the sense of the county as an entity. Among the earliest maps was the one drawn up for John Browne of the Neale in 1585. Gerard Mercator's large wall map of the British Isles, published in 1564, was among the first to include topographical details. This map and the work of other cartographers were synthesized in the maps of John Speed, published in Elizabethan times. It was not until the mid-17th century that maps were officially commissioned in preparation for the projected plantation of Connaught. William Petty was responsible for the Down Survey of Ireland, which showed the lands

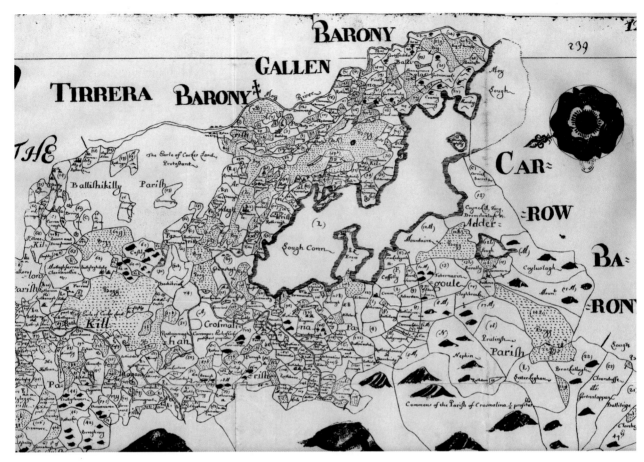

William Petty's map of the Barony of Tirawley, prepared in 1657 as part of the Down Survey of Ireland

throughout the country forfeited during the Cromwellian period. Co. Mayo, with the exception of the Barony of Tirawley, was excluded from the survey because suitable maps had already been prepared during the Strafford Inquisition, completed in 1635. In 1683, Petty's map of the Barony of Tirawley was published in his book *Hibernia Delineatio*. William Bald's *Maritime County of Mayo*, prepared under the auspices of the Grand Jury, was commenced in 1809 and completed in 1817. The first Ordnance Survey maps were published in 1838, providing intimate details of every county on the scale of 6 inches to the mile.

The land surveys of the 17th century utilised Mayo as an administrative division. The Grand Jury system was the earliest form of local government, replaced in 1898 by the County Council system, which also used the county divisions for administrative purposes. This county identity, together with various social and cultural activities, such as the organisation of sporting events and publication of regional newspapers, has contributed to the creation of Mayo as a physical and mental construct.

Symbols reflecting particular aspects of the county's heritage are incorporated in the official arms of Mayo County Council, granted by the Chief Herald of Ireland in March 1981. The arms were based on a heraldic device originally designed in 1960 by Michael J. Egan for the Mayo Gaelic

Official arms of Mayo County Council

A group of men at Muingerena, Mullet Peninsula, photographed by Charles Browne in 1885

The Gentleman of Ireland   *The Gentlewoman of Ireland*

The Civill Irish Woman   *The Civill Irish man*

The Wilde Irish man   *The Wilde Irish Woman*

'Civil and Wild Irish Men', woodcut by John Speed, published in 1600

Athletic Association Board.

The crest is a single slipped rose, with a stalk, on a green mount representing the Virgin Mary. The coat of arms has a shield with a bordure of gold. The nine green yew trees around the edge of the shield represent the nine baronies of the county (recalling that Mayo gets its name from the Gaelic *Maigh Eo* or 'plain of the yew tree'). The Patriarchal cross in the centre of the shield represents the Diocese of Tuam and the three Passion crosses below, the dioceses of Killala, Achonry and Galway-Kilmacduagh-Kilfenora. The large vessel on the waves recalls the proud maritime tradition of the county, with special reference to the sea-going O'Malley family. The arms are completed with the motto *Dia is Muire linn* (God and Mary be with us).

People and language

Mayo is one of the least populated areas of Ireland, with a density of 20 people per square kilometre. The population has traditionally been concentrated in the more fertile central region, while large areas, such as Erris, have remained sparsely inhabited. In common with the rest of the country, the population of Mayo has shown a general trend towards urban living, with 12% of the population living in towns of more than 5,000 people, according to the 1996 Census.

The archaeological excavations at the Céide Fields in north Mayo give us a remarkable insight into Mayo's earliest known people and establish the fact that an organised settled community first lived there some 6,000 years ago, in the Neolithic Period.

Although official population censi were not taken until the early 19th century, various estimates have been made over the centuries. Pre-Famine population growth in the west of Ireland accelerated in the second half of the 18th century and first half of the 19th. This population expansion necessitated massive reclamation and expansion into previously unsettled, less fertile marginal lands. The intense subdivision of land was made possible by the potato's ability to grow in nutrient-poor wet soils. A relatively small amount of land could provide enough potatoes to supply the nutritional needs of a growing family. The decline of the economy pushed people to become increasingly dependent on the potato alone, leading to the calamitous demise of the population as a result of the failure of the potato crop during the years of the Great Famine in 1846-50. The population of Co. Mayo fell by some 30% over the period 1841-51 – from 388,887 to 274,499 – due to death or emigration, with endemic emigration becoming one of the long-term legacies of the Famine.

From 1841 until 1971, Co. Mayo experienced a continuous decline in population. Then, in the period 1971-81, the first increase was recorded, bringing the population from 109,525 to 114,766. By 1986, only a minor increase was registered (to 115,184), followed by a drop to 110,713 in 1991 and a slight increase to 111,524 in 1996. Indications are that the population

Harvesting on the shores of Clew Bay

is on the rise again, reaching approximately 120,000 at the beginning of the 21st century.

Gaelic, the first official language of Ireland, evolved from a form of Celtic, the language of the Celts who came to Ireland between the end of the second millennium and 4th century BC. Over the centuries, the native Gaelic language was undermined by the various conquests and plantations, which resulted in the elimination of the Irish-speaking ruling classes and their replacement by the English-speaking Ascendancy. The Irish language became associated with poverty from the time of the Great Famine and as emigration continued, the number of Irish speakers began to decline. At the end of the 19th century, there was concern for the survival of the language. The establishment of Conradh na Gaeilge, the Gaelic League, in 1893 helped to revive the Irish language and Gaelic culture. Today, Irish remains the first, or everyday, language in a number of officially designated Gaeltacht areas throughout the country, including three regions in Mayo, each geographically separated from each other – Tuar Mhic Éadaigh (Tourmakeady) in the south of the county, Acaill (Achill) in the west and Iorras (Erris) in the north-west.

Tourmakeady Gaeltacht is located between Lough Mask and the Partry Mountains and was once part of the North Connemara – Co. Galway Gaeltacht until the county boundaries were altered in 1898. Up until the 19th century, the area was known by its Irish name of Sliabh Phártraí. When Thomas Plunkett, Archbishop of Tuam, replaced the Murrays as local landlord, he renamed it 'Tourmakeady' but despite his efforts to eradicate the Irish language, the area remained an Irish-speaking one. In 1905, Conradh na Gaeilge established the Irish college Coláiste Chonnacht in the area. More than twenty years later, one of the national Preparatory Teacher-Training Schools was also opened in Tourmakeady as a secondary school to train those likely to pursue a teaching career through the medium of Irish. Tourmakeady remained a strong Gaeltacht area right up to the mid-1950s, when Dr. Seán de Búrca wrote his book *The Irish of Tourmakeady*.

Achill Gaeltacht is comprised of the eastern part of the island and the Curraun Peninsula. Linguistic scholars claim that it is possible to detect the influence of Donegal Irish in the Irish of Achill. This influence, they suggest, dates to the time of Cromwell when the Irish speakers were expelled from Ulster and transplanted to Co. Mayo. The third and geographically largest Gaeltacht area in Mayo is in the Barony of Erris, though it is a long time since the whole barony was an Irish-speaking area. There are pockets of Irish-speaking communities throughout the area, such as Eachléim/Fál Mór, Gaoth Sáile/Dú Thuama and Dún Chaocháin. According to scholars, the Irish spoken here is closer to classical Irish than the Irish of Achill.

Gaeltachtaí Mhaigh Eo

Ceaptar gur tháing an Ghaeilge – céadteanga oifigiúil na hÉireann – ó theanga na gCeilteach, a tháinig go hÉirinn idir deireadh an dara mílaoise agus an cheathrú céad RC. Thar na céadta bliain d'imigh úsáid na teangan i laige de bharr gabháltais agus bochtaineachta. Tar éis an Ghorta Mhóir bhí ceangal í meabhar na ndaoine idir an Ghaeilge agus bochtaineacht. Le fás na himirce bhí an teanga ag dul i laige. Ag deireadh an 19ú céad bhí imní ann nach mhairfeadh an teanga. Chuidigh bunú Chonradh na Gaeilge, 1893, le hathbheochaint na Gaeilge agus an cultúr Gaelach.

Tá trí cheantar oifigiúla Gaeltachta ar leith i gCo. Mhaigh Eo: Tuar Mhic Éadaigh, Acaill agus Iorras. Tá Gaeltacht Thuar Mhic Éadaigh suite idir Loch Measca agus Sléibhte Phartraí agus roimh athrú na dteorainneacha sa bhliain 1898, ba chuid de Ghaeltacht Chonamara

Lighthouse on Achill Beg Island

Thuaidh i gCo. na Gaillimhe í. Go dtí an 19ú céad, b'é ainm Gaelach an limistéir sin ná Sliabh Phartraí. Nuair a chuir Ardeaspag Thuama, Tomás Pluincéad, deireadh le réim Mhuintir Mhuirithe, na Tiarnaí Talún áitiúla, thug sé ainm eile ar an gceantar: Tuar Mhic Éadaigh. Cé go ndearna sé a dhicheall cosc a chur ar labhairt na Gaeilge san áit, d'fhan an Ghaeilge beo. Sa bhliain 1905 bhunaigh Conradh na Gaeilge Coláiste Chonnachta sa limistéar sin. Fiche bliain ina dhiaidh sin osclaíodh scoil ghaelach eile — Coláiste Ullmhucháin d'oiliúint oidí scoile. Fuair na daltaí sa scoil seo ullmhuchán le go mbeidís ábalta múineadh trí Ghaeilge. Bhí Tuar Mhic Éadaigh ina ghaeltacht láidir suas go dtí lár na gcaogadaí nuair a scríobh an Dr. Seán de Búrca a leabhar *The Irish of Tourmakeady*.

Tá an Ghaeltacht in Acaill suite in oirthear an oileáin agus i leithinis an Chorráin. De réir scolairí teangeolaíochta, is féidir tionchar Ghaeilge Dhún na nGall a bhraith ar Ghaeilge Acla. Deirtear gur tharla sin, in aimsir Chromaill, nuair a ruaigeadh Gaeilgeoirí ó Chúige Uladh agus gur chuireadar fúthu in gCo. Mhaigh Eo. Freisin, bhíodh muintir Acla agus muintir Thír Chonaill ag obair le chéile ag piocadh fataí in Albain i dtús

*View of Aghagower village with
Croagh Patrick in the background*

an 19ú céad agus meastar go raibh tionchar ag an dá chanúint ar a chéile. Is í mBarúntacht Iorrais an tríú Gaeltacht agus an ceann is fairsinge cé gur fada an lá ó bhí an bharúntacht ar fad ina cheantar Gaeltachta. Tá pócaí láidre Gaeltachta sna ceantair seo: Eachléim/Fál Mór, Gaoth Sáile/Dú Thuama agus Dú Chaocháin. De reir scoláirí tá an Ghaeilge a labhraítear anseo níos clasaicí ná Gaeilge Acla.

The landscape revealed

The landscape of Mayo lies on a varied geological foundation, which significantly influences the vegetation, fauna and habitation patterns throughout the county. The oldest rocks in Ireland are found in Mayo, notably in the mountains along the Atlantic coast that are made up of igneous and metamorphic rocks. At Annagh Head on the Mullet Peninsula, there are resistant gneisses, over 200 million years old. The low-lying limestone plains of the Midlands extend into east Mayo and are overhung to the north by the mostly granite Slieve Gamph Range or Ox Mountains. The purple gemstones called amethysts were discovered during road-building in Achill Island during the mid-1960s and are still found today at the western tip of the island.

Following the last Ice Age, over 10,000 years ago, the landscape was moulded by the retreating ice into a mixed and varied terrain. High mountain peaks are found to the west and south of the county and two ancient mountain ranges divide at Clew Bay. A central corridor of fertile plains extends from Killala in north Mayo to the area east of Lough Mask in southern Mayo, crossed by a belt of rolling drumlins stretching westwards to Clew Bay. On reaching the sea, the sunken drumlins form a myriad of tiny islands in the bay. River valleys and lake basins are strewn over the landscape and the rugged indented Atlantic coastline, with its combination of precipitous cliffs and sandy beaches, fringes the north and west of the county, contributing to the natural beauty of the land.

Greatly influenced by the weather systems of the Atlantic Ocean, Mayo has been shaped continuously by weathering and erosion, producing a dramatic landscape. Since the arrival of the Neolithic farmers some 6,000 years ago, the cultural landscape has also been shaped continually by thousands of years of human activity. Climatic and human actions, including forest clearance, have combined to create extensive tracts of peatland in the north-west of the county.

The physical and cultural landscape of Co. Mayo has been recorded over the centuries by specialists in a variety of disciplines, including antiquarians, archaeologists, agriculturalists, naturalists, artists and writers. The combination of these studies provides glimpses of Mayo's past. Drawing on their own experiences, these individuals have interpreted different aspects of the same place. For example, John Luke's (1906-75) stylised view of Achill's Slievemore Mountain contrasts with the paintings of the same area by Paul Henry (1876-1958), an influential figure in the development of Irish landscape painting. Luke's painting was commissioned by the poet John Hewitt (1907-87), who gave it the title 'The Road to the West'.

Many painters have given us visual interpretations of the Mayo landscape. Early in his career, the artist James Arthur O'Connor (1792-1841) undertook a series of sixteen paintings of Westport House and environs, along with a series of four topographical views of Ballinrobe House. While living in Mayo in the early 20th century, Paul Henry produced many paintings that became instantly recognisable images

John Luke's painting 'The Road to the West', depicting Achill's Slievemore Mountain

Aerial view of Inishturk Island in 1967, showing lazy beds and ancient field systems

of the Mayo landscape. Other well-known artists, notably Jack B. Yeats (1871-1957), John Luke (1906-75), Louis Le Brocquy (1916-), Melanie Jellett (1897-1944) and Camille Souter (1929-), have depicted aspects of Mayo in their paintings.

Arthur Young (1741-1820), Alexis de Tocqueville (1805-59), Mr. and Mrs. Hall, William Hamilton Maxwell (1792-1850), William Makepeace Thackeray (1811-63), John Millington Synge (1871-1909), Heinrich Böll (1917-85) and Mayo-born George Moore (1852-1933) – all these writers have presented us with insights into Mayo's cultural and physical landscape. Other revealing pre-20th century records include the work of government officials such as Patrick Knight, a civil engineer in the early 19th century, and William L. Micks, First Secretary of the Congested Districts Board, established in 1891.

The Ordnance Survey Letters of Gaelic scholar John O'Donovan provide detailed commentaries on the histories of parishes and origins of place names, as well as original drawings of many antiquities throughout Co. Mayo. In 1824, the British Government decided to initiate a comprehensive series of 6-inch maps of Ireland. The project was supervised by Colonel Thomas Colby for the British Board of Ordnance, a military body responsible for the mapping. He

William Bald's map of Clare Island, published in 1830 as part of 'The Map of the Maritime County of Mayo'

employed Irish scholars, including O'Donovan, in the Topographical Department of the project to ensure the accurate recording of place names. These scholars examined written records, ancient and modern, and also undertook extensive fieldwork, generating a wealth of information on the country's local history, tradition, topography and archaeology. More than a hundred years later, in 1935, the Irish Folklore Commission was established and employed full-time folklore collectors to record the customs and traditions of Mayo.

The growth of popular interest in the natural sciences and archaeology during the Victorian period saw the formation of a huge variety of amateur Irish field clubs, historical studies and natural history groups. Amateur archaeologists continue to do much to record and interpret Mayo's rich archaeological remains. Thomas Westropp (1860-1922), Françoise Henry (1905-82) and Ruardhi de Valera (1916-78) were among the early professional archaeologists to undertake a systematic study of Mayo's past. Their work has been augmented by recent archaeologists, notably Peter Harbison, Séamus Caulfield, Christiaan Corlett, Gerry Walsh, Gretta Byrne and Leo Morahan.

Among the most significant photographers of the county were Castlebar-based Thomas Wynne (1838-93), Belfast photographer Robert Welch (1859-1936), employed by the Congested Districts Board, and the William Laurence Studio Photographers. These men provide wonderful photographic insights into Mayo at the turn of the

19th century. The Cambridge University Aerial Photographic Collection includes many fine photographs of Mayo from the 1960s and is an important means of studying the hidden archaeology and changing history of the landscape. More recently, award-winning Mayo photographers have vividly captured scenes of life in Mayo and some of their work is reproduced in this publication.

Among the most accessible work on Mayo's landscape is that of Robert Lloyd Praeger (1865-1953), the prolific environmentalist from Co. Down who is remembered for his books about the Irish countryside, including *The Way that I went* and *A Tourist's Flora of the West of Ireland*. Along with over a hundred field workers, Praeger collected material between 1909 and 1911 in what became known as the Clare Island Survey, a multidisciplinary action research project that did much to reveal the archaeology, flora and fauna of the island. The Royal Irish Academy published the findings of the survey in a series of 67 reports. A second Clare Ireland Survey commenced in 1991. The publications and documentary films of naturalists like David Cabot, Michael and Eithne Viney, and Éamon de Buitléar have brought new knowledge and interpretations of Mayo's natural history to a wide audience in recent years.

Illustration by Wendy Walsh of white clover, small cudweed, shoreweed and autumn hawkbit, growing on the shore of Lough Mask (from 'Flowers of Mayo')

Flora and fauna

Mayo boasts a diversity of wildlife habitats – coastal, mountains, lakes, woodland, fens, peatland, wetlands and pasture. Many of these habitats remain undisturbed because of their remote locations. They host a plethora of flora, some rare. The aquatic pale butterwort, great sundew and pipewort are noteworthy. Mayo's mountain slopes and coastal cliffs are home to St. Patrick's cabbage and the related kidney saxifrage, both among the select group of plants native to Ireland. Alpines, such as moss campion, starry saxifrage and purple saxifrage, have made their home in Mayo and live alongside Mediterranean plants, such as the green-winged orchid and autumn ladies' tresses.

Patrick Browne (1720-90) of Woodstock, Co. Mayo, was a pioneer botanist who was friendly with the renowned Carl Linnaeus of Sweden (who created the Linnean system of binominal classification for plants and animals). Browne was the author of a record of botanical findings, principally from Co. Mayo, published by Éamon de Burca in 1996 as *Flowers of Mayo*, with colour illustrations by artist Wendy Walsh.

Parts of Mayo, such as Erris and Achill Island, are devoid of tree cover today, but were once densely forested. This is known because petrified tree stumps have been found buried a few metres below the surface of peatbogs, suggesting that prior to the development of the bog, these areas were wooded. J.C. Curwen recorded that in Mayo in 1818, 'In passing through the bogs, we have frequently seen timber extracted from them. We had an opportunity of examining an oak about six feet in diameter and thirty in length, perfectly sound, it had been a fine tree

Illustration by Wendy Walsh of purple loosestrife at All Souls Church (c. 1747) in Crossboyne (from 'Flowers of Mayo')

and had recently been drawn from the bog'.

The English travel writer Arthur Young (1741-1820), in his *Tour in Ireland* during 1776-78, noted that there were no trees in Erris and recorded the story he had heard of a young man who saw a tree for the first time when he left the Barony of Erris.

In some parts of Mayo, conditions have allowed for the regeneration of woodlands or, in some cases, the survival of primeval forest of oak, elm and pine. These native tree species were joined in the 18th and 19th century by introduced species, such as beech, ash, chestnut, spruce and sycamore, together with exotic shrubs and flowers. In the 20th century, new imported tree varieties were introduced, such as sitka spruce, mainly for commercial purposes.

The Belleek Woodland is an example of a mixed woodland originally planted for commercial purposes. It contains a variety of hardwood species, including oak, ash, sycamore, lime, whitebeam and elm, as well as many coniferous trees. Today, it is an important amenity area around Belleek Manor, along the River Moy, with local walks providing an opportunity to view the flora and fauna.

A rich variety of wildlife, both common and rare, can be found throughout the county, including badgers, deer, foxes, hares, hedgehogs, minks, pine martens, rabbits, stoats and bats of the whiskered and lesser

Illustration by Wendy Walsh of blackthorn at Castle Bourke, inhabited from the 13th to 19th centuries, now a ruin (from 'Flowers of Mayo')

Ancient tree stumps petrified in Tourmakeady Bog

Mixed woodlands surround Moore Hall, at the edge of Lough Carra

Sessile oaks at Old Head, near Louisburgh, intermingled with rowan, birch, willows and conifers, are part of the only woodland along Mayo's Atlantic coast

Lush woodlands around Belleek Manor,
on the western bank of the Moy estuary

horseshoe species. Feral goats roam the lower western slopes of the Ox Mountains, near Foxford; so celebrated are they that a sculpture of them by Doug Hack has been erected in the town. The Mullet Peninsula and the meadows around Foxford provide a refuge for the endangered corncrake. The merlin, Europe's smallest falcon, and the red grouse, once plentiful, are both found among the heather in the higher ridges of the Ox Mountains. The red-necked phalarope, a rare and endangered bird, has made Annagh Marsh, near Belmullet, its most southerly breeding point. The common European buzzard has on occasions been sighted soaring above the countryside, searching out its prey.

The poem by Antoine Ó Raifteirí (1779-1835) *Condae Mhuigh-Eo no Cill Aodáin* ('County Mayo or Killeaden', translated by Dr. Douglas Hyde) recalls in one of its verses the variety of birds once found in Mayo:

The craggy cliffs along Mayo's
Atlantic coast provide nesting sites
for many types of sea birds

Cill Aodáin

There is a cuckoo and the thrush answering each other there
The blackbird and the ceirseach hatching over against them
The goldfinch, the woodcock, and the linnet in a cage there,
The snipe leaping up, and the swan from Rome,
The eagle out of Achill and the raven out of Kesh Corran,
The falcon from Loch Erne and the lark from the bog
And if you were to be there in the morning before rise of sun,
Sure you would hear every bird of them a-singing in the grove.

Tá an chuach 's an smólach ag freagairt a chéile ann,
Tá an londubh 's an céirceach ar gur os a gcomhair
An gúld-finse, 's creabhar 's an linnet I gcage ann,
An naosgach ag leimnigh a 's an eala ón Róimh.
An t-iorlach as Acaill 's an fiach dubh ó 'n gCéis ann,
An seabhach as Loch Éirne 's an fhuiseog ó 'n mhóin,
'S dá mbeitheá ann ar maidin roimh éirighe na gréine,
Go gcloisfeá gach éan aca ag seinm san 'ngróbh'.

W.H. Maxwell's *Wild Sports of the West*, published in 1832, has proved an enduringly popular account of Mayo's wildlife. Maxwell, Canon of the Tuam Diocese, befriended the Marquis of Sligo, who gave him use of his shooting lodge in Ballycroy, Erris, in the early 19th century. From this base, Maxwell recorded his adventures with the plentiful wildlife and espoused the magnificence of Mayo for the sports enthusiast. He writes:

> To look at a map of Mayo, one would imagine that Nature had designed that country for a sportsman. The westerly part is wild and mountainous; alpine ridges of highlands interpose between the ocean and the interior, and from the bases of these hills a boundless tract of

Carrowmore Lough, Erris

Nephin, Mayo's second highest mountain, rises 806 m (2,646 ft) above an otherwise flat landscape

heath and moorland extends in every direction. To the east, the face of the country undergoes a striking change – large and extensive plains cover the surface . . . This part of Mayo is justly held in high estimation as a hunting country.

Maxwell vividly describes the wildlife he finds around him in Erris:

In the calm of the evening I hear the shrill cry of the sand-lark, and in early dawn the crowing of the cock grouse. I see the salmon fling themselves over the smooth tide as they hurry from the sea to re-ascend their native river . . . I trace from the window the outline of a range of hills, where the original red deer of Ireland are still existing.

Physical features

Mayo's mountains differ in appearance and age. From Clew Bay to Bangor in Erris, the Nephin Mountains contrast with an otherwise flat skyline. Nephin itself, an imposing peak of impervious quartzite, is the second highest mountain in Connaught (Mweelrea being the highest), rising 806 m (2,646 ft) on the west side of Lough Conn. The Slieve Gamph

The Holy Mountain of Croagh Patrick
on the shores of Clew Bay

Range or Ox Mountains, on the east side of Lough Conn, is composed of granite, with some white quartz running through it. There is a limestone area within this range, at Croaghmoyle, which is similar, though much smaller, to the famous Burren of Co. Clare.

The Nephin Beg Range extends from Lough Conn to Achill Island, where Croaghaun Mountain ends in a sheer vertical drop to the Atlantic Ocean. Also on Achill, the majestic Slievemore dominates the island, reaching a peak of 671 m (2,201 ft). Schists, gneiss and quartzite make up the mountain ranges along the Atlantic coast.

Croagh Patrick or St. Patrick's Reek, the Holy Mountain, looks down 765 m (2,510 ft) over the numerous partially drowned drumlins in Clew Bay. This mountain, of rough sparkling quartzite, resistant to climatic change, has been exposed to the feet of millions of pilgrims as they wend their way along the centuries-old path of glittering white rock that leads to the summit. This path can be seen from great distances. On clear days, the oratory on top of the Reek is visible as a tiny extension to the mountain. From its peak, a magnificent panoramic view can be seen of the Atlantic Ocean, Blacksod and Clew Bays, the Nephin Beg Range and the Sheeffry Hills, interspersed with lakes. William Makepeace Thackeray, travelling in 1842, says that Croagh Patrick was:

> The most beautiful view I ever saw in the world . . . The sun was just about to set, and the country round about and to the east was almost in twilight . . . The bay and the Reek, which sweeps down to the sea, and a hundred islands in it, were dressed in gold and purple, and crimson, with the whole cloudy west in a flame.

Mweelrea, the triple-peaked grey mountain to the north of Killary Harbour, is the highest mountain in Connaught, rising 819 m (2,688 ft).

*A steel engraving by W.H. Bartlett/
J. Cousen, c. 1841, of Delphi Fishing
Lodge on the shores of Doolough*

Made of sandstone, slate and shales, it dominates the cluster of mountains
in the region, including the Sheeffry Hills, Ben Gorm Range and Partry
Mountains. Maamtrasna is the highest point in the Partry Mountains,
which consist of Ordovician slates and shales, some 500 million years old.
Deep valleys surrounded by mountains intersect the Partry range. The
Doolough Valley is one such area and was the scene of a great tragedy in
1849 during the Famine period. The high mountains around that lake give
an almost mystical feel and the area was called 'Delphi' by the Marquis of
Sligo, who claimed the site was reminiscent of the ancient Greek oracle's
home, north-west of Athens.

Mayo's coast is wild and rugged, broken by many sandy beaches,
spectacular cliffs and large inlets, running from Killala Bay in the north to
Killary Harbour in the south-west. The coast faces north to the Arctic
Circle and west across the Atlantic Ocean. The islands off Mayo are
numerous and full of archaeological remains, as well as relatively
undisturbed plants and wildlife.

Killary Harbour forms the border between the counties of Mayo and
Galway. This superb deep-sea inlet, surrounded by steep and high valley
walls, is the best example of a fjord in Ireland. It was formed during the
last Ice Age, some two million years ago, as glaciers moved over the
Partry Mountains towards the sea, deepening and widening the existing
river valley. At the end of the Ice Age, the ice melted and sea levels rose.
The valley was flooded and the fjord (meaning 'drowned river valley')
created. The area north of Killary Harbour had the reputation of being the
richest sanctuary for shellfish, such as scallops, on the west coast.

There are spectacular sea cliffs along the north Mayo coastline, from

Killary Harbour is a perfect example of a fjord, or drowned river valley, formed during the last Ice Age, some two million years ago

Bartragh Island, an important sanctuary for wild birds, stretches across Killala Bay, providing a protective lagoon on its landward side

Caher Island, site of ancient stone crosses and monastic ruins, has been a place of pilgrimage for centuries

Benwee to Downpatrick Head, featuring sea stacks and small islands off the coast. The individual figures of Kid Island, Pig Island, Illanmaster and Horse Island remain resistant to the beatings of the wild Atlantic. The remarkable 60 m (197 ft) sandstone pillar of Dún Bríste, a collapsed sea arch at Downpatrick Head, emerges defiant from the waves, as do the Stags of Broad Haven. The sandy island of Bartragh shelters Killala from the Atlantic Ocean, creating a lagoon in the bay.

Inishturk, the 'island of the wild boar', is a small island off the south-west coast, measuring 5 x 3 km (3 x 2 ml). It is formed of Ordovician sandstones and slates, which give the landscape an attractive rippled effect. It is home to a population of 90 people. Neighbouring Caher Island, 8 km (5 ml) off the coast, is of the same rock formation as Inishturk. It continues to be a pilgrimage destination on 15 August each year; otherwise, it is uninhabited except for the cattle and sheep grazing there. The much smaller island of nearby Inishdalla is a significant breeding ground for grey seals in the autumn months.

Clew Bay is a large area of open sea, indenting the south-west coast of Mayo. On the land side, the bay runs from Mulranny on the north shore to Louisburgh on the south. The bay itself is dotted with hundreds of partially submerged drumlins, dumped there after the last Ice Age when the glaciers melted. They form a myriad of tiny islands, supporting a great diversity of coastal and terrestrial habitats.

Clare Island lies across the entrance to Clew Bay and has an area of 8 x 5 km (5 x 3 ml). The high ridge of Croaghmore dominates the island, rising 463 m (1,520 ft) above the north-western shore. Robert Lloyd Praeger and his team, while conducting the first Clare Island Survey of 1909-1911, examined in great detail the island's geology, history, archaeology, place names, flora and fauna.

A Galway hooker sails out of Clew Bay, with Clare Island on the horizon

Over 393 native plants were recorded during that survey, including ancient tree stumps showing that Clare Island had been wooded at some stage centuries before. A second Clare Island Survey began in 1991, similar in scope to the original survey and supervised by the Royal Irish Academy. This survey has shown a decline in plant species on the island, probably due to changes in farming practices. But the island remains a bird-watcher's haven and one of the most environmentally varied areas in Europe.

Achill is Ireland's largest island, covering over 100 sq km (39 sq ml) and with a coastline of about 129 km (50 ml). It is disconnected from the mainland by a narrow channel of water, spanned by a road bridge since 1887. There are two great mountains on the island, almost of equal height: Slievemore on the north coast rises 671 m (2,201 ft) above sea level, while Croaghaun on the north-west coast falls dramatically from 668 m (2,192 ft) to the Atlantic Ocean between Achill Head and Saddle Head. Achill boasts the highest cliffs in Europe. There are high cliffs all along the coast around Croaghaun, while on the southern coast the Minaun Cliffs, overlooking Keel Strand, drop 250 m (813 feet) vertically into the sea. Spectacular views can be seen from here, including schools of passing dolphins and porpoises, and solitary basking sharks.

Achill probably gets its name from the Latin *aquila* for 'eagle'. The white-tailed sea eagle was once a familiar sight on the island, but is now extinct. A variety of smaller sea birds are still found, however, with great colonies of gulls and white terns, among others, nesting on the ledges of the sea cliffs.

Achill has many long sandy beaches, such as Doogort on the north side of the island with impressive seal caves nearby. The fine beach at Keem Bay is tucked below a headland cliff rising up 182 m (597 ft). A special conservation area lies between the beaches of Keel and Dooega on the

The long sheltered beach of Keem Strand,
Achill Island

Great basking sharks feed on plankton during the summer months in
Keem Bay

south shore of the island, offering protection to the sandy grasslands and their wildlife. Lapwings, snipe, curlews, gulls, ringed plovers and oyster catchers frequent these beaches.

A spectacular view of Achill's Keem Bay is visible from the road above the beach. During the summer months, basking sharks, also known as sunfish, can be seen feeding in the bay. There is a fishing ground off the Achill coast called Sunfish Bank. The fate of basking sharks is similar to many other marine animals: they were once plentiful off the Mayo coast and hunted for their fins (which were exported to Japan for soup) and their liver oil, of high quantity and quality (which was used to fuel lamps). In the 1950s, there were five shark-fishing companies operating in Achill, when basking sharks up to 10 m (33 ft) long and weighing some 6 tonnes were caught. By the 1960s, however, the sharks had become scarce and the companies closed.

The Inishkea Islands, off the south-west coast of the Mullet Peninsula, have been uninhabited by people since the early 1930s. But they remain an important home to over 200 species of plants and 85 species of migrating birds, including barnacle geese, peregrine falcons and endangered corncrakes. Half of the Irish wintering population of barnacle geese nest on these islands and they are also the breeding grounds for grey seals. The island of Inishkea North is low-lying, in contrast to Inishkea South with its hills of over 70 m (230 ft) high. Maps dating to the 17th century recorded a mythical island north of the Inishkea Islands, near Inishglora, the home of storm petrels. This island was often sought by explorers, but never found. It is, in fact, the elusive island of Hy Brasil.

Lighthouses were established as protective warning signals for the perilous coastline. Private lighthouses were first found along the coast in the early Christian period. During the 18th century, the Commissioners of Irish Lights was established to provide and maintain navigational aids for shipping around the Irish coast. Because of the indented nature of Mayo's coastline, many lighthouses were established – at Achill Beg, Ballyglass, Black Rock, Blacksod, Clare Island, Eagle Island (off the Mullet Peninsula)

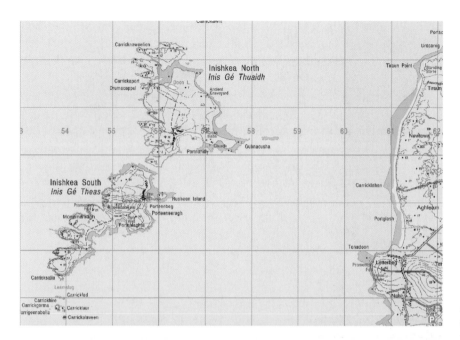

The Inishkea Islands, off the west coast of the Mullet Peninsula, are home to migrating barnacle geese, as their Irish name suggests — Inis Gé, meaning 'Goose Island'

Black Rock Lighthouse, automated since 1974, perches on the bleak island of Black Rock, north of Achill

Blacksod Lighthouse at Eachleim on the southern Mullet Peninsula

Blanket bog in Erris, with a view of the Nephin Beg range in the distance

and Inishgort in Clew Bay. All these lighthouses were once staffed with resident keepers, but after 1997, like others around Ireland, they became fully automated and monitored by computer. Staff now only visit them to carry out repairs.

Black Rock Lighthouse was built on the precipitous cliff of Black Rock, a tiny outcrop 12 km (7.5 ml) offshore, north of Achill Island. Work commenced in 1858 on the circular tower, which was built from stone cut from the rock. Completed in 1864, the lighthouse crew and their families lived there until 1893, when shore dwellings at Blacksod were completed. Black Rock Lighthouse was automated in 1974.

Blacksod Lighthouse is situated on the mainland, near the southern tip of the Mullet Peninsula. Completed in 1866, it was built of local cut granite. The lighthouse station converted to electricity in 1967 and two years later, in 1969, it became a helicopter base.

The Barony of Erris comprises north-west Mayo, as far south as Achill and Mulranny on the north shore of Clew Bay. The area consists in the main of an open, unbroken expanse of blanket bog, with only the Nephin Beg Mountains breaking the skyline. The bog stretches over the western landscape, cloaking the mountains and valleys, reaching the northern cliffs of Benwee Head and the collapsed sea arch of Dún Briste at Downpatrick Head. W.H. Maxwell describes Erris as a 'district of unspoiled natural beauty and into this landscape poets, painters, sportsmen and antiquarians have come in search of beauty, pleasure and knowledge'.

T.H. White (1906-64), who wrote *The Godstone and the Blackymor* based on his experiences during his time spent at Sheskin, describes the physical beauty of the Erris landscape:

> The river, shallow with summer, rippled in herring-bone patterns like the roof of your mouth, the colour of weak beer, cutting its winding way six feet below the level of the bog. And the bog

Lighthouse at Ballyglass on the Mullet Peninsula, north of Belmullet

Grey seals frequent the waters off the Mullet Peninsula and breed on the Inishkea Islands

stretched flat for miles and miles, a landscape out of Browning's *Childe Roland*. Round the rim of the saucer, there were the mountains, as bare, calm and empty as the bog . . . There was a minute waterfall or glide of water. The soft, tart, ale-coloured stream slid over the smooth stones from step to step, cool and glistening.

The Mullet Peninsula lies within the Barony of Erris, north of Achill. Long (20 km or 12.5 ml) and narrow, it is joined to the mainland by a small isthmus, between Broad Haven and Blacksod Bay, on which is sited the town of Belmullet. The peninsula, a flat treeless plain, is subject to extreme weather influences, leaving it windswept but resilient in the face of the harsh Atlantic.

Robert Lloyd Praeger, in his book *The Way that I went*, describes the Mullet as:

That remote peninsula, half bog, half sand, full of bays and queer lakes and outlying islets; treeless, sodden, storm swept and everywhere pounded by the besieging sea, beautiful on a fine day with wondrous colour over land and sea, desolate beyond words when the Atlantic rain drives across the shelter-less surface.

Grey seals and whales make their appearance in the waters around the Mullet Peninsula. W.H. Maxwell describes in his *Wild Sports of the West* how in Blacksod Bay 'a seal would suddenly raise his head above the surface, gaze for a moment at the boat, and when he had apparently satisfied his curiosity sink quietly from view'.

The Moy Estuary comprises an area of 1,200 hectares (2,965 acres) of tidal waters, with channels, sand bars and islands. It is a rich feeding ground for sea trout and teems with sand eels, herring fry, sprat and crustaceans. Sea trout, weighing up to 1.8 kg (4 lb), are caught on the fly in the season, from mid-April to early October.

The Moy River, straddling counties Mayo and Sligo, rises in Sligo and travels south-west to Ballylahan. From there, it flows north through

Ballina town – situated on the estuary of the River Moy, which flows into Killala Bay to the north

Foxford to Ballina, where the estuary stretches out to sea for 9.6 km (6 ml). Flanked by the Nephin Mountains to the west and the Ox Mountains to the east, the river is a total of 138 km (86 ml) long. In 1845, the flow of the Moy was altered from its natural course at Moyne Abbey to its present flow through Bartragh Banks. The river and its extensive tributaries drain a catchment area of over 2,000 sq km (772 sq ml), including the great loughs of Conn and Cullin. This natural drainage system results in improved agricultural land. The main Moy channel is deep and up to 40 m (131 ft) wide in the middle and lower reaches. It is well known as an excellent salmon river.

Lough Conn ('Hound's Lake') and Lough Cullin ('Holly Lake') are found in Mayo's low limestone plain, with the Nephin Mountains as a backdrop to the west. Drained by the Moy River, the two lakes meet at a narrow bridge of land aptly called Pontoon, a favourite place of artists and anglers alike. The Deel River is the main tributary of the Lough Conn/River Moy system and supplies both salmon and trout stocks to the Moy catchment area. Lough Cullin is really a part of the depression forming Lough Conn, but was cut off by a rocky ridge. The Manulla River is its main tributary. The wooded foreshore of the lake and surrounding areas include birch and holly, as well as old oak trees. Both lakes provide nesting grounds for the largest number of common scooter ducks found anywhere in Europe. The graceful mute swan, Ireland's only breeding swan, is also found at Lough Cullin, along with the Icelandic whooper swan, which winters on the lake and feeds in the nearby meadows around Foxford.

Lough Mask is the largest lake in Mayo in an area of great natural beauty. It is about 16 km (10 ml) long and covers an area of some 8,094 hectares (20,000 acres), lying on a bed of limestone. Its western shores are

The spectacular meeting of two lakes at Pontoon – Lough Conn (top of picture) and Lough Cullin – separated by a rocky ridge of land, spanned by a one-arched road bridge

overshadowed by the ancient shales and slates of the Partry Mountains. This lake is famous for its brown trout, pike and eel fishing. There are no salmon since the only outflow is an underground river that rises in the nearby village of Cong, the setting for the film *The Quiet Man*. Here, limestone chasms form an underground waterway connecting Lough Mask to Lough Corrib in the neighbouring county of Galway. During the Famine, a canal was built to provide a navigation channel between the two lakes. This was also intended to lower water levels during winter in the upper lake, Lough Mask. However, the scheme did not work because of the nature of the karst landscape – the limestone soaks up or 'swallows' water into underground streams.

To the north-east of Lough Mask is the much smaller Lough Carra, described in George Moore's novel *The Lake*, published in 1905. With a variety of limestone and wetland habitats, this lough is noted for its bird life, including breeding pairs of mallard and tufted duck, as well as teal, wigeon and shoveler.

Boglands of Mayo

The poet Louis MacNeice captures the mystery of the boglands of Mayo at nightfall in his poem *Sligo and Mayo*, published in 1939:

> *And when the night came down upon the bogland*
> *With all-enveloping wings*
> *The coat-black turf stacks rose against the darkness*
> *Like the tomb of nameless kings.*

Bog or peat is soil composed of over 90% water and the remains of plant materials that have not decomposed. Bogs are formed as a result of climate and human activity. Early farmers in Mayo cleared the forests to make way for agriculture, leaving the soil vulnerable to the Atlantic weather system. Increased moisture leached minerals from the soil, leaving an ideal acid environment in which mosses, heathers, lichens, grasses and sedges could thrive. When they died, these plants did not fully decompose due to the lack of microorganisms and oxygen in the soil. Their remains accumulated, eventually forming bogland.

In east Mayo, raised bogs were formed by an upward growth of accumulated layers of undecayed mosses and other plant remains. This makes the land appear higher than the surrounding countryside. Blanket bogs were also initially formed in wet depressions like raised bogs, but instead of accumulating, they overflowed and spread across the countryside, cloaking the mountainous and low-lying regions of north and west Mayo.

The word 'bog' is derived from the Irish word *bogach*, meaning 'soft'. Turf from the bogs traditionally supplied the fuel needs of the people. Tenants were allowed to cut turf owned by the landlord, but with strict conditions

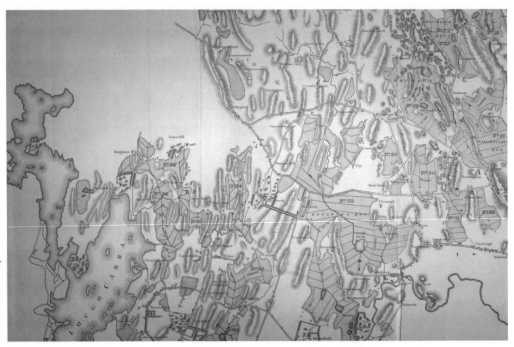

One of a series of detailed maps showing the bogs near Lough Carra, east Mayo, drawn up by the Commission on Bogs during 1809-13

*Cutting turf from a deep raised bog
near Westport*

attached. J.C. Curwen observed in 1818 the unusual design of the loys or
spades, used for cutting turf, that were peculiar to Mayo. A series of
beautifully engraved maps showing the bogs of Mayo in fine detail survives
from the early 19th century. The maps were the result of a survey of bogs
undertaken between 1809 and 1813 by a government-appointed Commission
on Bogs. Those working on the project included the engineers Alexander
Nimmo and William Bald. The purpose of the Commission was to enquire
into the nature and extent of bogs in Ireland and to assess the practicality of
draining and cultivating them for agricultural use. Bogs were regarded at
that time as wasteland, barriers to communication, useful only for rough
grazing and for fuel saved by hand-cutting. The Commission suggested
methods of reclamation of the bogs, including lines of drainage.

In recent years, boglands everywhere have decreased at an accelerating
rate due to extensive mechanised turf-cutting and reclamation of land.
Today, bogs are viewed as one of our most distinctive natural resources, to
be conserved and studied not only for their rich and diverse flora and fauna,
but also for the objects and landscapes they preserve from the past.

The Owenduff Nephin Beg National Park has been established within the
Bellacorrick Bog complex. The park incorporates the largest undisturbed
lowland blanket bog in the country and aims to protect its unique ecosystem
and landscape. The Wildlife Service has also declared 1,198 hectares (2,960
acres) of bog in the Knockmoyle/Sheskin area, between the Oweninny River
and Sheskin in north Mayo, as a National Nature Reserve. Other bogs in the

Bogs have a unique flora and attract a rich variety of wildlife

Watermint thrives in the wet conditions of boglands, filling the air with its aromatic scent

county have been recommended as National Heritage Areas and Special Areas of Conservation, including smaller raised bogs in east Mayo.

Bogs are often noted for their unique flora and fauna, producing an array of silver grey, pale pink, russet, purple, vermilion and golden-green colours that form a backdrop to the black turf. The common sponge-like sphagnum moss, grasses, heathers and sedges are all found on the blanket bogs of Mayo. The grasses tend to be of a tough nature, including purple moorgrass, deergrass, black bog rush, bull rush and reedmace. The bog vegetation provides nesting grounds for small birds, such as skylark, meadow pipit, dunlin and golden plover. The water pools in the bog are important resting grounds for water hens, ducks such as mallard and teal, amphibians such as the common frog and insects such as the non-biting midge.

Several types of heather are found in Mayo, including Mackay's heath around Bellacorrick and the rare St. Daboec's heath in the south and west of the county. Bell heather, cross-leaved heath and ling heather are excellent sources of nectar, attracting many insects and birds, and can be found on Clare Island, north of Mulranny, Killary Harbour and around Lough Conn. Foxes and mountain hares can often be found on the bogs, finding cover among the many ferns growing there, including royal, maidenhair and spleenwort.

The flowering bogbean, butterwort, tormentil, silverweed and bog asphodel also grow in bogs, while the aromatic scent of bog myrtle and watermint fill the air. Bog myrtle or sweet gale (*Myrica gale*) has many uses, including as a dye, an insect repellent or as a remedy. The carnivorous plants of sundew and bladderwort thrive around bog pools,

Protecting the natural environment, such as this unspoilt beach at Lacken Strand in north Mayo, is among the top priorities of Mayo County Council

trapping and digesting insects. The distinctive bog cotton sedges, once plentiful on cut-away bog, are now becoming scarcer. This is a problem for many birds that use bog cotton as a staple in their diet, including the Greenland white-fronted geese that winter here.

Local authorities increasingly play a role, in partnership with local communities, in managing the landscape of the county. Their role extends to protection of the environment, planning for visual effects that are empathetic to the environment and the creation of a sustainable countryside for those living in and visiting Mayo. In 2001, Mayo County Council Planning Department commissioned consultants to draw up Integrated Area Plans for Erris, Newport and Achill in order to examine these issues of environment, infrastructure, planning needs and sustainability. Under the auspices of Mayo County Council, the County Development Board undertook the compilation of *Maigh Eo — Le Cheile le Neart: 10 year Integrated Strategy for the Economic, Cultural and Social Development of County Mayo, 2002-2012*. Among the objectives of this strategic plan are to ensure the sustainability of the natural environment, as well as the protection and enhancement of the natural and constructed environment in consultation with the local community.

Chapter 2

People and Politics

A survey of Mayo's history provides glimpses of how power, politics and strife affected the daily lives of its inhabitants through the centuries. Mayo's first people arrived some time after 8000 BC, when melting ice had raised sea levels and effectively disconnected the land bridges that linked Ireland and Britain. The lifestyle of the earliest Stone Age hunters and gatherers changed little until about 4000 BC when Neolithic people came to the area and settled down to cultivate the land. These first farmers cleared the forests, using polished axes with sharp cutting edges, and sowed seeds in well laid-out fields. They grew cereal crops, including an early type of wheat, and harvested them. They kept cattle and raised stock, which could graze all year round because of the warmer climate of the time. They made pottery and lived in substantial timber houses, some of which were surrounded by dry-stone enclosures. They honoured their dead in great megalithic structures, many of which are still visible on the landscape today.

All this is known from the remains of the largest and oldest Neolithic field system in Europe, measuring over 1,000 hectares (2,500 acres), discovered in 1934 between Ballycastle and Belderrig on the north coast of Co. Mayo. The site, today known as Céide Fields, remained undisturbed for millennia beneath a covering of 2 to 4.5 m (6.5 to 15 ft) of bogland. Then, while cutting turf in 1934, a local school teacher called Patrick Caulfield discovered this hidden treasure. His son, the archaeologist Séamus Caulfield, surveyed the extensive system and began archaeological excavations in 1969. The Céide Fields Visitors' Centre near Ballycastle, opened in 1993, has interpreted the archaeological finds and recreated the daily lives of these early farmers. Séamus Caulfield has drawn attention to the high levels of social cohesion needed by these Neolithic farming communities for the large-scale clearance of woodland, the organisation of planned field systems and the building of the megalithic burial tombs in the area.

Mary Robinson, native of Ballina – former President of Ireland and UN High Commissioner of Human Rights

Spectacular site of the Neolithic Céide Fields on the north Mayo coast

Srahwee wedge tomb (known locally as Altoir), outside Louisburgh, dates to about 1800 BC

The well-preserved Ballina portal dolmen, known as 'The Four Maols'

The Neolithic people were the first to construct the impressive communal burial structures known as megalithic tombs. These probably also served as ritualistic sites and are known in local lore as 'Dermot and Grainne's bed' after the legend of the fleeing lovers. Archaeologists have divided these megalithic tombs into four types: court, portal, passage and wedge. The term 'megalith' comes from the Greek meaning 'great stone' and these tombs are constructed of large stones, often with several massive uprights covered by a stone roof or capstone. Inside, there are commonly one or more burial chambers. The structure would originally have been covered over by a heap of small loose stones, forming a cairn. In many cases, the cairn has disappeared and only the megalithic structure remains. Some Neolithic tombs continued in use into the later Bronze and Iron Ages, while others were first constructed in the Bronze Age.

The Ballina portal dolmen, situated on a low hill overlooking the River Moy, is known locally as 'The Four Maols', named after four former clerics who were buried here in the middle of the 6th century (*maol* meaning 'bald' in Irish). The monks were said to have murdered the popular Bishop of Killala and were, in turn, murdered by the bishop's brother because of an intrigue over the succession to the kingship of Connaught. Today, the dolmen consists of three large upright stones, supporting a massive capstone. Another large stone lying nearby may have been the original fourth support.

Megalithic tombs may have continued in use into the later Bronze and Iron Ages. Others, notably wedge tombs, may first have been constructed in the Bronze Age. But as time went on, the communal megalithic tombs were replaced by simpler, stone-lined burial chambers, known as cists. Each consisted of a 'coffin' made of stone slabs lining the inside of the dug-out grave, which was then covered over by rounded earth or a cairn of loose stones. The cremated human remains were placed in the cist, often accompanied by pottery and other objects. A series of cist graves has been found on an esker ridge at Ballinachalla, between Cong and Ballinrobe, dating to 2000 BC. Archaeologists discovered cremated bones, an inverted vase urn, a lidded vase and a flint knife in these graves.

A pottery vase-shaped food vessel found in a Ballinachalla cist grave, dating back 4,000 years

Stone circles generally date from the early Bronze Age (post-2000 BC) and consist of near-circular enclosures built of large upright stones set at prescribed distances from each other. They may have been used for ceremonial purposes and human burials. Mayo has many fine stone circles, including Dooncarton in Erris; Rathfran in north Mayo, consisting of sixteen stones, five of which now lie flat; and a group of three – Nymphsfield, Tonaleeaun and the Glebe – outside Cong village.

It is difficult to interpret the precise meaning and use of stone circles, stone rows and standing stones. They may have been used to mark the location of burial tombs or acted as commemoration stones or been the location and object of ritual practices. Some standing stones have been marked with the earliest Irish system of writing – ogham, dated to the 4th

Dooncarton stone circle, north of Pollatomish in the Barony of Erris

Breastagh ogham stone, near Lacken Bay in north Mayo

Pair of Bronze Age sun discs, found at Rappa Castle, Crossmolina

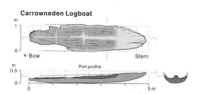

Plan of Carrowneden log boat, some 4,000 years old, found near Mannin Lake, Ballyhaunis

and 5th centuries. Ogham writing consisted of an alphabet of originally 20, and later 25, letters formed as slashes of varying lengths which were incised on standing stones. These stones were most likely for marking memorials or boundaries. Breastagh ogham stone, near Lacken Bay, is a Bronze Age standing stone, some 3 m (9 ft) high, which was later incised with ogham inscriptions.

Sun discs, made of decorated thin gold sheet, were among the first types of gold jewellery made during the Bronze Age. This was the period when gold production first began and gradually reached a superior standard of metallurgy and artistic excellence. Sun discs were discovered at Rappa Castle, Crossmolina, dating back to 2200 – 1800 BC. The decorations on these discs are similar to those on the cross-inscribed stone found in Leigue Cemetery, Ballina, which may be pre-Christian in date.

Another find in Mayo from the Bronze Age was the Carrowneden log boat. Discovered in 1996 on the margins of Mannin Lake, near Ballyhaunis, the boat dates back 4,000 years. Although only a portion survives – some 5 m (16.4 ft) long and 1 m (3.3 ft) wide – it was clearly a very large vessel and probably served a variety of functions, such as transporting turf, animals, people and their goods along the rivers and lakes of prehistoric Mayo.

In the Neolithic Period, houses tended to be rectangular in shape. The isolated farmsteads, or ringforts, of the Early Christian period (AD 500 - 1000), and their water-based equivalents called crannógs, tended to be circular. In 1993, prior to the building of the N5 Swinford by-pass, a ringfort was excavated by archaeologists of Mayo County Council at Lislackagh. Circular wooden houses were found inside the western part of the ringfort. They were initially assumed to be of Early Christian date, but radiocarbon dating put them firmly in the Iron Age (500 BC - AD 500), making Lislackagh the oldest ringfort found in the country to date. A smelting furnace, large quantities of iron slag and an iron knife were discovered within the ringfort, indicating that the inhabitants were smelting iron on the site and producing iron objects for their own use. Numerous other small finds were also unearthed, including bone, stone and blue glass beads, a broken lignite or jet bracelet, flint and chert implements, and pieces of copper. These objects are similar to the types of goods found in Iron Age burial sites.

Echoes of social and cultural life in pre-Christian Mayo have been revealed by archaeologists and by written records from the Christian period. Pre-Christian Mayo society was based around a social order with a strong warrior culture, where an early form of the Gaelic language was spoken and high status was afforded to the learned class.

Myths and legends grew up around these ancient people. In Ireland, prose sagas were the main form and Mayo features in many of these tales, celebrating extraordinary feats and battles. The sagas provide insights into aspects of the political geography of the period, the social organisation of the people, the importance of cattle in their economy and

Iron Age round house found inside Lislackagh Ringfort, near Swinford, excavated by Mayo County Council archaeologists in 1993

Eochy's Cairn, a passage grave located on Killour Hill, between Cong and Ballinrobe

their methods of combat. The texts, written in the Christian period, also give us the names of the ancient places of Mayo, such as Partraige in south Mayo and Ciarraige in east Mayo, and the ancient ruling families, including the Ui Briuin and the Ui Fiachrach.

Scholars have classified the prose sagas into separate cycles. The mythological cycle recorded in the *Book of Invasions* relates how the Tuatha Dé Danann defeated the giants known as the Fomorians. The Dé Danann were thought to have been deities of the pagan Irish, but when the sagas were written down in the later Christian period they were presented as tribes with supernatural powers.

Wilhelmina Geddes' stained-glass window, commissioned by the Museum and Art Gallery of Belfast, depicts the legend of the Children of Lir

The Ulster cycle includes the tale of *An Táin Bó Cúailnge* (The Cattle Raid of Cooley) with its Mayo associations. The tale is about a quarrel between Queen Medbh of Connaught and her husband Ailill about who had the greatest number of possessions and the subsequent invasion of Ulster by Queen Medbh to steal the brown bull of Cooley so that she could equal Ailill's famous white-horned bull of Connaught. Among the fiercest fighting groups in Medbh's army was the Domhnann Sept of Iorras Domhnann (Erris).

The mythological tale of *The Battle of Moytura* (from *Magh Tuire* meaning 'plain of the pillar') was written in the 9th century and describes a battle for control of Ireland, fought between the Fir Bolgs under their king, Eochaí, and the Dé Danann. Cong was suggested as a possible location for the great battle by scholars writing versions of this saga in medieval times because of the wealth of prehistoric cairns and stone circles found in that area. One of the best known monuments is Eochy's Cairn, a passage grave rising up from Killour Hill, half-way between Cong and Ballinrobe. It is named after the mythical King Eochaí, the last ruler of the Fir Bolgs, said to have been killed on the final day of the battle and buried here.

The well-known children's myth *The Children of Lir* was written in Christian times. According to the legend, the wife of the King of the Dé Danann bore two sets of twins, but later died. Her sister married the king and soon grew jealous of her stepchildren. She used her magic powers to turn them into swans, fixing three terms of three hundred years to be spent at different locations before returning to human form. They spent their first three hundred years on the Sea of Moyle, the second three hundred at Lake Deavarragh in Westmeath and their last three hundred off Iorras Domhnann (Erris). They found their resting place on Inishglora, an island in the Bay of Erris. Here, according to legend, they met the Christian missionary St. Brendan, who was associated with monastic sites on Inishglora and Cross Abbey on the Mullet. The saint's bell summoned the children back to human form and they were baptised before being buried together on the island.

The story of *The Children of Lir* was depicted by the celebrated artist Wilhelmina Geddes (1887-1955) in her striking stained-glass window, commissioned in 1929 as the stair window for the new Museum and Art Gallery of Belfast. It consists of eight panels in rich earthy colours. Geddes worked with the stained-glass studio *An Túr Gloine* (The Tower of Glass), a distinguished school of

Peter Grant's bronze sculpture of
Manannan Mac Lir, erected on
Castlebar's Mall in 1992

internationally recognised artists, founded by Sarah Purser. Geddes also designed a stained-glass window of St. Brendan for the 1924 British Empire Exhibition at Wembley, which was later installed in Curraun Church on Achill Island.

Manannan Mac Lir was the son of Lir, the Celtic god of the sea and the most spiritual divinity known to the ancient Gaels. His home was the land of promise and he was celebrated as a beneficent provider: all who feasted at his table achieved immortality. Mannin Lake, near Tourmakeady, was named after him, as was the Isle of Man. Like Neptune, Manannan was usually depicted driving a magic chariot over the waves and this is how he has been immortalised by Peter Grant in his powerful bronze sculpture, erected on The Mall in Castlebar in 1992. The sculpture was donated to Castlebar Urban District Council by Helen Hooker O'Malley, the widow of Ernie O'Malley, writer and Republican.

The introduction and spread of Christianity to Ireland from the 5th century is traditionally associated with St. Patrick, patron saint of Ireland. According to his own writings, Patrick was born in West Britain and brought to Ireland as a slave when he was sixteen. The earliest surviving biography of Patrick was written by Tírechán from

The Knappaghmanagh inscribed stone near Westport is of pre-Christian date, later inscribed with a Christian cross

Tirawley in the second half of the 7th century. The arrival of Christianity challenged the traditional high status of the learned classes. In Ireland it took on a monastic character, independent of Rome. Among the better known monastic sites in Mayo are those located at Balla, Cong, Errew, Meelick and on islands off the west coast. Typically, the early church sites were several acres in size, round or oval in shape and enclosed by dry-stone walls or earthen banks. These sites became centres of exchange – of goods, information and learning. The church building and the beehive huts, built as accommodation for the monks and visitors, were dry-stone constructions using the corbel technique. These early churches were replaced by medieval abbeys, built in the Romanesque style and later in the Gothic style. The church's patronage of the stonemason's art is much in evidence in the many ecclesiastical ruins throughout Mayo.

The political history of the county during this period is fragmented and remains somewhat obscure. The area of Mayo was under the sphere of influence of the Ui Fiachrach, a clan descended from the famous Niall of the Nine Hostages, the early 5th-century king of Tara. This clan was replaced in the 8th century by the rival dynasty Ui Briuin, who were also believed to be descended from a shared ancestor, in this case Brión, said to have been a brother of Niall of the Nine Hostages. From the Ui Briuin clan sprang the O'Connors, taking their name from one of their most successful warrior-kings, a man called Conchobar who died in 973.

Cross inscribed stone on the island of Inishkea North

Cross inscribed stone on Caher Island, still a place of pilgrimage in August each year

Cross inscribed stone on the west side of Duvillaun More island

By the 10th century, the O'Connors had established themselves as the principal provincial Kings of Connaught, acting as overlords in Mayo. Within the kingdom, there were many petty kingdoms whose rulers gave allegiance to their provincial king. The High King of Ireland was usually chosen from among the provincial kings. Rory O'Connor (d. 1198) became the last High King in 1166, a few years before the declaration of the Norman king as paramount Lord of Ireland. Like his father Turlough O'Connor (1088-1156), Rory was not only politically powerful, but also a generous patron of the church and the arts. Cong Abbey, for example, was built under his patronage.

In 1183 Rory abdicated and retired to Cong Abbey where he stayed for the remainder of his life. Rory's brother, Cathal of the Wine Red Hand (d. 1224), eventually succeeded him. During a relatively peaceful reign, Cathal managed to delay the expansion of the Anglo-Normans into the province despite the grant of Connaught to the Norman lord William de Burgo (d. 1205). Like other O'Connors before him, Cathal was also a patron of the church, founding Ballintubber Abbey in 1216, and like his brother Rory, he died as a monk, in the Cistercian house of Abbeyknockmoy in Co. Galway. His death brought about a renewed succession feud between the O'Connor clan, complicated by the arrival of the Normans in the province in 1235. Cathal's time as king is recalled in the poem *A Vision of Connaught in the Thirteenth Century* by James Clarence Mangan (1803-49):

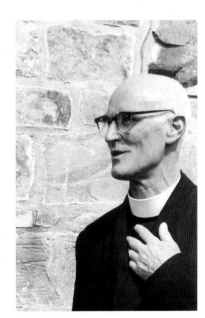

Father Charles O'Connor, of the royal O'Connor Don line, attended the celebrations marking 750 years of Ballintubber Abbey in September 1966

Depiction of Richard Mór, 'Lord of Connaught', from the 16th-century illuminated manuscript of the De Burgo family, 'Historia et Genealogia Familiae de Burgo'

De Burgo

William De Burgo
↓
Richard Mór (d. 1243)
Lord of Connaught
↓

Richard II   Walter (d. 1274)
Earl of Ulster
↓
Richard (d. 1326)
Red Earl
↓
John
↓
William (1312-1333)
Brown Earl
↓

Elizabeth   M.   Lionel, Duke of Clarence
Son of King Edward III

A Vision of Connaught in the 13th century

*I walked entranced
Through a land of Morn:
The sun, with wondrous excess of light,
Shone down and glanced
Over seas of corn
And lustrous gardens aleft and right.
Even in the clime
Of resplendent Spain
Beams no such sun upon such a land;
But it was the time,
'Twas in the reign,
Of Cáhal Mór of the Wine-red Hand.*

*Anon stood nigh
By my side a man
Of princely and port sublime.
Him queried I –
"O, my Lord and Khan,
What clime is this, and what golden time?"
When he – "The clime
Is a clime to praise,
The clime is Erin's, the green and bland;
And it is the time,
These be the days,
Of Cáhal Mór of the Wine-red Hand."*

*Then saw I thrones,
And circling fires,
And a Dome rose near me, as by a spell,
Whence flowed the tones
Of silver lyres,
And many voices in wreathed swell;
And their thrilling chime
Fell on mine ears
As the heavenly hymn of an angel-band –
"It is now the time,
These be the years,
Of Cáhal Mór of the Wine-red Hand."*

*I sought the hall,
And, behold! – a change
From light to darkness, from joy to woe!
King, nobles, all,
Looked aghast and strange;
The minstrel-group sate in dumbest show!
Had some great crime
Wrought this dread amaze,
This terror! None seemed to understand*

'Twas then the time,
We were in the days,
Of Cáhal Mór of the Wine-red Hand.

I again walked forth:
But lo! The sky
Showed fleckt with blood, and an alien sun
Glared from the north,
And there stood on high,
Amid his shorn beams, a skeleton!
It was by the stream
Of the castled Maine,
One Autumn even, in the Teuton's land,
That I dreamed this dream
Of the time and reign
Of Cáhal Mór of the Wine-red Hand.

There have been many variations of the Norman De Burgo family name since Robert de Burgo accompanied William the Conqueror from Normandy to the battle of Hastings in 1066. His descendant, William de Burgo, founded the family variously known as De Burgh, De Burca, Burke or Bourke. William's son, Richard Mór (d. 1243), manipulated the succession dispute of the O'Connors to his own advantage and invaded Connaught in 1235, claiming for himself the title 'Lord of Connaught'. Along with his other Norman allies, Richard Mór succeeded in reducing the power of the O'Connors while also making a politically astute match by marrying Hodierna, the maternal granddaughter of Cathal O'Connor. Despite its declining power, a bitter struggle for succession once again erupted among the O'Connor clan. In 1384, the royal family of O'Connor of Connaught split into two hostile factions: the O'Connor Ruadh (red) and the O'Connor Donn (brown).

A 19th-century print drawing of the
ruins of Ballylahan Castle, near
Foxford, built by Jordan d'Exter
in the 13th century

15th-century carved tomb at Straide Abbey

Walter de Burgo, Richard Mór's son, was granted the Earldom of Ulster in 1263 through his marriage to a daughter of the Norman lord, Hugh de Lacy. Walter's son, Richard (d. 1326), became known as the 'Red Earl' of Ulster and ruled almost half of Ireland. William De Burgo (1312-33), whom the Gaelic annalists called the 'Brown Earl', succeeded his grandfather Richard while still a minor. He was to be the last De Burgo Earl of Ulster. The title passed to Lionel, Duke of Clarence, when he married Elizabeth, the daughter of the Brown Earl. Despite Lionel's claim to the lands of Connaught, they remained in the hands of the junior branch of the De Burgo family, who kept control by adopting Gaelic customs, including succession rights, in order to protect their lordships.

Like the O'Connors before them, the De Burgos of Mayo became embroiled in fierce succession feuds. Edmond Albanach 'the Scot' (d. 1375), a grandson of Richard Mór, was the ultimate victor, defeating his cousin and opponent, Edmond the Bearded, whom he drowned at Lough Mask Castle in 1338. He adopted the title 'MacWilliam Ioctar' (a territorial overlordship title meaning northern or lower MacWilliam) and, despite continual warfare, his family dominated the area now known as Mayo, with the aid of Scottish gallowglasses, until the Elizabethan conquest in the 16th century.

From the De Burgos' principal military allies sprang the great Norman

PEOPLE AND POLITICS 45

families of Mayo – the Prendergasts, Stauntons, d'Exeters and d'Angulos. Many other settler families also gained lands in Mayo, including the Barretts, Lynnots, Walshes, Joyces and Merricks. The O'Malley clan was one of the few Gaelic families to retain their lands, aided by their maritime prowess and ability to shift allegiances with the prevailing political winds.

As a reward for his part in the Norman conquest of Mayo, Jordan d'Exeter received the Barony of Gallen. He built a number of defensive castles there to hold his newly acquired territory, with his principal stronghold at Ballylahan Castle, close to a fording point on the Moy. This castle is the oldest and largest baronial castle in Mayo – a fortress built in a strategic position to control and dominate the surrounding territories. Its twin-towered gateway was rounded outside the line of the curtain wall, but squared off behind it. The remains of many Norman castles are still visible throughout Mayo, some of them being repaired and altered in later centuries.

By the 15th century, the Normans, who were comparatively few in number and who had retained an almost wholly Gaelic tenantry, had effectively become *Hiberniores ipsis Hibernis* or 'more Irish than the Irish themselves'. After decades of war with their displaced Gaelic neighbours, the d'Exeters adopted Gaelic customs and the families of MacJordan and MacStephens emerged as branches of the d'Exeter family.

A 15th-century tomb at Straide Abbey, depicting contemporary figures in tailored clothes, illustrates how Norman and Gaelic dress styles had become integrated and suggests the greater social cohesion that had occurred between the two communities. The tomb carvings show a man (the donor) and his wife on either side of the piéta figure of the Virgin Mary with the dead Christ in her arms. The fine detail of the work, which in medieval times would have been painted, displays the high standard of tailoring in the clothes of the figures. The woman's clothes consist of a loose-fitting gown with a half round neck and tight-fitting sleeves, buttoned from the wrist to the elbow. She is also wearing a figure-of-eight looped belt around her waist and an Irish-style mantle. The man is dressed in a long one-piece tunic, belted around the waist and with tight-fitting sleeves, like the woman's dress. Three buttons close a vent in the skirt of the tunic, just below the belt. A tailored triangular hood breast piece covers his chest; the shoulder piece of the hood, characteristic of Irish dress, is also visible. The object hanging from his belt is thought to be a weaver's shuttle, an indication of his trade and source of wealth.

Tudor conquest of Mayo

In the 16th century, the Tudor monarchs began a re-conquest of Ireland. Henry VIII declared himself King of Ireland in 1541 and embarked on the first of the Tudor military campaigns. This had little impact on Mayo. But by 1570, during the reign of Elizabeth I, the Tudors began to have a real effect on political life in Mayo, gaining control of the county by the end of the Queen's rule in 1603. The late 16th-century woodcuts of John Derrick record, from an English perspective, the military campaign of the Lord

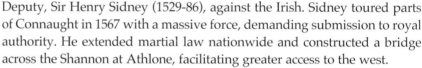

16th-century woodcut by John Derrick showing Sir Henry Sidney's defeat of the Irish

Line engraving by W. Van De Passe of Sir Henry Sidney, Lord Deputy of Ireland, who constituted Mayo as a county in the 16th century

Deputy, Sir Henry Sidney (1529-86), against the Irish. Sidney toured parts of Connaught in 1567 with a massive force, demanding submission to royal authority. He extended martial law nationwide and constructed a bridge across the Shannon at Athlone, facilitating greater access to the west.

Gradually the lordships system of the Normans was replaced with an English provincial administration. The Earl of Sussex (1523-83) constituted, or established, the province of Connaught. Sir Henry Sidney, Lord Deputy of Ireland, constituted the county of Mayo within Connaught under the 1569 Act 'so that her Majesty's laws may have free course'. The office of Lord President or Governor of Connaught was introduced to assert English law in the province. Sir Edward Fitton was the first of the English military men appointed to this position. Sir Nicholas Malby was appointed Military Governor of Connaught in 1576 and, two years later, replaced Sir Edward Fitton as Lord President.

Sir John Perrott (c. 1527-92) became Lord Deputy of Ireland in 1584 and introduced the 'Composition of Connaught' the following year. The Composition challenged the traditional relationship between local lords and their followers by introducing a taxation system requiring an annual payment to support the new Lord President of Connaught. The Composition Commissioners divided each territory into quarters or units of 120 acres (49 hectares) and made agreements between the Crown, landowners, freeholders and tenants concerning the annual taxes to be paid.

As part of the Composition, English customs replaced Gaelic customs. For example, the Gaelic law of succession by election was replaced by the

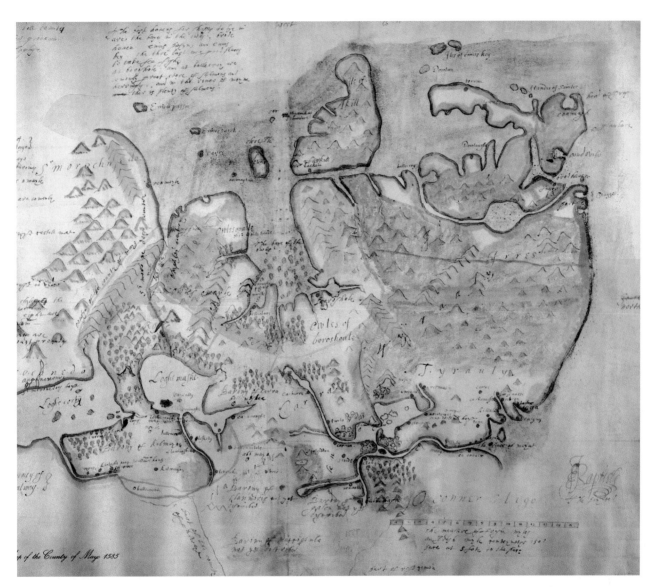

One of the earliest surviving maps of Mayo, prepared for John Browne of the Neale in 1585

English system of succession by the eldest son. During this changeover from the Gaelic to the English system of law, there was a period of transition while new inherited land titles were established. Theobald Dillon, a collector of Composition rent, was one of several English administrative officials who exploited the turmoil of the time to carve out an English-style estate in the Barony of Costello.

Richard Bingham, Lord President of Connaught from 1584 to 1596, established his authority militarily throughout the province. He intervened in the MacWilliam succession disputes, destroying the castles of the Bourkes (the descendants of the Norman De Burgos), hanging their leaders and ruthlessly curtailing their revolt. The Bourkes invited 2,000 Scottish mercenaries, known as redshanks, into Mayo, but Bingham massacred the Scots at the famous Battle of Ardnaree in September 1586. The 'Nine Years War' (1594-1603), which arose out of the threatened

Seán MacUilliam Mhic tSeaain became the MacWilliam Ioctar in the 16th century, as depicted here in the illuminated manuscript 'Historia et Genealogia Familiae de Burgo'

breakup of the Ulster Gaelic lordships, spread to Connaught, but this too was suppressed by Bingham. He gained a reputation as a tyrant and was imprisoned for a period by Queen Elizabeth for abuse of martial law. The tombstone of Richard Bingham at London's Westminster Abbey records that he was made Governor of Connaught, where he 'overthrew the Irish Scots, expelled the traitor O'Rourke, suppressed diverse rebellions and, that with small charges to Her Majesty, maintained the province in a flourishing state for thirteen years'.

Shane MacOliverus (d. 1580), also known as Seán MacUilliam Mhic tSeaain, was a descendant of Edmond Albanach 'the Scot' and became the MacWilliam Ioctar in the 16th century. Shane had an illuminated manuscript of the Bourke family history and genealogy prepared, possibly because of his proposal that he and his sons should be made English peers. His desire for English peerage suggests his acknowledgement of the Crown's growing dominance in the political affairs of Mayo.

Grace O'Malley: Pirate Queen

The O'Malley clan was one of the few Gaelic families to retain their Mayo lands after the Tudor conquest. Grainne Ni Mhaille, or Grace O'Malley (c. 1530-1603), is the most illustrious member of the family about whose deeds numerous accounts are recorded in Elizabethan State Papers. She is the subject of many legends and poems, and in the 19th century became a nationalistic symbol. She is remembered as the Pirate Queen and also as Granuaile, from the Irish *maol* meaning 'bald' – a reference to the short cropped hairstyle she adopted, so atypical for women of her day but which suited her rough, sea-faring activities. Grace was the daughter of Owen O'Malley, king of the O'Malley clan, hereditary lords of a territory that once stretched from Connemara to Westport and successful traders with continental Europe. But the O'Malleys were also pirates, claiming tolls and cargo from vessels that came into their territory.

Grace O'Malley was first married at the age of 15 to Donal O'Flaherty, whose family were Gaelic chiefs of Connemara. Some years later, Donal was murdered and Grace returned to her father's land. Her second marriage was to Richard an Iarainn Bourke, whose gaelicised Norman clan held the territory north of Clew Bay. Richard owned rich iron mines on his Burrishoole lands and was later to become the MacWilliam Ioctar. Grace secured her own livelihood from 'the land and sea'. She maintained stongholds on Clare Island and at Carraigahowley (Rockfleet), near

Newport, from where she commanded her own fleet of galleys. These small vessels, powered by sail and banks of oars, offered speed and versatility – the main weapons of the Pirate Queen's surprise attacks on unsuspecting cargo ships passing within her realm.

Grace's second husband died in 1583 and she claimed his property, even though Gaelic custom usually only allowed the widow of a deceased chieftain to inherit one-third of his possessions. When a year later, a new Lord President of Connaught, Richard Bingham, was appointed, Grace's local power and autonomy brought her under Bingham's scrutiny. He described her as 'for forty years the stay of all rebellions in the west' and did everything possible to curtail her power and the power of the Gaelic Lordships. He eventually succeeded in impoverishing the Bourkes and destroying Grace's dominance over the western coastline, virtually impounding her fleet.

In an unprecedented move, Grace appealed directly to the English queen. She wrote to Elizabeth in early 1593, providing a summary of her life and her destitute circumstances. In July of that year, she set sail for London to seek an audience with the queen. The meeting between the two women took place in September. Elizabeth and Grace conversed in Latin, the only language they had in common. Both were about 60 years of age, with strong minds and wills. Elizabeth agreed to Grace's sons inheriting their father's estate. She also agreed to the provision of maintenance for Grace for the remainder of her life from her sons' estates and that the amount be deductible from their taxes payable to the Crown for the estates. Grace also sought permission to continue to invade 'with sword and fire all Your Highness' enemies'. This, Bingham interpreted, somewhat correctly, would be used by Grace as an excuse to return to her ways of securing her livelihood 'by land and sea'. Grace had used her political astuteness to shift alliances and to navigate through the political turmoil and war that punctuated the transition from Gaelic to English law. Her aim had been to maintain her family's power base in Mayo and in this she was successful.

Grace O'Malley, the Pirate Queen, died in 1603, the same year as Queen Elizabeth coincidentally. Tradition says Grace is buried in the Cistercian Abbey on Clare Island. Certainly, the O'Malley coat of arms is in that abbey (and also at Murrisk Abbey), where a cut limestone slab bears the name 'O'Maille' carved in raised letters at the bottom and the family motto above – *Terra Mariq[ue] Potens* (Powerful on Land and Sea). The arms also feature the martial symbols of a boar and a stallion, poised as if leaping. The lower left quarter of the shield contains a galley, symbolic of the family's maritime exploits. The stone is carved to resemble woven material, expanding into carved decorations on either side of the shield.

Grace's son by Richard Bourke was called Tibbot-ne-Long or 'Theobald of the Ships' (1567-1629). He got his name from the story that he was born aboard his mother's ship during an enemy skirmish, after which, tradition holds, she immediately continued fighting her attackers. In 1585, Tibbot

A carving of Granuaile is carried as the figurehead on the State-owned brigantine, Asgard II, built in 1981 as a training ship

Woodcut depicting Grace O'Malley's famous meeting with Elizabeth I in September 1593 - from the cover of 'Anthologia Hibernica', 1793-94

The Jacobean-style tomb of Tibbot-ne-Long in Ballintubber Abbey

married Maeve, daughter of Charles O'Connor of Sligo. While many Gaelic lords left Mayo in the face of English expansion into Mayo, others adopted English customs and offered loyalty to the English crown in order to maintain their properties and positions of power. Tibbot sided with the English under Sir Conyer Clifford, Governor of Connaught, against rebellious Gaelic lords. For this support he was created a knight and then made Viscount Mayo in 1627. Two years later, he was murdered. He is buried in the sacristy of Ballintubber Abbey in a Jacobean-style tomb, which incorporates early medieval carvings with those of the early 17th century.

The emerging English system and changing lifestyle that followed the Tudor expansion into Mayo alienated many who lamented the loss of their Gaelic lords and way of life. When the Gaelic lords of Ulster, of whom the O'Neills and the O'Donnells were the most powerful, rebelled against the English crown in what became known as the Nine Years War, the Gaelic lords of Mayo, dissatisfied by the Composition of Connaught, joined their revolt. Defeat came at Kinsale in 1603 and many of the Gaelic lords departed for the Continent in the summer of 1607, in the episode known as the 'Flight of the Earls'.

A 17th-century Irish ballad, called 'The County of Mayo' by Thomas Lavelle, recalls the prosperity in Mayo before the protagonist was forced to emigrate as a result of the arrival of the new conquerors. The ballad was published in the monthly paper *A Broadsheet* in July 1903, translated by George Fox and accompanied by a hand-coloured illustration by Jack B. Yeats:

'The County of Mayo' by Jack B. Yeats shows an emigrant forced to leave his home in the 17th century

The County of Mayo

On the deck of Patrick Lynch's boat I sit in woeful plight
Thro' my sighing all the weary day and weeping all the night.
Were it not that full of sorrow from my people forth I go,
By the blessed sun, 'tis royally I'd sing thy praise, Mayo.

When I dwelt at home in plenty, and my gold did much abound,
In the company of fair young maids the Spanish ale went around.
'Tis a bitter change from those gay days that now I'm forced to go,
And must leave my bones in Santa Cruz, far from my own Mayo.

There are altered girls in Irrul now, 'tis proud they've grown and high,
With their hair-bags and their top-knots, for I pass their buckles by,
But it's little now I heed their airs, for God will have it so,
That I must depart for foreign lands, and leave my sweet Mayo.

'Tis my grief that Patrick Loughlin is not Earl of Irrul still,
And that Brian Duff no longer rules as lord upon the hill;
And that Colonel Hugh O'Grady should be lying dead and low,
And I sailing, sailing swiftly from the county of Mayo.

The Armada Room of Belleek Manor (now a hotel) was constructed from the timbers of the wrecks of the Spanish Armada that floundered off the Mayo coast in 1588

In 1588, Pope Sixtus V backed the Spanish Armada's attempted invasion of England as part of a Holy War against Queen Elizabeth, who had been excommunicated in 1570. When attempts to invade England were defeated by Sir Francis Drake's fleet, the ill-fated Armada escaped towards Ireland. Five ships were wrecked in stormy weather along the Mayo coast. The Spanish crews that survived the wrecks were largely slaughtered by either the Irish or the English. In September 1588, Sir Richard Bingham, Lord President of Connaught, reported that he had executed 800 men for collaboration with the Spanish. Owen O'Malley, Grace's father, is reputed to have killed the crew that landed on Clare Island. The crew that landed at Ballycroy occupied Doona Castle until another Armada ship, the *Girona*, picked them up and sailed north to Donegal, where they were again shipwrecked, after which there were no survivors.

Rebellion and settlement

Thomas Wentworth (1593-1641), Lord Deputy of Ireland (1632) and also Earl of Strafford, gave his name to the Strafford Inquisition. This inquiry into ownership of land in Co. Mayo, completed in 1635, was undertaken with the political purpose of confirming Charles I's title to Connaught. The Old English and Old Irish of Mayo formed an alliance, fearing that the inquisition would lead to a plantation of Connaught, similar to that already undertaken in Ulster, together with a concern about growing official intolerance of their Catholic religion. This alliance eventually led to some Mayo landowners participating in the armed rebellion that originated in Ulster in 1641.

Oliver Cromwell waged a brutal campaign against the native Irish in 1649-50

During the rebellion, Protestants sought protection from the Bingham family in Castlebar when the town surrendered to the Catholic forces. Safe passage to Galway was promised for a group of 100 Protestants, including John Maxwell, Bishop of Killala. Lord Mayo, the joint Governor of Mayo, escorted them as far as the county border. But at Shrule Bridge on 13 February 1642, while crossing into Co. Galway, the refugees were attacked and many killed. Lord Mayo was posthumously accused of ambivalence towards the rebels who carried out the massacre and of not protecting the refugees. His son, Theobald, was executed for his perceived role in the tragedy by Cromwellian soldiers in 1653.

Oliver Cromwell (1600-58) as Lord Lieutenant of Ireland campaigned throughout the country during 1649 and 1650. His brutal war against Catholicism and native political power stretched into Mayo. Military success was followed by the Cromwellian land settlement of 1652. This was a plan to repay, with grants of land, the Commonwealth soldiers and adventurers for their services. Displaced landowners from the rest of Ireland, if found to be innocent of rebellion against Cromwell, were offered the choice of 'To hell or Connaught'. In Connaught, the deposed landowners were given lands in four counties west of the Shannon, including Mayo (except the Barony of Tirawley, which was reserved for Cromwellian soldiers). The transplantation to Connaught also involved transplantation within Connaught and consequent changes in ownership of land there.

In order to facilitate the Cromwellian settlement, a survey of Irish land was undertaken in 1654 by the scientist and economist William Petty (1623-87). It was known as the Down Survey because of the practice of recording empirical information on site rather than tabulating survey findings. In Mayo, the only portion surveyed was the Barony of Tirawley. After the Cromwellian regime collapsed and with the subsequent restoration of the English monarchy in the form of Charles II in 1660, land holdings in Mayo were again altered. Those who had power and influence (such as Viscount Mayo and Viscount Dillon) were restored to their lands, but most were not so lucky. Some settlers who had been granted lands in the Cromwellian period were allowed to retain them.

The conversion to Catholicism of James II (1633-1701) in 1669 and his post-accession religious policies were viewed with suspicion by his English subjects. They sought to replace him in 1688 with the Protestant Prince of Orange, William III, husband of James' Protestant daughter, Mary (1662-94). Members of Mayo's landed class who supported James and the Jacobite cause included Manus O'Donel (one of the O'Donnells of Tirconnell who settled in Newport), the Brownes of the Neale, Colonel Dominick Browne of Castlemacgarrett (who commanded a regiment at the battle of Aughrim) and Theobald Dillon (seventh Viscount of Costello-Gallen).

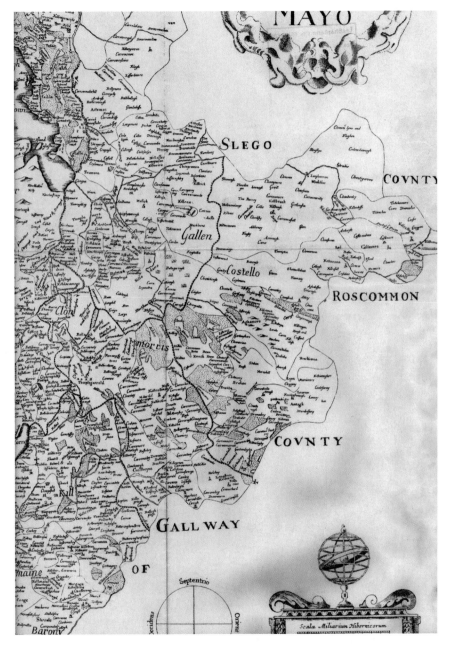

Petty's 1657 map of the Barony of Tirawley was the only part of Co. Mayo recorded in the Down Survey

Colonel John Browne of Westport raised two regiments within Co. Mayo for James II and supplied cannonballs to the army from his local iron works. He was a friend of Patrick Sarsfield (1655-93), was the first Lord Lucan and a colonel in the army of James II. The Jacobites were finally forced to surrender in 1691 and negotiate the Treaty of Limerick. Under its terms, Sarsfield and other Jacobite soldiers were forced to sail to France. They became known as the 'Wild Geese'. The episode is described in the poem *Farewell to Patrick Sarsfield* (Anonymous), translated by Frank O'Connor:

Ballinrobe House, one of many fine estates built in Mayo in the 18th century, painted by James Arthur O'Connor early in the 19th century

Killala Rangers' Volunteer Medal, awarded to Timothy O'Neal, 1778

South Mayo Militia's Volunteer Medal, awarded for Military Merit, 1793

Crossmolina Artillery Volunteer Medal, 1780

Farewell to Patrick Sarsfield wherever you may roam,
You crossed the sea to France and left empty camps at home,
To plead our cause before many a foreign throne
Though you left ourselves and poor Ireland overthrown.

Catholic hopes of religious freedom faded with the defeat of the Jacobite cause in 1691. The subsequent introduction of the infamous Penal Laws of the early 18th century commenced a period of religious repression and 'anti-popery'. Catholic tenants eked out a frugal existence on tiny holdings, with potatoes as the stable diet for the majority of the rapidly growing population.

Many of the landed gentry converted to Protestanism, in order to retain their estates, and became associated with the minority Church of Ireland. They consolidated their landed estates and remained prosperous throughout the 18th and early 19th centuries despite the economic uncertainty and the decline in the linen trade and agriculture, inaugurated by the ending of the Napoleonic Wars in 1815.

In 1776 British troops left Ireland to fight against the American colonists who had taken up arms in their bid for independence from the English. In Ireland, part-time military forces called the Volunteers were established locally throughout the country for the purpose of guarding against French invasion and preserving law and order in the absence of regular troops. Among the local Mayo Volunteers raised were the South Mayo Militia, Killala Rangers, Crossmolina Artillery and the Ballina and Ardnaree Volunteers. The Volunteer movement took on wider political importance when the Protestant Ascendancy in Ireland, influenced by the American War of Independence, pressed for a measure of self-government. The more radical Volunteers sought a degree of legislative independence for the Irish Parliament through the repeal of Poynings' Law and Declaratory Act. The success of these demands, achieved through a combination of menace and constitutional agitation, laid the

Oil painting by William Sadler depicting 'The French in Killala Bay' in August 1798

basis for what is inaccurately known as 'Grattan's Parliament' of 1783-1801. However, the failure of the parliament to introduce wider reform, combined with growing radicalism in the wake of the French and American revolutions, led to the gradual demise of hopes for constitutional reform and gave way to rebellion in 1798.

The 1798 Rebellion

The Rebellion or Insurrection of 1798 originated from the revolutionary ideas of the Society of United Irishmen, established in Belfast in 1791 by a group including the young Dublin lawyer, Theobald Wolfe Tone (1763-98). Their radicalism fused the ideas of modern democracy and ideals of equality and liberty, inspired by the Americans and French, with Irish patriotism. Uprisings first took place in Ulster and Leinster, although they were widely separated by distance and context. Both were savagely repressed by the military before an outbreak of hostilities occurred in Mayo.

On 22 August 1798, a French expedition of 1,000 men under the leadership of General Jean Joseph Amable Humbert (b. 1767) landed at Kilcummin, north of Killala. Matthew Tone, brother of Wolfe Tone, was on board General Humbert's ship when it sailed into Killala Bay. After landing, the French took over the residence of Bishop Stock, the Church of Ireland Bishop of Killala, as a temporary headquarters, before making

Plaque at Moore Hall, erected in 1957,
commemorates John Moore as President
of the Connaught Republic

their way to Ballina and thence cross-country to Castlebar. Stock's narrative of the event was published in 1800 and is an important record of 'the year of the French'.

The French were surprised by the lack of military training among the Irish who supported them. Nonetheless, over 3,000 Irish recruits joined their ranks on the march to Castlebar, many armed only with pikes and pitchforks. This Franco-Irish force marched along the remote west shore of Lough Conn over rough uneven ground. They passed Barnageeha (the Windy Gap) and arrived at Castlebar to face a startled British garrison under the command of General Lake. They broke through the Crown forces and moved from Staball Hill down Thomas Street to what was then the market place. From here, they took Castlebar Bridge, under the command of General Fontaine. With the rebels in pursuit, the Crown forces broke and fled in what became known as the 'Races of Castlebar'. Then fortune turned. The Franco-Irish forces were finally surrounded by English troops on 8 September 1798 at Ballinamuck in Co. Longford. Here, the French surrender was accepted, but some 2,000 Irish were massacred. Father Andrew Conroy, parish priest of Addergoole (Lahardane), and Father Manus Sweeney of Newport were hanged for their support of the French.

John Moore (1767-99) of Moore Hall, Lough Carra, joined the 1798 rebellion while a student of law in Dublin. He later became the first President of the newly declared Republic of Connaught. However, the republic was short-lived and Moore was imprisoned for over a year, dying in 1799 in a Waterford gaol while awaiting trial. He was buried in Ballygunner Cemetery in Waterford. In August 1961, his body was brought home to Mayo and re-interred in Castlebar on The Mall, where a memorial gravestone was erected.

The poet William Butler Yeats (1865-1939) set his play *Cathleen Ni*

Houlihan in Killala at the time of the French landing in 1798. The play tells the story of a poor old woman who comes to a peasant's cottage and persuades a young man to leave his sweetheart and join the French. The play caused a sensation in 1902 when it was first staged, with Maud Gonne in the lead role. Years later, to commemorate the events of 1798, a major television film was co-produced by three national broadcasting stations – Ireland's RTE, England's Channel 4 and France's FR3. The film, *The Year of the French*, which was made in 1982, was based on Thomas Flanagan's historical novel of the same name.

The only contemporary plaque commemorating the Rebellion of 1798 is incorporated into the wall of Castlebar's Christ Church, the Church of Ireland on Ellison Street. It was erected to the memory of five privates of the Fraser Highlanders who were killed in action in Castlebar on 24 August 1798.

The Rebellion of 1798 remained a potent event around which Republicans rallied for many generations. The 'Maid of Erin' monument, sculpted by T.H. Denning, was unveiled in Ballina for the centennial commemoration of the rebellion in 1898 by Maud Gonne MacBride (1866-1953), founder of the nationalist women's organisation Inghinidhe na hÉireann (Daughters of Ireland). In 1987, the monument was re-dedicated by her son, Seán MacBride (1904-1988), former Chief of Staff of the IRA (1936), founder of Clann na Poblachta (Party of the Republic), Minister for External Affairs in the first inter-party government of 1948-1951 and Nobel Peace Prize winner in 1974. The inscription on the monument reads:

> *Well they fought for poor old Ireland*
> *And full bitter was their fate;*
> *Oh! What glorious pride and sorrow*
> *Fill the name of ninety eight.*

(Above) 'The Maid of Erin' in Ballina by sculptor T.H. Denning, erected to commemorate the 1798 Rebellion

(Above left) A scene from the film 'The Year of the French', made in 1982, showing the Franco-Irish army crossing Palmerston Bridge, near Killala

*Spiorad '98 commemorative parade,
organised by Mayo County Council
Arts Squad in 1998*

*Commemorative parade held in
Castlebar in 1948 to mark the 150th
anniversary of the 1798 Rebellion*

On 1 August 1948, 150 years after the Rebellion of 1798, a commemorative parade 'for Mayo patriot dead and her gallant French allies' was organised in Castlebar. President Seán T. Ó Ceallaigh; Taoiseach John Costello, TD; Éamon de Valera, leader of the Opposition; Cahir Healy, MP from Northern Ireland; Hugh Delargy, representing the Irish in Great Britain; and a representative of the French Government – all officially saluted the passing parade along the West Mall. The military sections, marching in columns of three, included representatives of the Irish Army and the Mayo branch of the old Irish Republican Army (IRA). The parish contingents marched in columns of four and included bands from Castlebar, Kiltimagh, Foxford and Ballaghaderreen.

The bicentenary of the 1798 Rebellion was commemorated in 1998, with colourful and imaginative pageants and parades throughout Mayo. The Mayo County Council Arts Squad worked in partnership with community arts groups to create major street events, called *Spiorad '98*, which interpreted the context and events of the rebellion.

The Great Famine

Many travellers to Ireland in the 19th century commented on the destitution among the common people of Mayo. The writer William Makepeace Thackeray (1811-63), visiting the county on the eve of the Famine, commented that 'after a couple of months in the country, the stranger's eye grows somewhat accustomed to the rags; they do not frighten him as at first; the people who wear them look for the most part healthy enough'.

Between 1750 and the outbreak of the Great Famine in 1846, the population of Ireland grew faster than that of any other western

European country. Landlords were able to greatly increase rents as the demand for land grew and the expanding population was pushed to cultivate less productive areas, such as mountain slopes and bogland. However, marginal soils and small holdings (often as little as a quarter of an acre) could still produce potatoes in sufficient quantity to feed a family. When supplemented with skimmed milk, they offered a cheap and healthy, if monotonous, diet for the majority of Mayo's population. But any failure of the potato crop would herald disaster since the population had no cash reserves and could not avail of alternative food supplies. The potato harvest failed several times during the 19th century – critically in 1817, 1819, 1821 and 1831-32. But these disasters were dwarfed by the scale of the crop failure during the years 1846 to 1850 – the years of the Great Famine.

The Great Famine occurred at a time when Ireland formed part of the richest, most industrialised nation in the world, the United Kingdom. The Famine was a product of many factors, including four years of blighted potato harvests, the people's inability to acquire alternative food sources, the continued export of grain and the inadequacy of the government's response to the growing crisis. During the Famine, Mayo lost 30% of its population either through death or emigration. The long-term effect of the Famine impacted greatly upon the social and economic life of the people of Mayo for many generations.

The blight affecting the potatoes was first noticed in September 1845, but the real devastation dates from the autumn of 1846, the second year of the potato crop failure. At the time, no cure was known. Fifteen years after the Famine, it was discovered that the fungus *Phytophthora infestans* caused the blight; it could reproduce itself rapidly, infecting entire fields within hours. It was to take another 25 years before an effective cure was found, by the French scientist Professor M. Millardet who devised a mixture based on copper sulphate (bluestone) and hydrated lime to be sprayed on the growing shoots of the plants.

The only hope for the vast body of the starving Irish was to turn to the workhouses, which had been established under the Poor Law (Ireland) Act of 1838 to alleviate the distress of the 'deserving poor'. Under the Act, the country was divided into 130 (later 163) Poor Law Unions, as administrative districts. Five Unions with workhouses were initially established in Mayo – at Ballina, Ballinrobe, Castlebar, Swinford and Westport. The number increased to nine in the early 1850s, with additional workhouses at Belmullet, Claremorris, Killala and Newport. Each Union was governed by an elected Board of Guardians, who were responsible for the levying of rates to pay for the relief of the destitute and for maintaining a Union workhouse.

In Mayo, the Poor Law Unions comprised of extensive areas overwhelmingly populated by semi-destitute peasantry. The various Boards of Guardians went into arrears due to the non-payment of Poor Law Rates and looked to central government for assistance during the

19th-century print of 'An outside jaunting car in a storm', with ragged children begging for alms

A deserted house and the trace of lazy beds are all that remain of this family's small holding in Mayo

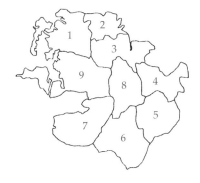

The nine Poor Law Unions of Co. Mayo, set up in the 1850s

1. Belmullet
2. Killala
3. Ballina
4. Swinford
5. Claremorris
6. Ballinrobe
7. Westport
8. Castlebar
9. Newport

Swinford Workhouse, one of George Wilkinson's standard designs, with a front block that housed receiving rooms on the ground floor and a board room on the first floor

George Henry Moore (1810-1870), a Mayo landlord who worked to relieve the distress of his tenants during the Famine

Famine years. Some of Mayo's Poor Law Unions were declared 'distressed' and financial assistance was given to Ballina, Ballinrobe, Castlebar, Swinford and Westport. But the response did not meet the scale of the need. Workhouses were designed in pre-Famine times to house 1.5% of the Poor Law Unions' population. During the Famine, they were unable to cope with the demands of the thousands of people who often walked miles to seek relief and who were frequently refused. The workhouse system was rigid: inmates were separated according to age and sex, and had to follow a severe disciplinary regime governing their diet and daily schedule. The system continued in varying forms into the early years of the Irish Free State and was replaced after 1923 by a system of County Homes for the old and infirm, and hospitals for the sick.

In the spring of 1846, Indian corn was imported into Ireland to help ease the crisis. It was known as 'Peel's Brimstone', after Prime Minister Sir Robert Peel and the burning pain it left in the stomachs of the hungry. Public works schemes were also introduced in 1846 to give employment so that the destitute could earn money to buy food. The works consisted of activities such as making roads, breaking stones, drainage works, pier and bridge building. The building of a canal connecting Mayo's Lough Mask to Galway's Lough Corrib was one of the many schemes undertaken. The purpose was to provide a navigation channel between the two lakes, but the canal was never used since the bedrock was limestone and it proved too porous.

The Castlebar newspaper *The Telegraph or Connaught Ranger* reported in June 1846:

> Numerous, and we regret to state, well-founded complaints, have been made to us from Turlough, Islandeady, Castlebar, Ballinrobe, Newport, Westport, Aughagower and Ballyhean, as to the manner in which Public Works are being carried out – but particularly the way in which the poor wretches employed on them are paid their wages. Many of those creatures, pale and haggard, have declared to us that for two, three, four and five weeks! they have not been paid their wages.

In August 1846, the same newspaper published a petition sent to the Right Hon. Lord John Russell, First Lord of the Treasury, following a public meeting 'of at least twenty thousand persons'. The petition was from the inhabitants of the parishes of Aglish, Ballyhean, Breaffy, Turlough, Islandeady, Touaghty, Drum, Rosslee, Ballintubber, Burriscarra, Kilmeena and Kilmaclasser. The newspaper reported:

> The meeting assembled in the open air, on the Green of Castlebar, beg leave to respectively submit to you that in consequence of the total failure of the potato crop of the present season, the great bulk of the people of these parishes, and of the county generally, are reduced to a state of utmost destitution, and that starvation with all its horrors must immediately ensue, and the people will, unless relieved, inevitably perish by hundreds and thousands.

A commemorative cross on the road to Delphi marking the scene of a famine tragedy in 1849

William Bennett, a member of the Religious Society of Friends (the Quakers), wrote an account of his visit to Mayo during the Famine. He entered a cabin in Belmullet and saw:

> Stretched in one dark corner, scarcely visible, from the smoke and rags that covered them, were three children huddled together, lying there because they were too weak to rise, pale and ghastly, their little limbs – on removing a portion of the filthy covering – perfectly emaciated, eyes sunk, voice gone, and evidently in the last stage of actual starvation. Crouched over the turf embers was another form, wild and all but naked, scarcely human in appearance. It stirred not, nor noticed us. On some straw, soddened upon the ground, moaning piteously, was a shrivelled old woman imploring us to give her something – baring her limbs partly, to show how the skin hung loose from the bones, as soon as she attracted our attention. Above her, on something like a ledge, was a young woman, with sunken cheeks – a mother, I have no doubt – who scarcely raised her eyes in answer to our enquiries, but pressed her hand upon her forehead, with a look of unutterable anguish and despair.

During 1846-47, the Religious Society of Friends, together with other charitable relief organisations (such as the British Association) and local relief committees, organised soup kitchens for the needy. *The Tyrawly Herald* reported in January 1847 that Ballina and Ardnaree Relief Committee had distributed 1,387 quarts of soup each day to 563 families at the expense of £23. In the same year, William Bennett reported that the school house in Rossport was fitted into a soup kitchen by the Religious Society of Friends to which 'the poor people came a very long way, from other districts, in the hopes of partaking of the bounty, and were not sent empty away'.

The National Famine Memorial at Murrisk, sculpted by John Behan

Certain landlords were callous in the extreme during the great poverty of the Famine years. For example, Sir George Charles Bingham, third Earl of Lucan, and Sir Roger Palmer were notorious for the mass evictions of their tenants. Other landlords, however, made great efforts to relieve the distress of their tenants, among them the Marquis of Sligo of Westport House, George Henry Moore (1810-70) of Moore Hall and Robert Lynch-Blosse of Balla. They collectively chartered a ship, the *Martha Washington*, to sail from New Orleans to Westport with 1,000 tons of flour on board for distribution among the poor. George Henry Moore also made provision for relief with the substantial £10,000 winnings he had obtained from his horse, *Corunna*, in the Chester Cup in 1846.

Doolough, in a remote part of west Mayo, was the scene of a terrible tragedy in March 1849. A large number of starving people gathered in Louisburgh to seek assistance from the local relieving officer. They were instructed to apply for relief to the Westport Poor Law Board of Guardians, who were meeting at Delphi Lodge near Doolough, a valley situated in the rugged Mweelrea mountain peaks. The people walked the 20 miles to Delphi overnight, but were subsequently refused assistance by the Board. Many perished as a result. This tragedy was commemorated for some years in the Famine Walk from Louisburgh to Delphi, and was supported by the Irish charity group Action from Ireland (AfrI), which aids famine victims throughout the world.

Mass emigration was a central feature of the Famine years and remained a long-term legacy for Mayo. Cargo vessels used to import goods were used on their return journeys to export people to the United States of America, Great Britain, Canada and Australia. Landlord-assisted emigration was introduced and the 'American wake' became a feature of Irish life. Deserted villages now became a familiar part of the Mayo landscape.

Passenger traffic across the Atlantic went unregulated during the early years of the Famine and desperate emigrants were frequently exploited. The *Elizabeth and Sarah* was such a vessel involved in the trade. It sailed from Killala in July 1846 bound for Quebec with 276 passengers aboard, 64 more than was officially allowed. Sanitary conditions were poor and there were no toilet facilities. The journey took eight weeks, double the estimated time. By the end of the voyage, over 40 passengers had died from overcrowding, lack of food, dehydration and unsanitary conditions. Such vessels rightly earned the name 'coffin ships'. It is therefore apt that the National Famine Memorial by John Behan is sculpted in the form of a coffin ship, with skeletal bodies overflowing from its decks. This poignant symbol, set on the shores of Clew Bay at Murrisk, was unveiled in 1997, on the 150th anniversary of the Great Famine.

In the ten years between 1841 and 1851, the population of Co. Mayo fell by some 30% – from 388,887 to 274,499. Since the Famine, successive censi showed a steady decrease in the county's population, to a low of 109,525 in 1971. The dramatic population decline can be clearly seen in one Mayo townland, Aghadrinagh, where a comparison of the pre-Famine 1839 Ordnance Survey map with the post-Famine 1900 edition of the map shows the number of houses severely depleted in the later map.

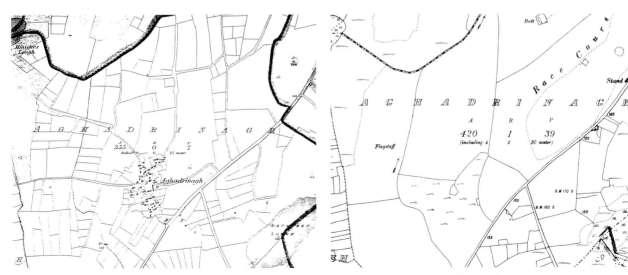

Ordnance Survey map of 1839 showing the densely populated townland of Aghadrinagh in Ballyheane parish

Ordnance Survey map of 1900 showing the townland of Aghadrinagh, now severely depopulated

The Land War and reform

Memories of the Great Famine were revived during the late 1870s as bad weather, poor crops and declining cattle prices produced an agrarian crisis in Mayo which left the people heavily in debt and unable to pay their rents. The crop failures resulted in spontaneous mass protest that was channeled, under the leadership of James Daly (1838-1911) and Michael Davitt (1846-1906), into the formation of the Land League in 1879. An historic meeting at Daly's Hotel on The Mall in Castlebar took place on 16 August 1879 and the Mayo Land League was established. It quickly grew into a national organisation, with Davitt taking the position of secretary and organising Land League branches throughout the country. It combined nationalists of all shades in one mass agrarian movement and received strong backing and financial help from emigrants and supporters in America. The tactics of the League included mass demonstrations in support of reduced rents, resistance to evictions and opposition to new occupants replacing evicted tenants.

Michael Davitt was born into the Famine in 1846. His family was evicted from their home at Straide and forced to emigrate to industrial Lancashire in England. There, like many Mayo emigrants before him, Davitt started work in the textile factories at a very young age. He lost his arm in an industrial accident, but was fortunate to be sponsored by a philanthropic businessman to return to school for a few years. He subsequently became an organiser of the Irish Republican Brotherhood and was connected with the 1867 Fenian Rising. He was sentenced to fifteen years' penal servitude in 1870 at Dartmoor prison. After seven years

An eviction scene in the west of Ireland, sketched by Aloysius O'Kelly and published in the Illustrated London News of March 1881

of harsh conditions, he was released and returned to his native Mayo, where he received a great welcome. Touring in the United States, he was reunited with his family who had emigrated to Scranton, Pennsylvania, a town now twinned with Ballina. On his return from America, he helped found the Land League.

Davitt was motivated in part by his own experiences of landlordism, which he recalled in the most famous of his six books, *The Fall of Feudalism in Ireland* (1904):

> Almost my first-remembered experience of my own life and of the existence of landlordism was our eviction in 1852, when I was about five years of age. The eviction and the privations of the preceding famine years, the story of the starving of Mayo, of the deaths from hunger and the coffinless graves on the roadside – everywhere a hole could be dug for the slaves who died because of 'God's providence' – all this was the political food seasoned with a mother's tears over unmerited sorrows and sufferings which had fed my mind in another land, a teaching which lost none of its force or directness by being imparted in the Gaelic tongue, which was almost always spoken in our Lancashire home.

James Daly (1838-1911) from Boghadoon, Lahardane, proprietor and editor of the Castlebar-based *Connaught Telegraph* newspaper, was one of the most notable defenders of Mayo's small farmers, although he was a relatively prosperous, large grazier farmer himself. He was educated by the Franciscan Brothers at Errew Monastery and later became a town councillor and Poor Law Guardian. He was one of the main organisers of the mass meetings of the land campaign in its early years. The first of these meetings was held at Irishtown, near Ballindine on the Mayo-Galway border on Sunday, 20 April 1879. Thousands of assembled tenants sought rent abatements because of their inability to pay following bad harvests. The people of Kiltimagh made a Land League banner of silk poplin for the Irishtown meeting, the front emblazoned with the words 'God save Ireland' above a harp, flanked by wolfhounds and with shamrocks all around.

In 1880, Captain Charles Cunningham Boycott (1832-97) became the first victim of the Land

The Land League banner of the Kiltimagh contingent at the Irishtown meeting in April 1879

Sketch of Land Leaguers tilling the farm of an imprisoned farmer, published in the Illustrated London News of May 1881

Sketch of police encampment in the grounds of Lough Mask House during the Boycott Affair, from The Graphic of November 1880

'The Affray at Belmullet' as depicted in the Illustrated London News of November 1881

League's public campaign of ostracisation of those who traversed its demands for fair rents. At the same time, Boycott unwittingly gave his name to a new word in the English language. It was the local priest, Father John O'Malley, who coined the word 'boycott' and it first appeared in print in an article by an American journalist, James Redpath, in October 1880. Within a month, the French newspaper *Le Figaro* reported that 'the Irish have invented a new word: they now say to 'boycott' someone, meaning to ostracise him'.

Boycott had come from Norfolk in 1857 to live at Corrymore House, near Keel on Achill Island. Then in 1873, he moved to manage the Lough Mask estate of Lord Erne, who resided in Fermanagh. He gained notoriety in the autumn of 1880 when he resolutely refused to lower rents despite a succession of bad harvests. The Land League commenced its campaign of ostracisation against him. The English newspapers, the *Daily Express* and *Daily Telegraph*, sympathised with his predicament and assisted in organising the 'Boycott Relief Expedition' between 13-27 November 1880, when 50 Ulstermen were recruited from Cavan and Monaghan as relief labourers to save Boycott's harvest. His ten acres of crops were altogether worth about £500. A large military force was maintained for the protection of the working party. An encampment was formed with 30 tents, complete with furniture and provisions, provided by the government and brought under escort from Ballinrobe to Lough Mask. Lady Louisa Knox (née Browne) of Cranmore House assisted the Boycott family by supplying timber for the fires. Despite such efforts, the boycott was not lifted – local people continued not to deal, trade, talk or work with the Captain. Thus, he and his family were forced to sell out and return to England, where Boycott died in 1897 at his home in Surrey. The Boycott affair attracted significant international publicity for the Land League campaign and was seen as evidence of the mass opposition to the landlord system.

Violent agrarian incidents were common occurrences during the years of the land war. The *Illustrated London News* of 12 November 1881 carried an illustration entitled 'The Affray at Belmullet', created from a sketch by Aloysius O'Kelly. The 'affray' took place when a process server, accompanied by 60 policemen, attempted to serve summons for rates on tenants at Grawkill, near Belmullet. Three hundred local people assailed the police with showers of stones as they ascended the mountain path leading to their village. The police attempted on several occasions to charge up the hill and eventually fired 24 shots at the crowd. An elderly woman and a young girl died while several others, including members of the police, were seriously injured. Twenty people were subsequently arrested and sent to Castlebar gaol.

The eviction of James Walsh's family from their home in Elmhall, Belcarra, on the instructions of Miss Harriet Gardiner (1821-92) in October 1886

The Ladies' Irish National Land League was formed in response to the British government's Coercion Act of 1881, which undermined the legality of the Land League and imprisoned its male leaders, including Charles Stewart Parnell, its President. The Ladies' organisation fell outside the terms of the Act and so continued the land campaign. The first committee of the Ladies' Land League included two women from Co. Mayo – Anne Deane from Ballaghaderreen (then in Co. Mayo), who was President of the Ladies' Land League for a period, and Beatrice Walshe of Balla. The organisation operated in difficult times, when there was an upsurge in evictions and the 'No Rent Manifesto' campaign, which was a strike against rent payment. The Ladies' Land League monitored evictions and provided relief to those affected, keeping detailed records on specially devised 'Eviction Forms'. They also organised resistance to land-grabbing.

From Kilmainham gaol, Charles Stewart Parnell, President of the Land League, negotiated the so-called Kilmainham Treaty. This brought about his release and that of other Land League leaders, as well as the repeal of the Coercion Act in exchange for an end to land agitation. Finally the process of ending landlordism through legislation had begun, with laws introduced from 1885 onwards.

The dismantling of landlordism was not the end of the land question in Mayo. In 1899, a new organisation, the United Irish League, was launched in the county – the cradle of constitutional revolutions. Founded by William O'Brien (1852-1928) and John Dillon (1851-1927), both Members of Parliament, the objective of the United Irish League was to oppose large ranches held by graziers.

William O'Brien, MP and Cork journalist, founded the newspaper *The Irish People* to promote the ideas and activities of the United Irish League.

Eviction forms, devised by the Ladies' Irish National Land League, recorded individual details of evictions in 1881

Sketch of 'O'Brien on the rack turned by Lord Sligo', published in the Freeman's Journal of June 1900

The District Nurse at Geesala, south of Belmullet, employed under the Lady Dudley Nursing Scheme

He lived for a time in Westport, where his wife recorded aspects of their three years spent at Mallow Cottage in her books *Under Croagh Patrick* (1904) and *My Irish Friends* (1937). John Dillon, a radical liberal, was the elected MP for Mayo East from 1885 to 1918. Along with John Redmond (1856-1918), he was at the centre of the Home Rule negotiations in the early 20th century, the purpose of which was the restoration of an Irish parliament in Dublin with responsibility for most domestic issues.

The United Irish League put forward the imprisoned John O'Donnell as their candidate in the first Mayo County Council elections in 1899 and in the parliamentary election for the Mayo South seat left vacant after Michael Davitt resigned. O'Donnell's candidacy was opposed by Major John MacBride (1865-1916), who was supported by the leadership of the Irish Parliamentary Party. The opposing candidates reflected the local and national disunity among the various strands of nationalism.

Arthur Balfour, Chief Secretary for Ireland at the time, established a new agency in 1891 – the Congested Districts Board. This was set up to encourage agriculture and industry in destitute parts of the country along the western seaboard. The Board was described by some as an attempt to 'kill Home Rule with kindness'. (The question of Home Rule dominated Irish political life between 1870 and 1920.) The Board's first task was to compile 'base line reports' on 84 selected districts (this number was later increased) in 8 western counties, including Mayo. The latter had the largest area surveyed (893,480 statute acres) and the largest population (143,201 in 1891), but one of the lowest Poor Law Valuations per head of population (18*s* 3*d*). The intention was that these reports would be used later to measure the progress of the Board's various works, which included the purchase and redistribution of land, and the development of fisheries, agriculture, infrastructure and support for industries, such as the Foxford Woollen Mills.

The ending of the land war did not however eradicate all the difficulties confronting the people of Mayo. The 20th century brought growing concern for social and public health. Among the earliest schemes established was the Lady Dudley Nursing Scheme, set up by Lady Dudley, the wife of the Lord Lieutenant, to employ nurses in the poorest parts of Ireland through funds raised by private subscription. The nurses in the scheme were particularly well trained and promoted cleanliness and healthy living. They were given a bicycle and equipped with surgical implements and medical stores. They were frequently called upon to set bones, dress wounds and perform operations. Thirteen such nurses were initially employed under the scheme and, in the absence of suitable accommodation, the Congested Districts Board provided loans to build houses for them.

Consumption or tuberculosis (TB) was one of the main threats to health at the turn of the century. Newspapers advertised cures and remedies, but in the early years there was little hope of recovery. In the early 1900s, Lady Aberdeen, the wife of the Viceroy of Ireland, founded the Women's

'Ireland A Nation' – a formal group portrait of Mayo Nationalists, photographed by Thomas Wynne, c. 1900

National Health Association to fight TB. The 'War on Consumption' incorporated a van touring the west, using exhibitions to promote pure food, pure milk and cleanliness, but the disease persisted.

Mayo County Council proposed the appointment of a Tuberculosis Medical Officer, noting that the 'insidious disease is claiming large numbers of victims in the county'. Some decades later, sanatoria for TB sufferers were opened around the county, including Belleek Manor in Ballina in the 1950s. For 30 years from 1924, Creagh House near Ballinrobe was known as 'St. Theresa's Sanatorium for Consumption Patients'. Despite best efforts, the disease ravaged its victims and when the sanatorium went on fire in 1939, it proved difficult to find volunteers, other than the diligent staff, to fight the flames – such was the dread of TB.

The revolution in land ownership resulted in a degree of material prosperity. This, in turn, provided the opportunity for renewed interest in Gaelic culture, including Irish history, literature, music, art and, most particularly, Gaelic games and language. This growing awareness created the sense of a culturally distinctive 'Irishness', which supported the demand for national independence. Conradh na Gaeilge, the Gaelic League, was founded in 1893 under the presidency of Dr. Douglas Hyde (1860-1949), who became the first President of Ireland (1938-45). The League sought to preserve Irish as the national language, encourage the study and publication of Gaelic literature and cultivate modern literature in Irish. Hyde insisted that the Gaelic League should avoid party politics. Along with other cultural organisations, it became a part of the broad movement that sought Ireland's economic, social and political independence.

Dr. McHale Corps of the National Volunteer Movement 1912-1916, photographed by J.J. Leonard near Lahardane

Major John MacBride, executed in May 1916, along with the other leaders of the Easter Rising

As a result of the work of the Gaelic League, hundreds of Gaelic enthusiasts travelled to Mayo and other parts of the west of Ireland where Irish was still spoken to learn the language. Tourmakeady was entirely Irish-speaking at the beginning of the 20th century and an Irish Summer College was established there to promote learning of the language. Sir Roger Casement (1864-1916) was the school's guiding spirit. Among members of the Gaelic League to attend the college was Éamon de Valera (1882-1975), President of the first Dáil, founder of Fianna Fáil and President of Ireland for two terms, from 1959 to 1973.

Towards independence

The land question undoubtedly dominated the hearts and minds of the people at the end of the 19th century and into the early 20th. But other political issues also engaged them. The Easter Rising of 1916 against British rule in Ireland was largely a Dublin affair, with Mayo's local authorities initially passing resolutions condemning the Rising. The response of the government, notably the execution of the leaders, won country-wide public sympathy for their cause. This was reflected in Mayo, with new local authority resolutions retracting the initial condemnation.

Major John MacBride (1865-1916) was one of the fifteen executed in Kilmainham on 5 May 1916 in the aftermath of the Rising. MacBride, born at Westport Quay in 1865, emigrated to South Africa in 1896. There he worked in the mines and was also active, along with Arthur Griffith (1871-1922), in organising the Irish Society in Johannesburg, which formed the Irish Transvaal Brigade. He was wounded at Ladysmith while

Dr. Kathleen Lynn of Cong (seated, front row on right) in the summer of 1916 with other women involved in the Easter Rising

fighting for the Boers during the Boer War in 1899. In 1903, he married Maud Gonne (1866-1953) in Paris. She, a life-long political activist, was immortalised in W.B. Yeats' love poems and MacBride is also remembered in his poem *Easter 1916*. MacBride is commemorated today on Westport's Mall with a bronze bust by the sculptor Peter Grant.

Another Mayo participant in the 1916 Rising was Dr. Kathleen Lynn (1874-1955). She was born at Cong, where her father was the local rector, and throughout her life combined her medical work with campaigning for feminist and nationalist movements of the day. Active in the Votes for Women Campaign, she acted as medical attendant to the suffragettes during their militant hunger strike campaign in 1912. A member of the Irish Citizen Army, she was Chief Medical Officer and a Captain during the 1916 Easter Rising, with responsibility for medical planning and supplies to the Citizen Army's stations during the fighting. She later served as Surgeon-General to Sinn Féin and was elected to its Executive (of 24 persons) at the 1917 convention. In the same year, she served as Vice-President of the Irish Women Workers' Union. This remarkable woman always considered medicine as an important tool for social improvement. She was only too aware of the preventable medical problems faced by those living in Dublin's slums. Along with Madeline Ffrench Mullan, she founded St. Ultan's Hospital for Infants in Dublin in 1919 and it became the first hospital to introduce the BCG vaccine for the prevention and control of tuberculosis in 1936.

The seeds of World War I (1914-18) were laid in the colonial ambitions, incipient nationalism and dynastic tensions developing among European countries at the start of the 20th century. These factors were aggravated by commercial rivalries, which led eventually to the outbreak of war in 1914. For various personal and political reasons, many young Mayo men were among those who joined the British Army in what was supposed to

Private John Roach (front row, 3rd from right) was awarded the Distinguished Conduct Medal for conspicuous gallantry in action during World War I, pictured outside Castlebar Courthouse in 1918

be 'the war to end all wars'. Over 400 Mayo men died fighting in that war. In the shadow of the new political atmosphere that emerged after the 1916 Rising, those soldiers were quickly forgotten. Those who returned home were frequently treated as outcasts. Nonetheless, hundreds of local people turned out when Private John Roach of the Connaught Rangers was awarded the Distinguished Conduct Medal for conspicuous gallantry in action. His bravery involved volunteering to obtain more bombs when his unit's supplies were exhausted and using his own initiative to organise an attack on the enemy.

A general election was called in Ireland in December 1918 after World War I ended. Nationally, there was an overwhelming majority of Sinn Féin candidates elected. All four seats in Mayo fell to Sinn Féin with huge margins, with the leader Éamon de Valera victorious over Ballaghaderreen-born John Dillon of the Nationalist party. The execution of the leaders of the 1916 Rising and the Conscription Bill of 1918 contributed to the support for Sinn Féin. After their election, the Sinn Féin TDs (or MPs) refused to take their seats at the Westminster Parliament, following their policy of abstention, and those who were not in gaol established an independent parliament in Dublin – the first Dáil Éireann. It met on 21 January 1919 and elected a Republican government. This was also the day that the first shots of the Anglo-Irish War or War of Independence were fired by the Irish Volunteers. They took an Oath of Allegiance to the Dáil in August of that year and adopted their new name – the Irish Republican Army (IRA).

The growing support for the Republican cause in Mayo is evident in a banner which the Kilkelly Sinn Féin Cumann (established in 1915) made in memory of Thomas Ashe in 1918. He was a native of Co. Kerry and a Commandant in the 1916 Rising, dying in September 1917 from force-feeding while on hunger strike. The banner was used on many political occasions, often accompanied by the Kilkelly Fife and Drum Band. Among the first outings for the banner was to Ballaghaderreen to support Éamon de Valera when he addressed a rally there during the 1918 election. The last time the banner was used was when Seán Lemass spoke in Kilkelly at a rally in 1944.

In the War of Independence (1919-21), the guerrilla warfare campaign of the Irish Republican Army depended on local initiatives to establish 'flying columns' of men permanently under arms on manoeuvres. The IRA's tactics included the burning of the barracks of the Royal Irish Constabulary (RIC) to force their evacuation and withdrawal from the targeted areas. All of Ireland was policed by the RIC, under the direct control of Dublin Castle. The locally recruited RIC were reinforced in 1920 by a new RIC Auxiliary Division comprised of ex-Army officers and by a force of new recruits drawn mainly from among the lower ranks of former British soldiers. This latter force became known as the Black and Tans because of the odd assortment of uniforms initially supplied to them. The numerous atrocities for which they were responsible established a brutal reputation for the force. Mayo people like Richard Walsh from Balla helped to procure arms for the Republicans from England during the War of Independence. He later became a member of Mayo County Council and then a Fianna Fáil TD and Senator.

The 'Remember Thomas Ashe' banner, made for Kilkelly Sinn Féin Cumann in 1918

The war in Mayo

Mayo-born Ernie O'Malley (1897-1957) was initially an Irish Republican exponent of the physical force tradition, who later became an author, poet and art critic. Born in Castlebar, O'Malley spent his summers at Rosbeg, Westport. In 1907, his family moved to Dublin, but he was to return to

British forces stationed at Westport, c. 1920

*Ernie O'Malley in 1929, photographed
by Edward Weston in Carmel,
California*

Mayo in the 1930s to live at Burrishoole Lodge in Newport. His two autobiographical volumes, *On Another Man's Wound* and *The Singing Flame*, are important accounts of the revolutionary period of 1916-23. His book *Raids and Rallies*, based on a series of articles in the *Sunday Press* newspaper, was published posthumously.

O'Malley joined the Volunteers soon after the 1916 Rising and quickly established himself as a natural leader. He interrupted his medical studies in 1918 and joined the IRA, becoming one of its full-time organisers and working alongside leading IRA men Dan Breen and Seán Treacy. O'Malley was firmly against the 1921 Anglo-Irish Treaty and was appointed Director of Organisation for the Anti-Treaty Republican forces, led by Éamon de Valera. In April 1922, he participated in the take-over of the Four Courts in Dublin. The bombardment of these buildings in June by the pro-Treaty forces saw the commencement of the Civil War. O'Malley acted as Assistant Chief of Staff of the Republican forces, responsible for Leinster and Ulster. He was badly wounded during his capture in November 1922. While still in prison, he was elected TD for Dublin North in August 1923 and in November he participated in a 41-day hunger strike. After his release in 1924, he was in poor health and travelled throughout continental Europe to recuperate. He returned to his medical studies in 1926, but these were interrupted again when in 1928 he went on a fund-raising tour of the USA on behalf of the *Irish Press* newspaper, which de Valera was in the process of establishing for the Fianna Fáil party. He returned to Ireland in 1935 and married the American artist Helen Hooker.

In 1938, after leaving his medical studies for a third time, O'Malley moved to Mayo where he farmed for some years, as well as photographing Early Christian monuments and collecting folklore around Clew Bay. He also pursued his literary interests as editor of *The Bell* and artistic pursuits in writing art criticism and organising a Jack B. Yeats' exhibition in Dublin in 1945. In 1951, he acted as an assistant to John Ford, the film director, in the making of *The Quiet Man* at Cong and in a second film in 1956.

During the War of Independence, the Mayo Brigade of the IRA was divided into four – the North, South, East and West Brigade Columns. In North Mayo, 50 volunteers and officers were engaged in active service and most of their action took place around Ballina and Bonniconlon. These, therefore, were also the areas that bore the brunt of reprisals. In Spring 1921, Michael Kilroy of Newport formed the West Mayo Brigade Column from what had been independent battalion columns in Castlebar, Westport and Newport. Kilroy was leader of this Flying Column, which undertook numerous surprise attacks including those at Westport and Newport on 18 May 1921. The main body of the brigade took up an ambush position at Kilmeena the next day. Five members of the brigade died, with several others badly wounded, and

one member of the police force was killed as a result of the two-hour engagement between the IRA and the RIC and Black and Tans. Another member of the West Mayo Brigade was killed a few days later at Skirdagh. Then, on 2 June 1921 at Carrowkennedy near Westport, Kilroy's Flying Column ambushed a large convoy of RIC and Black and Tans, forcing them to surrender. The brigade collected 25 rifles, 25 revolvers, a Lewis machine gun, 5,000 rounds of ammunition and boxes of bombs. In the days following, thousands of British troops were deployed in Mayo and the greatest round-up of IRA suspects ever seen in the west took place.

Three weeks after the Carrowkennedy ambush, the 31 members of Kilroy's Flying Column of the West Mayo Brigade were photographed by J.J. Leonard in what is considered one of the finest photographs of an active service unit during the War of Independence. The image was captured at Derrymartin on the southern slopes of Mount Nephin at 11.45pm on the evening of 21 June 1921 (the longest day of the year), with no light but the 'light of Heaven'. The four men inset in the corners of the photograph are members of the Flying Column who were on duty at the time.

Kilroy's Flying Column of the IRA's West Mayo Brigade, photographed by J.J. Leonard at 11.45pm on 21 June 1921. (Back row) Michael Kilroy, Tom Ketterick, Edward Moane, John Gibbons, J. Walsh, Paddy J. Cannon, Paddy Lambert, Jim Kelly, J. Doherty, B. Malone, Jim Rush and Joe Ring.
(Middle row) M. Naughton, Ned Hogan, Jim Harney, Dan Sammon, Jack Keane, Jack Connelly, Richard Joyce, Patrick McNamara and Willie Malone.
(Front row) Dan Gavin, Tom Heavey, Johnnie Duffy, Jack McDonagh, P.J. Kelly, Jim Moran, Jimmy Flaherty, B. Cryan and Michael Staunton.
(Lying in front) Dr. J.A. Madden.
(Insets, clockwise from top left) P. Duffy, J. Baker, T. Ainsworth and M. Gallagher.

Lewis gun captured by Kilroy's Flying Column of the IRA's West Mayo Brigade at the battle of Carrowkennedy, 2 June 1921

Unveiling ceremony at Kilkelly in June 1972 of the monument to the East Mayo Brigade, sculpted by Yann Renard Goulet

Republican courts, like this one in Westport, were held all over the country between 1919 and 1921

In May 1921, the South Mayo Brigade, under the leadership of Tom Maguire from Cross, ambushed British troops at Tourmakeady. A major battle developed and five RIC men were killed. The British troops finally withdrew and the RIC were forced to evacuate their barracks at Derrypark (which looked down on Lough Mask) and Kinnury. The IRA strategy was to strain the British by forcing them to police these evacuated areas with patrols which would then be vulnerable to ambush. In June 1921, Tom Maguire was elected Sinn Féin TD for Mayo. He was a member of the anti-Treaty forces during the Civil War and was elected as a Republican TD in 1922 and 1923 for Mayo South, remaining on the IRA Executive until 1927 when he resigned. He adhered to the view that the Second Dáil (1921-22) was the legitimate government of the Irish Republic.

The engagements of the East Mayo Brigade included the capture of Swinford RIC Barracks, various ambushes at Callow, Foxford, Killasser and Carracastle, an attack on Ballaghaderreen Barracks and an engagement with the Black and Tans at Charlestown in which a large consignment of weapons was seized. In June 1972 near Kilkelly, the East Mayo Brigade was commemorated in a striking monument of a solitary figure, cast by the Breton sculptor Yann Renard Goulet. Among the longest surviving members of the brigade were John Snee and Peadar Duignan, the brigade's Training Officer. Snee was born at Barcull, Kilkelly, and joined the 3rd Battalion of the East Mayo Brigade in 1921. He volunteered for full-time active service with the brigade's Flying Column. His unit, along with most of the Western forces, were opposed to the Treaty. In his memoirs, Snee recalls the time he spent in prison at the Curragh during the Civil War.

From 1919-21, voluntary arbitration courts were established by the Republicans to replace official courts. The first public session in the country was held in Ballinrobe in May 1919. Martin Michael Nally from Balla was one of the District Justices in these Republican or Dáil Courts. Nally was a member of Mayo County Council from 1918 and also of Claremorris Rural Council. He was elected Cumann na nGaedheal TD for Mayo South in 1923 and in all subsequent elections until 1943. The success of these courts made it possible to encourage the boycott of official county courts. Solicitors, like James Garvey of Westport, received letters from both the British and the Republicans warning them not to participate in the opposing courts.

The War of Independence ended in a truce in July 1921 after which the Anglo-Irish Treaty was negotiated. The Treaty established the Irish Free State as a self-governing dominion within the British Commonwealth. As a result of the Treaty, Sinn Féin split into two factions – those who

James Garvey, the Westport solicitor, like others in his profession, received notices from both British and Republicans, warning him not to participate in enemy courts during the War of Independence

Two Mayo members of the IRA in 1921

supported the Treaty and the newly established Free State, and those who rejected the Treaty on the basis of Ireland's continued subordination to the British Crown. The Civil War between pro- and anti-Treaty forces started in June 1922 when the pro-Treaty troops shelled the headquarters of the anti-Treaty troops in the Four Courts in Dublin. The war continued up until May 1923 when the pro-Treaty supporters formed the first government of the Irish Free State. This episode is one of the great tragedies of Irish history. Former comrades who had fought side by side in the War of Independence against Britain now fought against each other in a bitter conflict, which left a deep imprint on the political scene for many decades.

The pro-Treaty Free State Army (also known as the Regulars or National Army) fought the anti-Treaty Republicans (or Irregulars) in a guerilla war for control of Co. Mayo. Michael Kilroy opposed the Treaty and was on the Executive of the anti-Treaty IRA. He became Officer Commanding of the Western Command of anti-Treaty forces during the Civil War. He was elected Republican TD for Mayo South in 1923 and elected to Mayo County Council in 1925. He joined Fianna Fáil and was elected TD in June and September 1927, 1932 and 1933. Despite the initial numerical superiority of the Republicans in the Civil War, they adopted a

*National Army Captain Tom Healy
of Pontoon (front passenger side),
killed along with Volunteer Seán
Higgins of Foxford by the Irregulars
at Glenamoy in 1922*

defensive strategy, having limited amounts of arms and ammunition and being without facilities to hold captured prisoners.

One encounter in September 1922 involved 150 Irregulars attacking Ballina with an armoured car, 'Ballinalea', which had been previously captured from the National Army. The Irregulars took arms and ammunition from the garrison and left the town in two groups. Some made their way towards Bonniconlon; others went to Killala and on to Ballycastle and Belderrig, finally reaching Glenamoy. The National Army were ambushed by the Irregulars at Glenamoy, losing six men in the ensuing battle. Among them were Captain Tom Healy from Pontoon and Volunteer Seán Higgins from Foxford. As a result of such engagements and losses, the government responded by introducing large-scale internment and from September 1922 the death penalty was introduced for those found with illegal arms. Among those arrested were six young men from South Mayo, who were executed in Tuam, Co. Galway. The Civil War finally came to an end in May 1923.

A Free State

The first Commissioner of the new unarmed police force of the Free State government was Michael Joseph Staines (1885-1955) from Newport. At an early age, he became actively involved in the Gaelic League and the Irish Volunteers, becoming a member of the Supreme Council of the Irish Republican Brotherhood. He took part in the Easter Rising of 1916, for which he was interned at Frongoch in Wales. After his release in 1918, he was elected to Dublin Corporation and Dáil Éireann, later becoming a member of the Senate from 1922 until 1936. In February 1922, he was appointed Commissioner of the Civic Guards, the new police force. He was succeeded by General Eoin O'Duffy.

Pictured here in his Irish Volunteer uniform, c. 1914, Michael Staines of Newport fought as a staff officer in the GPO in 1916

The word 'Eire' dug into the mountain side at Downpatrick Head warned fighter pilots of World War II that they were in neutral territory

The first election in the Irish Free State was held in August 1923. In Mayo North, two Republicans and two members of Cumann na nGaedheal were elected. In Mayo South, two Republicans and three members of Cumann na nGaedheal were elected. In 1927, Fianna Fáil was founded and in the elections that year Cumann na nGaedheal retained two seats in Mayo North, while Dr. J.A. Madden (one of Kilroy's Flying Column in 1921) held one of the Republican seats for Sinn Féin and the other went to P.J. Ruttledge of Fianna Fáil. In Mayo South, Cumann na nGaedheal lost a seat to Labour and Fianna Fáil won both Republican seats. In the 1937 election, the Mayo North constituency was reduced from four seats to three and Fianna Fáil held their two seats. In Mayo South, there was no change in party representation. In 1943, two members of Clann na Talmhan (Party of the Land) were elected to the Dáil for the first time – representatives Dominick Cafferky and Joseph Blowick gained their seats from both Fianna Fáil and Fine Gael.

Clann na Talmhan had been founded in 1938, with support mainly from the western seaboard. The party primarily represented the grievances of small farmers, many of whom were unable to sustain their families and were forced to leave the land and emigrate. At one stage, Clann na Talmhan had eleven members in the Dáil. The Mayo representatives of the Clann na Talmhan party in the Dáil included party leader Joseph Blowick of Belcarra, who served as Minister for Lands in two inter-party governments, Dominick Cafferky (Kilkelly), Bernard Commons (Balla) and Tommy O'Hara (Foxford). The party was also represented on Mayo County Council by Michael Corley, Michael Fadden, Peter McGrath and Martin Carney.

Emigration

In the years following independence, the Mayo population had continued to decline because of the lack of employment opportunities in the county. The population fell from 172,690 in 1926 to 161,349 in 1936 and to 133,052 by 1956. These were lean years in Mayo – years of hardship, poverty and decline. Most people were dependent on agriculture for a living, but income was low and still had to be supplemented by emigrants' remittances or savings from seasonal work in England. Mechanisation and economies of scale for production meant the number of people engaged in farming steadily declined and emigration was rampant. This trend was exacerbated by national and international factors, such as Ireland's Economic War of 1933-38 with Britain and by World War II.

For generations, emigrants from Mayo took the boat to Britain and North America. The shipping lines that advertised fares for emigrants had many agents in the county. The Laird lines from Ballina and Westport travelled to Glasgow and Liverpool, while the Cunard line sailed via Liverpool to New York. The Charlestown journalist and author John Healy wrote two books, entitled *Nineteen Acres* and *Death of an Irish Town* (later republished as *Nobody Shouted Stop*), which comment powerfully on the social history of Mayo in the 1950s and '60s. He tells the story of the deprivation and neglect endured by many Mayo people at that time. In *Death of an Irish Town*, he poignantly records the demise of the commercial and social life of Charlestown as a result of the large-scale emigration:

> John 'yes-boy' Durkan's is closed. No one knocks on Teresa Cassidy's counter any more . . . jovial Jim Gallagher's is no more. Jack O'Donohue's is closed . . . and Tom McCarthy's place. And James Parson's place. And the saddler Vesey . . .

Healy goes on to record that the morning train passing through Charlestown to Dublin was known as the 'emigrant train':

> Morning after morning in the 1940s they went, in droves like cattle . . . The train would pull into Charlestown to a crowded platform . . . The train carried away thousands of emigrants and did more to assist emigration from County Mayo than any other single agency.

The novelist Heinrich Böll (1917-85), who lived on Achill Island in the 1950s, echoed the desolation of emigration in his book *Irish Journal*, translated from German by Leila Vennewitz:

> Those farewells at Irish stations, at bus stops in the middle of a bog when tears blend with raindrops and the Atlantic wind is blowing.

In recent years, the story of emigration from Mayo has come full circle and many former emigrants are now returning home, while other nationalities are immigrating to live in Mayo. Local GP Dr. Jerry Cowley

Manulla Junction 1941 – in the words of John Healy, the train 'did more to assist emigration from Co. Mayo than any other single agency'

initiated the Safe Home Programme in 1984. This imaginative scheme actively seeks to return older Irish people who emigrated many years ago and who supported the economy when their efforts were badly needed, but who are now in need of care. As part of this initiative, a purpose-built community housing project, St. Brendan's Village in Mulranny, was opened, which has now become recognised as a model for the care of older and disabled people. It offers people the opportunity of staying in their own local community rather than being displaced to institutions further afield. This project has been a powerful tool for rural regeneration and is now the largest local employer in the area.

Public administration

Mayo as a unit of administration dates from the late 16th century, although the Grand Jury system was not imposed until the 17th century. The Grand Jury was an assembly of 23 leading landowners, nominated by the current High Sheriff of the county. They met twice yearly, at Spring and Summer assizes. Originally, their responsibility was exclusively related to criminal law functions. They gradually acquired administrative duties for the so-called 'fiscal business'. This included responsibility to make provision for the construction or repair of roads, bridges and piers. The Grand Jury also employed a number of officials, including the Secretary of the Grand Jury and the County Surveyor. Finance for these expenses was raised via the Grand Jury Cess, which was an assessment or tax levied on property within the county. Although substantially reformed by the Grand Jury (Ireland) Act of 1836, the system was inefficient mainly due to the fact that the Grand Jury lacked continuity and could not therefore own premises or machinery. This meant that works undertaken under the auspices of the Grand Jury had to be undertaken by contract.

St. Brendan's Village in Mulranny provides a continuum of support in the local community for older people

The modern system of local government dates from the Poor Law (Ireland) Act of 1838. The county was divided into Poor Law Unions – first five and later nine – vested with statutory powers for the relief of destitution through the workhouse system and after 1847 also by outdoor relief. After the Famine, the Poor Law Unions were given powers to provide basic medical care in the form of the dispensary system. Major reform of the system came with the Local Government Act of 1898, which established Mayo's County Council, Rural Districts Councils and Urban Districts Councils. The Rural Districts Councils were abolished by the new State in 1925 and their functions absorbed by the County Council. The Urban Districts Councils at Ballina, Castlebar and Westport continued in operation and were renamed Town Councils in 2002, retaining responsibility for local planning, maintenance and some services.

Mayo County Council first assembled in the Grand Jury Room of the County Courthouse in Castlebar on 22 April 1899. The 1898 Act introduced democratic elections for the first time, although it was some years before universal suffrage was introduced. A number of Acts expanded the services provided by the Council and reformed its structure, creating the position of County Manager to exercise executive functions while the elected councillors retained reserved functions which determine policy and finance. New functions were added to the Council's responsibilities, including environmental matters and county planning and development, while the Health Act of 1970 removed responsibility from the Council for the health services to the regional Health Boards.

In 2002, Co. Mayo was served by 31 County Councillors, elected from seven electoral areas. The Council has responsibility for protection of the environment, fire protection, agricultural services, planning, road maintenance, enhancing the cultural and artistic life of the community,

Staff of Mayo County Council photographed on the retirement of the County Manager, Liam MacLochlainn, in 1971

tax and refuse collection. The Council headquarters is based in Castlebar and there are nine Area Offices located in towns across the county. A process of reform, entitled 'Better Local Government', was introduced for all local authorities in Ireland in 2001. Under this programme, Mayo County Council restructured its senior management team with the introduction of six 'Directors of Services'. Three Directors of Services have devolved responsibility for the supra-areas of the county – Castlebar/Ballinrobe/Claremorris, Westport/Belmullet, and Ballina/Swinford. Three other Directors of Services have responsibilities for the areas of Capital Works, Corporate Affairs, and Community and Enterprise within the central Council structure. Under the process, elected members of the Council have been given an enhanced role in the formation of policy in partnership with representatives of the social partners. A programme to implement the process of devolution of the County Council services on an area basis was also initiated in 2002.

Ministers from Co. Mayo

Over the years, many individuals from Mayo have contributed to the national political scene and formed government policy. Among these were the TDs who represented Mayo constituencies and held ministerial portfolios:

Joseph McGrath (1888-1966): Born in Dublin, Joseph McGrath became an accountant for the ITGWU trade union and took part in the 1916 Rising. He was elected first in 1918 in Dublin and later for Cumann na nGaedheal in Mayo North in 1923. He resigned from government in 1924, pursuing a successful business career as Director of Labour on the Shannon Hydroelectric Scheme during the 1920s and as founder of

Waterford Glass, Donegal Carpets and the Irish Hospitals Sweepstake. He was also a breeder and trainer of race horses and well known in the racing world.

Ministerial portfolio:
Minister for Labour and Minister for Industry and Commerce in the Provisional Government, 1922
Minister for Industry and Commerce in the Free State Executive Council, 1922-24

James Fitzgerald Kenney (1877-1956): Born in Ballyglass, and of Clogher House, Claremorris, James Fitzgerald Kenney was called to the Bar in 1899 and later became King's Counsel. He was elected as Cumann na nGaedheal TD for Mayo South in 1927 and thereafter until 1944.

Ministerial portfolio:
Parliamentary Secretary to Minister for Justice, 1927
Minister for Justice, 1927-32

Patrick Joseph Ruttledge (1892-1952): Born in Ballina, Patrick Joseph Ruttledge was a solicitor and active in organising the Republican Courts of 1920-21. He was elected Sinn Féin TD for Mayo North in 1921 and opposed the Treaty. He was elected anti-Treaty and Republican TD for Mayo North in 1922 and 1923. He was Chairman of Ballina Urban Council between 1919 and 1932, and Chairman of Mayo County Council from 1922 to 1926. He was a founder member and Vice-President of Fianna Fáil. He was re-elected Fianna Fáil TD at both elections in 1927 and at every subsequent election until his death in 1952.

Ministerial portfolio:
Minister for Lands and Fisheries, 1932
Minister for Justice, 1933-39
Minister for Local Government and Public Health, 1939-41

Joseph Blowick (1903-70): Born in Belcarra, Joseph Blowick was a farmer and became leader of Clann na Talmhan in 1944. He was elected as Clann na Talmhan TD for Mayo South in 1943 and re-elected in every subsequent election until 1965. His main achievement as Minister for Lands was the encouragement of forestry schemes.

Ministerial portfolio:
Minister for Lands, 1948-51 and 1954-57

Patrick J. Lindsay (1914-93): From Geesala, Belmullet, Patrick J. Lindsay was called to the Bar in 1946. Elected for Fine Gael in the Mayo North constituency in 1954 and 1957, he was a controversial figure in the Dáil and published his anecdotal autobiography, *Memories*, shortly before his death in 1993. He was Master of the High Court from 1975 to 1984.

Ministerial portfolio:
Parliamentary Secretary to the Departments of the Gaeltacht and
   Education, 1956
Minister for the Gaeltacht, October 1956-57

Michael Moran (1912-83): Born in Ross, Castlebar, and educated locally
at St. Gerard's College, Mícheál Ó Moráin became a solicitor and was
first elected as a Fianna Fáil candidate in the Mayo South constituency
in 1938. Elected in every subsequent election until 1973, he was
responsible for the decentralisation of the Department of Agriculture
and the re-location of some of its sections to Davitt House in Castlebar.
He was Minister for Justice during the run-up to the Arms Crisis in
1970 when two government ministers were alleged, and subsequently
acquitted, of being involved in arms trafficking and using government
money to supply arms to the Irish Republican Army for the defence of
the nationalist population in Northern Ireland.

Ministerial portfolio:
Minister for the Gaeltacht, 1957-59
Minister for Lands, 1959-68 (and Gaeltacht, 1961-68)
Minister for Justice, 1968-70

Seán Flanagan (1922-93): Born in Ballyhaunis, Seán Flanagan was a noted
footballer and captained the winning All-Ireland teams in 1950 and
1951. A solicitor, he was elected as Fianna Fáil TD for Mayo South in
1951 and at each subsequent election until 1969, in which year he was
elected for the new constituency of Mayo East and again in 1973. He
was elected to the European Parliament for Connaught-Ulster in 1979.

Ministerial portfolio:
Parliamentary Secretary to Minister for Industry and Commerce, 1965-66
Minister for Health, 1966-69
Minister for Lands, 1969-73

Henry Kenny (1913-75): Born in Castlebar, Henry Kenny worked as a
national school teacher and a farmer, as well as being a noted footballer
and member of the Mayo All-Ireland winning team of 1936. He was
elected Fine Gael deputy for Mayo South in 1954 (Fine Gael had not
held a seat there since 1944) and subsequently re-elected in 1957, 1961
and 1965. He was elected in the new constituency of Mayo West in 1969
and 1973. The by-election caused by his death in 1975 saw his son,
Enda Kenny, elected.

Ministerial portfolio:
Parliamentary Secretary to Minister for Finance, 1973-75

Denis Gallagher (1923-2001): Born in Curraun, near Achill Island, Denis
Gallagher was a national school teacher and renowned for his tireless

work in the community. A founder member of the Achill Fishermen's Co-operative and the Federation of Sea Fishing Co-operatives, he was greatly admired for his promotion of the Irish language and was involved in the establishment of Údarás na Gaeltachta. In 1954, he unsuccessfully stood for Clann na Poblachta in the Mayo North constituency, but won a seat in 1973 in the new Mayo West constituency as a Fianna Fáil candidate. He backed George Colley in the Fianna Fáil leadership contest of 1979 and was subsequently demoted from Charles Haughey's new cabinet, but later appointed a Minister of State in several administrations. He retired from national politics in 1997 and continued with his local community work by founding the Achill Development Committee.

Ministerial portfolio:
Minister for the Gaeltacht, 1977-79
Minister of State at Department of Industry, Commerce and
  Tourism, 1980-81
Minister of State at Department of Social Welfare, 1982
Minister of State at Department of the Gaeltacht, 1987

Seán Calleary (1931-): Born in Ballina and son of Phelim Calleary, Dáil Deputy for Mayo North (1952-69), Seán Calleary studied engineering at University College Galway. He was a keen rugby player, playing with the Galwegians and for Connaught during 1952-60. First elected to the Dáil in 1973 as a Fianna Fáil deputy representing Mayo East, he remained a TD until 1992.

Ministerial portfolio:
Minister of State at Department of Labour and Department of the
  Public Service, 1979-81
Minister of State at Department of Trade, Commerce and Tourism,
  October-December 1982
Minister of State at Department of Foreign Affairs, with special
  responsibility for Overseas Aid, 1987 and re-appointed in 1989

Paddy O'Toole (1938-): From Ballina, Paddy O'Toole was a national school teacher. He was the Taoiseach's nominee to the Senate from 1973-77. He was first elected to the Dáil in 1977 as a Fine Gael candidate for Mayo East. He lost his seat in the 1987 election. While a TD, he was responsible for the purchase for the State of the famous salmon Moy Fishery, including the Ridge Pool at Ballina.

Ministerial portfolio:
Minister for the Gaeltacht, 1981-82
Minister for the Gaeltacht and Minister for Forestry and Fisheries,
  1982-86
Minister for Defence and the Gaeltacht, 1986-87, with additional
  portfolios for Fisheries and Tourism, January-March 1987

Padraig Flynn (1939-): Born in Castlebar, Padraig Flynn was first elected to the Dáil in 1977 as Fianna Fáil deputy representing Mayo West. A long-standing public representative, he was a member of Mayo County Council from 1967-87 and Vice-Chairperson from 1975-77, and is especially remembered in Mayo for the excellent road system around Castlebar. He held a number of ministerial posts until becoming a member of the European Commission in 1993, with responsibility for Social Affairs and Employment.

Ministerial portfolio:
Minister of State at Department of Transport and Power, 1980-81
Minister for the Gaeltacht, 1982
Minister for Trade, Commerce and Tourism, 1982
Minister for the Environment, 1987-91
Minister for Justice, 1992
Minister for Industry and Commerce, 1992
Member of the European Commission, responsible for Social Affairs
    and Employment, 1993 and re-appointed 1995-98

Enda Kenny (1951-): Born in Castlebar and son of Henry Kenny, Fine Gael deputy since 1954, Enda Kenny was first elected to the Dáil in 1975 at the Mayo West by-election following the death of his father. Formerly a national school teacher, he has been a member of Mayo County Council since 1975. He was the Fine Gael Chairman of the Economic Affairs Committee in 1991-92 and a member of the New Ireland Forum during the same period. In 2002, he was elected leader of the Fine Gael party.

Ministerial portfolio:
Minister of State at Department of Education and at Department of
    Labour, with special responsibility for Youth Affairs, 1986-87
Minister for Tourism and Trade, 1994-97

Jim Higgins (1945-): Born in Ballyhaunis, Jim Higgins was first elected to the Dáil in 1987 as a Fine Gael representative for Mayo East, having previously been a Senator, on the Labour Panel from 1983-87 and a Taoiseach's nominee in June 1981-February 1982. Formerly a community school teacher, he became a member of Mayo County Council in 1979.

Ministerial portfolio:
Minister of State at Department of Finance, February-May 1995
Minister of State at Department of the Taoiseach and at Department
    of Defence, and Government Chief Whip, 1995-97

Tom Moffatt (1940-): Born in Ballina, Tom Moffatt is a medical doctor as well as the holder of many athletic titles for Mayo, Galway and Connaught. He has played Gaelic football at club and university levels, and remained active in the game as an administrator and medical

Paul O'Dwyer turning the sod in 1974 for the O'Dwyer Cheshire Home, built on the grounds of his family home at Lismirrane, near Swinford

officer. He has been a Fianna Fáil Dáil deputy since 1992, when he won the Mayo East seat left vacant by the resignation of Seán Calleary.

Ministerial portfolio:

Minister of State at Department of Health and Children, with special responsibility for Food Safety and Older People, 1997-2002

Mayo natives have also held ministerial portfolios when representing other constituencies. Among the more recent representatives are:

Emmett Stagg (1944-): Mayo-born Labour Party member, Emmett Stagg was first elected in 1987 to Dáil Éireann, representing Kildare. He served as Minister of State at the Department of the Environment with responsibility for Housing and Urban Renewal between 1992-94 and also as Minister of State at the Department of Public Enterprise with responsibility for Energy and Nuclear Safety between 1994-97.

Bernard Durkan (1945-): A native of Killasser, Swinford, and member of Fine Gael, Bernard Durkan was first elected to Dáil Éireann in 1981, representing Kildare. He was Minister of State at the Department of Social Welfare with special responsibility for Information and Customer Services and the Integration of the Tax and Social Welfare Codes from 1994 to 1997.

Pat Rabbitte (1949-): From Ballindine, Pat Rabbitte was first elected to represent Dublin South-West in Dáil Éireann in 1989 as a Workers' Party candidate. He was Minister of State to the Government and at the

Noel Dorr (left) from Foxford, former Secretary-General, Department of Foreign Affairs, with Professor Iognáid Ó Muircheartaigh, President of NUI, Galway, on the occasion of his conferment with an honorary Doctor of Law degree in June 2001

Department of Enterprise and Employment with special responsibility for Commerce, Science, Technology and Consumer Affairs from 1994 to 1997. He was elected leader of the Labour Party in 2002.

Mayo natives have made important contributions to both national and international political developments in a variety of roles. Among the noteworthy was **Thomas J. O'Connell** (1883-1969), a native of Bekan, near Ballyhaunis. He was leader of the Labour Party between 1927 and 1932, and was Secretary of the Irish National Teachers' Organisation (INTO) during the period 1916-48. He was first elected to Dáil Éireann for Co. Galway in 1922 and later represented Mayo South from 1927-32.

On a wider international stage, **Paul O'Dwyer** (1907-98), from Lismirrane, Bohola, emigrated to New York in 1925 and became a prominent figure in New York political life. A lawyer by profession, he was an active humanitarian and civil rights advocate. He was also President of the New York City Council and New York Commissioner to the United Nations. He retained his links with Mayo and in 1971 donated his ancestral home to the Cheshire Home Foundation. He also significantly assisted in fund-raising for the new centre for the disabled, built on the site.

Noel Dorr (1933-), from Foxford, has made a very important contribution to contemporary Ireland and the wider global community. He had a long and distinguished career in the Department of Foreign Affairs, where he served as Secretary-General from 1987 to 1995. Among other positions he held were the Irish Permanent Representative to the United Nations in New York in 1980, President of the United Nations Security Council in April 1981 and August 1982, and Ambassador of Ireland in the United Kingdom from 1983-87. The esteem in which his work was held was reflected in the roles accorded to him in the drafting of EU Treaties and as Government representative on the 'Carlson Committee' concerning reform of the United Nations.

Among the most distinguished Mayo-born political figures are the former Taoiseach Charles J. Haughey and former President Mary Robinson. **Charles J. Haughey** (1925-) was born at Mountain View, Castlebar, and was first elected to Dáil Éireann in 1957, when he topped the poll in the Dublin North-East constituency. His first ministerial appointment was as Parliamentary Secretary to the Minister for Justice during 1960-61. He was Minister for Justice (1961-64), Minister for Agriculture and Fisheries (1964-66), Minister for Finance (1966-70) and Minister for Health and Minister for Social Welfare (1977-79). In December 1979 until June 1981, and again from March-December 1982, he was Taoiseach. When Fianna Fáil returned to power in 1987, he again served as Taoiseach for a further two years. He remained leader of the party until 1992.

The most distinguished living Mayo native is **Mary Robinson** (1944-), who was inaugurated the seventh President of Ireland on 3 December 1990. Born Mary Bourke in Ballina, she was a barrister by profession and appointed Reid Professor of Criminal Law in Trinity College Dublin when she was 25 years of age. She was elected to Seanad Éireann as a representative of the University of Dublin between 1969-89. She served on many parliamentary committees and was a member of Dublin City Council from 1979-83. With her husband, Nicholas Robinson, she founded the Irish Centre for European Law in 1988. In 1997, after almost seven years as President of Ireland, she took up the appointment of United Nations High Commissioner of Human Rights and travelled the world in active service for humanity, retiring from the position in 2002.

Remembering the Past

Mayo's present social and economic life has been shaped in many ways by its past. In 1993, a year-long festival to celebrate 5,000 years of rural settlement, culture and heritage took place in Co. Mayo. The festival was a tribute to the resourcefulness of the people of Mayo and a catalyst for creating a climate of confidence and pride in the future development of the county, which may be very different from, but which draws upon, the past.

President Mary Robinson receiving the Freedom of the County from Padraig Hughes, Mayo County Secretary, and P.J Morley, Cathaoirleach of Mayo County Council, in 1991

There has been an interest in the lifestyle and folk tradition of Mayo over the centuries. The poet William Larminie (1849-1900) published an early collection of folktales in 1893. Muriel Gahan (1897-1995), founder member of the Arts Council and active member of the Irish Countywoman's Association, strongly promoted folk crafts. The Irish Folklore Commission, founded in 1935, had full-time folklore collectors operating in Mayo, including Tomás Búrca, Mícheál Ó Sírín and Liam Ó Coistealbha, followed in the 1970s by Professor Séamas Ó Catháin of the Department of Irish Folklore, University College Dublin. Their studies, recording the customs, traditions and ways of working that infused the pattern of country life, enable us now to recall a past that is vanished.

At the start of the third millennium, the story of Ireland's rural past is told in the exhibitions at the National Museum of Country Life, set beside Turlough House within the beautifully restored gardens of Turlough Park. Opened in 2001, the museum presents the skills, labour, lives and spirit of traditional society nationally. It recalls a world that was seemingly unchanging for generations, but which has moved in almost one generation from living reality to memory. The collection evokes appreciation and celebration of life on the land and sea, and is a poignant reminder to us of the history of survival on the landscape which earlier generations helped to form and of which we are now custodians.

Chapter 3

Religion and Pilgrimage

The people of Mayo have a long tradition of spiritual and religious expression. Court tombs and other megalithic structures built by prehistoric people are possibly the earliest surviving sites of spiritual ritual. The Christian tradition became established from the 5th century onwards when St. Patrick, the patron saint of Ireland, is said to have brought Christianity to Mayo. He is associated with many Christian monastic sites in the county, as well as the holy mountain of Croagh Patrick (known locally as the Reek) and the ancient pilgrimage route along the Tóchar Phádraig (Patrick's Causeway).

Over the centuries, many pagan rituals were absorbed into Christian customs. For example, today's annual pilgrimage to Croagh Patrick, which takes place on the last Sunday in July each year, replaced the ancient Celtic harvest festival of Lughnasa, which was held in honour of the pagan god Lugh in August. Other pre-Christian rituals that became part of the church's calendar include bonfire night on 23 June (eve of the feast day of St. John the Baptist), pilgrimages to holy wells and rituals relating to waking the dead.

The Mayo countryside is rich in ecclesiastical ruins. Among the most visually imposing are the medieval abbeys, often located near lakes and rivers. The monastic orders responsible for these abbeys were introduced into Mayo with the coming of the Normans in the 13th century. Augustinians, Franciscans, Dominicans, Cisterians and other orders came from continental Europe and dramatically altered church organisation and architecture in Mayo. The large Romanesque and Gothic abbeys constructed by these orders replaced the earlier native church buildings. The monasteries thrived for some 300 years as the focus of spiritual life, centres of learning, communication, trade and commerce. Their destruction came with the Reformation, under the reign of Henry VIII (1509-47) and, later, his daughter Elizabeth I (1558-1603).

The suppression of the monasteries continued in the Confederation years of 1641-49. The decline continued in the Cromwellian period, with

Errew Abbey in north Mayo, once the leading religious centre of Tirawley

A mosaic in Aghagower Church depicts St. Patrick blessing a pilgrim, with Croagh Patrick in the background

the arrival of Oliver Cromwell's forces into Mayo in 1649-50. The Protectorate under Cromwell and his son, Richard, further weakened the position of Catholics in Ireland. The restoration of Charles II in 1660 raised hopes of religious freedom, but these faded with the defeat of the Jacobites in 1690. The subsequent introduction of the infamous Penal Laws of the 18th century began a period of repression and 'anti-popery'. Continuing into the 19th century, the Church of Ireland became associated in the popular mind with one section of the population – the Ascendancy. Many Church of Ireland churches were built or rebuilt throughout Mayo during this time, in the distinctive 'tower and hall' style still visible on the landscape today. A combination of political factors and the emergence of a newly confident Catholic Church, after emancipation in 1829, led to a period when relations between the Christian churches reached a low ebb. Catholics were compelled to pay tithes to support the minority Church of Ireland and this remained a source of public grievance until the disestablishment of the Church in 1869.

In the years after the Great Famine (1846-50), remittances from emigrants abroad financed a programme of Catholic church building on a grand scale. In the towns, nuns were particularly associated with education and health care provision. The buildings constructed to fulfil these social functions were the largest and most dominant architectural structures in the county, apart from the houses of the landed gentry. The devastation of the Famine encouraged what historians call the 'devotional revolution'. Traditional religious practices, which had endured through Penal times, were increasingly replaced by practices centred on the church building, such as devotions, novenas, processions and benediction. These were promoted by Missions given by the Vincentian, Redemptorist and Jesuit orders. The reported apparition of the Virgin Mary at Knock in 1879 inspired devotion there and today Knock Shrine has become a global centre of pilgrimage, recognised as one of the major Marian shrines in the world, with over 1.5 million visitors each year.

Throughout the 20th century, the parish structure provided a sense of community identity, particularly in rural areas. Schools, public houses, post offices and shops were often located near the church. From the late 19th century, the Gaelic Athletic Association (GAA) was organised on a parish basis and this helped to reinforce parish allegiance. Religious practices continued to evolve throughout the 20th century. The annual pilgrimage to Croagh Patrick, revived in 1905, has retained its popularity and symbolism nationally, at a time when religious practices centred on church buildings began to decline. Many local roadside grottos were erected in the county after the Marian Year of 1954. Mayo-born Fr. Patrick Peyton (1909-92) from Attymass drew inspiration for his popular family rosary crusade throughout the USA from his own childhood experiences of reciting the rosary at home each night with his family. Famed for his phrase 'The family that prays together, stays together', Fr. Peyton staged hundreds of radio and television shows in the USA with well-known stars of Broadway and Hollywood, and he founded the popular programmes *Family Rosary* and *Family Theater*. More recently, another priest, Fr. Kevin Hegarty, has founded and edits *Céide* magazine in Mayo. Described as a magazine presenting a 'review from the margins', it publishes articles on Catholic social debate and spiritual exploration.

Early Christian times

From his own writings in the *Confessio*, we learn that St. Patrick was born in West Britain into a Romano-British family. He was brought to Ireland as a slave at the age of 16 and escaped six years later to the continent, where he was ordained. While there, he had a vision in which the Irish beseeched him to return to them. He recognised the voices of people who lived beside the wood of Fochluth, near the western sea (Foghill above Lacken Bay may be an anglicisation of 'Fochluth'). The poet Sir Aubrey de Vere retells this story in his *Legends of Saint Patrick*:

> *'It was the cry of the children that I heard*
> *Borne from the black wood o'er the midnight seas-*
> *On Fochluth wood'. Thus speaking, he arose*
> *And, journeying with the brethren towards the west,*
> *Fronted the confine of that forest old.*

The earliest surviving biography of Patrick dates from the late 7th century and was written by Tírechán, a bishop from Tirawley, Co. Mayo. This biography concentrates on Patrick's activities in North Connaught and gives the first account of the saint's famous retreat on the top of Croagh Patrick in AD 441, fasting and praying for 40 days and 40 nights of Lent.

On 7 March 1990, a stone statue of St. Patrick was erected in Westport's Octagon. Sculpted by Ken Thompson in Portland stone, St. Patrick is depicted as a young shepherd boy, dressed in contemporary Roman clothing. Relief carvings decorate the Doric pillar on which the statue stands, showing incidents in the life of the saint and inscriptions from the *Confessio*, including with some irony the following:

> *I am Patrick*
> *A sinner*
> *Most unlearned*
> *The least of*
> *All the faithful and*
> *Utterly despised*
> *By many.*

The Church founded by St. Patrick was isolated from Rome's direct influence and developed its own monastic character, with clans supporting their local bishops and priests. The ecclesiastical site of **Moyne Abbey**, near Shrule, is typical of many early Christian sites and may have been one of the original monasteries founded by St. Patrick in the 5th century. The building is surrounded by a 'moyne' or precinct, oval in shape and encircled by a massive dry-stone wall, enclosing several acres of land.

St. Brendan the Navigator, seeking his 'Hy-Brasil', established monastic sites in the 6th century on the islands off the west coast of Mayo, including Inishglora. In the words of the poet Gerald Griffin (1803-40):

St. Patrick, sculpted by Ken Thompson in 1990, now stands atop the Doric pillar as the centrepiece of Westport's Octagon

Aerial view of Moyne Abbey, near Shrule, clearly shows the 'moyne' or precinct of the site

Men thought it a region of sunshine and rest,
And they called it Hy-Brasil, the isle of the blest.

The remains of St. Brendan's settlement on the now uninhabited island of Inishglora consist of church ruins, beehive huts, a monastic wall and inscribed stone slab crosses. Early stone churches of this period were constructed using the corbel technique of fitting stones together, without the use of mortar. Each successive layer of stones projected slightly inwards, resulting in walls and roof of one construction, often described as resembling an upturned currach. The earliest churches were probably built in the same form and on the same scale, but constructed of timber. These churches were later replaced by dry-stone structures, which, in turn, were replaced by stone buildings using mortar in their construction. The remains of St. Brendan's Oratory on Inishglora, in rectangular box design, may have replaced an earlier structure since mortar was used to bind its walls, suggesting that it is probably later than the 6th century.

There are many beliefs and miracle properties associated with ancient monastic sites. It is said of the holy well on Inishglora that 'if a woman, of any age, take water from the well, it will instantly turn into red worms'.

The sand or clay from this island is believed to have peculiar properties that banish rats. It is also said that human remains will not perish on the island. Roderick O'Flaherty (1629-1717) in his book *Ogygia*, published in 1793, relates:

> *In Innisglora, on Erris shore,*
> *Should we the bodies of our sires explore,*
> *We'd find them blooming, fresh and fair;*
> *No human flesh can rot or perish there.*

(Above) St. Brendan is depicted in the right panel of this stained-glass window by Harry Clarke, one of a series of eight adorning St. Mary's Catholic Church in Ballinrobe

(Above right) Monastic remains on Inishglora, photographed in about 1900

A stained-glass window representation of St. Brendan, created in 1925 by Harry Clarke (1889-1931), in the medieval-inspired Arts and Crafts tradition, is one light in his series of eight two-light windows in St. Mary's Catholic Church in Ballinrobe. The Harry Clarke Studios also made windows for churches throughout the county, including Cong, Kilmaine, Newport and Westport. Another beautiful stained-glass representation of St. Brendan was created by the renowned artist Wilhelmina Geddes (1887-1955) and can be seen in Curraun Church on Achill Island.

Mayo Abbey, founded by St. Colman at the end of the 7th century, developed into the most famous religious and educational centre in Connaught. When the area that became known as Co. Mayo was defined in the 16th century, it took its name from this abbey, known as Maigh Eo or 'plain of the yew tree'. The Venerable Bede, historian of the early medieval English church and people, documents that the monastery was founded following a dispute in the 7th century over the calculation of the date of Easter and other doctrinal issues. Bishop Colman, with his

Aerial view of the vicinity of Mayo Abbey

The graveyard at Mayo Abbey beside the 1845 church, built on the site of the 7th-century abbey

followers, resigned from their monastery on the island of Lindisfarne, off the English coast, as a result of the dispute. They travelled first to Inishbofin, off the Galway-Mayo coast, and subsequently founded a monastery at Maigh Eo (today's village of Mayo Abbey), near Claremorris. They came to own over 1,000 acres of land in the area known today as Kilcolman or 'church of Colman'.

Bishop Colman and his followers may have sailed from Lindisfarne to Inishbofin in a simple currach. To test this theory and to mark the anniversary of the death in AD 597 of Donegal-born St. Columba, the staff of Kilmartin House Trust in Scotland constructed a light, but durable currach in the grounds of Mayo Abbey in 1997. The boat was made of six types of wood and covered in cured hides. It was successfully sailed from Co. Antrim to Argyll in Scotland and from there to Iona.

When the Synod of Kells organised the dioceses in Ireland in 1152, the See of Tuam became an Archbishopric and Mayo became a diocese, spanning from Claremorris to Achill. Adam Magauran was possibly the last bishop of the diocese. He was slain in 1593 by the troops of Sir Richard Bingham, Lord President of Connaught in 1584-96. By 1632, the diocese of Mayo was united with Tuam.

In the 15th century, an Augustinian monastery was founded on the Mayo Abbey site, which was 'abounding in means and revenue'. Under Elizabethan rule, this monastery was dissolved into secular hands. In the early 19th century, Eneas McDonnell (1783-1858), Westport-born novelist and Catholic politician, wrote of the destitution of the Mayo Abbey population and their inability to raise funds for a new parish church. On the eve of the Great Famine, a new parish church, built from the ruins of earlier buildings and with assistance from abroad, was consecrated in 1845.

Medieval high crosses are not generally found in Co. Mayo, with exceptions such as the fragment of a high cross discovered at Mayo Abbey. This fragment probably dates from the 9th century. It consists

(Top) Currach constructed in 1997 to re-enact the 7th-century voyages of St. Columba to Iona and St. Colman to Mayo

(Above) Fragment of a high cross found at Mayo Abbey, probably dating from the 9th century

(Right) The round tower of Aghagower survives today at a height of 16 m (53 ft)

of a decorated high cross head, made of red-yellow sandstone. The short block-end arms contain circular 'armpits' without the ring characteristic of high crosses. It is very weathered, with only faint traces of carved interlace ornamental designs and a Christ figure. The most unusual feature of the Mayo Abbey cross head is the lion-figure crouching on top of the cross. This was an image used to symbolise the resurrection of Christ and was associated with Columban monasteries.

Round towers, or *cloigthithe* (bell houses), are associated with 11th- and 12th-century monastic sites. The sheer height of these structures, usually well over 15 m (50 ft), would have made them visible for miles around. Modern scholarship suggests that they acted as guides or

(Top) The classic round tower of Killala stands 26 m (85 ft) high, complete with its conical cap

(Above) Only 10 m (33 ft) of the round tower of Balla survive today, though it was probably originally 30m (98 ft) high

(Above left) The round tower of Turlough stands 23 m (75 ft) high, adjoined today by a roofless, cruciform-shaped 18th-century church

The round tower of Meelick rises
22 m (72 ft) above a hillside graveyard

landmarks for pilgrims in their journeys to various monastic sites to venerate the relics of the saints. Earlier scholars had put forward the theory that they were places of sanctuary for the monks in times of attack.

There are five surviving round towers in Co. Mayo and one miniature representation of a round tower in Rosserk Franciscan Friary.

Medieval abbeys

Today, despite their ruinous state, the architecture, craftsmanship and beauty of Mayo's medieval abbeys are still much admired. The remains of these great buildings – founded by many different orders including the Augustinians, Cistercians, Dominicans and Franciscans – are conspicuous on the landscape, particularly in the south and east of the county. Ballintubber and Ballyhaunis Abbeys are exceptions in that they were both reconstructed and remained in use into the present century.

From about the 10th century, Irish churches began to be built in the Romanesque style. Though in ruins today, some features remain, such as the round-headed doorway of **St. Derbhile's Church** in Fallmore, on the southern tip of the Mullet Peninsula. This small, now lonely and isolated church is built of local granite, probably in the 11th century. Although much weathered, traces of incised lines are still visible on the doorway and interlaced ornament can be seen on the doorjamb. The church is dedicated to St. Derbhile, whom *The Annals* refer to as Derbhla de Iorras of the royal line of Fiachra, son of the King of Ireland. To the north-east of the church is St. Derbhile's 'bed' or grave, and further to the north is the Holy Well of the saint, reputed to provide cures for eyesight problems.

The 12th-century **Cong Abbey** was a foundation of the royal O'Connor family, possibly built by Rory O'Connor (d. 1198), the last native High King of Ireland. It was built on an earlier 7th-century monastery founded on the site by Fechin of Fore. Local tradition maintains that Rory O'Connor, who died after thirteen years in canonical orders at Cong, is buried beneath the chancel window. Cong was once a bishopric named among the five sees of the province of Connaught.

Cong Abbey's fame is due in part to its exquisite processional cross. Dating from the early 12th century, it is made of oak and decorated with gilt bronze, gold filigree, gems, glass and niello. The intricacy of the

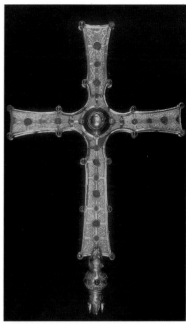

The exquisite early 12th-century Cross of Cong

Romanesque-style doorway of St. Derbhile's Church, Fallmore, on the Mullet Peninsula

Romanesque doorway at Cong Abbey

design, together with the gracious curves in the arms and shaft, place the Cross of Cong among the great masterpieces of Irish medieval metalwork. The inscription in Irish, found on the narrow sides of the cross, states that 'In this cross is preserved the cross on which the founder of the world suffered'. Other inscriptions give details of the cross' patrons and the craftsmen who made it.

The late Romanesque style of Cong Abbey can still be seen today in a number of splendid early doorways, which have a distinct French influence and some of the finest stone sculpture preserved anywhere in the country. The capitals bear classic acanthus leaves and the round-headed doorways are studded with decorative zig-zag patterns. The remains of the cloister provide an insight into the beauty and superior craftsmanship that once graced this abbey. Built in 1220, but later reconstructed, the capitals of each round-headed arch in the cloister are carved with classically inspired grooved plant leaves. The pillars may have been an early example of the dumb-bell pier, which later became almost universal in church architecture throughout Ireland.

In about 1500, one of the O'Malley clan is thought to have built **Clare Island Abbey** for the Order of St. Bernard of Clairvaux on the site of a former Carmelite abbey. This Cistercian abbey consists of a simple single-storey nave, adjoined by a chancel with an upper storey. As was the custom of the period, the living accommodation of the monks was integrated into the church building on the upper floor.

A unique feature of Clare Island Abbey are the medieval frescos on the chancel walls. These depict human and animal forms in vivid shades of scarlet, orange red, chocolate brown and golden yellow. Bands of yellow and blue paint encircle the walls above the frescos and there are also signs of the chancel vault having been painted with imitation groin-ribs and corbels. An extensive preservation programme has been carried out on these frescos under expert supervision.

Remains of the cloister at Cong Abbey

(Above) Medieval frescos in the chancel of Clare Island Abbey

(Above left) Ballintubber Abbey – 'the abbey that refused to die'

In 1216, Cathal Crobderg O'Connor, son of Turlough O'Connor and brother of Rory O'Connor, the last High King of Ireland, founded **Ballintubber Abbey** for the Augustinian monks on the site of an older Patrician church along the pilgrimage routeway of the Tóchar Phádraig. Cathal was a notable patron of the arts and endowed many monasteries, including the Cistercian Abbey at Abbeyknockmoy in Galway where he was to die a monk in 1224. Cathal's attachment to the Cistercians may in part explain the fact that the plan of Ballintubber Abbey is Cistercian in style, but without the usual aisles.

Ballintubber has become known as 'the abbey that refused to die'. Despite its dissolution and destruction over the centuries, it is the only abbey to remain in continuous use since its foundation in the 13th century. Many attempts were made to restore it during the 19th century. In 1846, restoration began under Archbishop John MacHale (1791-1881) of Tuam. Then, in 1889, the architect George Ashlin re-roofed the chancel, crossing the transept. The abbey was finally completely restored in 1966 for the 750th anniversary of its foundation. The restoration of its Romanesque and early Gothic architectural details provides an insight into how the abbey may have looked when first built.

The beauty of Ballintubber Abbey can be seen in its chancel, where delicate shafts rise from the walls at a point about shoulder height, their fine lines contrasting strikingly with the massive roof ribs above. The original 13th-century stone slab altar is still used today, although the Stations of the Cross, telling the story of Christ's passion, have been replaced by ones created by the artist Imogen Stuart.

Jordan d'Exeter founded the Franciscan friary of **Straide Abbey** in the 13th century, which was transferred to the Dominican Order within a few years. The chancel of Straide Abbey probably dates from its foundation, although

Carved stone tomb at Straide Abbey

the east window has obviously been altered, possibly in the 15th century. The rest of the church, including a magnificent carved stone tomb, is dated to the 15th or early 16th century.

The tomb niche has an elaborate canopy, below which there are two fine carved panels. The first panel shows the Wise Men bearing their gifts, together with a carving of Christ displaying his wounds. The second panel contains the figures of the donor, a bishop and the saints Peter and Paul. The donor, who is kneeling, was possibly a weaver, suggested by the shuttle-like object hanging from his belt. John Dillon (1851-1927), MP and agrarian reformer, erected a 19th-century monument in the niche of the tomb for his relative Anne Deane, President of the Ladies' Land League.

Hugh O'Malley founded **Murrisk Abbey** in 1457 for the Augustinian Friars and it became a noted centre of learning. Among its pupils was the famous Pirate Queen, Grace O'Malley (c. 1530-1603), who, despite her robust lifestyle, was a most educated woman, capable of debating in Latin with Queen Elizabeth during their meeting in London in 1593. Grace was also married in Murrisk Abbey, where an O'Malley coat of arms can be seen today. Built on the shores of Clew Bay, with Croagh Patrick rising behind, the abbey buildings are L-shaped, with the domestic buildings located to the north of the church building. The south wall of the nave contains unusual battlement features. The abbey also contains a fine five-light east window with delicate bar tracery.

A series of poems was written in the 18th century in which the authors rivalled each other on the beauty and value of their respective abbeys. Fr. William Bourke's poem, written in 1730, is translated as *The Friar's Farewell to Murrisk* and compares the beauty of Murrisk Abbey with the Augustinian Abbey at Ballyhaunis. Fr. Bourke's unfavourable comparison provoked a reply from Seán Ó Moráin, who was probably a member of the Ballyhaunis Augustinian community. Sheila Mulloy, Westport historian, provides the English translation for both these poems.

(Opposite) Restored chancel of the 13th-century Ballintubber Abbey, as photographed in 1966

*Elegant five-light east window
of Murrisk Abbey*

The Friar's Farewell to Murrisk

*Farewell to you lovely Murrisk,
So tranquil and mild,
And to the fine lordly mountains
That rise up on all sides.
As I walked on the strand there,
The curlew's refrain,
Was sweeter than all the music,
On this side of the plain.*

*I promised to obey,
The friars placed over me,
And to submit my desires,
To those of the community.
This is what has left me,
Condemned here to long craving,
For I would never have left Murrisk,
And its beautiful havens.*

*If I can hold out,
Until the cuckoo's call beguiles,
I will then go to Murrisk,
And rest there a while.
The folk here are not,
The pleasant wise company I knew,
But are like idols of oak,
With an axe rough hewn.*

Mo shlan leat, a Mhuruisg

Mo shlán leat, a Mhuruisg bhreagh, shéimhigh, shuairc,
'S do na sléibhtibh breagha meala bhí a ndeas is a dtuaidh,
Bu bhinne liom guth crotaighe a' siubhal ar an tráigh
Na ceólta na cruinne an taobh-seo den Chlár.

Gheall mé gan amhras úmhlacht don chléir,
Is mo thoil féin a shéanadh ar a toil-san go léir.
Ise sin a d'fhág mise insa tír seo go buan,
Nó ní thréighfinn-se Muruisg ná aoibhneas na gcuan.

Má mhairim-se féin go ngoiridh an chuach
Rachad-sa go Muruisg is déanfad ann mo chuairt;
Níl na daoine annseo mar chleacht mise saothamhuil ná suairc
Ach mar íomháigh de dhair choille a snoidhfidhe le tuaigh.

Reply from Seán Ó Moráin

*There is hard twisted heather,
West on the Reek,
There is cold there and rain,
Wind, frost and sleet.
We ate no winkles,
Or limpets from stony strands,
But smooth wheaten bread,
And beer was at hand.*

The remains of the 15th-century Murrisk Abbey lie in the shadow of Croagh Patrick

Were it not my respect,
For my God in Heaven,
And his blessed priests,
To whom all powers were given.
I wouldn't let pass,
This slight to my place of birth,
From any living person,
Or from you, Father William Bourke.

Freagra le Seán Ó Moráin

Bíonn fraoch cruaidh, casta thiar ar a gCruaich
Bíonn sioc uirthi, fearthainn, gaoth, sneachta is fuacht,
Ní faochain a chleachtamar-ne ná báirnigh cladaigh chruaidh
Ach arán sleamhain cruithneachta, 's ní raibh sugh na heórna uainn.

Mur mbéinn-se a' géilleadh do Rígh na ndúl,
Is dá chléir ro-bheannuighthe ag ar fhág sé gach cumhacht
Ní leigfinn féin masladh na tíre ar fad' un siubhal
Le aon neach dhá maireann, ná leat-sa, a Athair Uilliam a Búrc.

De Burgo – O'Malley chalice of 1494

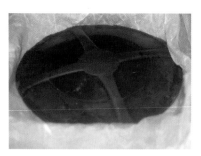

*The late medieval Mias Tighearnain
or Dish of St. Tighearnan*

Medieval Mayo plate

The De Burgo – O'Malley chalice, which now forms part of the National Museum of Ireland collection, is the earliest surviving piece of dated domestic Irish plate. According to the Latin inscription written around the base line, Thomas de Burgo and Grace O'Malley 'caused' the chalice to be made in 1494. The 'Grace O'Malley' mentioned was the great grandaunt of the famous Pirate Queen, Grace O'Malley or Granuaile, who also married into the same gaelicised Norman family of Bourke (De Burgo). The chalice itself is Gothic in style, consisting of a plain cup with a distinctive knob on the stem and an octagonal pyramidal shaped foot with incurved angles.

The late medieval Mias Tighearnain (Dish of St. Tighearnan) is a well-preserved religious plate item with Mayo connections. This shallow circular dish is decorated inside and out with crosses of arms of equal length. A circular setting of cast gilt silver with a broad rim is found in the centre of the front of the dish. The Mias is thought to have been made during the period of the Barrett patronage of Errew Abbey. It then passed from the possession of the O'Flynn family, the erenachs or guardians of the church lands at Errew, into the hands of the Knox family of Rappa Castle, Ballina, in the late 18th or early 19th century. Knox's tenants took oaths on the Mias as a means of settling disputes. It was sold in London in the 1930s and subsequently acquired by the National Museum of Ireland.

The Franciscan friaries of Rosserk and Moyne, located close to each other in north Mayo, are easily identifiable from a distance by their tall, narrow belfry towers, typical of Franciscan houses. **Rosserk Abbey** was a Third Order Franciscan friary, founded by the Joyce family in about 1440 on the site of an earlier church. The church lies south of the cloister and has a central tower and southern transept, with two chapels and a sacristy cupboard. The refectory and dormitory are located around the cloister above vaulted basements. In 1590, Rosserk Abbey was destroyed on the orders of Sir Richard Bingham, Lord President of Connaught during 1584-96. The lands were held in secular hands first by the Earl of Thomond and later, in 1635, transferred to the Earl of Cork.

Moyne Abbey, beside the River Moy in north Mayo, with its belfry tower of nearly 27 m (90 ft), was built for the Franciscans of the Strict Observance in 1460. Although founded by the Barretts, a Norman-Welsh family, the Bourke family became its principal patron. The Observant friars were strongly opposed to the Reformation and were closely identified with Gaelic opposition to Tudor expansion. Moyne may have been a novitiate for all Observant houses in the country. The friary was raided in 1578, but continued intact until 1590 when Sir Richard Bingham destroyed the building and dispersed the community. A small number of friars remained attached to the abbey until 1800.

The intact belfry tower of 15th-century Moyne Abbey rises some 27 m (90 ft) from the main church

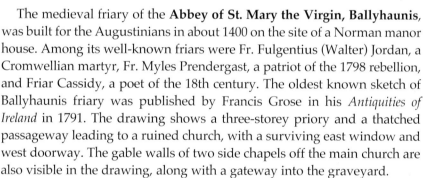

Ballyhaunis Abbey, sketched by T. Cocking for Francis Grose's 1791 book 'Antiquities of Ireland'

The medieval friary of the **Abbey of St. Mary the Virgin, Ballyhaunis**, was built for the Augustinians in about 1400 on the site of a Norman manor house. Among its well-known friars were Fr. Fulgentius (Walter) Jordan, a Cromwellian martyr, Fr. Myles Prendergast, a patriot of the 1798 rebellion, and Friar Cassidy, a poet of the 18th century. The oldest known sketch of Ballyhaunis friary was published by Francis Grose in his *Antiquities of Ireland* in 1791. The drawing shows a three-storey priory and a thatched passageway leading to a ruined church, with a surviving east window and west doorway. The gable walls of two side chapels off the main church are also visible in the drawing, along with a gateway into the graveyard.

Religious persecution and revival

The Skingin Chalice was donated by Fr. Skingin to the Augustinian Abbey of St. Mary the Virgin in Ballyhaunis. This attractive example of the Irish silversmith's craft was made in Galway in 1648. The crucifixion is engraved with simple light strokes on the base and the ornate central knob is decorated with eight fleur-de-lis, a sign of French influence. The Latin inscription around the base is translated as 'Pray for Father Roger Skingin who had me made for the use of the Convent of Ballyhaunis in the year of the Lord 1648'. The Augustinian friar, Fr. Fulgentius Jordan of Ballyhaunis, may well have used this chalice before he was martyred in 1649 by Cromwell's army. But the chalice was saved, perhaps aided by its design which allows it to be unscrewed into two parts and so more easily be concealed.

The dissolution of the monasteries in Mayo and the subsequent distribution of their property to secular hands commenced during the

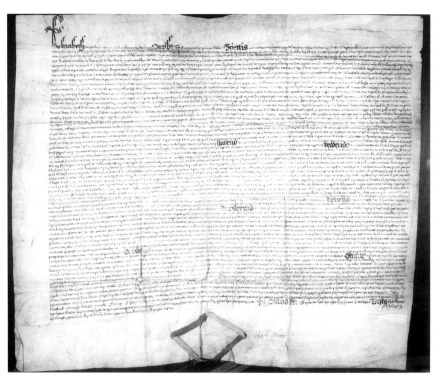

(Top) The Skingin Chalice, made in 1648

(Above) Seal of Elizabeth I, attached to the letter-patent to Edmund Barrett

(Above right) Letter-patent of Elizabeth I, granting the property of former religious houses to Edmund Barrett

reign of Elizabeth I. Buildings and lands were granted by a series of letters-patent to individuals or bodies. One such Elizabethan grant was made in favour of Edmund Barrett of the monastic termon (or hospital) of Castlecarra, Co. Mayo.

Following Cromwell and the later defeat of the Jacobites, a period of severe religious repression for Catholics in Ireland began in the 18th century with the introduction of the infamous Penal Laws or Anti-Popery Acts. Among the key measures of these laws were those that affected the rights of Catholics to hold property, in effect excluding them from political power since such power derived from the ownership of property. Other legal provisions affected education, military service abroad and the right to vote. Further measures required the clergy to register and also outlawed future ordinations. There are many folk tales of priests illegally celebrating mass at remote sites during these times of religious repression. Denunciation by informers was a constant danger, particularly where a 'priest catcher' lived locally. Among the most notorious of these was John Mullowney, alias Seán na Sagart, who was murdered at Ballintubber while hunting down a priest.

Small wooden crucifixes, known as penal crosses, were acquired by pilgrims visiting Lough Derg in the 17th and 18th centuries. One such cross, dated 1744, was discovered in Abbeyquarter, near Ballyhaunis. Carved from a solid piece of timber, it has the typical short crucifix arms with the Christus in relief, surrounded by symbols of the Passion. On the reverse side, the date of 1744 is carved in large figures running

down the shaft, indicating the year the pilgrim visited Lough Derg.

Another religious practice was that of the 'pattern', which is possibly a corruption of the word 'patron'. Patterns were communal visits to holy sites associated with the patron saint of a district on that saint's feast day. Holy wells, churches and graveyards were visited on such pattern days by people from far and wide, many having walked long distances to attend. Pilgrims performed 'Stations', which consisted of walking around a holy site, often in bare feet and sometimes on their knees, stopping at various points to say a prescribed number of prayers. Traditionally, holy wells were places to which people turned in prayer to seek cures for ailments and for blessings. Offerings of medals, pieces of cloth, flowers or coins were frequently left at the well as a sign of thanksgiving for the cure or blessing received.

One of these patterns was recorded in an article and accompanying sketch in the newspaper *The Graphic* in January 1875. Entitled 'Pattern Day at Balla', the pilgrims are shown carrying candles and making their way past Balla Round Tower on their knees to the nearby Holy Well of Tobar Phádraig.

When a person died it was traditional to hold a wake for them, during which the family, friends and neighbours remained with the corpse through the night. These wakes were also traditionally festive gatherings when people engaged in pipe-smoking and story-telling, singing and dancing, as well as ritual games of ancient origin. The caoineadh, or keen, was a wailing lament for the dead and was always a feature at wakes in Mayo. This keening tradition pre-dates Christian times and was

(Above left) The Holy Well of St. Derbhile at Fallmore Church on the Mullet, photographed by C.R. Browne in about 1885

(Above) Front and back of a penal cross, found at Abbeyquarter, Ballyhaunis and dated 1744

*'Pattern Day at Balla', as depicted in
The Graphic of January 1875*

*Burriscarra Graveyard, near
Ballintubber Abbey*

frequently commented upon by foreign travellers. The English writer Arthur Young, for example, described the caoineadh in Mayo as being done in a 'most horrid manner'.

Catholic and Protestant traditions

Archbishop John MacHale (1791-1881), a native of Tobbernaveen, Lahardane, was also known as the 'Lion of the West'. Among his earliest memories was the French marching through Lahardane in 1798 on their way to Castlebar. Following the rebellion of 1798, he retained the memory of the hanging, on a charge of treason, of Father Andrew Conroy, the priest who had baptised him. MacHale was to become the first bishop to complete his education in Ireland since before the Penal Laws of the 18th century. In 1820, under the pen name Hierophilos, he put forward many Catholic grievances, especially those concerning education, in a series of open letters to the national press and developed a nationwide reputation for his active campaigning for Catholic emancipation. He was a gifted Irish language scholar. He was created Co-adjutor Bishop of Killala and later elevated to the position of Archbishop of Tuam in 1834.

Archbishop MacHale was staunchly opposed to what he saw as the proselytising activities of the Reverend Edward Nangle on Achill Island. He made an official visit to Achill in 1854 and established a Catholic school and monastery at Bunnacurry, administered by the Franciscan Order. He also established other schools on the island in reaction to the evangelical Church of Ireland Mission established by Reverend Nangle at Dugort in 1833. Commonly known as the Colony, this settlement was a planned undertaking by the Irish Church Mission Society 'for the purpose of establishing and conducting, in the island of Achill, the first missionary settlement which had ever been established among the native Irish using the Irish language'. Bishop Thomas Plunkett of Tourmakeady was an

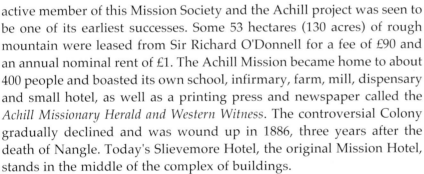

(Above) Archbishop John MacHale,
the 'Lion of the West'

(Left) Franciscan Brothers at
Bunnacurry Friary, Achill, at the
end of the 19th century

active member of this Mission Society and the Achill project was seen to be one of its earliest successes. Some 53 hectares (130 acres) of rough mountain were leased from Sir Richard O'Donnell for a fee of £90 and an annual nominal rent of £1. The Achill Mission became home to about 400 people and boasted its own school, infirmary, farm, mill, dispensary and small hotel, as well as a printing press and newspaper called the *Achill Missionary Herald and Western Witness*. The controversial Colony gradually declined and was wound up in 1886, three years after the death of Nangle. Today's Slievemore Hotel, the original Mission Hotel, stands in the middle of the complex of buildings.

The Sisters of Mercy, Sisters of Charity and Sisters of St. Louis were among the orders that provided education to girls and influenced women's devotional practices throughout Co. Mayo from the end of the 19th century. Despite the relative restrictions under which they worked in the early years, the nuns did tremendous work in the fields of education and training, later to be replicated in the provision of health care within the county.

The Sisters of Mercy came to Mayo in 1842 and opened their first convent in Westport. They established themselves quickly and other convents were soon opened in Castlebar, Ballinrobe, Swinford, Claremorris, Louisburg and Tourmakeady. The habits worn by the nuns changed little over the 100 years between the foundation of their Order and the early 1950s. Specific measurements were provided for all clothing. The habit was made of black serge, reaching from the throat to the feet and pleated around the waist with a train of 41 cm (16 in). The inner sleeves fitted close to the arms and were covered by large, wide outer sleeves. The veil was made of black crepe, while the novices wore white calico. The coif around the face was made of white calico, with a rigid cloth inserted straight across the forehead. The cincture, or belt, was made of black leather, 5 cm (2 in) wide. Rosary beads were also worn on the cincture and

Lithograph of the evangelical Church of Ireland Mission, or Colony, established at the foot of Achill's Slievemore in 1833

professed Sisters wore a brass crucifix, about 10 cm (4 in) long.

The Methodist leader John Wesley (1703-91) first visited Mayo in 1756 on his circuit of Ireland. His controversial and very public ministry drew crowds and applause as well as opposition and dissension. By the end of the 18th century, Methodist chapels were built in Turlough and on Westport's South Mall. The latter was replaced in the late 19th century by a cut-stone church with lancet windows in the neo-Gothic style, which was deconsecrated in 1961. Wesley himself laid the foundation stone for Castlebar's first Methodist chapel in May 1785, built on the east side of The Mall. The medieval tradition of including living accommodation for the Minister as an extension of the church building was incorporated into the Castlebar church.

The Church of Ireland underwent a revival in Mayo in the first half of the 19th century. Many churches were built or refurbished during the early decades and again, in a smaller wave of construction, after the disestablishment of the Church in 1869. Many of these new churches, mainly of the Gothic 'tower and hall' variety, were built on older ecclesiastical sites or close to the demesnes of landlords. Turlough Church is typical of the confident style: cruciform in plan, with a tall square bell tower, it was built in 1820 and enlarged in 1824. Today it serves a small, but vibrant community.

The Church of Ireland church in Castlebar was completed in 1739 and

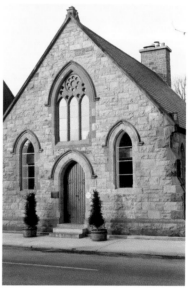

(Above) Former Methodist Chapel on Westport's South Mall

(Above left) Sisters of Mercy at Ballinrobe Convent in about 1900

renovated in 1807. Dr. Richard Pococke (1704-65), Church of Ireland Bishop of Ossory, antiquarian and travel writer, toured Ireland in 1752 and recorded religious practices, agricultural improvement and industrial development. His accounts were published in his book *Tour in Ireland*. He describes the construction of the Church of Ireland church at the junction of Ellison Street and The Mall in Castlebar. The distinctive clock tower feature was added during the early 19th-century renovations. Ellison Street is named after the Rector who ministered there in the late 18th century.

The Reverend Walter Blake Kirwan (1754-1805) was the Church of Ireland Dean of Killala in 1800. He was the son of Pat Kirwan of Galway and Mary Blake, daughter of Walter Blake of Galway and niece of the Primate of Armagh, Dr. Anthony Blake. They were related by marriage to the Blakes of Towerhill, who resided at Clooneen in Burricarra parish. The Reverend Kirwan was recognised as an eloquent preacher early in his career. However, he left the Catholic Church in 1787 and was ordained as a Church of Ireland minister. Because of his passionate orations, he was much sought after for charity sermons seeking to raise funds for various causes. The scene of one of his sermons, aimed at fund-raising for a Dublin orphanage, was recorded in a contemporary drawing by Hugh Douglas Hamilton – the Reverend Kirwan is seen in full dramatic pose, while a number of young ragged orphans are gathered around at his feet.

A revival in the building of Catholic churches occurred towards the close of the 18th century. Designed in plain vernacular style, they were constructed at a time of great hardship and usually consisted of simple structures in a T-plan or cruciform shape, in keeping with other local buildings. The historical and architectural importance of churches of this period has been recognised in recent times; previously, they were demolished or simply abandoned. The architecturally restrained church

Methodist Chapel on the east side of The Mall, Castlebar

(Above) Clock tower of Christ Church, overlooking The Mall, Castlebar, built in 1739 and later renovated

(Right) Turlough Church of Ireland, built in 1820, is typical of the Gothic 'tower and hall' style

at Straide is typical of the period. Attached to the 13th-century Dominican Abbey, it was probably built in the early 19th century, using cut stone from the older abbey. It was used until 1916, when the more modern Church of Saints Peter and Paul was consecrated. In the 1940s, the north transept of Straide Church was demolished and the former church was used as a dance hall until the 1970s, when it fell into temporary disuse. The church was reconstructed and opened in October 2001 as the Michael Davitt Museum.

The foundations of a new Catholic church in Castlebar had been laid in 1872, but work soon came to a standstill. Then, in 1897, work commenced on a new church, to be called Our Lady of the Holy Rosary, designed by Walter G. Doolin. A storm destroyed part of the building in 1899 and the project was not completed until 1901. It was the largest church to be designed by Doolin and featured the typical Gothic style he favoured, with flanking monumental gateways. However, the church was not completed to its original design and the planned tower was never incorporated. James Pearse, a stonecarver and the father of Patrick Pearse, a leader of the 1916 Rising, made the ornamental screen at the back of the altar. Archbishop McEvilly dedicated the church in October 1901. The railway companies provided special trains for the large crowds attending the dedication ceremony and offered passengers reduced fares.

St. Patrick's Church in Newport is built in the assured style of the early 20th century. It is the most celebrated of Rudolph Butler's churches, designed in an adapted Hiberno-Romanesque style on the site of an earlier church. It is faced in local red sandstone, with carved Dunfries sandstone at

Charity sermon by the Reverend Walter Blake Kirwan to raise funds for a Dublin orphanage

the entrance, complemented by a roof of green slates. Inside, the central aisle of the church is barrel-vaulted and held up by slender columns.

In the early 20th century, stained-glass windows created by native craft workers were appearing in churches throughout the country. In Newport, the 'Last Judgement' was installed, created by the Harry Clarke Studios. Windows from this famous studio are found in many churches throughout Mayo and supplanted those from the Mayer Studios of Munich, which were once popular. Today, the latter are found, for example, in Ballina Cathedral and the Church of Ireland in Castlebar.

Liturgical festivals were common in the 1950s and '60s. They were significant events in the lives of the people of the parish. National school children dressed for the day and congregated with their Bishop and priests at their local Cathedral to engage in religious devotions. In later years, the parish community congregated in smaller groups in their local

(Above) Straide Church, typical of the early 19th-century vernacular style

(Above right) Workers on the site of the Church of Our Lady of the Holy Rosary, Castlebar, completed in 1901

(Right) Hiberno-Romanesque St. Patrick's Church, Newport – its doorway inspired by the medieval doorway of Galway's Clonfert Abbey

deanery, where they were visited by their Bishop.

Confraternities, such as the Sacred Heart of Jesus, were popular in Mayo in the 1950s. They were made up of guilds, originally segregated by sex, which met monthly. The attendance of members was recorded in a roll book and subscriptions paid for pious purposes, such as the purchase of religious banners, hymn and prayer books. At the meetings, members recited the rosary, listened to sermons and sometimes received benediction. The social as well as the religious aspects of these events made them attractive to participants.

Foxford members of the Confraternity of the Sacred Heart of Jesus, c. 1923

The Ballyhaunis Mosque, built in the early 1980s

Mayo's only mosque is located in the town of Ballyhaunis. Designed in a plain style except for the dome, which is typical of mosque architecture throughout the world, complete with shortened pointed spike, the mosque was built in the early 1980s for immigrants who arrived from Pakistan, Syria and Palestine to work at the Halal Meat Processing plant. The plant was later taken over by Glanbia and continued to employ many of the former Halal employees. The Muslim community gathers for worship on Friday, the Holy Day, and the prayer leader, the Imam, leads

Mass being celebrated outside the modern oratory in Knock

prayers from the Qur'an (Koran), the Holy Book of Islam. Children also receive their religious instruction on that day.

Knock Shrine

In August 1879, fifteen people reported seeing, over a period of two hours, an apparition of the Virgin Mary, accompanied by St. Joseph and St. John the Evangelist, at the south gable of their parish church in Knock, the Church of St. John the Baptist. They also described seeing an altar at the gable of the church on which a cross, a lamb and angels were visible. A special ecclesiastical commission examined the witnesses in 1879 and another commission in 1936 examined the survivors. These commissions found that the 'testimony of the witnesses, taken as a whole, was trustworthy and satisfactory'.

As news of the apparition spread, pilgrims flocked to Knock. Many cures were reported and those who claimed cures left their sticks and crutches at the gable wall. The Reverend Bartholomew Cavanagh, Parish Priest of Knock-Aghamore at the time of the apparition, kept a diary of all the reported cures. In March 1880, the *Weekly News* began publishing extracts from his diary. By the end of 1880, he had recorded 300 cures.

Pilgrims removed the plaster and cement from the gable wall as relics and souvenirs. In the autumn of 1880, the Apparition Gable was given a new coat of cement and an iron railing erected to provide protection. In thanksgiving for the remarkable recovery of her eyesight in 1880, Miss McKee donated a gift of a Portland stone statue of Our Lady. Today, this stands at the head of the

The south gable of the Church of St. John the Baptist in Knock, site of the apparition in 1879

grave of Monsignor James Horan (1911-86), who did so much for the development of Knock and is often referred to as the 'builder of Knock'.

An oratory at the Apparition Gable was first erected in 1940, to be replaced in 1979 and again in 1992. The interior of the 1940 oratory was constructed of Connemara marble and housed statues of the Virgin Mary, St. Joseph and St. John. The modern oratory provides seating for 150 people and new statues, created by the Roman sculptor Professor Lorezo Ferri, depict the original apparition scene of 1879.

The first significant Papal recognition of Knock Shrine occurred in the Marian Year of 1954. In that year, Pope Pius XII created a new Feast of the Queenship of Mary. As part of the celebrations for that occasion, Marian shrines around the world were invited to send a banner to Rome. The banner from Knock Shrine was among 400 sent and one of only 20 especially selected to be presented to His Holiness at St. Peter's Basilica. The Pope decorated the Knock banner with a special gold medal minted for the occasion.

Twenty years later, in 1974, Pope Paul VI blessed the foundation stone for the new Church of Our Lady, Queen of Ireland, to be built at Knock. A slab of Carrara marble, from the famous quarries north of Rome, bears the inscription 'Pope Paul' in blue lettering. In 1979, the centenary year of the apparition, Pope John Paul II reached the 'goal' of his journey to Ireland when, on 30 September, he came as a pilgrim to Knock Shrine. He prayed and celebrated mass with a congregation of almost half a million people and raised the status of the church to full Basilica of Our Lady, Queen of Ireland. On that day, Pope John Paul presented a Golden Rose

Pope John Paul II during his visit to Knock in 1979

Monsignor James Horan holds the Golden Rose presented to Knock Shrine by Pope John Paul II in 1979

to Knock Shrine, a token of special reverence and devotion that has only occasionally been conferred by popes and which can be traced back to Honorius III in the 13th century. Held in an ornate sterling silver vase, the gold-leaf rose surmounts a cluster of branching smaller roses and leaves. The rose is regarded as the queen of plants and a symbol of Mary. Indeed, one of the witnesses of the 1879 apparition at Knock stated that he saw 'on her brow, a beautiful rose'.

Knock Shrine has today become a global centre of pilgrimage, with over 1.5 million visitors each year, and is recognised as one of the major Marian shrines in the world. The old church is now part of an extensive complex of buildings housing a range of activities, including pilgrimage, a marriage introduction bureau and a folk museum. Permanent shops have replaced the temporary stalls selling religious souvenirs, while new hotels cater for visitors' needs.

Croagh Patrick

The Holy Mountain of Croagh Patrick was once on an ancient pilgrimage route stretching along the west coast of Ireland from Kerry to Donegal, with Mayo's Caher Island as one of the places of worship along the way. Another ancient route led from the east along the Tóchar Phádraig (Patrick's Causeway), which probably originally commenced at the prehistoric royal site of Rath Cruachain in Co. Roscommon and passed westwards through Aghagower to Croagh Patrick. Today's annual pilgrimage to Croagh Patrick, revived in 1905, takes place on the last Sunday in July each year, known locally as Reek Sunday. Traditionally, local people make their own pilgrimage on the last Friday in July, known as Garland Friday, possibly from the tradition of wearing garlands of flowers.

Today, the main route is rather shorter than in former times, consisting of a three-mile path, called the Casán Phádraig, that rises steeply up the mountain side from the village of Murrisk, on the southern shores of Clew Bay. The path, made of glittering white quartzite, worn and polished by pilgrims over thousands of years, winds its way to the summit, 765 m (2,510 ft) above sea level. The way can be slippery and dangerous, yet many modern pilgrims still go barefoot. Ash walking sticks aid others on their journey. Up until 1974, the pilgrimage used to take place at night. Pilgrims would arrive by train in Westport and be ferried to Murrisk in a continuous fleet of buses running from afternoon to midnight. Private houses in Westport would serve teas and refreshments to the passing pilgrims. In recent times, an annual pilgrimage has also been revived along part of the Tóchar Phádraig, between Ballintubber Abbey and Croagh Patrick.

The old Irish name for Croagh Patrick describes it well – *Cruachan Aigli*, meaning 'conical mountain' or alternatively 'mountain of the eagle' (although *Aigli* could also refer to a person). Below the mountain on the shores of Clew Bay are the ruins of Murrisk Abbey, built by the O'Malley

View of Clew Bay from Croagh Patrick

Pilgrims have been climbing Croagh Patrick for centuries and continue to do so to this day; this photograph records the 1956 pilgrimage

family for the Augustinian monks in 1475. The monks of Murrisk took charge of the Croagh Patrick pilgrimage, which was previously in the charge of the monks of Aghagower.

In 1905, shortly after Dr. John Healy became Archbishop of Tuam, an oratory was built on the summit. The building contractor, Walter

The patterns of ancient stone walls and buildings are visible under the snow blanket seen here covering the summit of Croagh Patrick

Heneghan of Louisburgh, used local materials carried up the mountain by donkey for the construction. An estimated 10,000 people attended the dedication ceremony, brought by trains specially scheduled by the Midland and Great Western Railway Company. Peter MacConville's brass band played at the dedication.

Excavations by Mayo County Council archaeologist Gerry Walsh in the 1990s revealed the remains of an early Christian oratory on the summit of Croagh Patrick. This oratory, dating to between AD 430 and 890, was constructed using the drystone corbel technique, similar to that used in the famous Gallarus Oratory on the Dingle Peninsula in Co. Kerry.

The performance of penitential exercises on Croagh Patrick, known as the 'Stations of the Reek', has evolved over many centuries. Today, there are essentially three stations. Traditionally, the first station is at Leacht Benin (Benin's stone or grave), which was named for Benin, one of St. Patrick's disciples. This station now takes place at the statue of St. Patrick, a few hundred yards up the mountain. The second station is traditionally at Leaba Phádraig (Patrick's bed) on the summit of the Reek. The 19th-century writer William Makepeace Thackeray described this station as 'a shapeless heap of stones' around which the pilgrims walked. In more recent times,

Kilgeever Holy Well, for some the last Station on their pilgrimage to Croagh Patrick

Bronze Age cairns, known in recent times as Reilig Mhuire, on the west shoulder of Croagh Patrick

pilgrims walk around the oratory, built in 1905. The third station is Reilig Mhuire (Our Lady's Cemetery), located down from the summit on the western shoulder of the Reek. Thackeray described it as consisting of 'three stone heaps', which today we know are Bronze Age cairns or burial sites, indicating the ancient traditions of the Holy Mountain.

In the past, many pilgrims to Croagh Patrick would conclude their pilgrimage at Kilgeever Holy Well, located between Croagh Patrick and Louisburgh. Pilgrims would circle the well, in bare feet or on their knees, as they formed their intention or made their request, after which they knelt and prayed. They would continue praying while walking to the flagstones to the south of the well and then return to circle and pray again at the well.

Chapter 4

Landed Gentry

The stone castles introduced by the Normans in the 13th century, often surrounded with defensive curtain walls, were a means of maintaining military control over conquered areas. Ballylahan Castle on the River Moy, near Foxford, is a fine example of such a structure. From the 15th to 17th centuries, landowners built fortified tower houses, with defensive features such as battlements, loophole windows and surrounding bawn walls. These tower houses can still be seen at Kildavnet, Achill Island, Carraigahowley outside Newport, Castleburke at Lough Carra and Ballinrobe Castle. Then, in the more peaceful 18th century, no longer in need of fortified dwellings, a revolution occurred in the architectural style of the houses of the aristocracy and gentry – one that was to last until the end of the 19th century. The solid tower houses gave way to elegantly designed homes.

The 18th century was a relatively prosperous period in Ireland for the landed classes. Secure with rental incomes from their tenanted estates, they built large houses as their country seats, designed by well-known architects and surrounded by well-planned gardens and open parklands. The houses were filled with the means for gracious living, including fine furniture, silver, glass, ceramics, paintings and beautiful plasterwork. Gone were the days of the semi-fortified dwellings of the landed classes – the age of the fully domestic country house had come.

These country houses are generally associated with the Neo-classical style of architecture, popular during the Georgian period. Westport House, Enniscoe House in Crossmolina, Moore Hall at Lough Carra, Ballinamore House in Kiltimagh and Ballinrobe House – all were inspired by ancient Roman architecture, preserved and made popular by Andrea Palladio (1508-80) in the 16th century and enjoying a revival in 18th-century Georgian England. Characteristically, these houses share a central block design of two or three storeys in height, almost as high as long, built over a sunken basement. The central façade was given emphasis with the inclusion of a portico extending over the entrance doorways, often flanked with windows or columns. Enniscoe

Belleek Castle Hotel, Ballina, 2001 – originally called Belleek Manor, it was built in 1825 and designed in the Tudor Revival style, mixed with Gothic Revival

Westport House, c. 1760, looking east from the sea, from a painting by George Moore

House in Crossmolina, for example, was built with a pedimented tripartite doorway, complete with Doric columns and side windows.

Architecturally, the 19th century was the age of revivals. In addition to Gothic and Celtic, people took an interest in other styles of the past. Belleek Manor, Ballina, (known today as Belleek Castle Hotel) was built in 1825 and was designed in the Tudor Revival style, mixed with Gothic Revival. Victorian houses of the period include Turlough Park House and the late Victorian baronial addition to Ashford Castle, as well as the baronial houses of Mount Falcon (built in 1870 outside Ballina), Errew Grange in Crossmolina (itself modelled on Mount Falcon) and Breaghwy House in Castlebar. Other examples include the late 19th century Creagh House, situated close to Loughs Mask and Carra near Ballinrobe, which was built in the Italianate style of Samuel Ussher Roberts (1813-92).

From the 18th century onward, the houses of the landed classes were surrounded by meticulously landscaped parkland, within a demesne that contained the lands farmed by the landlord. Landowners increasingly aimed at achieving a formal country landscape around their fashionable houses. They were also responsible for extensive tree-planting that gave Mayo many of the graceful broadleaf mature trees still standing today. Castlemacgarrett Estate, outside Claremorris, home of the Oranmore and Browne family, was famous for its trees – conifers, oaks, limes, sycamores, golden willows, horse chestnuts and beeches. William Makepeace Thackeray (1811-63) noted in 1842 the thousands of fine trees in the landscaped grounds of Westport House. Athavallie House in Balla, today a school, was another Mayo country house set in splendid parkland with carefully planted trees, including elm, larch, copper and silver beech.

In the Victorian period, the gentry continued tree-planting programmes, drawing attention to the beauty of individual trees. They developed pleasure gardens with formal geometric plant beds cut into smooth lawns that they filled with brightly coloured annuals surrounded by firm gravel paths. The Victorian interest in gardening stimulated landowners to grow unusual and imported species, and to experiment with plant breeding. These labour-intensive gardens required an array of staff and greenhouses to support the production of bedding plants, while walled gardens, built out of view of the house, provided vegetables, fruit and cut flowers. The craze for follies and gazebos – a further development of the landscape idea – also took hold on some Mayo estates.

Some of the great Mayo landed families and their country houses are highlighted on the following pages. Through these families, we get an indication of their extensive national and international connections, their travels and occupations, marriage alliances and social pursuits, as well as their generous patronage of the arts, made possible by the wealth derived from their tenanted estates.

The Brownes of Westport House

Colonel John Browne (c. 1640-1711) was the first of the Brownes of Westport House to settle in the area. A lawyer and also a colonel in the army of the Catholic king James II during the Williamite War, he was prominent in drafting the 1691 Treaty of Limerick which ended the war. He was the second son of Sir John Browne, first Baronet of the Neale. He was also the great grandson of John Browne, born in Sussex, who came to Mayo in 1580 as part of the Elizabethan conquest of Mayo and who described himself as the first Englishman 'in living memory' to settle there.

Colonel Browne acquired vast estates in Mayo and Galway, and built the first Westport House on the site of a ruined castle which had once belonged to the old Gaelic O'Malley family. He married Maud Burke, daughter of Theobald Burke who was the third Viscount Mayo and descendant of Grace O'Malley or Granuaile, the Pirate Queen. Westport, at that time, was called Cathair na Mart (stone fort of the beeves). Colonel Browne's son, Peter (1670-1724), built Westport Harbour. Peter's son John (1709-76), named after his grandfather, decided on the ambitious project of removing the old Cathair na Mart village to make a landscaped parkland around the newly commissioned Westport House and then of building the new planned town of Westport. This project was continued by his son, Peter (1730-80).

John Browne (1709-76) was brought up a Protestant in order to retain the family estates. He was elevated to the peerage in 1760 with the title of

(Above) John Denis Browne (1756-1809), first Marquis of Sligo

(Above right) Front and south-facing side of Westport House

Baron Mount Eagle; he was later made Viscount Westport in 1768 and finally created Earl of Altamont in 1771. He conformed to the ideals of the English agriculturist Arthur Young (1741-1820), supporting innovative agricultural practices and the development of the linen industry locally. His grandson, John Denis (1756-1809), supported the creation of the United Kingdom of Great Britain and Ireland through the Act of Union in 1800 and was created the first Marquis of Sligo (the title of Mayo was already in use). Despite changing fortunes and circumstances, Westport House has remained in the Browne family to the present day. In the 1980s, the tenth Marquis of Sligo, Denis Edward, opened the house and grounds to the public and has developed the estate into a popular attraction for visitors. This has enabled the family to maintain their Palladian home.

Commissioned by John Browne (1709-76), Westport House is one of the great Georgian houses of Ireland. It was built in 1731 of grey limestone in the Palladian style and to the design of Richard Castle (1690-1751), an architect of German origin whose name was originally Cassels. He became one of the most prolific architects of the period and popularised Palladian architectural principles. He designed such great houses as Russborough House in Co. Wicklow, Carton House in Co. Kildare and Leinster House in Dublin (today the seat of the Oireachtas).

Originally, Westport House consisted of a single, east-facing block house of two storeys with seven bays, over a half-sunken basement, built with quality cut stone and designed with small windows, making the house appear larger. After his marriage to Elizabeth Kelly, heiress to sugar plantations in Jamaica, Peter (1730-80), the second Earl of Altamont, enlarged the house considerably by adding a further three sides to it, probably to the design of Thomas Ivory. The house was now a square built around an open courtyard, which was later enclosed by a roof.

Howe Peter Browne (1788-1845), second Marquis of Sligo, had a passion for archaeology. One of his better known exploits was his

*Entrance to Westport
House, on the east-facing
side dating from 1731*

involvement in an excavation in Mycenae in 1812, during which the two
great 3,000-year-old columns from the doorway of the Treasury of
Artreus were removed. He spent four months in gaol for bribing British
sailors to assist with the transportation of these antiquities. The columns
remained in the basement of Westport House until 1906 when the sixth
Marquis presented them to the British Museum in exchange for replicas.
In 1943, these replicas were erected on the south-facing side of the house.

   The entrance to Westport House is through the central façade in the
original east-facing block, dating from 1731. The entrance is composed of
a tripartite arrangement of door and window openings under a pediment,
an arrangement prominent in many of Richard Castle's designs. Below
the pediment and above the door and windows are three carved masks of
satyrs.

(Above) James Wyatt's plasterwork is an exquisite feature of the dining-room of Westport House

(Right) Coronet belonging to the second Marchioness of Sligo, wife of Howe Peter Browne

Castle's design is retained in the gracious entrance hall, complete with parquet floor and barrel-vaulted ceiling. The central Victorian staircase is made of Sicilian marble, beautifully framed by the double Doric frieze. George Wilkinson (1820-96) designed the staircase in 1857 for George Browne, third Marquis of Sligo. C.T. Fuller's larger-than-life 1865 marble *Angel of Welcome* greets those entering the house from a niche on the half-landing above the first flight of stairs. The image of an eagle, the family's motif, is incorporated into the bronze balustrade, made by Skidmore of Coventry, England.

In 1781, John Denis, third Earl of Altamont and later first Marquis of Sligo, employed the English architect James Wyatt (1746-1813) to complete the interior of Westport House. His elegant plasterwork motifs were inspired by the paintings discovered at the archaeological sites of Pompeii and Herculaneum. His plasterwork was cast from moulds and set in low relief, featuring Neo-classical repeating figures and garlands in oval and circular medallions. Although later renovations removed much of Wyatt's plasterwork throughout Westport House, it survives in magnificent detail in the dining-room.

In the 18th century, mahogany replaced oak as the preferred wood for furniture. The mahogany in the two matching dining-room doors came from the family's estates in Jamaica. A large dish-ring decorated in rococo style was part of the dining-room's table setting, which contributed to an impressive display on the table by elevating the dishes and also serving the practical function of keeping hot dishes from marring the expensive mahogany surface.

The Brownes of Westport were well connected and would have attended such Royal events as the accession of George IV (1762-1830) to the throne. On these ceremonial occasions at the English Court, formal dress was worn, with the ladies wearing coronets. One of the latter survives from the time, probably first worn by the Marchioness of Sligo Hester Kate, wife of Howe Peter Browne (1788-1845), second Marquis of Sligo. The shamrocks in the coronet represent the fact that it was worn by the holder of an Irish title. Sophia-Charlotte, mother of Howe Peter, was the daughter of Richard Howe (1726-99), First Admiral of the Fleet. Through his mother, Howe Peter had an entrée to the Royal family and he befriended the Prince Regent, the future George IV, who was a generous patron of the arts and later became godfather to Howe Peter's eldest son.

Howe Peter, although better remembered for his interest in Regency high life and archaeology, had another side to his character. As Governor of Jamaica, he was presented with a silver candelabrum in 1828 in recognition of his support for the emancipation of slaves in Jamaica. The candelabrum is decorated symbolically at its base with a former slave holding up his child, suggestive of a new-found freedom. The stem of the candelabrum is a palm tree, with its fronds extending from a central branch decorated with Neo-classical inspired bell flowers, surmounted by a pineapple.

The Moores of Moore Hall

The Moores of Moore Hall claimed descent from Sir Thomas More (1478-1535), executed by Henry VIII and declared a saint in 1935. George Moore (1729-99), second son of John Moore of Ashbrook, commenced building a house at Muckloon, beside Lough Carra, in 1792, which became known as Moore Hall. He made his fortune in the wine and brandy trade between Alicante in northern Spain and Galway. His son John (1767-99) joined the rebellion of 1798 in Mayo and was appointed President of the short-lived Republic of Connaught, but died while imprisoned in Waterford. He is remembered today by a plaque on Moore Hall, erected in 1957, and a memorial gravestone on The Mall in Castlebar, where his body was re-interred in 1961.

Moore Hall passed to John's brother, George (1770-1840), an historian who married Louisa Browne, niece of the second Earl of Altamont of Westport House. Their son, George Henry Moore (1810-70), inherited Moore Hall. A famous steeplechaser in his youth, George Henry became a prominent statesman and Member of Parliament for Mayo. During the Great Famine (1846-50), he acted with enormous charity and was a supporter of the Tenant Right Movement. His son, George Augustus (1852-1933), originally intended to become a painter and was associated with the French Impressionists in Paris. Instead, he became a distinguished writer, publishing 35 books in all. He was part of the Irish Literary Revival of the late 19th and early 20th centuries and one of the founders of the National Abbey Theatre in Dublin, together with W.B. Yeats and Lady Augusta

Candelabrum presented to Howe Peter Browne as Governor of Jamaica in recognition of his support for the abolition of slavery

Oil painting by John B. Yeats of George Augustus Moore (1852-1933), writer and part of the Irish Literary Revival movement

Gregory, among others.

On the death of his father in 1870, George Augustus inherited Moore Hall and its estate of over 4,860 hectares (12,000 acres), but he chose to live in London. George's younger brother, Colonel Maurice Moore (1854-1939), lived in Moore Hall – the last of the Moores to do so since it was burned down in 1923 during the Civil War. Colonel Moore served with the Connaught Rangers in the Boer War and is credited as the founder of the Irish Volunteers, later serving as a Senator in the new Irish Free State. George Augustus sought compensation from the State after Moore Hall was burned. He claimed a total of £16,289 13s. 6d. in respect of the buildings, furniture, china, engravings and books that were destroyed. He received only £7,000. He died in London in 1933 and his ashes were brought back to Mayo, to be laid to rest on Castle Island in Lough Carra.

Moore Hall is magnificently located, with a fine view of Lough Carra,

The imposing façade of the ruins of Moore Hall, built during the 1790s and burnt in 1923 during the Civil War

as described in George Augustus Moore's novel *The Lake*. Designed by John Roberts, the imposing square Georgian house is three storeys high, with a pillared portico. Inside, the house was once decorated with Italian plasterwork and panelled oak walls throughout the reception rooms. Its extensive library reflected the wide interests of the Moores.

In his entertaining autobiography *Hail and Farewell*, George Moore describes Moore Hall, where he lived until 1879:

> Moore Hall had always seemed to me a Mansion House inferior to Clogher and Tower Hill. But it is superior to either, for it was built in 1780 [sic], and it was with a sense of relief that I have heard from the Colonel in Dublin that the roof had been raised by my father after winning some big races. The old roof was fifteen feet lower, and the slates that covered it were the small green Irish slates like tiles mortared together. I learnt from him that it had never been completely water-tight, and constant leakage having rotted the beams, the roof had to be raised. So my antipathy to this eighteenth-century house was to some extent justified. It was no longer eighteenth century; its eighteenth-century proportions had been spoiled by the new roof . . . But I had always liked the imposing flight of the steps, the iron railings, the pillared balcony, and the hall with its Adams ceiling, and should have liked the rooms on either side better if they had not been decorated in accordance with Victorian taste.

In the same book, George Moore vividly describes the power of the 'big house' in the Ireland of former times:

(Above) George Moore's grave on Castle Island in Lough Carra

(Above right) Castlebar House was the new home of the Earls of Lucan during the 19th century

Moore Hall was built in feudal times . . . a big square house on a hill, to which the peasants came every morning to work . . . We were kings in those days; little kings, but kings for all that, with power of life and death as has been said and truly, for we often sundered wife and husband, sister from brother; and often drove away a whole village to America if it pleased us to grow beef and mutton for the English market. And in those days the peasants were afraid to thatch their cottages lest their rent should be raised, nor was there one peasant in our villages or in the Tower Hill villages worth a ten-pound note . . . The landlords have had their day. We are a disappearing class, our lands being confiscated, and our houses are decaying or being pulled down to build cottages for the folk. All that was has gone or is going. Moore Hall represents feudalism.

The Binghams of Castlebar

In the late 16th century, John Bingham (a brother of Sir Richard Bingham, Governor of Connaught from 1584 to 1596) acquired Castlebar Castle and surrounding land from the Norman family of De Barry, who had owned the land since the 13th century and gave their name to the town of Castlebar. The Binghams adapted the castle and lived there until it was destroyed by fire in 1798. Nearby, they built an unpretentious two-storey, five-bay, late Georgian house, set in beautiful landscaped gardens. The house and grounds were sold in 1924 to the Sisters of Mercy for use as a school.

In the first half of the 18th century, Sir John Bingham married Anne Vesey. She was the granddaughter of William Sarsfield, who was the brother of Patrick Sarsfield (1655-93) – Earl of Lucan and colonel in the army of James II, forced to flee Ireland after the Jacobite defeat in 1691. Sir John's son, Charles Bingham, became Baron Lucan in 1776 (he chose the title 'Lucan' in deference to his family's connection with Patrick

Sir George Charles Bingham (1800-88), third Earl of Lucan, known as 'the Famine Earl'

Sarsfield) and was created Earl of Lucan in 1795. Charles' daughter, Lavinia, married the second Earl of Spencer (the family of the late Princess Diana), after whom Spencer Street in Castlebar town is named.

Sir George Charles Bingham (1800-88), who succeeded as third Earl of Lucan in 1839, is dubbed 'the Famine Earl' and was described as a cruel tyrant, responsible for widespread evictions from his Castlebar estate during the period of the Great Famine in 1846-50. His contemporary, Finlay Dun, author of *Landlords and Tenants in Ireland* (1881), quoted the anti-Catholic sentiments of the Earl, recording him

Drawing room of Enniscoe House, built in the early 18th century and today one of the Heritage Houses of Ireland

as saying that 'he would not breed paupers to pay priests'. Sir George was recalled as Commander of the Cavalry in 1854 after the disastrous blunder of the 'Charge of the Light Brigade' at Balaclava during the Crimean War, which resulted in heavy casualties. However, his son George, the fourth Earl of Lucan, was well liked and is remembered for presenting The Mall – a beautiful green, bordered by trees and formerly the Lucan's cricket pitch – to the people of Castlebar in 1888. The seventh Earl of Lucan, Richard John, was born in 1934 and succeeded to the title in 1964. He disappeared from his London home in 1974 and remains at large, sought by the police in connection with the murder of the family nanny, Sandra Rivett.

The Jacksons of Tirawley

Enniscoe House, near Crossmolina, is located in an attractive setting under Nephin Mountain, with a magnificent view of Lough Conn. The interior is decorated in original Georgian and Victorian styles, and retains fine plasterwork throughout the house. For example, the oval hall with its central staircase is lit from above by a glazed dome, which is surrounded by graceful foliage and oval medallions of classical figures. A German artist recently restored the decorative plasterwork, using organic paint to assist its conservation. Enniscoe House is one of the Heritage Houses of Ireland and is today the home of Susan Kellett, a direct descendant of the original owners. Mayo North Family Heritage Centre is situated within the estate and incorporates a museum of rural life and a family history research centre.

In the 17th century, Francis Jackson, an officer in Cromwell's army, received 20,250 hectares (50,000 acres) in Tirawley, previously owned by the Bourkes of Norman descent. The Jackson family built a three-storey house in the early 18th century, which was later incorporated into the present-day Enniscoe House, built less than a hundred years later by Colonel George Jackson. The 1798 rebels, accompanying Humbert's French forces from Killala to Castlebar, occupied the house for a short time. Some months later,

(Above) Wedding dress of ivory silk, worn by one of the Ormsby ladies in the early 1800s

(Above centre) Bridesmaid dress of cream silk, belonging to the Ormsby family

(Above right) A fashionable cotton nursing or day dress, now in the Ormsby family collection in Canada

Colonel George Jackson participated in the slaughter of the Irish rebels, some 2,000 men, defeated at Ballinamuck in Co. Longford on 8 September 1798.

The Ormsbys of Ballinamore

The Ormsbys came to Mayo during the reign of Elizabeth I. Initially, they settled in the 14th-century castle built by Jordan d'Exeter. Later, in the second half of the 18th century, they built Ballinamore House, near Kiltimagh. After the Ormsbys emigrated to Canada in 1935, the house was successively owned by the Sisters of St. John of God and Western Care. It now serves as a private nursing home.

The Ormsby family of Ballinamore House presented a magnificent collection of early 19th-century dresses to the Royal Ontario Museum in Canada. The collection includes a fine wedding dress of ivory silk, which was probably at the cutting edge of fashion for the period. Worn in the early 1800s by one of the Ormsby ladies, it is not known where the dress was made or ordered from – possibly from Dublin, London or Castlebar. It could also have been made locally by a tailor using the latest fashion plates. The stiffened stand-up collar of the dress falls in two points over the shoulders, reminiscent of a 17th-century doublet. The bodice is gathered to the waistband. The puffed sleeves are banded with wide ivory satin armbands. The hemline is padded, serving to give a fullness to the skirt rather than the straight line of previous years. The padded hem also held the dress out from the body and kept the silk fabric from 'floating'.

Also included in the Ormsby collection is a cream silk bridesmaid dress of the 19th century. It has the 'inverted triangle' look that was influenced by 17th-century styles. The bodice is complemented by a full triangular-shaped skirt, pulled tightly at the waist by a wide belt. The sleeves are described as 'gigot' or 'leg of mutton', typical of the style and contributing to the 'inverted triangle' shape of the upper part of the body. The sleeves were reinforced with buckram to keep them in shape and a pad was strapped to the upper arm to ensure the sleeve was held out. The lower part of the skirt was decorated with frills, held up at regular intervals with pleated satin. The extended pleated satin is held in place with bows, adding an attractiveness to the dress made full by the padded hemline.

A fashionable example of a 19th-century plain cotton nursing or day dress has also survived from Ballinamore House. The dress' double collar was detachable and designed to be worn with a boat-shaped collar that left the shoulders bare. The sleeves were tacked down at the shoulders to enhance the style of the wider neckline and give a softer appearance, but would also have been held out from the body by pads or stiffeners. The soft shape of the skirt tends towards the bell shape popular in the following decades.

The Fitzgeralds of Turlough

John Fitzgerald of Gurteen in Waterford lost his Waterford estate as a result of the Cromwellian land settlement in the 17th century. He later procured Turlough Estate, outside Castlebar, which had been previously owned by Walter Bourke of Norman descent. John Fitzgerald's great grandson, George, was a captain in the Austrian Army and married Lady Mary Hervey, a sister of Frederick, the fourth Earl of Bristol and Bishop of Derry. George commissioned a painting of himself and his two sons, George Robert and Charles Lionel, from the famous German-English painter Johan Zoffany (1733-1810). This was completed, signed and dated 1764, and shows George tenderly embracing his younger son, Charles Lionel, while his eldest son, George Robert, flys a kite. Charles Lionel later inherited the estate at Turlough and married Dorothea Butler, the eldest daughter of Sir Thomas. He also became a colonel with the North Mayo Militia.

George Robert (1748-86), eldest son of George Fitzgerald, grew up to be known as the 'Fighting Fitzgerald'. He was the most infamous of the Fitzgerald family. After Eton, he joined the army and, in 1770, married Jane, daughter of William Connolly of Castletown, Co. Kildare, Speaker of the Irish Parliament. She died young and in 1782 George married Sydney Vaughan of Carrowmore, Co. Mayo. George became known for his recklessness and constant trouble-making, which included kidnapping his father in a dispute over money and inheritance. He is reported to have had the unusual habit of bringing a pet bear with him in

George Fitzgerald of Turlough, with his two sons, George Robert (right) and Charles Lionel, painted by Johan Zoffany in 1764

the front seat of his coach which he used to terrorise people. He had bitter quarrels with his neighbours, Lord Altamont of Westport and Lord Lucan of Castlebar, but it was his dispute with Patrick Randall McDonnell of Chancery Hall, Ballyvary, a Justice of the Peace, that was to cost him his life. George Fitzgerald was sentenced to death after being found guilty of the murder of McDonnell and was hanged outside the old Castlebar gaol on The Mall on 12 June 1786, 'dressed in a ragged coat, of the Castletown hunt, a dirty flannel waistcoat and drawers'. He was afterwards taken down and buried at midnight in the family vault at Turlough.

The present Turlough Park House was completed for the Fitzgeralds in 1865. The original, bow-fronted 18th-century house was abandoned and is now in ruins inside the present entrance gates. Sir Thomas Newenham Deane, the Cork architect, designed Turlough Park House, five years after his partner, Sir Benjamin Woodward, died. Deane also built the Church of Ireland in Westport and the National Museum of Ireland in Dublin's Kildare Street.

Turlough Park House has been described as of High Victorian Ruskinian Gothic design and combines architectural styles popular in the

19th century. The two-storey façade is symmetrical, rising to a high pitched roof with dormer windows. The house is constructed of local limestone and contains bands of smooth and rough stones. An attractive open Gothic porch is located at the front and the house extends to include a stable block and courtyard wing. A lean-to vinery glasshouse, heated with a solid fuel boiler, was later built on the south side of the stables. Inside, the principal staircase is designed to pass above the hall door, so that its half-landing passes a superb stained-glass window, which incorporates the Fitzgerald coat of arms and is designed with triple trefoil-headed lights, surmounted by quatrefoil lights.

Turlough Park presents an outstanding example of Victorian landscape design and contains many typical features of the period, some of which are unique in Mayo. The gardens were landscaped over a 300-year period by the Fitzgeralds and contain several constructed features, such as the artificial lake which is approached from the house by Neo-Italianate grass terraces incorporating limestone steps. The Park also contains many rare trees, including some fine mature broadleafs. In front of the house, formal flowerbeds were cut into the lawns to display brightly coloured annuals and perennial roses, popular in Victorian times. The gardens around the house were decorated with classical-inspired urns and rustic garden furniture, redolent of the period.

The walled garden of Turlough Park, like many Victorian gardens, was located out of view of the main house. Vegetables for the table and flowers cut to adorn the house were grown here. Fruit trees, probably peaches, plums and nectarines, were trained and supported on the garden walls. Bedding plants were begun in the glasshouses and later

The front of Turlough Park House, built in 1865, with its formal gardens and manicured lawns

The walled garden of Turlough Park

moved to the various flowerbeds visible from the house. There is a single door entrance in the north wall and a large arched service entrance of double doors in the east wall (to the right of the workmen in the photograph). A pump may have been the garden's only water supply.

Mayo County Council purchased Turlough Park House and its surrounding 12 hectares (30 acres) in 1991 at the suggestion of Christy Lawless, local historian, who saw the potential of the historic property and park. In a partnership involving the National Museum of Ireland, the Department of Arts, Heritage, Gaeltacht and the Islands, the Office of Public Works and Mayo County Council, Turlough Park House has been developed as the National Museum of Country Life – the National Museum of Ireland's first Division outside Dublin. The gardens have also been restored and are now listed among the 'Great Gardens of Ireland'. The purpose-built, four-storey museum exhibition building was designed with regard to the dominance of Turlough Park House, the landscaped parkland and the view of Turlough Round Tower, standing 23 m (75 ft) high.

The Guinnesses of Ashford Castle

Ashford Castle is located beside the picturesque village of Cong, on an isthmus between Lough Mask and Lough Corrib. Today, it is a hotel of international renown. The oldest part of the castle dates back to the 13th century and was built by the De Burgo family of Norman descent. They were granted lands that had formerly belonged to the Gaelic O'Connor family. In the 16th century, Sir Richard Bingham, Governor of Connaught, took over the castle and built his own fortified house within the original defensive walls.

Colonel Dominick Browne of Castlemacgarrett, outside Claremorris, acquired Ashford Castle in 1715. He built on a French-style château to Bingham's fortified house and the family used this new extension as a shooting lodge and holiday residence. In 1855, Sir Benjamin Lee Guinness purchased Ashford Castle and its estate of 2,835 hectares (7,000 acres) from Lord Oranmore and Browne. Sir Benjamin was one of the brewery family whose success story had began in 1759 when Arthur Guinness took over a brewery at St. James' Gate in Dublin. He switched from brewing ale to producing a thick, dense heavy 'porter', with a characteristic dark body and creamy head.

Sir Benjamin's son, Arthur Edward Guinness (1840-1915), inherited Ashford Castle in 1868 and later became a peer, choosing the title Lord Ardilaun. Over a period of 30 years, he rebuilt Ashford Castle in Victorian baronial style, using local grey limestone to the designs of James Franklin Fuller (1835-1924) and George Ashlin (1837-1922), both prolific architects working in Ireland. Arthur continued his father's major landscaping project around the castle. This work involved resettling the tenants in new houses in other parts of the estate. Hundreds of locals were employed in drainage, road-building and planting schemes throughout the grounds, which resulted in 40 km (25 ml) of private roads, wooded avenues and landscaped gardens secluded from the outside world.

Aerial view of Ashford Castle

James Franklin Fuller was also responsible for the dramatic grand entrance to Ashford Castle. He designed a late Victorian, castellated, six-arched bridge, with two octagonal turrets at one end and a castellated gateway at the other, complete with arrow slits and surmounted by a gigantic 'A' (denoting the family title of Ardilaun) and a Baron's coronet.

Follies and pastimes

Follies and gazebos were built at a distance from the country houses of the gentry, with the dual purpose of providing shelter at a viewing point on the estate and also to act as a destination for an excursion or picnic.

Although the country house of the Barons of Kilmaine has long since disappeared, two follies survive in its grounds – a stepped pyramid and a

The dramatic entrance bridge to Ashford Castle, designed by J.F. Fuller in the late 1800s

Stepped pyramid in the grounds of Kilmaine House, erected in 1750 by Sir John Browne to the memory of his brother, George

temple. Sir John Browne, first Baronet of the Neale, erected the miniature model of the pyramids from a plan given to him by his brother-in-law, James Caulfeild (1728-99), first Earl of Charlemont. Caulfeild was responsible for several important classical architectural projects, including the building in Dublin of the Casino in Marino and Charlemont House on Parnell Square. The nine-tier pyramid was formerly crowned by a lead statue of Apollo. The nine steps rise to a height of 10 m (33 ft), from a base of over 13 m (43 ft) in width. On the rise of the fourth step, a cut-stone plaque bears the Latin inscription:

TEMPLUM FORTITVDINIS
MEMORIAE DILECTISSIMI FRATIS
GEORGII BROWNE ARMI. HVIVSCE
PATRIAE QVONDAM DECUS & TVTAMEN
VIXIT AD 1750.

Translated, this means: 'A temple of fortitude, To the memory of a dearly beloved brother, George Browne Esq., Late glorious protector of this fatherland, Died 1750.'

Sir John Browne's other surviving folly is an unusual temple, made up of six Doric columns arranged in a hexagonal shape and supporting a finely carved roof. The temple rests on a stone base, which is actually the roof of a crypt. Below, the crypt consists of a series of stone arches, buttressing the walls and acting as support for the columns of the temple above.

Belleek Manor, outside Ballina, known today as Belleek Castle Hotel,

(Above) The Hunt assembling outside Ashford Castle, Cong, c. 1974

(Left) The Hunt at Hollymount House, c. 1900

was built in about 1825 as the home of Francis Arthur Knox-Gore, who was created a Baronet in 1868. On his death in 1873, he was buried in the grounds of the demesne beneath a striking monument erected by his son, Sir Charles James. The crown-like structure is made of cut stone and stands 9 m (30 ft) high on a mound surrounded by a deep, but waterless moat. Belleek Manor remained the property of the Knox-Gore family for over a century. It subsequently passed first to the Beckett family, then to Mayo County Council and, in more recent years, to the hotelier Marshall Doran.

Hunting and shooting were favourite pastimes of the gentry in the 19th century. Most of the great houses of Mayo supported stables and employed a large number of servants to care for their horses and hounds, including farriers for shoeing and saddlers for making tack. There was a set dress code for those participating in the hunts, which were also great social occasions around which hunt balls and other events were organised. These events were important dates in the social calendar of the landed classes, who otherwise generally lived some distance from others of their class.

Lord Ardilaun's estate at Ashford, near Cong, undertook a tree-planting programme to attract woodcock and other birds suitable for shooting. The game books from Lord Sligo's estate in Westport record that over 10,000 birds were bagged over a four-year period in the first decades of the 20th century.

The Knox-Gore Monument, set in the grounds of Belleek Manor

Chapter 5

Farming the Land

Patterns of farming were superimposed on the landscape of Mayo over thousands of years. The earliest farmers arrived in the Neolithic Period, some 6,000 years ago, and developed extensive field systems. Those in the north of the county were uncovered by archaeologists in 1969, having remained hidden and undisturbed beneath a blanket of bog for millennia. This Neolithic site in north Mayo, known as the Céide Fields, is among the best preserved of its type in Europe.

Ringforts are numerous and visible on the Mayo landscape today. They were the homes of farmers who lived there in the Early Christian period (AD 500 – 1000). These circular enclosures, housing single farmsteads, were constructed of earthen banks or stone walls, and varied in size, being on average about 30 m (98 ft) in diameter. Wealthy farmers also lived in crannógs, or semi-artificial islands built in lakes and marshy areas, which would have required more labour and materials to construct. These Early Christian farmers were predominantly involved in pastoral farming, although some crops would also have been grown. Cattle were very important in their society and the county features in the 8th-century prose saga *An Táin Bó Cúailnge* (The Cattle Raid of Cooley), the central theme of which is a cattle raid. This epic, although based on events in the preceding centuries, can also be interpreted as reflecting the period in which it was written.

After occupying parts of Mayo in the 13th century, the Normans introduced a form of feudalism based on English practices. Under this system, people had clearly prescribed social and economic obligations towards their overlords. Although some were serfs, others lived as freeholders, working their own land and the lands of their masters, whom they supplied with part of their harvest. The Normans also introduced new farming practices and the traces of their medieval field systems are still visible today in places such as Mayo Abbey.

Land use in Mayo, its cultivation and productivity, while dependent on climatic and environmental factors which changed over time, has also been affected by political and economic factors. From the end of the 17th

Drystock farming is the principal agricultural activity in Mayo today

Members of the travelling community –
the Murray Family, photographed by
Fr. Browne in 1938 near Urlaur

century, a pattern of large estates emerged. These were owned by a handful of landlords and worked by tenants who were given leases ranging from one to 21 years. Small tenant farmers became increasingly dependent on subsistence agriculture, which in many cases did not provide the income needed to pay the annual rent or to purchase necessary supplies. Some people were able to earn an income by migrating for seasonal work to the eastern counties or to Scotland or England. Others made some cash through illicit whiskey-making or spinning and weaving. Mass emigration followed the Great Famine of 1846-50 and, in the decades after, many emigrants sent money from North America, Australia and England to relatives in Mayo. These remittances were a significant source of income for those who remained at home.

During the second half of the 18th century and the first half of the 19th, Mayo's population growth accelerated, reaching approximately 389,000 people on the eve of the Great Famine – more than three times the size of the current population. This increased population necessitated massive reclamation and expansion into previously unsettled, marginal land. The intense subdivision of land and expanding population was made possible by the potato, which could be grown on relatively small plots of land in sufficient quantities to supply the nutritional needs of a family. The potato became the staple food of the poorer classes, with disastrous results when the crop failed. This happened several times in the early decades of the 19th century, producing local famines, most notably during 1831-32. However, a series of crop failures in the years 1846-50 – the Great Famine – had calamitous, immediate and long-term effects on the people of Mayo.

Periodic bad potato harvests continued in the years following 1850,

*Ruins of the 'Deserted Village'
on the slopes of Slievemore, Achill*

with the spectre of famine always hovering closeby. In 1879-81, local famines again occurred within the county and, in response, the Land League was founded at Daly's Hotel in Castlebar in August 1879, with its inspirational slogan of 'The Land for the People'. This popular movement quickly became a national force and succeeded in bringing about dramatic changes in the system of land ownership. The Land Act of 1881 acknowledged the interests of both the tenant and the landlord in the land. This was followed by subsequent Acts that introduced schemes enabling tenants to purchase their existing holdings, thereby establishing ownership for those who worked the land.

In 1891, the government established the Congested Districts Board for Ireland, the first of a series of initiatives to tackle the 'problem' of the West. The Board created a landscape of small, consolidated holdings of about 8-10 hectares (20-25 acres) for individual families, who were to be housed in dispersed rather than clustered communities. After the foundation of the Irish Free State in 1922, further initiatives were taken to improve Irish agricultural and rural life. The Land Act of 1923 divided up the remaining estates still controlled by landlords. The new Agricultural Credit Corporation (ACC) provided loans for farm improvements and government inspectors helped to raise the quality of farm produce. However, grievances remained and a new political party, Clann na Talmhan (Party of the Land), was founded in 1938 to address the continuing difficulties of small farmers in the west of Ireland. The party presented itself as following in the footsteps of the Land League. It achieved significant electoral success in Mayo in the 1940s and '50s, and retained representation on Mayo County Council until 1968. Belcarra farmer Joseph Blowick (1903-70) became the leader of Clann na Talmhan in 1944. He served as Minister for Lands in two inter-party governments

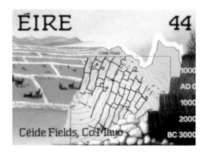

Aerial view of north Mayo's Neolithic farm landscape, reproduced in a commemorative stamp by An Post in 1993

during 1948-51 and 1954-57, and oversaw the rejuvenation of the Land Commission and the introduction of massive drainage schemes (including the Moy Scheme) and afforestation programmes.

Considerable changes occurred in farming during the 20th century. Since the 1930s, the number of people engaged in agriculture and farm holdings has steadily declined. In 1975, there were 24,500 farms in Mayo; that number collapsed to 11,000 in 1991, with a corresponding amalgamation and enlargement of farm holdings. In terms of farmer numbers, the total number of full-time farmers declined from 10,300 in 1991 to 6,900 in 1999; the corresponding figures for part-time farmers show an increase from 4,500 to 5,200 in the same period. The overall decline in the number of full-time farmers working in Mayo was accelerated by the mechanisation of farming practices, introduced from the 1940s, and by the need for increased productivity. Rural electrification from the 1950s generated major changes in farming, as well as in the social life of Mayo. The daily lives of households in rural areas were transformed from the 1970s by the availability of pipewater supplies from community-organised Group Water Schemes and County Council-organised Regional Water Supply Schemes. Farming became increasingly mechanised – hand-milking was replaced by milking machines, while potato-pickers and grain silos came on the market. Most significant was the advent of the tractor, which dramatically changed farm life and necessitated the enlargement of field sizes. The change from a labour-intensive fodder system of hay-making to a mechanised system of silage-making has completely altered the pattern of summer work on Mayo farms.

In the absence of alternative employment, changes in agriculture contributed to the continual haemorrhage of people from Mayo. In response, a committee was formed in Charlestown which evolved into the Defence of the West Movement, less formally known as 'Save the West'. The focus of the campaign was to preserve the Western small-farmholder class. John Healy, the Charlestown author and journalist, expressed some of the sentiments of those concerned with the depopulation of rural Mayo in a series of articles in *The Irish Times* newspaper. The series was later published in his classic book *Death of an Irish Town* in 1968 and republished in 1988 under the title *No One Shouted Stop*.

Ireland's membership of the European Union since 1973 has played a major role in the shaping of farming trends within Mayo. Initially, EU policy encouraged intensification of production, particularly of livestock, by guaranteeing prices. Subsequently, policy changed to making direct payments to farmers under a system that decoupled the land from production. In recent years, EU farm policy has viewed the land as a vital environmental resource, to be preserved rather than overexploited. The 1994 Rural Environmental Protection Scheme (REPS) was introduced to support environmentally friendly farming practices.

Agriculture remains an important industry in Mayo today, engaging almost a quarter of the county's workforce. The trend is towards fewer

A ringfort on the slopes of Croagh Patrick, dwelling place of a substantial farmer of the Early Christian period

but larger farms, employing less people. Grassland-based livestock predominates in Mayo, with drystock cattle farming the most important enterprise, followed by dairying and sheep production. Farmers on small holdings are no longer able to make a living solely from farming and so must supplement their income in various part-time ways, such as seasonal agri-tourism, off-farm factory work, transfer of the land to other uses like forestry or recreation, and diversification into organic farming.

The agricultural practices described in this chapter continue to be increasingly replaced by new methods of farming. Organisations such as Macra na Feirme, Teagasc (formerly the county committees of agriculture) and farmer-owned co-operatives, such as Connacht Gold (formerly the North Connacht Farmers' Co-operative), have been to the fore in debating, documenting and influencing the changes that have taken place in Irish agriculture.

Farming settlements

The first people who came to Mayo, some 9,000 years ago, lived by hunting and gathering. Evidence of organised farming dates from Neolithic times, about 6,000 years ago, and is strikingly seen in the archaeological site now known worldwide as the Céide Fields, between Ballycastle and Belderrig on the north coast of Co. Mayo. These first Mayo farmers cultivated the land, kept domestic animals and grew cereal crops. They developed grasslands by clearing the forests and most likely used the wood for fuel and for building their houses, boats and barrels. They created well-organised field systems, which may have been used for hundreds of years, by dividing the land into regular strips with parallel dry-stone walls and right-angled cross walls. Archaeologist Séamus

Interior of a traditional 19th-century thatched farmhouse on Hennigan's Heritage Farm at Killasser, near Swinford

Caulfield, who started excavations in 1969, uncovered large pasture fields of 2-5 hectares (5-12 acres), suggesting all-year-round grazing of livestock, which would have been possible in the slightly warmer climate of that period.

The Neolithic people of Mayo probably lived in rectangular houses made of wood. Evidence of the oldest surviving house of this type has been found at Ballyglass in north Mayo and its plan has been recreated at the Céide Fields Visitors' Centre. The plan of this early house is echoed in the elongated rectangular houses again common in Mayo at the end of the 19th century, although circular houses (in the form of cashels, ringforts and crannógs) were the usual form of structure in the intervening period.

There were, over time and in different regions of Mayo, variations in the style, construction and materials used in house building, depending on what was available locally. The relatively better houses of the 19th century were modest single-storey structures, rectangular in plan and one room deep. They were built using local materials of stone or mud, with thatched roofs of straw or rushes. At the end of the 19th century, the Congested Districts Board found that of the 2,297 houses in Erris, only 512 had more than one room. Traditional houses gradually evolved into three-room houses, either elongated by additions to the building or by adding internal walls to divide the rooms.

The one-room houses were often shared with animals due to the absence, on most farms, of suitable accommodation for livestock, the building of which may have increased valuation and rents. The ruins of the 'Deserted Village' on Achill Island consist of almost 100 of these one-room homes, aligned north to south on the southern slopes of Slievemore, and are today a poignant reminder of the community that once lived there from the 17th century. Edward Newman, who travelled throughout Ireland in 1840, described the houses he saw in Achill:

This Island of Achill is more like a foreign land than any I have visited; the natives reside in huts. They are without chimneys or windows, and the roof seems continuous with the walls. The interior is generally undivided, and is tenanted by men, women, children, pigs and poultry and often goats and cows.

Traditionally, the fireplace was the focal point of the house and was generally located near a gable wall. Before chimney flues were introduced in the late 19th century, the smoke holes in the thatch did not create enough draft to clear the smoke from the building, which meant that houses were constantly filled with smoke, a point often noted by travel writers of the period. Near the fire, there was usually an 'out-shot' or box-like projection (also known as the hag or cailleach) built into one of the walls of the house, in which a bed was accommodated, closed off from the room by a curtain.

Thatching – the traditional practice of roofing houses with perishable natural materials, such as straw, rushes, heather and reeds – was the norm in Mayo until the 1930s, when thatched roofs were replaced with sheets of galvanized metal or slates. Traditionally, roofs were thatched with whatever materials were available and in a style that suited the local weather conditions. Thus, there was great regional variation in thatching materials and construction methods. In more prosperous and affluent times, thatchers were a highly specialised group of craftsmen, skilled in various thatching styles. Before the thatch was fixed in place, a layer of sods or 'scraws' was usually first laid on the roof timbers to support it. In one method of thatching, the thatch was then pinned to the scraw with 'scollops' or wooden pegs made of willow, hazel, briars or other available wood. However, in some coastal areas, as a precaution against high winds, another method was employed whereby the thatch was tied down

This thatched house in the Knock area is an example of a traditional farmstead. A reek clamp of turf is located along the boreen laneway leading to the farmyard house. Outhouses for cattle are situated near the house, beside which a shed full of hay and a clamp of fodder are also found. On the other side of the house, an orchard of fruit trees and rhubarb plants are visible. Behind the house are yet more fruit trees and a vegetable garden of freshly dug potato ridges and beds of cabbage and more rhubarb. In the fields behind the house, some late hay has been shaken out to dry and marks left by hay-cocks after they were removed are visible.

by ropes, crossways and lengthways to form a net, and, in some cases, weighted and secured by stones. This latter method, common in Achill and Erris, was described by Patrick Knight in his book *Erris in the Irish Highlands*, published in 1836:

> [The thatch], instead of being confined in the usual way by scollops, is thrown loosely on, and bound down by ropes across the house from eve to eve, there tied to pegs, or loose stones lying on it, and sometimes by cross ropes from gable to gable, in the form of a net, about four inches asunder.

Survival on small farms

Potatoes had the capacity to thrive in the wet acidic soils of Mayo and came to be the single crop for the majority of the population in the years before the Great Famine of 1846-50. A small plot of land could provide enough potatoes to support a family for ten months of the year. On the eve of the Famine, the majority of Mayo's exceptionally dense rural population (recorded at 388,887) depended on the potato.

In pre-Famine Mayo, many people lived in clachans or villages of clustered dwellings, which accommodated all those living in a townland. The people generally followed the rundale system of communal farming, which utilised a large 'in-field' for cultivation, sited beside the clustered housing, and a larger 'out-field' for cattle grazing. The in-field consisted of tillage strips of good and poor land in which each family grew crops, such as potatoes and oats. The strips were marked, but not physically separated. Cultivation in lazy beds was the usual method, consisting of a

Lazy beds at Doogort, Achill Island, as photographed in 1855

The skeletal ruins of the 'Deserted Village', surrounded by medieval field systems superimposed with pre-Famine lazy beds, on the southern slopes of Achill's Slievemore mountain

series of drainage channels in between raised seed beds. The out-field was physically divided from the in-field by a stone wall and was used for grazing cattle. Their manure was used for maintaining the fertility of the in-field. Cattle numbers were restricted according to the collop or Gaelic measure, which was the estimated amount of grass needed by one cow. The land was reallocated frequently to ensure equal sharing and to adjust to population growth.

Frederick Cavendish (1777-1856), reformer, proprietor and editor of *The Connaught Telegraph*, gave evidence before the 1843 Devon Commission investigating the state of agriculture in Ireland. He reported that all the mountain farms of Mayo were held in rundale and that he was of the opinion that the bulk of the petty sessions' work arose from squabbling about the subdivision of the land.

The practice of storing and preserving butter by burying it in bogs has a long tradition in Ireland, reflecting the importance of milk and other dairy products in the diet of the people. The lack of oxygen in bogs enables most materials to be preserved for an indefinite time. Before being buried, the butter was usually wrapped in a cloth or skin container and placed in a cask or vessel hollowed out from a single piece of wood. So-called 'bog butter' dating from medieval times has been found preserved

(Above) Dooagh on Achill Island, as photographed in 1948, was a traditional village of clustered dwellings

(Above right) Traditional cluster of houses on the banks of the Moy at Belass, Foxford, c. 1900

in bogs in good condition. The fat in the butter alters with time and its appearance and flavour change. When found, the bog butter is a hard yellowish-white substance, somewhat like cream cheese in texture, and usually contains an abundance of cow hairs.

Butter-making was an important occupation in Mayo homes up to the 1950s. After that time, shop-bought butter became the norm. Prior to the 20th century, the cream was skimmed by hand from the top of the milk and then covered with muslin cloth overnight to let it ripen. When milk separators became available in the 1900s, the separation process was speeded up. When the cream was 'ripe', churning began. Many types of churn were used, but the most popular were the dash or plunger churn and the barrel churn. After churning, the butter was washed several times, then salted and moulded into shape.

There were many piseógs, or superstitions, associated with the churning which, it was believed, must be followed in order to ensure that the butter production would not be spoilt. Those visiting a house when churning was taking place had to take a turn at the churning. In some areas, visitors could not leave the house until churning was fully complete. In other areas, if a visitor entering the house did not say 'God bless the work', it was interpreted as a sure sign that the churning was going to fail.

For many centuries, farm labourers seasonally left Mayo from Spring to Christmas. They went to the east of Ireland, Scotland and England to find work as harvesters in order to earn cash to pay the rent and other bills back home. Seasonal migration from Mayo continued well into the second half of the 20th century.

Aloysius O'Kelly (1851- c. 1928), illustrator and painter, contributed a series of articles and drawings to the *Illustrated London News* in the 1880s. His image of 'Irish Harvesters on their way to England', published in May 1881, is typical of scenes he witnessed while in the West and offers a

realistic and sympathetic portrait of the circumstances of the majority of Mayo people at the time.

The playwright John Millington Synge (1871-1909) took a coach from Ballina at four o'clock one morning in 1905 and later described meeting harvesters walking from the West, making their way in heavy rain carrying scythe handles and little bundles tied in red handkerchiefs. Their destination was Ballina town, from where they hoped to embark on ships going to Liverpool or Glasgow. On arrival, they would spread out through the countryside in small groups, seeking work together. A ganger, usually Irish and often from Mayo, organised work for them picking potatoes or weeding turnips. The conditions under which they lived were very basic and improved little with time. Both men and women slept in barns and outhouses, with hardly any privacy and little or no sanitary facilities.

Later in the 20th century, Peadar O'Donnell (1893-1986), the Donegal writer and social reformer, buried in Swinford graveyard, highlighted the terrible conditions under which the harvesters or 'tatie hokers' (potato-pickers) worked. These conditions were occasionally brought to light by such tragic events as those that occurred in September 1937 at Kirkintilloch near Glasgow. On that occasion, ten boys from Achill Island, working as harvesters, burnt to death in their bothy or cabin. They had been locked in overnight, as was the practice.

Many people engaged in the making of poitín or poteen as a means of supplementing their income. Distillation of this illicit whiskey was routine throughout Mayo until the mid-19th century. The effects of Fr. Matthew's temperance campaign and the vigilance of the Revenue men eventually discouraged the practice. But in some areas of Mayo, poteen-making continued up to modern times. Poteen is distilled from oats or barley and sometimes potatoes. The still is central to the manufacturing process. It is generally of tin or copper, and usually has

(Above) Wooden vessel containing bog butter, buried in medieval times and found preserved in Tumgesh Bog, near Swinford

(Above left) 'Irish Harvesters on their way to England', sketched by Aloysius O'Kelly and published in the Illustrated London News of May 1881

A posed photograph, taken by Thomas Wynne, of a woman in possession of an illegal poitín still, surrounded by arresting officers of the Royal Irish Constabulary, c. 1900

a capacity of 91-136 litres (20-30 gallons). The ingredients are heated to boiling point in the still, causing them to evaporate through a tin worm, or coiled metal tube, stretching from the head of the still into a vessel full of cold water. When the gases from the worm are condensed by the cold water, they return to liquid form and the end result is whiskey. The more times the alcohol is distilled, the less impurities remain and so the better the whiskey.

There are many folk stories and superstitions connected with poteen throughout Mayo. It was commonly held that the first drops of poteen should not be consumed but left for the fairies in order to ensure successful distillation on future occasions. It was also used medicinally and was considered an excellent remedy for all sorts of aches and pains, strains and sprains, when rubbed on externally.

Wool production was a family or village affair, commencing with the shearing of the sheep around the end of May. Washing and drying of the wool followed and in the winter months the wool was teased and oiled to soften it. It was then carded or combed to remove tangles and made into smooth rolls in preparation for the spinning stage of the process.

The ancient spindle and whorl method of spinning was improved by mounting the spindle horizontally on a wooden frame and driving it by a band attached to a wheel. Spinning wheels came in a variety of sizes; the 'big spinning wheel' was once the most common throughout Mayo.

Thread or yarn was made on the tail opposite the big wheel through a number of simultaneous processes. The end of a roll of wool was passed between the finger and thumb of one hand and the other hand was used to work the wheel; the thread was moved evenly over and back, spinning the yarn. When sufficient yarn was spun, a ball of wool was made. When

Spinning, usually using the 'big spinning wheel', was a home industry involving the women of the house, as recorded here in Erris by Charles R. Browne, c. 1885

sufficient wool was available, it was taken to the weaver who made it into material such as flannel, frieze or blanket cloth, to which he often gave twill, herringbone and diamond patterns. Journey-tailors would came periodically to homes to make the material into suits of clothes and other garments.

Booleying – from *buaile* meaning 'milking place' – was the practice of moving cattle from May to October from lowland fields to mountain pastures to avail of the good grazing there. During the summer, the cows were milked and butter was churned, with some of the butter being stored in the bog for later use. Booleying, known internationally as transhumance, was practised as late as the 1940s on Achill Island, one of the last places in Mayo to continue this ancient custom.

Francis Walker's painting of a 'booley house' in Achill in 1904 gives an impression of summer booley accommodation. Generally, temporary huts were made of stone and turf, roofed over with bog timber and turf. Sometimes, the stone huts were made more permanent by using the ancient stone-corbelling technique, resulting in houses shaped like the old beehive monastic dwellings of the 6th century. The 17th-century stone houses of Achill's 'Deserted Village', abandoned by the late 19th century, were also used as summer booley accommodation.

Evictions and clearances

Mass evictions and the clearance of tenants from the land, including their dwellings and tillage plots, followed the Great Famine of 1846-50 as Mayo landlords sought large grazier tenants who would provide more lucrative drystock cattle farms to supply the growing urban centres in England and Ireland. In response to high rents and evictions, mass meetings of small

A 'buaile' or booley house on Achill, painted by Francis Walker in 1903

(Opposite, above) Evicted tenants sit, with their belongings, in protest or despair outside the gates of their former landlord

(Opposite, below) 19th-century line drawing by A. Nicholl showing pastoral farming in the raised land above Westport House and town, against the dramatic backdrop of Croagh Patrick and Clew Bay

tenant farmers and landless labourers were held throughout Mayo – in Irishtown, Westport, Claremorris, Balla and elsewhere – culminating in the formation of the Land League in Castlebar in August 1879. The Land League quickly became a national organisation, campaigning for better conditions for tenant farmers and ownership of the land by the tenants.

John Forbes noted on his travels in Mayo in 1853 that:

> The new system of consolidation . . . was here strongly indicated by the comparatively small amount of corn land, the great extent of pasture ground; and still more unpleasantly by the ruined walls and roofless homes that marked our tract [road] on either hand as we proceeded through the territories of Lord Sligo and Lord Lucan, the great proprietors of the district . . . The system of consolidation of farms has been carried to a considerable extent in the vicinity of Ballina. One proprietor has dispossessed all the cottagers, except about six over a tract of 15,000 acres; but like Lord Lucan [of Castlebar], he has not yet obtained tenants for the large farms thus created.

The campaigning and agitation on the land question undertaken by the Land League was continued with the founding of the United Irish League (UIL) in Westport in 1898 by William O'Brien (1852-1928) and John Dillon (1851-1927). The UIL's objectives were to agitate against the amassing of large tracts of land by graziers and to campaign for the redistribution of grass ranches among small farmers. The

J.J. Leonard's humorous photograph nonetheless captures the serious anti-grazier message of the United Irish League

photographer J.J. Leonard caught the anti-grazier feelings, prevalent in the late 19th and early 20th centuries, in his close-up picture of a cow with a placard around her neck, reading:

NOTICE
This land we'll have it we must get,
So do not 'low' or mourn,
Upon the high road you must go
Never to return.
GOD SAVE IRELAND

Leonard annotated his photograph with the words, 'The land for the people and the road for me', echoing the message on the placard.

William O'Brien, MP and Cork journalist, founded the newspaper *The Irish People* to promote the ideas and activities of the UIL. He lived for a time in Mayo, where his wife wrote a book on the events of their three years spent at Mallow Cottage in Westport. The UIL dominated the first County Council elections in 1899 and also ran in the parliamentary election for the South Mayo seat left vacant after Michael Davitt's resignation that year.

Congested Districts Board and Clare Island

After completing his tour of the West in 1890, Mr. Arthur Balfour, as Chief Secretary for Ireland (and later to become British Prime Minister in 1902-05), proposed to his government that the people there needed special help 'in order to lift them out of the slough of misery to which they had been condemned by the force of circumstances over which they had little or no control'. Thus the Congested Districts Board was established in 1891 to initiate long-term improvements in agriculture and lifestyle in the west of Ireland. Congestion was seen, according to Balfour in a speech made in Liverpool in November 1890, as 'a population not congested in the sense of being crowded, but congested by not being able to draw from their holdings a safe and sufficient livelihood for themselves and their children, whose condition trembles constantly on the verge of want, and when the potato crop fails, goes over that margin and becomes one of extreme and even dangerous destitution'. The Board sought to improve conditions through the amalgamation of small holdings, improved agricultural practices and development of supplementary sources of income. The Department of Agriculture and Technical Instruction took over some of this work after its establishment in 1899. After the founding of the Irish Free State in 1922, the Congested Districts Board was replaced by the Land Commission, which resettled migrants from Mayo to new farms in the Midlands so as to consolidate and increase the size of western farms.

In 1895, the Congested Districts Board acquired Clare Island for £5,486 from the O'Donnell Estate. It was the Board's first experiment in buying and distributing land to tenants. The island was at that time

Aerial view of Clare Island showing the striped farms introduced by the Congested Districts Board in the late 1890s, superimposed on the older rundale field system

home to 700 people who practised the rundale system of farming. Like the Digby Estate in Erris and other estates in Mayo, the Board remodeled the island, creating 77 new enlarged farms. These retained the rundale principle of providing access for each farm to all soil types by creating 'ladder' or striped farms. The new farms consisted of fields that ran in narrow strips from the mountain to the sea coast. As part of the project, the fields were enclosed by the construction of up to 80 km (50 ml) of stone walls, marking farm boundaries and separating the farms from mountain commonage. This arrangement had a striking impact on the landscape. An aerial photograph of Clare Island, taken in 1965, shows the indelible patterns of the various systems of agriculture over the centuries – the lazy beds, the rundale system and the superimposed striped field system of the Congested Districts Board introduced in the late 1890s.

On Clare Island, as throughout Mayo, the Board initiated the building of isolated, individual houses on each farm, as opposed to the traditional clustered settlements. Houses were built according to specified plans, with slate or tile roofs instead of the usual thatch. The Board encouraged changes in other traditional practices, too, such as

*The old and the new on Clare Island –
traditional stone, thatched cottages were
replaced by modern slate-roofed houses
built by the Congested Districts Board*

*Clare Island, dramatically located
at the entrance to Clew Bay
off Westport, provides an ideal
case-study of the changing farming
landscape*

the relocation of the dung heap from the front of the house and the
removal of animals from the house into separate outdoor
accommodation. The Board sent out agricultural advisors to instruct
people on new methods of crop rotation, to introduce new animal
breeds and to encourage the production of a wider range of crops.

Four years after the Congested Districts Board remodeled Clare
Island, the tenants purchased their farms with land annuities, made

'Top of the Hill' by Grace Henry,
showing women of Achill in the 1920s

available under the various Land Acts. These loans, taken up all over
the country, were given on generous terms and were repayable over
68½ years. Later, they caused hardship indirectly for farmers when,
in 1932, Éamon de Valera, leader of Fianna Fáil, refused to continue
repayment of the land annuities to the British government. This
precipitated the six-year Economic War with Britain and, since it was
the main market for Irish agricultural goods, farmers' incomes were
severely affected during this period of 1933-38.

Today, Clare Island is home to about 150 people. The island
community has felt the effects of the decline of small-scale farming,
although the development of a fish farm offshore and agri-tourism
help sustain the community, which engages two teachers in its
national school.

Romantic Mayo

In the late 19th and early 20th centuries, the small owner-occupied farms were labour-intensive and living conditions were basic and hard-won. Romantic images of Mayo and the West were created in literature and art in the early 1900s. These images were compatible with the distinctive cultural heritage and identity favoured by the new Irish State, which hoped to root families on the land and support small farming communities. In Mayo, the majority of farm holdings remained at less than 20 hectares (50 acres) at the end of the 20th century.

The paintings of Paul Henry (1876-1958) between the years 1910-19 were inspired by life on Achill Island. He had taken up residence there with his wife Grace, also a painter, and presented strong romantic images of Mayo's farmers, embodying dignity despite poverty and hard physical toil. His paintings captured Mayo's beautiful landscapes and became instantly recognisable by their dramatic cumulus clouds and blue mountains. Reproductions of his Mayo paintings were hung in railway

'The Potato Diggers' by Paul Henry depicts rural toil set against the dramatic Mayo landscape

stations throughout the country to advertise the Great Southern Railways and were influential in popularising a romantic image of Mayo.

Grace Henry also captured the spirit of the people in her painting 'Top of the Hill', formerly entitled 'Achill Women'. Her picture shows the clothing worn by the local women, with the red tones of the shawls contrasting with the subtle surrounding colours of the uncultivated landscape. Paul Henry, in his autobiography *An Irish Portrait*, published in 1951, recalled that the women's clothes were mostly made of coarse homespun flannel, dyed a vermilion colour that changed with wear, weathering and washing.

The idealised aspirations of small farming communities, popular in the mid-20th century, were echoed in the Davitt and Parnell commemorative stamp, issued by the Post Office in 1946. This stamp marked the centenary of the birth of two great leaders – Straide-born Michael Davitt (1846-1906), founder of the Land League, and Charles Stewart Parnell (1846-91), MP and President of the Land League. The stamp was designed by R.J. King and featured the figure of a ploughman tilling the soil against the background of Mayo's distinctive Croagh Patrick mountain, with the legend *Tír agus Teaglac* (Country and Homestead). Using the image of Croagh Patrick was perhaps reflective of the central role that Mayo had played in the Land League – founded in 1879 in Castlebar.

The Davitt – Parnell commemorative stamp, issued in 1946

Pastoral farming

Animals were traded many times during their lives, making cattle fairs an important feature of farming life in Mayo for many centuries until they were gradually replaced by indoor marts from the 1960s. Calves were reared to be sold at local fairs and then traded again at larger fairs, such as the Ballinasloe Fair in Co. Galway. The English travel writer Arthur Young noted in his *Tour of Ireland 1776-1778* that 800 bullocks from the Barony of Tirawley in north Mayo were sold annually at the great fair in Ballinasloe. At such fairs, the cattle were generally bought by large grazing farmers in the Midlands and eastern counties, where they were fattened up before being exported as part of the 'provisions trade' to England.

Fair days have a long tradition in Mayo. Among the three oldest recorded fairs were those at Ardnaree, Ballinrobe and Crossmolina. Ardnaree, Ballina, was granted a patent in 1612 for a fair to take place on the feast day of St. Augustine and the following day (28th and 29th August). Ballinrobe's patent was granted in 1605 and made provision for a three-day fair, beginning on Whit Monday. A patent of 1633 allowed a two-day fair to take place in Crossmolina, commencing on Ascension Thursday. Livestock fairs continued on the streets of certain towns in Mayo until the late 1970s. Shop-owners took the precaution of erecting barriers in front of their premises on fair days to protect against the throngs of cattle, sheep and other animals milling around. Today, smaller livestock and horse fairs remain a regular feature in some towns, with added attractions, such as stalls selling clothes, plants and household goods.

In 1973, on the eve of Ireland joining the EEC, a group of agricultural

(Above) Cattle quenching their thirst in the River Moy at Ballina town in 1948

(Above right) Belmullet Fair, as it was in the late 1890s, with the women in traditional long dresses, shawls and plaid scarves

Balla Fair, photographed in the early 20th century

co-operatives amalgamated to form the North Connacht Farmers' Co-operative (NCF) in order to offer a wider range of services to farmers and to act as an advocate of the smaller farmer. NCF marts opened throughout Mayo and offered new outlets for the sale of livestock at places such as Balla, Ballinrobe, Ballyhaunis, Swinford, Westport and Ballina. The marts put an end to the traditional fair days. Cattle production has increased in recent decades, with 80% of farms now involved in drystock cattle farming.

Sheep, suited to rough ground, were kept in Mayo mainly for their wool. Traditionally, the wool was either sold directly to spinners or to dealers at a local market. Sheep farming became a significant enterprise in Mayo during the 1980s and '90s, until the continental market peaked. Since the late 1990s, the numbers of hill sheep have declined as a result of government directives

Pigs were once an important feature of the Mayo rural economy

Bringing home the flock

aimed at limiting the destructive consequences of overgrazing.

From 1910, sheep-dipping for sheep scab became compulsory. Initially, farmers resisted the order and the archives of Mayo County Council record several applications from the Royal Irish Constabulary for authority to prosecute for non-compliance. In time, farmers banded together to build communal village sheep-dipping stations. The local authority continues to be responsible for ensuring that disease control and treatment measures are implemented.

Traditionally, tenants who were wealthy enough kept a pig. In the 18th and 19th centuries, pigs were fed on potatoes and sold for cash to pay the rent. In good times, the pig was slaughtered at home. The salted or smoked meat, preserved in sealed barrels, provided the family and neighbours with a supply of meat for several months. Today, pigs are generally found only in a few relatively large commercial pig and sow units throughout the county. Concern about the environmental impact of waste from pig factories has constrained the expansion of the industry.

Although coming relatively late to Mayo, dairying was the first branch of agriculture to come under the organisation of the Irish Co-operative Movement. Where creameries existed, they offered a secure outlet for milk sales and receipt of the all-important 'creamery cheque'. Traditionally, women played a central part in milk production on the farm, often taking charge of cleaning the churns and delivering the milk directly to the creamery by donkey and cart, and later by tractor and trailer. In some cases, the women's independent cash income was severely reduced if the creamery cheque was posted to 'the man of the house'. Today, bulk containers from the creameries collect and deliver the milk directly from farms to the creamery.

(Above) Women traditionally delivered milk to the creamery by donkey and cart

(Above right) Bill Noone's milk delivery bicycle, photographed by Fr. Browne in Foxford in 1938

Milk, direct from the farm, was traditionally distributed door-to-door and carefully measured into the customers' own vessels. Mr. Bill Noone of Foxford was well known for his milk deliveries by bicycle, 'twice daily'. He was continuing the business begun by his father, Michael, who had used a pony and trap to carry 55-litre (12-gallon) containers of milk around the locality. Bill Noone's children continued the milk rounds before and after school right up to the early 1960s, after which time local farmers began to bottle and deliver their own milk. In more recent decades, pasteurising regulations brought about the establishment of centralised milk plants and delivery services, thus ending the direct milk-delivery operations.

Weigh stations and separating stations for milk were established at Balla, Castlebar, Claremorris, Ballinrobe, Killala and Belmullet. The Balla Creamery was typical of the simple design of these early plants. Its various separators, churns and other processes were powered from a stationary steam engine driven by turf. At the separating station, the cream would be separated from the milk and used to make butter. The skimmed milk was returned to the farmer, who would use it for feeding the calves. The Balla Creamery closed in 1942, when it was taken over by Tommy Joe McWalter. He changed the nature of the operation from manufacturing to packing butter, which was bought in bulk and retailed under the 'Manor' brand. The business has remained in the McWalter family, who operate a distribution centre for Mitchelstown products and Galtee Foods. Like Balla, many other smaller creameries also closed when milk processing became increasingly concentrated in larger, modern plants. Today, most of Mayo's dairy herd is found in the north and east, within the catchment area of Connacht Gold (formerly the North Connacht Farmers' Co-operative). The North Connacht Farmers' Co-operative was

Balla Creamery, c. 1900

instrumental in encouraging farmers to practically double their milk production between 1973 and 1983 – the year milk quotas were introduced by the European Union.

Cereal farming

Each year, from February onwards, fields were ploughed by farmers in preparation for sowing new crops. Until at least the 18th century in Mayo, the spade or hand-plough (rather than the horse-drawn plough) was the usual method of tillage, a practice which dates back to the Bronze Age. Originally, crops (usually oats) were sown by hand by casting seeds on to ridges and then covering them with earth from the furrows or dykes. Travel writers in the 18th century commented on the archaic custom of 'ploughing by the tail'. This involved using a straw rope to attach a wooden plough to the horse's tail. From the farmer's point of view, the method had the advantage of reducing damage to valuable ploughs and other farm implements since the horse would automatically stop when it met an obstruction. In more modern times, wooden ploughs were

The National Ploughing Championships include awards for ploughing with horses, as seen here during the 2000 competition on Finnegan Farm, Garryduff, Claremorris

John Proctor's sketch for the Illustrated London News of 1880, entitled 'Harrowing under difficulties: Mountain farm in Co. Mayo'

replaced by iron ones and horses gave way to tractors.

The *Illustrated London News* of January 1880 published a sketch by artist John Proctor, showing a man and a woman harrowing the soil of a mountain farm in Mayo, at a spot 'close to Pontoon Lough, on the road between Castlebar and Ballina, near the ridge on the mountain called The Rocks'. The man leads a horse, most likely borrowed or hired for the day's work, pulling a harrow over the ground to break up the soil for an oat field. The stones and boulders, which are too large to be moved by hand, block the progress of the harrow. It is guided and lifted by the woman, who is holding it by a rope made of straw. The accompanying report states that:

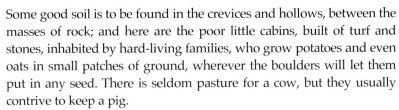

(Above) Donkey with empty pardógs, traditionally used for carrying animal manure

(Left) Fr. Browne's photograph entitled 'Spraying Jimmy', showing a Crossmolina man in the 1930s spraying the potato crop

Some good soil is to be found in the crevices and hollows, between the masses of rock; and here are the poor little cabins, built of turf and stones, inhabited by hard-living families, who grow potatoes and even oats in small patches of ground, wherever the boulders will let them put in any seed. There is seldom pasture for a cow, but they usually contrive to keep a pig.

A photograph by Fr. Browne, SJ, called 'Spraying Jimmy', taken in the Crossmolina area in the 1930s, captures the common practice of spraying potatoes with a mixture of copper sulphate (bluestone) and hydrated lime or washing soda. These chemicals help to prevent potato blight, but this was only discovered in the late 19th century – some 40 years after the cataclysmic Great Famine of 1846-50. Potato blight was an ever-present threat. Travelling though Mayo in 1905, John Millington Synge (1871-1909) noted the eagerness of the people to avail of any method that might save their crops. He learnt of one old woman who could not afford to buy a machine to spray her crops, but was found out in her field with a bucketful of the solution, sprinkling her potatoes with an old broom.

Cattle manure was an essential and valuable commodity for farming. So important was manure that farmers traditionally set up the dung heap beside the front door of their houses to provide evidence to the landlord that they had the means to fertilise the land. Pardógs were the traditional baskets (similar to turf creels) used for putting out farmyard manure on the drills of potatoes and other crops. Like creels, they were made from sally rods, cut from the willow in November. They differed from creels in that the bottom of the pardóg could be opened to deposit the load where

Donkey carrying a load of seaweed, as painted by Paul Henry during his time in Achill

it was required. The bottom piece was attached to one side by a home-made hinge, while the other side was kept closed with the help of a rod or bolt known as a sloidín. When putting out the manure, two baskets were strapped to either side of a donkey. It was important that the closing rods of both baskets were opened simultaneously, otherwise the uneven load would topple the beast. Today, slurry tanks are used to spread the manure, which comes from slatted houses where the animals are kept during the winter.

Seaweed was also highly valued as a fertiliser. Regulations allocated collection rights for this resource, which was often carried up to five miles inland from the coast, either by hand or on the backs of donkeys. The addition of lime to acid soils also helped increase productivity. Lime kilns, usually of circular shape and made of stone, were found in many townlands. They were filled with alternate layers of turf and limestone. This was burned to produce the lime for fertiliser and whitewash, as well as for making mortar. The practice of fertilising the land with lime and seaweed declined with the importation of guano in the mid-19th century and the increased use of artificial manures.

Farmers would set aside fields as meadows and harvest them traditionally in June or July each year. In more recent times, silage might be harvested a second time in early autumn. The traditional yield from

Saving the hay during the drying process, as photographed by Fr. Browne in 1938 at Keel, Achill Island

meadows was hay, but it is now much less important than silage as a winter fodder. Up until the early 19th century, the sickle was used for harvesting. Then the scythe was introduced, which increased productivity although it was more difficult to use. By the end of the 19th century, scythes had been replaced by mowing machines. After the hay had been cut with the scythe, it was left on the ground to dry and turned occasionally with forks. Then it was built into cocks, secured with ropes made of hay. These cocks stood in the meadow for up to two months and were then brought to the farmyard on donkey- or horse-drawn carts, where they were built into large hay stacks or ricks. In recent times, the cocks would simply be stored in a hay shed.

(Above) Tractors and silage harvesters have replaced scythes and hay cocks in today's meadows

(Right) Mr. Quigley of Snugboro making traditional hay cocks

Harvest time traditionally involved whole families working together in the fields

An early threshing machine, photographed by J.J. Leonard, Lahardane, c. 1930

Harvesting oats and barley traditionally involved grasping a bunch of stalks in one hand and cutting them with the hook of a sickle in a sawing action with the other. Women generally had the task of tying the fallen stalks into sheaves. These were then arranged in stooks and left to dry for several weeks. The stooks were piled together into stacks and later transported to a barn. Traditionally, a *meitheal* or reaping party got together for this work in September. The gang was made up of farmers from the local townland, assisting each other with the harvest. Despite mechanisation of the process, this communal approach to harvesting continued in many areas of Mayo.

Before the arrival of the threshing machine, grain was separated from the stalks by hand using specialised tools. The tied sheaves of corn were supported on a flat surface and, in an operation called scutching, the sheaves were methodically hit with a stone or stick to remove most of the grain from the stalks. The loose sheaves were then spread on the floor and, with rhythmic blows from a flail, the remainder of the grain was removed. The flail was a simple but effective tool, made up of two sticks, one longer than the other, tied together about four inches apart, so that one could swing and act as the beater and the other could be held steady. When the flailing was finished, the stalks were gathered together into bundles and used later in a variety of ways – for weaving, sleep mats (known as 'shakedowns'), winter bedding for livestock, thatching material, constructing household furniture and many other useful objects, such as horse collars and ties and tethers for animals. Examples of these objects can be seen in the National Museum of Country Life in Turlough, outside Castlebar.

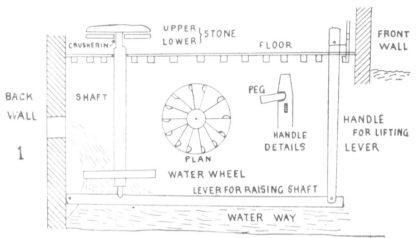

FLATLEY'S MILL.

(Above) Among the farm implements on display at Hennigan's Heritage Farm, Killasser, are (from left to right) the loy, steeveen, flail and slane – all in common use up to the 1960s

(Above right) Plan of Flatley's Horizontal Mill, near Ballyhaunis, showing the mechanics of the water wheel and stones

The final part of the operation was winnowing or separating the husks or shells from the grain, which was done by hand, using a sieve. Winnowing machines eventually replaced this time-consuming work. Then, in 1930, threshing machines were introduced, powered by steam engine, and incorporating in a later design the winnowing function. These labour-saving machines were generally owned by contractors, who brought them by tractor from one farm to the next.

Before the harvested grain could be used as food, the seed had to be milled and ground into meal or flour. Rotary stone querns were used from medieval times for this purpose. A rotary quern consisted of two flat circular stones, placed one on top of the other. The upper stone had a hole bored through its centre and a wooden handle was inserted and secured. Then, while the lower stone remained stationary, the upper stone was turned by the handle, grinding the grain that was poured slowly through the hole. The ground grain fell out between the edges of the two stones and was collected.

The ruins of small water-powered mills dot the Mayo countryside. They were used mainly in the medieval period and were sometimes owned collectively by groups of farmers. Flatley's Horizontal Mill at Cullentra Lake, near Ballyhaunis, was still working at the beginning of the 20th century. This type of mill was later replaced by vertical wheels. In both types of mill, water, directed from a mill pond or lake, forced the wooden mill wheels to rotate. They were connected by a long wooden shaft to two flat mill stones above. Just like the old rotary querns, the grain was poured in and ground between the stones. Milling grain became a widespread industry throughout an otherwise non-industrial Co. Mayo. Grain was milled not only for local consumption, but also to supply distant markets. Technological developments, such as metal wheels and the introduction of diesel-powered mills, increased output and exports.

*Pastoral farming remains the backbone
of contemporary agriculture in Mayo*

European Union and farming today

Ireland's entry in 1973 into the European Economic Community (EEC), latterly the European Union (EU), was viewed with great expectation by Mayo farmers, who hoped that membership would open up larger markets with guaranteed prices for Irish products. Within a decade, farm produce was in oversupply throughout Europe and quotas were placed on agricultural production, including, most famously, milk quotas introduced in 1983, which checked increased production.

The EU's reforms of the Common Agricultural Policy (CAP) during the 1990s have resulted in a change of European agricultural policy. Price supports were withdrawn in favour of direct payments supports for those in disadvantaged areas, such as farmers in Mayo. In 1995, Mayo farmers received an estimated IR£42 million in direct payments, paid as part of a policy designed to combat overproduction. The challenge became the establishment of farming practices and methods to manage and protect the landscape and environment. In the first four years after its introduction in 1994, 4,500 Mayo farmers joined the Rural Environmental Protection Scheme (REPS). This involved a five-year agreement between individual farmers and the Department of Agriculture and Food to promote environmentally friendly farming practices, designed to protect the environment, flora, fauna and archaeology of the farm area.

Chapter 6

Transport and Communications

In Mayo, roads began as simple paths and tracks created by people travelling continuously along the same route, sometimes laying down wood and plant materials to create a more permanent trackway. One such ancient routeway, the Tóchar Phádraig (Patrick's Causeway), pre-dates St. Patrick in the 5th century and is thought to have originated at Rath Cruachain in Co. Roscommon and continued as far as Croagh Patrick, outside Westport. Despite such early routeways, Co. Mayo remained largely without a connecting transport system until the 18th century when each parish became responsible for the roads in its own area, resulting in a wide variation in standards and maintenance throughout the county.

In 1777, George Taylor and Andrew Skinner carried out a survey of roads in Co. Mayo, when the road system was expanding and the number of horses, both private and hired, were on the increase. Their maps show an impressive network of roads, although of considerable variation in quality. Arthur Young recorded in 1776 that the road from Killala to Castlebar was 'vile and stony'. Some years later, James McParlan, who prepared a statistical survey of Co. Mayo for the Royal Dublin Society in 1801, reported that, overall, he found relatively good roads throughout Mayo.

The population of Mayo expanded significantly from the late 18th century until the Great Famine of 1846-50. The increased occupation of more marginal lands brought an increase in access lanes and routeways throughout the county. From the late 17th century, Grand Juries, composed of landowners or their agents, met twice yearly. Among their responsibilities were the so-called 'fiscal' items of business, which included making provision for the construction or repair of roads, bridges and piers. Finance for these projects was made available through the 'presentments' voted by the Grand Jury. These were formal allocations of money to a

Car outside the Railway Hotel in Westport, c. 1910

The ancient route of the Tóchar Phádraig is still followed by pilgrims walking to the holy mountain of Croagh Patrick

contractor in payment for specific projects, mainly financed by the Grand Jury Cess. Various bodies, such as the Board of Works and the Postmaster General, often called upon Grand Juries to maintain specific roads.

In the 19th century, the authorities saw the construction of roads as a means of enabling greater trade and industry within the county, as well as a means of denying a place of refuge to the lawless. Relief works included road-building and were introduced during times of particular distress to provide a small income for the destitute. Some relief roads became known locally as 'Famine roads'.

The establishment of Mayo County Council in 1898 coincided with the arrival of the motor car and the corresponding increased demand for an improved road system. Maintaining roads suitable for cars and other motorised machines, which was a central feature of the new Council's work, became increasingly expensive with the cost of road surface materials and machinery. The Council received funding from the 1909 Vehicle and Driver Taxation Act, introduced to provide funds for modernising and improving the road system. The advent of World War I put a stop on such central government resources and, in the following years, roads and bridges became targets of the Mayo Brigades of the Irish Republican Army during the War of Independence in 1919-21. During the 20th century, the road system improved as resources again became available and infrastructure increasingly became a priority at local, national and European level. Castlebar-born Padraig Flynn, TD and EU Commissioner, is especially remembered for the excellent road system around Castlebar.

At the start of the 21st century, Mayo County Council was responsible for 6,272 km (3,895 ml) of roads – 136 km (85 ml) of national primary roads, 271 km (168 ml) of national secondary roads, 590 km (367 ml) of regional roads and 5,275 km (3,275 ml) of local roads. The road works of the county are organised and supervised by the County Engineer, supported by nine District Engineers and offices. Road-building and maintenance is carried out by over 250 permanent employees, with approximately the same number being indirectly employed.

The conical mountain of Croagh Patrick, rising 765 m (2,510 ft) above sea level, has been a place of pilgrimage for many centuries. In the 5th century, St. Patrick followed an ancient routeway to the mountain, now known as the Tóchar Phádraig, and today, pilgrims still walk part of this same route each year, between Ballintubber Abbey and Croagh Patrick.

The Taylor and Skinner maps of Co. Mayo were published in 1778 in a convenient, hand-sized book, with the maps arranged in single or double columns for ease of reference. The maps were extremely detailed and show a complex network of major and minor routes. Also shown are the country seats of the landed gentry, who supported the mapping project by taking out subscriptions. Comparison with a modern roadmap shows that some of the 18th-century roads have declined into lesser routes today.

In his book *Sketches in Erris and Tyrawley*, published in 1841, Caesar Otway describes, in humorous detail, the occasion in 1799 when an English Brigade-Major was invited by the landlord, Major Bingham, to travel into Erris to inspect the small volunteer yeomanry corps, raised in 1796 on the Shaen Estate. In order to get to his destination, the Major travelled through the old and only pass into the area, as approached from Newport. Otway describes the pass as one on which 'no mortal-made carriage could have ever exercised a wheel upon its track'. A guide, who spoke Irish and knew the area, accompanied the Major. They hired ponies 'accustomed to bog-trotting and to the ins and outs of the country' and crossed the mountain with relative ease. They continued their journey following the tóchar, which Otway describes as 'a routeway comprising of a foundation of interwoven brambles, hazels, furze and even heath, which were surfaced with turf sods'.

The ponies trod lightly and picked their way along this routeway before descending into the boggy glens and flat land, with its

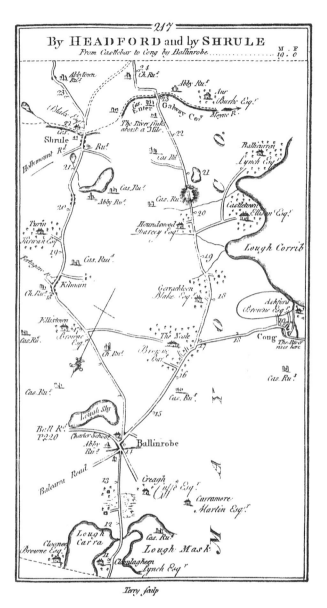

Taylor and Skinner's map showing roads leading into Ballinrobe in 1778

(Above) The Brigade-Major transported into Erris in 1799, as described by Caesar Otway

(Above right) Binghamstown, established in the 1820s, was superseded by Belmullet as the main market town on the Mullet Peninsula

'treacherously quaking and soft' surface. The travellers met a spot where the tóchar had sunk into the bog and the animals refused to go on. The Major's guide made his way across the difficult spot, leaping from tussock to tussock, and when there was none he 'cut a scraw with a gowl gob' and threw it before him and stepped lightly across so as not to sink, until he reached firmer ground. 'Not so the major; a tall, stiff, non-elastic man, who might be defined as *Homo valde perpendicularis*, cased in a tight cavalry jacket, tight buckskin breeches, tight over-knee boots.' The Major, noble no more, perched on the flank of the pony that had been placed on its side and, with 'a long pull, a strong pull, and a pull together', the pony with the Major was dragged by straw ropes across the quagmire. A soaring eagle looked on at how a Brigade-Major was transported into Erris in 1799.

John Bingham and Henry Boyle Carter, inheritors of the Shaen Estate, were the two principal landowners in Erris. In the 1820s, they developed the towns of Binghamstown (An Geata Mór) and Belmullet (Béal an Mhuirthéad) in tandem with the construction of roads into Erris. In early 1823, the first two-wheeled vehicle passed through Binghamstown to the extremity of the Mullet Peninsula and by 1824 the road was passable for carriages of all kinds. However, Binghamstown decayed as it was replaced in importance by the town of Belmullet. Belmullet was situated on the 'new road' at the narrowest part of the isthmus between the bays of Broad Haven and Blacksod. According to the engineer Patrick Knight, in his 1836 book *Erris in the Irish Highlands,* a post office was established in Belmullet in the 1820s and 35 newspapers were delivered with the post, which came initially three times weekly and later daily.

Knight also records that Alexander Nimmo, the renowned Scottish engineer, was sent from Dublin in 1822 to complete road works, begun in 1819, to link Belmullet and Blacksod Point to the Castlebar road. A branch

*The Ballina to Belmullet
Express, c. 1900*

road was extended from Bangor to Tulloghan Ferry and a road was
constructed from Ballycastle to Belderrig between 1822 and 1827. This
was extended as far as Glenamoy in 1830 and subsequently to near
Belmullet, opening a channel of communication along the north coastline
to the Mullet Peninsula.

It was not always easy for travellers to find what they considered
suitable transport to take them around Mayo. Horses, donkeys and carts,
ponies and traps, and later bicycles remained the principal means of
transport until after World War II. They were then gradually replaced by
motor cars, which made their appearance in small numbers in the early
1900s. John Barrow, in his book *A Tour around Ireland: Through the Sea
Coast Counties in the Autumn of 1835*, described his discomfort at having to
travel in the 'Swinford car' to Castlebar. He had hired this horse-drawn
vehicle for 10s. because the only alternative was to make a trip of 25 km
(15 ml) on the mail coach to Ballina and from there by coach to Castlebar.
He describes the 'Swinford car' as a cart with two tall wheels, without
sides and without ends. The driver was seated on the shaft and Barrow
crouched within inches of the horse's tail, seated on his travel bag and
wrapped in his cloak to protect him from the elements. They travelled on
'slowly and steadily at the rate of 3 or 4 miles an hour, reaching Castlebar
on a fair day'.

(Above) The 'Swinford car' consisted of a shaft between two tall wheels, as experienced by John Barrow in 1835

(Above right) Horse-drawn side car, c. 1901, in which passengers sat back to back, facing outward

'Going to the Market' by Jack B. Yeats shows a long-car travelling towards Clew Bay

The jaunting-car was a more sophisticated form of travelling, designed in the early 19th century and capable of carrying four passengers and a driver. It was the typical mode of transport hired by more wealthy travellers up until the early decades of the 20th century. The spoke-wheeled uncovered jaunting-car evolved from the side-car, in which passengers sat back-to-back, resting their feet on wooden foot-rests. The body of the jaunting-car was mounted on springs, with only two wheels underneath. The two long wooden seats were placed lengthways, so that the passengers sat facing out sideways while travelling. There was an elevated driver's seat in the front, although some cars would not be fitted with this luxury in which case the driver would sit on one of the passenger's seats and control the vehicle from the side.

Cycling was once a popular leisure sport among the 'well to do'

The use of horses and ponies for transport supported local employment and required the combined efforts of a number of specialised craftsmen, including tanners for the leatherwork of the harnesses, carpenters for the woodwork of the car and wheels, and blacksmiths for the metalwork of the horses' shoes or slippers, and iron for the wheels.

Jack B. Yeats (1871-1957) in his painting 'Going to the Market' captured a fine view of Clew Bay in the distance and an open-topped, four-wheeled long-car, driving locals, at an average speed of 6 to 7 miles per hour, to the market. The long-car evolved as a four-wheeled version of the two-wheeled side-car or jaunting-car. The painter Paul Henry (1876-1958) wrote in his autobiography, *An Irish Portrait* (1951), that the last long-car he saw in Ireland was the one to Dugort when he arrived to take up residence on Achill Island in the early 1900s.

Cycling became popular at the end of the 19th century. Initially a leisure sport, bicycles, including the popular penny farthings, were used for making excursions to beauty spots and places of antiquity. But later, bicycles became an important and affordable means of everyday transport for the majority of people in Mayo throughout most of the 20th century until the now-ubiquitous motor car replaced them. Women were as quick as men to avail of this new method of transport, but they favoured tricycles and bicycles with no crossbars so as to accommodate the long skirts in fashion at the time.

During the 1920s, Mayo County Council bought the Fowler Steam

(Right) The old and the new – horse and trap with penny farthing bicycles in Castlebar, c. 1900

(Below right) The Gráinne Ní Mháille steam road locomotive, restored by Mayo County Council

Road Locomotive, which became nicknamed the *Gráinne Ní Mháille*. The engine had previously been used to draw canons in London during World War I and was later sold to Mayo County Council via Northern Ireland. The *Gráinne Ní Mháille* engine is approximately six horse-power and weighs 10.5

tonnes. In 1924, the Council bought a new engine from Dublin, which is currently painted in the distinctive red and green colours of Mayo. These engines were used to crush road material and to pull equipment during road construction. In the late 1980s, Mayo County Council restored both engines and, in 1991, the *Gráinne Ní Mháille* won first prize at the Steam Rally in Stradbally, Co. Laois. They are now stored in the Machinery Yard of Mayo County Council, which is part of the Council's Road Construction Department.

The earliest group passenger transport service in Co. Mayo began in the early 19th century, between Clifden and Westport, and was part of the Bianconi Car Service. This service of horse-drawn road cars was pioneered in Ireland by the Italian emigrant Charles Bianconi (1786-

Castlebar-native Padraig Flynn, TD and European Commissioner (4th from right), with Joe Beirne, County Engineer (2nd from right), and other staff members of Mayo County Council Roads Department at the opening of the N5 in 1991

Ballina Main Street in 1946, showing the increasing popularity of cars but still plenty of bicycles on the as-yet uncongested street

1875). The service was next extended to Achill, prompted in part by visitors to the settlement of the Irish Church Mission Society (known locally as the Colony), established in 1833. Later, the Midland and Great Western Railway company took over the Bianconi Car Service between Clifden and Westport, and from 1910 the company operated a motor vehicle service between these towns, which proved of great significance in developing tourism in west Mayo.

Development of the road system in Mayo accelerated rapidly in the 20th century. Travel became increasingly dependent on roads rather than rail. In 1913, there were 100 cars and 143 motor cycles registered in Mayo, although the licence duty for the same year was paid only in respect of 19 cars and 32 cycles. By the 1920s, there were some 250 cars and motor cycles on the roads of Mayo. After World War II, cars became increasingly popular. In 1999, there were 4,881 new cars alone registered in the county. The ever-increasing number of privately owned cars has had a tremendous impact on travel patterns and lifestyles. People now travel regularly by road from dormitory towns and suburbs to such urban centres as Castlebar, Ballina and Westport. Maintaining and developing the road system of the county is a major component of Mayo County Council's responsibilities. The Council takes care of some 6,272 km (3,895 ml) of roads and has undertaken substantial road capital projects.

(Top) John D. Clark and Richard Glancy of the Mayo County Council Roads Department, examining plans for Castlebar Distribution Roads in June 1992

(Above) Knock International Airport Access Road opened in February 2000

(Above right) The introduction of taxi plates in 2001 made taxis more visible in Mayo's towns

Bridges

There are many old and interesting bridges in Mayo. One such is the Clapper Bridge, west of Louisburgh at Burlehinch near Killeen, thought to date from medieval times and possibly one of the oldest bridges in the county. It was known locally as the Colony Bridge, after the Church of Ireland settlement in that area. Of similar construction to bridges found in Devon and Cornwall, this clapper bridge, built for pedestrians, was made at a place on the river where the water depth was generally low. It is the largest complete clapper bridge in Ireland, stretching 50 m (164 ft) across the river. Its 37 arches are superbly constructed in the primitive clapper style, each made of a clapper or flat limestone slab, about 0.6 m (2 ft) wide, resting on a pier of about the same height above the river bed.

The stone, one-arched Pontoon Bridge was built over the narrow strait that links Lough Conn and Lough Cullin when a post or mail line to Sligo came into operation. A pontoon, or temporary bridge of flat-bottomed boats, was previously in place at this strait and hence the name 'Pontoon' stuck to the permanent bridge. The name could also derive from the anglicisation of the Irish *Bun Dá Abhainn*, meaning 'the bottom of two rivers'.

Up until the end of the 19th century, Achill Island remained separated from the mainland. The high levels of seasonal migration and the importance of developing market towns emphasized the necessity for a permanent link across the narrow channel. Finance for a bridge was acquired through subscriptions collected by an interdenominational committee. A swing bridge, pivoting on one central pier, was officially

The Clapper Bridge at Burlehinch, west of Louisburgh

Steel engraving of Pontoon Bridge in 1842, still a favourite spot for anglers fishing Loughs Conn and Cullin

opened by Michael Davitt, founder of the Land League, in 1887 and named after him. This bridge served adequately for 60 years, but then changes in modes of transport necessitated a wider roadway. In 1947, the old bridge was abandoned and, the following year, a new bridge opened, again called the Michael Davitt Bridge, built alongside and south of the original bridge. The new bridge was the largest bridge structure to be undertaken by an Irish construction company at the time, with J.C. McLoughlin of Pearse Street, Dublin, carrying out the work. Mayo County Council is responsible for maintaining the 'new bridge' and employs local residents to operate the swing partition to ensure the safe

(Top) The original swing bridge over Achill Sound, opened in 1887 by Michael Davitt

(Above) A bus of the Great Southern Railway company squeezes over the Michael Davitt Bridge at Achill, photographed by Fr. Browne before the original swing bridge was replaced in 1947

passage of high-masted vessels passing through the strait.

The seven-arched Burrishoole Bridge, crossing the Burrishoole channel, was built in the 18th century as part of the roadway between Newport and Mulranny. Then, in 1950, the road was re-routed along the former railway line to the north, located further downstream. The railway line, which ran from Westport to Achill, had been in operation from the 1880s until 1939. A bridge along its route carried trains over the Burrishoole channel and it was this bridge that was widened in 1950 to accommodate road traffic and replace the old Burrishoole Bridge route. By the 1990s, however, the high level of salt in the atmosphere had eroded the steel of the former railway bridge and, in 1998, Mayo County Council replaced the bridge's deck. While this work was being completed, road traffic was once again routed over the old Burrishoole Bridge.

Until the early 1980s, residents who lived on the far side of the Ugool Suspension Bridge near Bellacorrick were unable to bring their cars to their homes without taking a longer, alternative upstream route, which could only be crossed when the river was low. In 1982, Mayo County Council demolished the old suspension bridge and built a new Ugool Bridge, a single-lane fixed reinforced bridge.

Maritime transport

The currach is the traditional rowing craft that has been used along the west coast of Ireland for many centuries for fishing and transporting goods and passengers, both animal and human. Popular because of their

(Above) Photographed at the old Ugool
Suspension Bridge some years before it
was demolished are Mayo County
Councillor J.T. Barrett of Bangor, and
two local residents – Tom Carolan and
Martin McAndrew

(Above left) The seven-arched Burrishoole
Bridge, built in the 18th century

proven sea-worthiness and cheapness of construction, currachs were built
'upside down' or in an inverted position, with semi-circular wooden or
wicker ribs attached to a light wooden frame. Cattle hides were used to
cover the frame, made waterproof with coats of hot tar. The same method
is used today to build currachs, the only difference being that man-made
materials are now used to cover the frame. Currachs were never sailed;
they were always rowed, handled comfortably by three strong men and
lifted out of the water on their shoulders when not in use.

Variations in currach styles evolved, with particular styles taking on
the name of the area in which the boats were built. The Achill currach,
for example, is a little over 6 m (20 ft) in length, while the Belderrig
currach is slightly larger and the Inishkea model slightly smaller. The
design of the Inishkea currach is midway between the primitive earlier
vessels and the innovative double gunwale of later currachs, such as the
Achill model.

Access to Clare Island, at the mouth of Clew Bay, could once only be
gained by a long boat journey after which passengers disembarked at
poor landing facilities on the island. According to the *Parliamentary
Gazetteer of Ireland* (1846), 'A small pier was built in a little shady bay at
the east end, by Sir Samuel O'Malley's father, but it consisted of only a
wall about 7 feet thick and 228 feet long, covers a cove of only 300 feet by
150, mostly shallow and rocky, and possessing, even at pier-head, no
greater depth than 9 or 10 feet . . . A small creek, called Luchny, near the
west end is sometimes used as a landing place for boats'. The *Gazetteer*
also noted Mr. Alexander Nimmo's plans for improvements to the pier.

(Top left) Fr. Browne's photograph of people on the way to Clare Island, c. 1938

(Top right) Fr. Browne's photograph of a landing on Clare Island

(Above) Group of villagers and currachs at Dooagh, Achill, photographed in about 1900

In 1841, Clare Island had a population of 1,500 people; today, that is reduced to 150. Traditionally, the islanders used several types of vessel for fishing and transportation of goods, animals and people, including pucáns (heavily built carvel boats), hookers, currachs and other rowing boats, and more recently the Achill yawl (a carvel-built sail boat). Today, two ferry boats travel the 5.6 km (3.5 ml) between Roonagh Quay, near Louisburgh, and the main pier on Clare Island, which had successive improvements made to it over the years. Each ferry can carry up to 100

Two ferry boats ply the route between Clare Island and the mainland at regular intervals each day

passengers and the trip takes about 20 minutes. A mailboat also travels between the mainland and Clare Island four times a week and is licensed to carry up to 12 passengers.

Railways

The Midland and Great Western Railway (MGWR) of Ireland extended the railway system into Mayo towards the end of the 19th century. The MGWR was formed in the 1840s and was the third largest railway company in the country. In 1925, it amalgamated with other railway companies to form the Great Southern Railway.

The building of the railways provided employment for thousands of people and brought great prosperity for many years. The railways assisted trade, facilitating the transportation of farm produce to new markets outside Mayo and the importation of foreign dry goods into the county. Livestock trains carried cattle bound for England to Irish ports. The railways also provided a valuable passenger service for tourists and emigrants alike, as well as bringing seasonal workers to and from the harvest fields of England and Scotland.

The Ballyhaunis – Claremorris – Castlebar line, built in 1862, was the first railway line laid in Mayo in the standardised 5 feet 3 inches wide gauge. Some 2,000 people were employed in bringing the railway to Ballyhaunis. Many of those who came to work on the construction made their homes in the county when the work was finished. In 1866, Castlebar was linked to Westport and from 1874 until 1901 a passenger service operated from Westport to Westport Quay. The Westport line was extended to Mulranny in 1894 and to Achill a year later. The Achill line was one of the so-called 'Balfour Lines', named after Arthur J. Balfour,

The Westport – Achill railway line opened in 1895. Photographed here in 1911, the train travels past Mulranny Station on the shores of Clew Bay

Chief Secretary for Ireland during the years 1887-91, who introduced the Act providing State assistance for the construction of narrow gauge lines to disadvantaged areas. Railway construction continued in the 1890s, with lines extending from Claremorris to Ballindine and Ballinrobe.

North Mayo was first serviced in 1869 by a railway line from Manulla Junction running on to Ballyvary and thence to Foxford, which was, in turn, connected to the Claremorris – Castlebar line. Four years later, Foxford was linked to Ballina and 20 years later Ballina was linked to Killala. The Waterford and Limerick Railway was responsible for another line which also headed north from Claremorris, making stops at Kiltimagh, Swinford and Charlestown, after which it continued on to Curry in Co. Sligo. The first trains passed through Charlestown on 1 October 1895 and were welcomed by enthusiastic crowds.

Plans for other railway lines in Mayo never came to fruition. In the early years of the 20th century, there was much debate and speculation in Mayo County Council about the possibility of a rail link from Dublin to Blacksod Bay, where it would terminate at a proposed transatlantic shipping terminal. However, World War I commenced and the project was shelved.

In the early 20th century, small-scale dedicated industrial railway lines were built to facilitate the transportation of goods by individual companies. The Irish Industrial Mineral Company, for example, based on Achill Island, constructed a 2-foot gauge line which ran six miles from their whitestone quarry to Keel Harbour. This line was used between 1910 and 1916 to transport ore to the harbour, from where it

The first train arrived at Mulranny Station in July 1894 and the area prospered for some years as a tourist destination

was shipped by hooker to the grinding mill at Westport Quay. Railway lines were also constructed in Bellacorrick in 1958 and Bangor Erris in 1964 to assist the transportation of peat harvested by Bord na Mona for use at the Electricity Supply Board power station in Bellacorrick.

Upon occasion, trains were put on for special purposes. Such was the case in 1894 when a group of over 30 harvesters from Achill drowned in Clew Bay. Their hooker had capsized while carrying a full load of passengers to the steamship in Westport that would bring them to Scotland. A special train was brought into operation to transport the bodies of the victims home for burial in Achill's Kildavnet Cemetery, even though the Achill railway extension was still under construction at the time of the accident. Forty-three years later, in September 1937, another special train was put on to return the bodies of ten young boys to their native Achill. They had been working as harvesters in Kirkintilloch, near Glasgow, and had been burnt to death when their bothy or cabin, into which they had been locked for the night, had caught fire. Two weeks later, on 30 September 1937, the Achill line closed for both goods and passengers, and the tracks were removed shortly afterwards.

These disasters had been prophesied in the 17th century by Brian Rua Ó Ceabháin from Inver in Erris, who, it was said, was granted knowledge of the future after showing great kindness to a poor widow. He had foretold of the coming of the railway to Achill, describing carriages on iron wheels with smoke and fire. He prophesied that the first and the last trains to the island would carry home the dead.

Individual towns prospered with the arrival of the railways. The first train arrived at Mulranny, on the north shores of Clew Bay, on 16 July 1894, quickly making it a significant tourist destination. When Irish railway companies became involved in the hotel business, the

The viaduct at Knockranny, Westport, one of the viaduct bridges along the Westport – Achill railway line

luxury Mulranny Hotel opened in 1897. From 1898, a combined rail and hotel ticket was available. The hotel was equipped with every modern convenience of the time, including electric light, and by 1900 hot and cold water baths were also available. Patrons had access to sandy beaches and the use of the hotel's boats and golf links.

Newport Station, also on the Westport – Achill line, consisted of a series of small-scale, orderly, attractive buildings, designed to be functional. The Viaduct Bridge, carrying the railway over the Brown River, was built to the highest engineering and architectural specifications of the day and was completed in 1892 at a cost of over £7,000. It is still a resplendent feature on the Newport landscape today. A similar viaduct to that at Newport is located at Knockranny, also on the former Westport – Achill railway line.

By the 1950s, the general trend was towards closing railway lines rather than constructing new ones. Some railway lines initially ceased their passenger service and then later also discontinued their freight service. The Westport – Achill line finally closed in 1937. Islandeady, Balla and Bekan were among the stations closed in Mayo on the Westport – Dublin line. The last passenger trains on the line to Charlestown stopped in June 1963, although the freight train continued until 1975 when the station was completely closed. Foxford Station, on the Ballina line, received a reprieve: after being initially closed in 1963, it was later reopened in the 1980s and continues in operation today.

(Top) Newport Station in the early 1900s, with the entrance to the Viaduct Tunnel in the background

(Above) Tullamore – Westport return ticket, dated 26 July 1981

(Above left) View over Clew Bay from Mulranny

Aviation

Castlebar has a long history of aviation. William Munnelly of Castlebar and James Mee of Mullingar, who later settled in Castlebar, were among the members of the Royal Flying Corps, forerunners of the Royal Air Corps, who landed regularly in Castlebar during World War I. After the war, pleasure flights came into vogue and this interest eventually developed into Castlebar Regional Airport. In August 1966, a private airport at Castlebar, with a landing strip of over half a mile long, was opened with the financial backing of two Mayo brothers, Peter and Hugh Ryan. A four-seater plane, chartered by Bobby Smith and Frank Gill of the Royal Blues Showband from Claremorris, was the first to land on the new airstrip. Some years later, in 1972, the first successful transatlantic flight from Castlebar departed.

A transatlantic flight from Castlebar had first been attempted on 28 August 1927. Undertaken by Terry Tully from Carracastle, an experienced pilot of the Royal Flying Corps, he flew a sponsored flight from London – Ontario – London in the 'John Carling' airplane. Unfortunately, the flight never made its destination and the crew and craft disappeared without trace.

In November 1978, the first small plane landed on the 640 m (700 yards) airstrip at Belmullet. This community-sponsored airstrip was taken over in the early 1980s by Údarás na Gaeltachta, which had been supportive of the project from the start. The local community

Pilots and maintenance crews of the Royal Flying Corps, set up in May 1912, photographed in Castlebar

Minister Michael Moran (2nd from right), with Councillor Joe Chambers, Mayo County Council (2nd from left), at the opening of Castlebar Airport in 1966

had worked with Údarás to purchase 5 hectares (12 acres) of land for the airport, which was initially intended as a means of attracting industrial investors to the area. In recent years, it has contributed to the development of a growing tourist trade.

Knock International Airport opened on 30 May 1986 and the inaugural passenger flights, organised by Knock Shrine Society, brought pilgrims from Knock to Rome. This remarkable airport was pioneered by Monsignor James Horan (1912-86), a local clergyman, who saw it as a development essential to the future of the west of Ireland. He argued that smaller airports were for wealthy people, whereas regional and international airports enabled large passenger jets to carry ordinary people at lower rates, more frequently and over longer distances. Against the odds, Monsignor Horan worked for many years on the project, raising funds locally and also obtaining substantial government financial backing, and managed to see the airport built on a bleak bog outside Kilkelly. Sadly, he did not live to see the impact of the airport on the region. The Monsignor died in Lourdes in August 1986, a few months after the official opening of the airport. His remains were the first to be flown home to the new international airport.

(Above) Monsignor James Horan (right) with Taoiseach Charles J. Haughey, at the opening of Knock International Airport in May 1986

(Above left) The first transatlantic flight from Castlebar Airport departed in 1972

(Left) The first small plane landed in Belmullet in 1978

Postal service

From the mid-17th century, the service routes of the Royal Mail radiated out from Dublin. However, it would be more than a century before they came in any comprehensive way to Co. Mayo. Among the earliest post offices opened in the county were those at Killala, Newport and Castlebar. Rathlackan, Dugort, Westport, Kilkelly and Ballyhaunis post offices were opened before 1845. In the early years of the postal service, mail was delivered to post offices by foot or horse, mail-cart or stagecoach; in the days before rural postal deliveries began, recipients would visit their local post office to collect any mail awaiting them. The Postmaster-General had a responsibility to survey and map roads used by mail coaches and to suggest improvements to the Grand Juries, who were responsible for roads until the introduction of the County Council system in 1898. When the railways came to Mayo, they became an important means of transporting the mail.

W.H. Maxwell, author of *Wild Sports of the West*, first published in 1832, stayed for some time at Croy Lodge, Ballycroy, on the Erris Peninsula. According to Maxwell, his foot-postman followed a rugged horse-path through the hills to Ballycroy which, although seldom used in his time, was in the 1780s the only means of communication between Erris and the southern baronies.

By the mid-19th century, the Royal Mail Penny Post service was available throughout Ireland. It offered a more affordable service to the general public, requiring payment from the sender of the letter rather than from the recipient, as was previously the system. Post offices began to offer many services besides the delivery and sending of mail. They became centres of activity for all levels of society in towns and villages throughout the county, presenting opportunities for people to socialise on a regular basis. From 1861, the Post Offices Savings Bank was introduced to post offices everywhere and became increasingly popular. The old age pension was introduced in 1908 and was paid through post offices. Then, from 1912, post offices took over responsibility for the telegraph and telephone services. From the 1950s, telephone kiosks were installed outside post offices throughout the country, providing the first public telephones in many areas.

Mail continued to be delivered by foot or horse, mail-car or stagecoach until the early 20th century. Charles R. Browne, who undertook an ethnographic study of the Erris Peninsula, photographed a mail-car changing horses at Bangor Erris in 1885. The driver is seen covering the goods on the back of the car, while a tired horse is being led away, to be replaced by fresh horses. Fresh

The Achill and Nevin [Nephin] Royal Mail delivery car brought mail to the sub-post office at Dugort to service the Missionary Settlement on Achill Island

Changing mail-car horses at Bangor Erris, photographed by Charles R. Browne in 1885

teams were introduced at designated stops along all postal routes, as well as at coaching inns in the larger towns, such as Daly's Hotel in Castlebar and the Courthouse in Balla, both probably former coach houses. Unlike mail-cars, stagecoaches were covered cars and doubled as passenger transport, capable of carrying up to 20 people inside and outside the car. The early mail stagecoaches were protected by military detachments, armed with blunderbusses.

John Howard Pentland, Senior Surveyor and later one of three Principal Surveyors of the Architectural Department of the Board of Works, is credited with designing the post offices in Westport and Castlebar at the end of the 19th century, when many larger towns began to provide purpose-built post offices. The well-proportioned arcade of Westport Post Office reveals Pentland's love of classical architecture. The three semi-circular arches in the front of the post office building are in the tradition of the arcaded market houses along the Mall in Westport, but are far larger in size. A distinguishing feature of the Castlebar Post Office on Ellison Street are the large, ornate wrought-iron scrolls that hold up the gutters. The design of the building compensates for the slope on which it was built and the horizontal layering of red brick and grey stonework gives an attractive liveliness to the post office.

From the early 20th century, the postman on his bicycle was a familiar and welcome sight throughout Mayo. Doing his job in all kinds of weather, he provided a significant social service by bringing news to isolated villages and farmsteads. J.M. Synge (1871-1909), travelling through Erris in 1905, reported his experiences in a series of articles in the *Manchester Guardian* and *The Shanachie*; these were later republished in his 1911 book called *In Wicklow, West Kerry and Connemara*. He wrote that 'one could see white roads in the distance – often relief roads – twisting among the hills, with no one on them but a man

Swinford Post Office, c. 1900

Many local post offices were run from people's homes, such as Breaghwy (Breaffy) PO, outside Castlebar

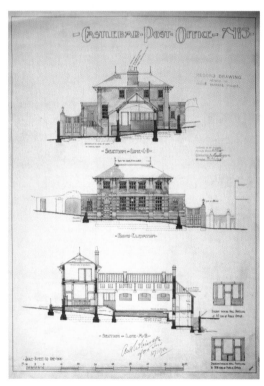

Board of Works 1901 architectural drawings of Castlebar Post Office, design attributed to John Howard Pentland

here and there riding in with the mails from some forlorn village'. From the 1960s and '70s, postal workers on bicycles began to be replaced by drivers in mail vans. This led to an initial reduction in the number of staff employed since it was said that one motorised postal worker could perform the work of 2.5 non-motorised workers. Nowadays, An Post offers a wide range of services, directly employing over 200 people throughout Co. Mayo, in addition to the sub-post office staff employed on a contract basis. 'Rationalisation' of existing services is expected in the coming years, with consequent social effects.

Newspapers

Before newspapers were widespread, town criers were engaged by advertisers to communicate news of forthcoming events to the public, such as an auction or the arrival of a circus in town. Throughout Mayo, well into the 20th century, town criers continued to announce local events and public notices. A town crier would make his way through the town, ringing a bell to attract people's attention and calling out the news in a loud voice, reading from information sheets or posters provided by the advertisers. Jack Cassidy (d. 1987) was the last Town Crier in Castlebar; his father, Bill, had been the Town Crier before him.

From the late 18th century onwards, newspapers began to spread throughout Ireland. There were about 20 provincial newspaper titles in Co. Mayo alone. These early newspapers carried very little local news; instead, their reports were copied from national and British newspapers. Some were dedicated to the promotion of particular causes, such as the *Achill Missionary*

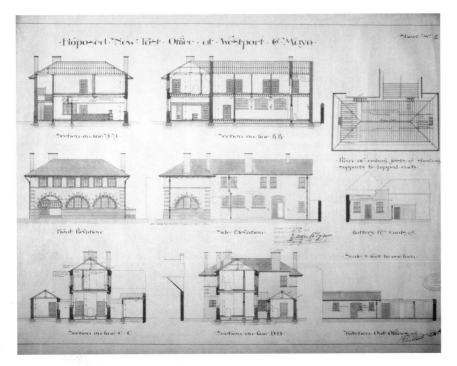

Herald and Western Witness, which was printed and published between 1837 and 1868 at the Missionary Settlement on Achill Island, with the stated objective 'to expose the doctrinal and practical abominations of popery'. The short-lived *Aegis or Western Courier*, published from Castlebar in 1841, supported the Temperance Movement founded by Father Matthew, who was concerned at the incidence of drunkenness among the poorer classes. The earliest newspapers held in Mayo County Library are a January 1823 issue of the *Ballina Impartial* and a January 1828 issue of the Castlebar-published *Mayo Constitution*. The latter was a Conservative newspaper, supportive of the British establishment. One of its editors was William Hamilton Maxwell, rector in Balla and author of *Wild Sports of the West*. Only a few provincial newspapers have survived to modern times.

The Connaught Telegraph holds the record for being the oldest surviving provincial newspaper in Ireland, commencing publication on 17 March 1828, under the masthead *The Telegraph or Connaught Ranger*. Frederick Cavendish (1777-1856) founded the paper to provide a nationalist voice for the region. He is remembered as a champion of the poor and oppressed. In 1845, the paper reported the appearance of the potato blight and foresaw the calamity that was to unfold. Ten years later, the paper promoted the Tenant Right Movement with enthusiasm. The paper flourished in the 1870s under the proprietorship of James Daly (1838-1911), the agrarian reformer, founder member of the Land League and the paper's most celebrated editor. Renamed *The Connaught Telegraph* in the 1870s, it was an advocate of the objectives of the Land League and publicised the early mass meeting in Irishtown in April 1879. Daly sold the newspaper to one of his employees, Thomas H. Gillespie (1874-1939), at the end of the 19th century and became a full-time farmer.

(Above) Tom Watson, Ballyvary postman, delivering mail in Dangan More in 1950

(Above left) Architectural drawings of Westport Post Office, design attributed to John Howard Pentland of the Board of Works

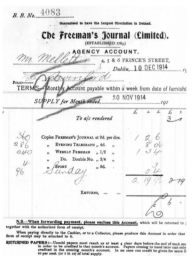

(Top) Jack Spain, Foxford's Town Crier, making an announcement in 1938

(Above) Invoice dated 1914 for copies of The Freeman's Journal received by Mellett's Newsagency, Swinford

Thomas Gillespie remained editor for the next 40 years and continued to reflect concern for the land issue, espousing the cause of the United Irish League. Since then, the paper has stayed in the Gillespie family under the separate editorships of brothers Bernie, Tommy, Alfie and Richard Gillespie. Richard's son, Tom, became editor in the 1990s.

In 1883, a group of businessmen assembled in the sacristy of St. Muredach's Cathedral in Ballina with the idea of establishing a newspaper with a strong nationalist outlook. The first issue of *The Western People* was published on 16 July 1883 with Patrick Smyth as editor – a local schoolteacher and closely identified with the fledgling Gaelic Athletic Association (GAA). The paper's first manager was Terence Devere. He was the great-grandfather of Terry Reilly, who became editor in 1977. *The Western People* attained one of the highest circulations among regional newspapers in the country and in 1995 became part of Thomas Crosbie Holdings of Cork, publishers of *The Cork Examiner* (now *The Irish Examiner*) since 1841.

The Western People incorporated *The Ballina Herald* in 1963. The latter started life as *The Tyrawly Herald* and was among the earliest newspapers published in north Mayo. It had a Unionist flavour and was variously owned by the Ham, Richey and Joynt families. R.W. Joynt was not only the proprietor, but also editor, reporter and printer. He renamed the paper *The Ballina Herald* and, under his editorship, it had a reputation of being a bright and newsy broadsheet with a good literary style.

(Above left) Frederick Cavendish, founder of The Telegraph or Connaught Ranger (now The Connaught Telegraph) in 1828

(Above centre) Terence Devere, first manager of The Western People

(Above) William Doris, joint founder and first editor of The Mayo News in 1892

(Left) Letterhead of The Connaught Telegraph in 1913, then under the proprietor and editor Thomas H. Gillespie

The first issue of *The Mayo News* was published in December 1892 by two brothers, William and P.J. Doris, from their printing works in Westport's James Street. William Doris was the first editor of the paper; he was also the first Secretary of the United Irish League, founded in Westport in 1898. Thus, editorially *The Mayo News* had an intentional nationalist outlook and reflected the political aspirations for Home Rule and reform of the land laws. Doris served variously as vice-chairman and chairman of Mayo County Council from 1899-1910. In 1910, the paper supported his successful candidacy for the Irish Party for the Mayo West seat in the House of Commons. His time in Parliament was cut relatively short as a result of the rapid growth in Sinn Féin's popularity following the 1916 Easter Rising, which was supported in *The Mayo News* under the editorship of P.J. Doris, causing a fraternal rift. Many years later, *The Mayo News* was the first Mayo newspaper to be published in tabloid format. From the 1960s, the paper came to be regarded as the leading sports paper in the county, covering even the smallest fixture, especially in west Mayo.

Chapter 7

Towns and Services

Mayo's network of towns has developed in response to a variety of factors, including economic, social and religious requirements as well as administrative necessities. Each town evolved its own architectural style and character, shaped by these influences. The history, function and development of Mayo's towns can often be discerned from the layout of the streets and the street names, from the presence of public buildings and the location and style of residential housing, public amenities and workplaces.

The earliest incipient towns were associated with ecclesiastical establishments, which served as patrons of the arts and developed as centres of intellectual life, trade and exchange. Early ecclesiastical centres, such as Cong, Balla and Ballinrobe, are today small towns, while Mayo Abbey, Aghagower and Ballintubber are villages. The Anglo-Normans arrived in the 13th century and added to the development of the urban landscape in the county. The English plantations of the 16th and 17th centuries saw the development of towns around military strongholds. In the more peaceful times of the 18th century, landlords oversaw the planning of towns and investment in commercial buildings. Westport was planned in the 18th century, while the planned towns of Belmullet and Charlestown emerged in the 19th century.

According to business directories of the 19th century, Ballina, Ballinrobe, Castlebar, Killala, Swinford and Westport were the chief business towns of the county. Ballina, Killala and Westport were trading ports; Castlebar was the county town; Swinford was a market town; and the military barracks stimulated the growth of Ballinrobe. Claremorris and Ballyhaunis emerged as leading Mayo towns after the Great Famine because of their location on the newly developed rail and road routeways.

Many Mayo towns have evolved from a simple single-street pattern, housing a street of shops providing a range of services. All towns had a 'Shambles' Street, a makeshift area of workshops, slaughterhouses and manufactories. Workhouses, barracks, courthouses and railway stations were among the new 19th-century public buildings. Religious orders

View of modern day Castlebar from Staball

were responsible for the appearance of architecturally imposing urban schools and convents. Modern public building programmes resulted in the construction of hospitals, libraries, town halls and public housing. Commercial factories, along with marts which replaced the open-air fairs, are more recent additions to towns. Cinemas, swimming pools, hotels and spaces for the performing and visual arts are among the modern leisure buildings found in the towns of Mayo. Shop fronts, banks and public houses have altered their appearance over the centuries, but have endured as features of the streetscapes in all towns.

The development of towns is an integral part of the heritage of the county, although Mayo has retained a low-density, largely rural-based population. The most notable shift in the county's population during the period 1986-96 was the growth of the urban districts of Ballina, Castlebar and Westport. In 1996, Ballina and Castlebar had populations of over 6,500 each. The populations of Westport and Claremorris were 4,253 and 1,914, respectively. Some of the more notable Mayo towns are described below, with an outline of their history and development. The selection is based on the number of inhabitants, as well as factors of local importance.

Ballina

Ballina town, or *Béal an Átha* (mouth of the ford), is situated in Kilmoremoy parish, named for the ancient monastic site of Cill Mhór na Muaidhe (the great church of the Moy), where Olcán, a disciple of St. Patrick, founded a church. The remains of the church and enclosure are still visible today at Leigue Cemetery on the Killala road. Within the enclosure, a cross inscribed stone has been identified as the Lia na Manach (stone of the monks), as mentioned in the 7th-century *Tripartite Life of St. Patrick*. Similarly designed gold discs, dating to the Bronze Age, were also found in the area and point to the great antiquity of the cross inscribed stones, which may pre-date the arrival of Christianity in Mayo.

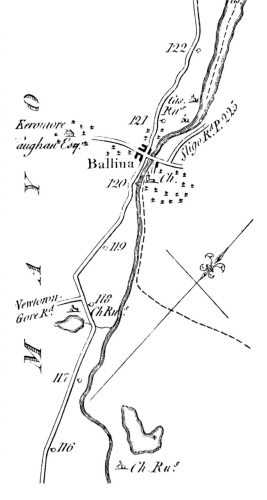

Taylor and Skinner's map of the roads into Ballina, published in 1778

Ham Bridge over the River Moy in Ballina

Ballina nestles on the Moy plain, with the Ox Mountains to the east and Nephin to the west. A town of character and charm, it is now the largest town in Mayo and the third largest in Connaught, after Galway and Sligo. Ballina forms a major regional centre situated on the intersection of two national routes for the north Mayo – west Sligo area. The town developed as a small sea port and market town on the estuary of the River Moy, expanding after the construction of The Quay in 1836. In the early 20th century, coal, tar, timber, cement and food (such as tea, coffee and fruit) were listed among the items imported into Ballina. It became a significant port for the export of livestock to Great Britain until the outbreak of World War II. The Quay is currently used primarily for pleasure boats.

Ardnaree, Bunree and The Quay are the oldest parts of Ballina town and were originally part of Co. Sligo until the Local Government Act of 1898. A medieval ringfort is among the earliest habitation sites discovered at Ardnaree. The native Irish later built a defensive castle on the same site. The remains of the magnificent doorway of the Augustinian Abbey, dated to 1427, can still be seen on the east bank of the river, beside the Neo-Gothic-style St. Muredach's Cathedral, the foundation stone of which was laid in 1827. The Ardnaree area was disturbed by the English conquests of the 16th and 17th centuries, the most notable event being the Battle of Ardnaree in 1586.

In 1723, the Lord Baron of Tirawley established the linen industry in

*(Above) Ballina Courthouse,
built in the 1840s*

*(Right) Low tide on the River Moy,
below Ham Bridge, Ballina c. 1900*

*Firework display during
the Ballina Street Festival, 2000*

Ballina by bringing a colony of weavers from the north of Ireland to the town. He also secured a patent for fairs and markets, which increased trade to the developing town. From the mid-18th century, Ballina also became a garrison town with the erection of the Military Barracks in 1740, which further contributed to the local economy.

Samuel Lewis, author of *A Topographical Dictionary of Ireland*, noted the expansion of Ballina, then the principal port of the county in 1837. Early in the 19th century, the building of the five-arched Ham Bridge accelerated growth of the town across the Moy. Better quality building materials arrived through the port, such as slate from North Wales, and the town experienced a building boom.

The architecture of Ballina changed in the 19th century, when many of

Bridge Street leading to Garden Street,
Ballina, c. 1900

the town's original buildings were replaced with Georgian façades. Several significant new public buildings appeared in the growing town, including the Workhouse (built in 1835) and the Courthouse and Bridewell (built in the 1840s). The railway came to Ballina in 1873 and ensured the vitality of the town, which became an important commercial centre for the farming community from a wide hinterland.

Ballina is built along the famous Moy, one of the finest salmon rivers in Europe. It is the town's single most significant asset. Salmon weirs were re-erected on the falls of the river at Ballina in 1850 at a cost of £1,500 and were used to catch great quantities of fish, which were shipped to Dublin and Liverpool. Since 1998, the weirs have ceased to trap salmon. Today, an opportunity to fish at the Ridge Pool, a premier site for salmon, is keenly sought by anglers from all over the world. The Ballina Salmon Festival, held each summer, has evolved into the Ballina Street Festival and now ranks among Ireland's premier festivals, attracting over 100,000 visitors a year to the north Mayo region for events such as Heritage Day and the Mardi Gras parade. Below Ballina, the Moy is tidal and the town offers the last bridging point on the river before it enters the sea at Killala.

Pearse Street, the busy commercial centre of Ballina, was originally known as Knox Street after a leading landlord family in the area. After the establishment of the Irish Free State in 1922, Ballina Urban District Council changed the town's street names to honour those patriots killed in the Republican cause since 1798. Among the names changed were Gore Street to Lord Edward Street, Arran Street to Tone Street, King Street to O'Rahilly Street, and John Street to Casement Street.

(Above) View of Castlebar in the 1900s from Staball, associated with the 1798 'Races of Castlebar'

(Right) Castlebar's narrow Castle Lane, as it was in the early 1900s

(Opposite) The Mall - Castlebar's public green, shaded with trees and used for leisure, arts and sports events

Castlebar

Castlebar, Mayo's county town, is centrally located at the junction of roads from Westport, Claremorris, Foxford, Newport, Ballina and Erris. The town gets its name from the castle built there by the Norman De Barry family in the 13th century. They dominated the territory until the 16th century, when they were displaced by the Binghams, originally from Sutton Bingham in Somerset. The town grew up around the castle, which was destroyed by fire in 1798 and a military barracks erected on the site.

The Binghams recognised the advantages of developing Castlebar and the town was incorporated by James I in 1613. Sir Charles Bingham, who became the first Earl of Lucan in 1795, assisted the development of the linen trade in the area. The pre-Famine *Parliamentary Gazetteer of Ireland* records Castlebar as 'a town of one principal street, nearly a mile in length, from which several smaller streets and lanes diverged'.

Among Castlebar's most attractive features is The Mall – a pleasant, open green, shaded with trees over a century old, and used as a public space for leisure, arts and sports events. In 1888, George, the fourth Earl of Lucan, donated the green, once the cricket pitch of the Bingham family, to the people of Castlebar. Some of the town's most important public buildings are situated around The Mall. The former Methodist Church, the foundation stone of which was laid by John Wesley in 1785, was built in Neo-Romanesque style and sited on the east side. Also on the east side is Daly's Hotel, where Michael Davitt founded the Land League in 1879. The Courthouse, on the corner of the north side of The Mall, was built in 1820 and was possibly designed by George Papworth. Its imposing classical fluted Doric columns, constructed from cast iron, were designed by George Wilkinson and erected in 1860. A 1798 commemorative monument and a memorial tombstone for John Moore, President of the 1798 Connaught Republic, are both located on the west side of The Mall. Overlooking The Mall from the west side are the modern headquarters of Mayo County Council, Áras an Chondae, opened in 1989 on the former site of the Mayo County Infirmary.

Castlebar, the administrative centre of the county, was traditionally a busy market town, the focal point of which was Market Square. Saturday was market day and agricultural produce from the surrounding area was sold there right up to the 1960s. The market continues today on a small scale, with the addition of travelling clothes merchants. Many large supermarkets have now located in Castlebar, making it a bustling shopping town.

(Above) Market Square, Castlebar, c. 1970

(Above right) Fine trees on The Mall, Castlebar – mute testimony to the Bingham family who donated the green to the town

In addition to being a vibrant commercial centre, Castlebar was once a significant garrison town, with an imposing military barracks and a separate cavalry barracks on the site of the present Garda Station. The only part that remains of the building that housed the cavalry are two stone lions, which once stood on the pillars leading into the barracks and now stand at the entrance to the Garda Station. The military brought important additional income to the town, as well as diversity. They introduced new leisure activities, popularising sports such as rugby and cricket, and influenced fashions in clothing, household goods and furnishings. The records from Wynne's Circulating Library and Newsagency suggest they also supported newspapers and other reading materials, which would not otherwise have circulated in the town.

The military barracks in Castlebar, Westport and Ballinrobe were based on similar plans and layout, and built in classical style. The barrack buildings were grouped around large open spaces, used for drilling and marching, the military training of the day. The Castlebar Army Barracks was built in 1834 to house 1,000 men. In 1891, the soldiers billeted in the barracks swelled the population of Castlebar to 3,558 people. Although burned during the Civil War, the barracks was restored after World War II and is currently used by Fórsa Cosanta Aitiúil (FCA), the reserve defence force.

Castlebar's town gaol was originally located at the corner of Ellison Street and Castle Lane. Later, in 1786, it was re-sited on the east side of The Mall. It was in that year that the infamous George Robert Fitzgerald was hanged outside the gaol. Some years later, many 1798 rebels, including Fr. Conroy of Lahardane, were hanged on the same spot. In 1835, the gaol was again moved, this time to a site on the Westport Road. William Makepeace Thackeray described that gaol as being 'like a stately

Fair Day in Castlebar's Army Barracks in 1950

Gothic castle but for the legend above the gate, which reads "Without Beware, Within Amend"'. It was eventually demolished in 1932 and the original buildings of the General Hospital were then built on the site.

There were various gaols in different parts of Mayo over the years, including Cong, Ballinrobe and Ballintubber. The latter two are recalled in a rhyme once popular throughout schoolyards in Mayo:

Shake hands, brother,
You're a rogue and I'm another,
You'll be hanged in Ballinrobe,
I'll be hanged in Ballintubber,
You'll be hanged with a rope,
I'll be hanged with a rubber,
The rubber will break
And I'll be safe
But you'll be hanged forever.

*(Top) Castlebar gaol, c. 1900,
before it was demolished in 1932
to make way for the County Hospital,
now Mayo General*

*(Above) Thomas Wynne's photograph of
the condemned man Edward Walsh, two
weeks before his execution in 1873*

The last execution to take place in Castlebar gaol was that of Edward Walsh on 19 August 1873, hanged for the murder of his wife. Two weeks before the execution, local photographer Thomas J. Wynne was allowed to photograph the accused. Wynne used the picture as a business opportunity to advertise the sale of 'a very interesting and instructive Pamphlet giving a description of his [Walsh's] life and career from his birth to his unfortunate end'.

Westport

Westport, in the parish of Oughaval in the Barony of Murrisk, is one of Ireland's few planned towns and one of only three in Mayo (the others being Belmullet and Charlestown). It became the setting for the novels of the writer George A. Bermingham, a pseudonym for Canon James Owen Hannay (1865-1950), Rector of Westport during the period 1892-1913. The town was laid out as an adjunct to the Marquis of Sligo's Westport House in the 18th century and is idyllically situated at the head of Clew Bay, in the shadow of Croagh Patrick. Careful planning can be seen in the town's spacious streets around the canalised River Carrowbeg, flowing through the tree-lined Mall. A heritage town, Westport's architecture is one of its many attractions. Among the most appealing buildings is the Holy Trinity Church, built in 1872 and influenced by Gothic Revival style.

The canalised River Carrowbeg flows through Westport's Mall

Throughout the medieval period, the Gaelic family of O'Malley dominated the area that was later to become known as Westport. John Browne (1709-76), first Earl of Altamont, removed the old Cathair na Mart (stone fort of the beeves) village to create a landscaped parkland around his newly commissioned Westport House and he began the construction of the planned town of Westport. His son, Peter (1730-80), continued the project. Credit for planning the new town is given to the Georgian architect James Wyatt (1746-1813), although other architects also contributed to its design. In 1838, the town was described as 'one of the most neat, regular, well-kept, and aggregately pleasant small towns of Ireland'.

Westport was a significant market town, attracting farmers from a wide hinterland who were eager to sell their produce and bring their livestock to The Quay for export. As late as the 1920s, rural women would come to Westport on market days wearing their traditional, long black clothes. These were homespun and worn with petticoats under the skirts, often red or another bright colour, and in the winter many wore an extra knitted layer.

The Octagon, once a fashionable shape for public spaces, housed a tall Doric pillar in its centre upon which once stood a statue of George Clendining (1770-1843), agent for the Brownes of Westport House, merchant banker and agent for the Bank of Ireland. During the War of Independence, the statue of Clendining was deliberately damaged by gunfire and later removed in the 1940s. A stone statue of St. Patrick, dressed in Roman attire, was erected on the pillar in March 1990.

The Quay, Westport, c. 1910

Market day in Westport, c. 1900, with the statue of George Clendining atop the Doric pillar in the background

Peter Browne (1670-1724) began the building and development of Westport Harbour. The commercial buildings and warehouses were built in the 18th and 19th centuries near the rear entrance to Westport House in order to facilitate the handling of the town's extensive trade in provisions, corn and linen. The Customs House, with its attractive half-moon windows, was built in the early 1800s as an office for the port's customs officials. The Westport Harbour Board maintained the docks area and dredged the channel to allow ships to enter this tidal port.

The Market Square,
Claremorris, c. 1900

Westport Quay, some 1.3 km (1 ml) to the west of Westport town, became an important tourist and day-excursion area when it was linked by passenger rail service to the town in 1874. The line was closed in the early 20th century, but tourists continued to travel there by car to enjoy, among other things, the hot seaweed baths of the Bath Hotel, one of the main attractions of Westport Quay until they closed in the 1950s.

Claremorris

The Barony of Clanmorris began to emerge as a geographical entity from early Christian times, long before its formal constitution by the Normans. Archaeological evidence of prehistoric habitation is plentiful in the countryside around the town. In Norman times, the area was given the name of Claremorris or *Clar Cloinne Mhuiris*, meaning 'the plain of the family of Maurice'. This refers to the famous Norman invader, Maurice de Prendergast, who came to Ireland with Strongbow in 1170 and was given a grant of this area. The estate passed to the Fitzgerald family and remained in their hands until the Williamite War at the end of the 17th century.

By the end of the 18th century, the town of Claremorris, on the Ballyhaunis to Castlebar road, was well established around its market square. Its development as a leading town in Mayo in the latter half of the 19th century was due to its location on the rail network. Claremorris Station opened in 1863 on the Great Northern and Western line, sponsored by Lord Lucan, running from Westport to Athlone.

In 1864, Geoffrey Browne built Castlemacgarrett House, outside Claremorris, shortly after his marriage to Mary Prendergast, the daughter of the previous owner of the estate. The house later became the seat of Lord Oranmore and Browne. Today, Castlemacgarrett is a private nursing home.

(Above) Castlemacgarrett House, outside Claremorris, built in 1864

(Above right) Claremorris' main street, now named D'Alton Street in honour of Claremorris-born Cardinal John Francis D'Alton, Catholic Archbishop of Armagh and Primate of All Ireland from 1946 to 1963

Denis Browne (1763-1828), MP for Mayo, resident magistrate and local landlord at Claremorris, came to live at Claremont House (later Mount St. Michael's Convent) shortly after the 1798 rebellion. The Kirwan family had originally built the house in Georgian style in the early 18th century. The much-feared Denis Browne tightly controlled Claremorris town and was notorious throughout the county. He acquired the nickname Donncha an Rópa (Denis of the Rope) during the 1798 rebellion when, as High Sheriff of Co. Mayo, he dealt severely with those who had participated in the rebellion or helped in any way. In 1903, Dr. Douglas Hyde collected the song *Na Buachaillí Bána* about Denis Browne and published it as a song ascribed to the poet Antoine Ó Raifteirí:

The Whiteboys

If I got your hand, it is I would take it
But not to shake it, O Denis Browne,
But to hang you high with a hempen cable
And your feet unable to find the ground.
For it's many's the boy who was strong and able
You sent in chains with your tyrant frown;
But they'll come again, with the French Flag waving
And the French drums raving to strike you down!

Na Buachaillí Bána

A Dhonncha Brúin 's deas do chraithfinn lámh leat
Agus ní le grá duit ach le fonn do ghabháil (góail)
Cheanglóinn suas thú le rópa cnáibe
Agus chuirfinn mo 'Spír' ido bholg mór.
Mar is iomaí buachaill maith chuir tú thar sáile
Thiocfas anall fós is cúnamh leo
Faoi chultaibh dearga agus hataí lása
'S beidh an droma Francach a' seinm leo!

Brabazon House, home of the Brabazon family who developed Swinford in the late 18th century

Swinford

Swinford, or *Béal Átha na Muice*, is a late 18th-century town, situated on the main Castlebar – Dublin road on a tributary of the River Moy. Evolving as a market town for the rural hinterland, it was developed by the Brabazon family, originally from Leicestershire, who obtained land in the area during the 17th-century Cromwellian settlement. Their estate was purchased by the Congested Districts Board after the Great Famine and their home, Brabazon House, was finally demolished in 1980 by the Western Health Board. It is now the site of Áras Attracta, a centre for the intellectually challenged. Part of the Brabazon Estate is now a public park, which accommodates Swinford's 9-hole golf course.

Swinford once held a market four times a year – in February, May, August and December. Before the opening of the railway line in 1895, it was a leading town for the sale of perishable farm produce, especially butter. On market days, cattle and pigs arrived into the town in droves and goods of all sorts were on sale from nailers, tinsmiths, carpenters and handymen.

The dramatist J.M. Synge, somewhat unflatteringly, described the character of the smaller towns of Mayo, giving Swinford a special mention:

> If one goes into Swinford or Charlestown, for instance, one sees a large dirty street strewn in every direction with loose stones, paper and straw, and edged on both sides by a long line of deserted-looking shops, with a few asses with pannier of turf standing about in front of them. These buildings are mostly two or three storeys high, with smooth slate roofs, and they show little trace of the older sort of construction that was common in Ireland, although there are often a few tiny and miserable cottages at the ends of the town that have been left standing from an older period. Nearly all towns of this class are merely trading centres kept up by the country people that live around them, and they usually stand where several main roads come together from large, out of the way districts. In Swinford, which may be taken as a good example of these market towns, there are seven roads leading into the country, and it is likely that a fair was started here at first, and that the town as it is now grew up afterwards . . . On market day, early in the morning, old men and women . . . crowd into the town and range themselves with their asses and carts at both sides of the road, among the piles of goods which the shopkeepers spread out before their doors.

Workhouses were the principal means of providing relief to the poor in the 19th century. They were built to the design of the English architect George Wilkinson (1813-90). The former admission block of Swinford Workhouse currently houses Swinford District Hospital. Behind the front building is one of the best-preserved mass Famine graves in the country, where 564 victims were buried – a poignant reminder of the devastation caused by the Great Famine.

Market Street, Swinford, in the 1920s

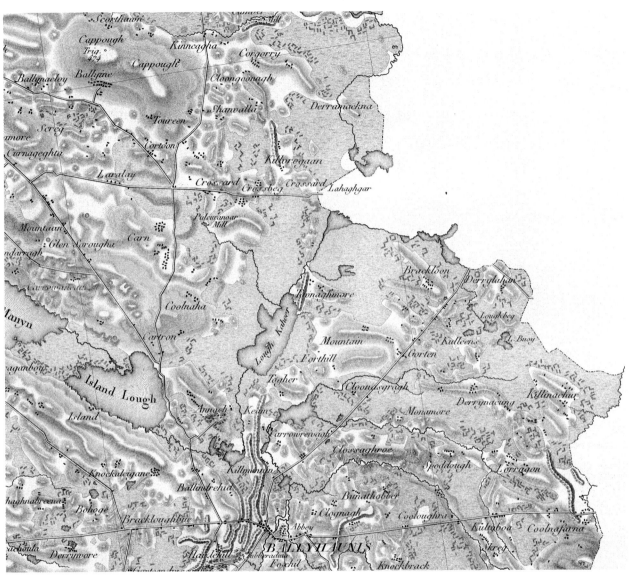

Bald's map of Mayo, completed in 1817, showing the hinterland around Ballyhaunis

Ballyhaunis

A busy modern market town, Ballyhaunis is located in the Barony of Costello, which borders Sligo and Roscommon. The name of the barony derives from the Norman family D'Angulo (or Nangle), who obtained land in the area in the 13th century and soon changed their name to the Irish MacCostelloe. The family retained control of the area around Ballyhaunis until the late 16th-century Tudor conquest, when Sir Theobald Dillon superseded them as the principal landowner and introduced common law to the area.

The name 'Ballyhaunis' is an anglicised version of *Beal Átha hAmhnais*, which literally means the 'ford-mouth of strife'. The Irish name is preserved in the popular song *Máire Bheal Átha hAmhnais*, the original

Bridge Street, Ballyhaunis, c. 1900

*Main Street, Ballinrobe, in the early
20th century*

version of which is thought to have been written by poet and Augustinian
Friar Cassidy or Tomás Ó Caiside – *An Caisideach Bán* (c. 1705-75). The
town is thought to have grown up around the Augustinian Abbey
founded by MacJordan, a descendant of the MacCostelloe family, which,
according to the Mayo historian H.T. Knox, was founded 'a little before or
after 1400 probably'. It has also been suggested that the origins of the
town date from the 13th century when the Norman Fitzgerald family built
a castle on the site which had previously been occupied by the native Irish
and which later became known as Abbey Hill. The Augustinian friars
were given 60 hectares (150 acres) at Abbeyquarter by the Nangle family
and from here they ministered to the people and ran a school, an
infirmary and a farm. The Abbey, as a great centre of learning and
commerce, contributed significantly to the expansion of the town.

By the 1800s, Ballyhaunis had become a thriving market town and centre for the local linen industry. In the second half of the century, several small industries had developed including those related to joinery, milling and weaving, as well as a number of bakeries. The economic expansion of the town was reflected in the development of Knox Street and Upper Main Street. Further expansion followed with the opening of the railway station in 1861, while more recently, in the early 1980s, Halal Meat Packers (later taken over by Glanbia) brought additional jobs to the town. Ballyhaunis is also the headquarters of Mayo's largest regional radio station – Mid-West Radio (MWR).

Ballinrobe

Ballinrobe, or *Baile an Rodhba* (town on the Robe), sited east of Lough Mask on the road between Galway and Castlebar, developed around a 7th-century church built on the River Robe, which runs through the town and gives it its name. Initially one of the parishes ruled from nearby Cong Abbey, Ballinrobe became established after the arrival of the Normans in the 13th century. The Augustinians built an abbey there in the 14th century under the patronage of the De Burgos. The town has been central to the political history of the county as an important base for the different rulers and administrators. After the arrival of the Normans, the Ballinrobe area belonged to the Fitzgeralds until the early

Soldiers photographed in Ballinrobe Army Barracks, c. 1900

14th century, when it passed to the hibernicised Bourkes whose power was later challenged by the Elizabethan conquerors. In the mid-17th century, the area was granted to James Cuff from Somerset, clerk to the Cromwellian Commissioners at Loughrea. The Cuff family, who lived at Creagh House, sold the old Norman castle beside the River Robe to the War Office in 1821 as a military barracks. In the early 19th century, travel writer J.C. Curwen observed that Ballinrobe was a 'neat little town' that appeared to have been 'recently much increased by new buildings, constructed of limestone with attractive doorways'.

In 1837, Ballinrobe consisted of one principal street from which others diverged, containing houses that were nearly all well built and slated, with 'many of handsome appearance'. The original uses of the streets are suggested by their names – Glebe Street was originally Church of Ireland property and Cornmarket was the market place for wheat, oats and barley.

Ballinrobe functioned as a garrison town, housing separate cavalry and infantry barracks from the early 19th century until 1922. New prosperity was brought to the town when, in 1892, a railway station linked it with Claremorris and the Midland and Great Western Railway network. Some of the harsher aspects of growing up in poverty in Ballinrobe in the 1940s are recalled in Noel Browne's book *Against the Tide*, published in 1986.

Crossmolina

Crossmolina, or *Crois Mhaoilina*, translated as 'O'Weeleeney's Cross' or 'O'Malina Cross', gets its name, according to Gaelic scholar John O'Donovan, from the ancient Irish landowner before the arrival of the Norman families, the Barretts and the Bourkes. The town is on the River Deel, 13 km (8 miles) west of Ballina and less than 1.5 km (1 ml) from Lough Conn, in the Barony of Tirawley and overlooked by Nephin Mountain. The River Deel, a focal point of the town, is one of the major salmon spawning arteries in the Moy system and has been enhanced in recent years by work on the river banks and bridge. Traditionally, Crossmolina was a market town and there were two fair greens in the town. On market days, the town filled with cattle and sheep from the surrounding farms. The principal landlords in the area were the Jacksons, and later the Pratts, of Enniscoe House, as well as the Ormsbys, Knoxs, Gore-Knoxs and Ormes.

The area surrounding Crossmolina is rich in historic sites and associations. The ruins of Abbeytown Abbey lie 1.5 km (1 ml) north of Crossmolina and to the east, in the grounds of Castle Gore, are the ruins of the 16th-century Castle Deel. There is a heritage centre and genealogical service at Enniscoe House, 3 km (2 ml) south-east of Crossmolina. The ruins of Errew Abbey are at the north end of a peninsula in Lough Conn, 10.5 km (6.5 ml) south-east of the town.

View of Crossmolina town,
overlooked by Nephin Mountain

Fresh fish, sold on the streets
of Crossmolina in 1938

The pump in Crossmolina's town square, photographed by Fr. Browne, c. 1938

Foxford

Foxford, or *Béal Easa* (ford mouth of the waterfall), is situated on the River Moy and overlooked by the Ox Mountains to the north-east. The development of Foxford owes much to the Sisters of Charity, who established a convent there in 1891. Mother Morrogh-Bernard, the Mother Superior, started the famous Providence Woollen Mills a year later. For most of the 20th century, the buzzer on the mill's clock tower could be heard for miles around, punctuating the life of the town – calling people to work and signalling their breaks and end of the working day. The Sisters of Charity also influenced the social life of the town, founding the Foxford Brass and Reed Band in 1897. The handball court was built in 1901; men and women's club rooms were built in 1915 and a music school opened in 1923. Today, the Foxford Woollen Mills Visitors' Centre presents a history of the mill and life in the town through an ingenious and compelling tour.

The town and surrounding district are an angler's paradise, with salmon fishing on the river and trout in the nearby lakes. Among the famous people who were natives of the Foxford area were Admiral William Brown (1755-1857), the poet Frederick R. Higgins (1890-1941) and Michael Davitt (1846-1906), from the nearby village of Straide. William Brown was the founder of the Argentine Navy, remembered in Foxford

Foxford's Providence Woollen Mills, established in 1892 by the Sisters of Charity

The town of Foxford developed around a fording point over the River Moy

(Above) Jackie McKenna's lime wood sculpture, 'Taking Flight', unveiled in Kiltimagh in 1993

(Above right) Main Street, Kiltimagh, c. 1900

by a bronze bust by the Argentinian sculptor Vergottini. A plaque on the wall of the Church of Ireland commemorates F.R. Higgins. The Foxford public library was named in memory of Michael Davitt and a museum in Straide recalls his life and achievements.

Kiltimagh

Kiltimagh, or *Coillte Mach* (outer woods), gave its name to the epithet 'culchie' to refer, in a derogatory manner, to migrants from the town. The term later developed to mean all people from outside Dublin. Kiltimagh expanded when George Browne, the local landlord, started a market there at the end of the 19th century. Fr. Denis O'Hara (1850-1922), parish priest of Kiltimagh from 1888 until his death in 1922 and also a member of the Congested Districts Board from 1893, initiated much development in the town. He oversaw the building of a new church in 1888, together with a town hall and cottage hospital (the latter was converted to a Garda Barracks in 1925 and is now a retirement home run by the Western Health Board). Fr. O'Hara invited the Sisters of St. Louis to Kiltimagh in 1897 to provide education and training, particularly for girls. He also spearheaded the development of a sewage and gas system for the town.

Kiltimagh has produced a number of outstanding sportsmen over the years, including World Handball Champion Jim Kelly (1909) and Olympic athlete Seán Lavan (1924 and 1928). The parents of Gene Tunney, World Heavyweight Champion (1926), also came from Kiltimagh. The town also became well known for its musical tradition and in 1935 the first radio broadcast from Mayo was a concert from the St. Louis Convent. The first cinema opened in 1944 and the first ballroom in 1961. Despite its decline in the mid-20th century, resulting in high emigration, Kiltimagh has developed as a modern town with new industries, facilities and services. One of the organisations associated with this recent revival was the Kiltimagh Integrated Rural Development, launched in 1989, the work of which has became the subject of a number of documentaries and publications.

Kiltimagh prides itself in preserving its 19th-century townscape,

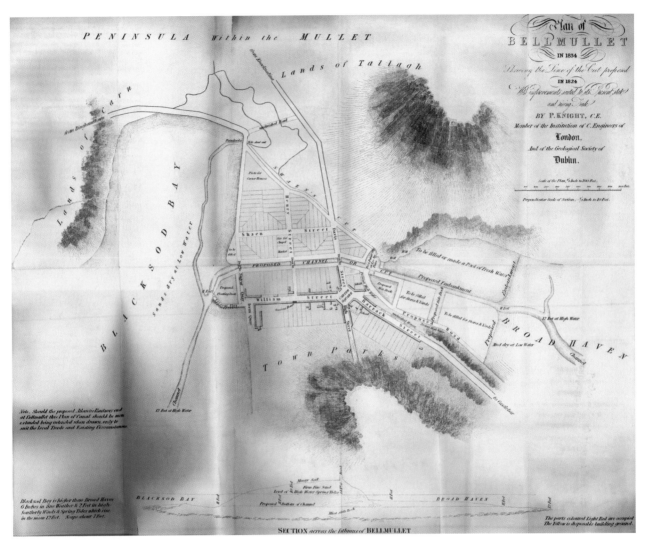

Patrick Knight's plan of Belmullet, published in 1836

reviving traditional crafts while also enhancing the quality of modern life. Many projects have been undertaken by a range of voluntary and statutory bodies to enhance the visual attractiveness of the town and to provide public facilities and services. In 1984, the Town Hall Theatre was opened. A children's adventure playground and a sculpture park have been opened, with exhibits by local, national and international artists. The Community Centre sports complex opened in 1988 and in 1989 Thomas Flatley of Boston, a native of the parish, officially opened the Town Museum in the old railway station office. Services cables have been placed underground, giving the town a more attractive aspect. One of the memorials in the modern town square honours Antoine Ó Raifteirí, born nearby at Killedan, who was the last of the great Gaelic bards. Kiltimagh hosts several pageants and festivals, such as the 'Coillte Come Home' festival of 1968, which drew thousands to the town, and the annual St. Patrick's Day Pageant, recognised as one of the best in Ireland.

*Ag coiméad an teanga beo – using the
language on the streets of Belmullet*

Belmullet

John Bingham and Henry Boyle Carter, inheritors of
the Shaen Estate, were the two principal
landowners on the Mullet Peninsula in the Barony
of Erris. In the 1820s, they developed the towns of
Binghamstown (*An Geata Mór* or 'big gate') and
Belmullet (*Béal an Mhuirthead* or 'mouth of the
Mullet') in tandem with the construction of the road
lines into Erris. Bingham built a road to the
extremity of the Mullet Peninsula and in early 1823
the first two-wheeled vehicle passed along it. He
also obtained a patent for holding fairs and markets
at the new town of Binghamstown, west of the
remains of Cross Abbey. But Binghamstown
gradually declined and fell into decay as it was
replaced in importance by the new town of Belmullet with its more
strategic location.

Belmullet was sited on the 'new road' at the narrowest part of the
isthmus leading to the Mullet Peninsula, between the bays of Broad
Haven and Blacksod. There were only three houses in the town when the
first wheeled vehicle arrived there in 1823, but ten years later it boasted
185 houses, together with corn stores, shops and hotels. A central square,
named after the town's developer, Henry Boyle Carter, forms a main
feature of the town. As the town grew, five new streets were laid out,
including Barrack Street where a police station was built. The prosperity
of the new town was largely a result of the Napoleonic Wars and its
strategic location between the two bays, which were connected on the
west side of the town by a canal. Belmullet continues to develop today
and is to be a centre for the decentralisation of Mayo County Council staff
and services.

Charlestown

Charlestown, today a busy market town on the borders of Mayo and
Sligo, began as a planned town built in 1845 under the auspices of Charles
Strickland, agent of Lord Dillon. Strickland started by offering a prize of
£100 – a fortune at the time – to the person who completed the first house
in the new town. John Mulligan was the winner and by 1851, despite the
Great Famine, 22 houses had been completed and 6 more were under
construction. They were all built to specific standards laid down by
Strickland. Over the following decades, the town evolved to its current
pattern of three streets converging on the town square.

Lord Dillon's (and hence Strickland's) interest in developing
Charlestown arose from the need for a market for his tenants' produce.
The only local market was at Bellaghy on the adjoining Knox Estate and
the tenants of that estate were, naturally, receiving more favourable

The erection of a market weigh hook and scales in Charlestown's main street led to bitter legal wrangles between the Dillon and neighbouring Knox Estates in the late 1840s

Members of the Charlestown Little Theatre Group, rehearsing a scene in their production of 'The Emigrants', written by Gerry Murray, local publican and county councillor, and filmed by RTÉ in 1986

treatment, being offered first choice to sell their produce and obtaining better prices. As soon as Strickland erected a weigh hook and scales in the new town, Knox successfully sued him on the basis that he had illegally established a market, having no permit for the device. In defiance, Strickland re-erected the scales within a short distance of where it had initially stood. Knox sued him again and the whole legal process was repeated on a number of occasions. In the end, Strickland's persistence and determination triumphed and Charlestown became an established market town.

Public buildings followed, with the erection in about 1870 of the town's two-storey RIC Barracks; Charlestown Station received its first passenger train in 1895; and the Town Hall was built in 1900. However, during the

(Right) Killala's historic round tower rises 26 m (85 ft) above the surrounding town

(Below) Aerial view of modern Killala, with the round tower in the centre of the town

mid-20th century, an almost imperceptible decline overtook the town. Through the writings of journalist John Healy (*see Bibliography*), the story of the town's high emigration rate and decay became synonymous with the economic decline rampant in many small towns at the time. Healy's prose reflected his anger and his hopes for the future of his town and for rural Ireland generally. In recent years, Charlestown has begun to achieve some of the economic and social progress for which he wished.

Killala

Mayo has a long maritime history, with recorded trading links to France and Spain going back to medieval times. Killala – north of Ballina and east of Ballycastle, sited at the point where the River Moy enters the sea at Killala Bay – was a rich and thriving sea port, with its principal trade recorded in 1837 as the exportation of oats and barley, and importation of planks, iron, tar, slates, flax seed, herrings and sugar. However, trade shifted to Ballina from the late 1830s, when that port was improved and a channel opened for shipping into the town. Killala today is a bustling resort town, gateway to the Neolithic Céide Fields further north and best remembered as the site of the French invasion under General Humbert in support of the Irish Insurrection of 1798, immortalised in Thomas Flanagan's historical novel *The Year of the French*.

Killala also has a long ecclesiastical history. The Irish name of the town, *Cill Alaidh*, refers to a church founded here by St. Patrick in the 5th century. Sometime between the 8th and 12th centuries, the distinctive round tower was built, which beckoned pilgrims to the area. This round tower, in the centre of the town, is complete with conical cap and rises to a height of 26 m (85 ft). It is one of only five such surviving towers in the county. Repairs to Killala's tower were made in 1841, including the resetting of missing stones in the cap, and again in 1882-83 by the Board of Works.

When the Irish Church was reorganised in the 12th century, Killala became the Seat of the Diocese of Killala. The large Franciscan abbeys of Moyne and Rosserk were established near Killala in the mid-1400s and thrived until the destruction of their buildings by Sir Richard Bingham, Lord President of Connaught, in 1590. The ecclesiastical importance of the town continued after the Reformation, when in 1670 the old cathedral was demolished and a new one built for the Church of Ireland, incorporating fragments of the medieval church.

Knock

Knock, originally named *An Cnoc* (the hill), was renamed *An Cnoc Mhuire* (hill of Mary) in May 2001 as a 'millennium present' by order of the Minister for Arts, Culture, the Gaeltacht and the Islands after the name change was sought by local residents. The town is one of the leading Marian shrines in the world today, attracting over 1.5 million visitors each year. The southern gable of the church in Knock was the scene of a

After the reported apparition in 1879 in Knock, the town grew as a pilgrimage centre, with street stalls providing souvenirs and religious memorabilia

reported apparition of the Virgin Mary, St. Joseph and St. John the Evangelist in August 1879 and is today the focal point of the shrine. In 1976, the Basilica of Our Lady, Queen of Ireland, was built with accommodation for 20,000 people. On 30 September 1979, Pope John Paul II came as a pilgrim to Knock Shrine, the goal of his journey to Ireland. Knock International Airport, outside Kilkelly, was opened in 1986, due largely to the efforts and work of the visionary Monsignor James Horan (1911-86) who promoted Knock as an international pilgrimage centre.

Newport

Newport, at the north-east corner of Clew Bay, was established in the early 18th century by the Medlycott family through their lessee, Captain Pratt. Pratt introduced linen manufacturing to the town under the management of immigrant Quakers. James Moore, agent for the Medlycott Estate, formally laid out the Quay at Newport in the late 18th century. The town prospered for many years, but later fell into decline as it was superseded as a port by Westport in the 19th century.

At the end of the 18th century, the Medlycott Estate was taken over by the O'Donel family who built Newport House, overlooking the harbour, which is now a luxury hotel. The O'Donels prospered for a time in the area, but after the Great Famine of 1846-50, they were forced to sell their lands through the Encumbered Estates Court.

Newport has many attractive architectural features, including the seven-arched Viaduct, built in 1892 to carry the Westport to Achill railway line, and the merchant buildings, constructed by the

entrepreneurial Carey family after the Great Famine. Martin Carey of the same family made a donation of £10,000 towards the cost of building the magnificent St. Patrick's Church that overlooks the town. Rudolph Butler designed the church in Celtic Revival Hiberno-Romanesque style and included a doorway inspired by Clonfert Abbey in Co. Galway. Inside, the three-light east window of the 'Last Judgement' by Harry Clarke, commissioned in 1927, is considered to be among his finest masterpieces.

Newport has developed into an angling and deep-sea fishing resort, served by the Newport and Burrishoole Rivers, Loughs Beltra and Feagh, and Clew Bay itself. At nearby Furnace, the Salmon Research Visitors' Centre tells the story of *The Salmon – King of the Fish*.

(Top) Newport House, today a luxury hotel, was once the home of the O'Donel family

(Above) Newport's Viaduct, built in 1892 to carry the railway over the Brown River, with St. Patrick's Church overlooking the town

Shops and markets

In the late 19th century, there was usually only one family-owned drapery and dry goods shop in the small towns and villages of Mayo. These businesses sold an extraordinary collection of items and were usually the only central buyer for local home products, such as eggs, chickens and butter. These shops were run on a system of credit, with bills being paid off after the sale of farm produce in the autumn or when the harvesters returned at Christmas time with their wages from Scotland or

'The Country Shop', sketched by Jack B. Yeats in 1905, was inspired by his visit to Belmullet

elsewhere. Once cleared, a new account was opened. Shopkeepers thus acted as creditors, effectively loaning out large sums of money during lean months, and the local people were dependent on them.

An ink and watercolour sketch by Jack B. Yeats, done in 1905, the year he visited Co. Mayo, illustrates a typical country shop of the time. The shopkeeper was based on a Mrs. Jordan whom he met in Belmullet. The painting shows the eclectic range of objects available for sale. Mirrors,

boots, candles, brooms, animal traps and lamps hang from the ceiling. Cloth, spices and sweets are stacked on the shelves and rosary beads hang down behind the shopkeeper. The weighing scales on the counter suggest that the shop also stocked flour, sugar and tea, and other items that were weighed out and wrapped in brown paper for customers. The woman customer appears reluctant to hand over money from her bag to the somewhat stern-looking shopkeeper.

In the 19th century, shops frequently doubled as public houses, with half the premises given over to serving alcohol, mostly porter, and lit by oil lamps and candles. Often the shopkeeper was also the local undertaker and ran the post office. Fair days and market days were held weekly or monthly in towns throughout the county. They were welcomed social occasions, as well as offering opportunities for buying all sorts of goods and animals, and for selling home produce and homespun clothes. Items made by local artisans could be bought, such as barrels, churns, wood bowls, spoons and butter prints made by the local cooper. Willow panniers and baskets and metalwork goods for farm and home were also available. Meal and flour were on sale, as well as sugar, tea, hardware and drapery supplies, imported from Manchester, London and Glasgow. Second-hand clothes, furniture and household items imported from England were popular at auctions in more recent times.

Today, the impact of increased mobility and transport has seen the replacement of small local shops by centralised supermarkets and convenience stores, offering extended service hours. Supermarkets provide new ranges of convenience and pre-prepared foods, sought by modern consumers in an era when home-grown produce seems a rarity and busy working and social lives favour the selection of time-saving products.

(Above left) Logo of the family grocer and publican 'M. Henry of Charlestown', whose business traded until the late 20th century

(Above right) 1879 publican's certificate granting M. Henry a 6-day licence for the sale of beer, cider and spirits

(Above) Mullin's Supermarket in Shrule, typical of today's convenience stores that have replaced many small local shops

Health provision

The County Hospital, opened in 1938, was built at a cost of £100,000 in Castlebar on the site of the former county gaol. Since then, the services provided by the renamed Mayo General Hospital have expanded dramatically. Hospital support is also provided by District hospitals at Ballina, Swinford and Belmullet. Specialist care is provided by the Western Health Board for the treatment and care of sufferers from Alzheimer's disease at St. Anne's, Castlebar, and for people with learning difficulties in Áras Attracta, Swinford.

Workhouses had negative connotations in the popular mind because of their association with famine and fever. After the establishment of the Irish Free State in 1922, the workhouses were closed, but in each county one building was retained as the County Home for the elderly and infirm. In Mayo, Castlebar Workhouse was deemed the most suitable for conversion to this purpose and in 1922 the newly formed County Board of Health invited the Sisters of Mercy to take charge of the residence. It was replaced in 1973 by a purpose-built community nursing centre, known as the Sacred Heart Home.

In 1865, the Board of Works built the Mayo Lunatic Asylum on the outskirts of Castlebar town, beside the then town gaol (now the site of Mayo General Hospital). The asylum was renamed several times - as the Castlebar and District Lunatic Asylum, then the Castlebar District Mental Hospital and finally in the 1950s as St. Mary's Hospital. In its early years, the Governors of the asylum were drawn from the titled gentry of the county and a resident medical superintendent managed the daily running of the establishment. When the County Council was established in 1898, a committee replaced the Governors and this, in turn, gave way to the Western Health Board, established in 1971, which took over the control of health affairs in the county.

'Arts in Health Programme' at the Sacred Heart Home, Castlebar

The original buildings of the Mayo Lunatic Asylum were designed by George Wilkinson in 1860. They were made of local limestone to resemble a series of plain townhouses and were arranged around a more ornate, Italianate-style central block. In the 1950s, the main gates of the asylum, then called St. Mary's Hospital, were demolished and then the outer walls taken down in the 1960s, both symbolic gestures to the emerging style of psychiatric care, whereby patients increasingly live in professionally supported homes in their own communities. The closure of St. Mary's as a psychiatric hospital was announced in 2002 and it has now become home to the Galway – Mayo Institute of Technology, which incorporates an Institute of Medical Science.

Mayo Lunatic Asylum on the outskirts of Castlebar, c. 1900

Children delivering turf to the Mayo Lunatic Asylum, c. 1920

The modern headquarters of Mayo County Council, Áras an Chondae, opened in 1989, overlook Castlebar's Mall from the west side

Mayo County Council's 'Town Improvement Programme' has encouraged enhancement of many towns and villages throughout the county since 1992

Mayo County Council

Mayo County Council's mission is to maintain and improve the quality of life for all the people living in Mayo and to make the county an even more attractive place for people to visit, invest and work in. Established under the Local Government Act of 1898, the role of Council was expanded and further defined by subsequent Acts. The Council is made up of an Executive, consisting of management and staff, and the Elected Members (Councillors), a structure that provides for both popular representation and efficient discharge of services. In its early years, the priority services provided by the Council were in the areas of road development, housing provision and sanitary services. These priorities have expanded to include environmental protection, agriculture, education, health and welfare, recreation and amenities, culture and the arts, as well as enterprise and development incentives.

In 1989, the staff of Mayo County Council moved to their new headquarters on the site of the Old Infirmary on Castlebar's Mall. The design of the three-story building was intended to harmonise with the traditional types of construction prevalent in the town. By the end of the 20th century, the Council was spending close to €90 million (IR£70 million) per annum on discharging its statutory duties and providing essential services. It is the single largest employer in the county, with a staff complement of 1,000 people, and its wages, salaries and pensions contribute €25.4 million (IR£20 million) annually to the local economy.

Mayo County Council has generated enhancement plans to develop towns throughout the county. These plans focus on the issues of derelict buildings, landscaping, development of amenity areas, colour schemes, car parking and other community needs and services. The Council's 'Town Improvement Programme' commenced in 1992 and has promoted the development of many towns and villages.

Mayo County Council has had a significant impact on the fabric of housing and services throughout the county. Besides supplying essential services, such as water and sewerage, housing schemes and in-fill housing have been built in many towns. Voluntary housing bodies have also supplied urban housing with the support of the local authorities. The Council also funded the first residential travellers' halting site in Castlebar, which opened in May 1995.

The Sanitary Services section of Mayo County Council supplies new and improved public water supplies. Over recent decades, work has been ongoing on a number of water supply schemes, including those for Achill, Erris and Ballycastle. The Ballinrobe water towers were constructed in 1991-92 at a cost of £3.5 million and with a capacity for 2,273,000 litres (500,000 gallons). The towers provide storage and control facilities for the Partry to Ballinrobe portion of the Lough Mask Regional Water Supply Scheme. This scheme supplies treated water from Lough Mask to the Castlebar region and to a majority of the South and East Mayo catchment area. Raw water is pumped from the shores of Lough

Ballinrobe's water towers, constructed in 1991-92 as part of the Lough Mask Regional Water Supply Scheme

Mayo's Fire Service retains 130 fire fighters, with headquarters in Castlebar

Mask to a high-level treatment works at Tourmakeady, from where it is fed gravitationally to the supply areas. The construction of the scheme commenced in 1979.

The Fire Service in Mayo consists of a retained brigade employing approximately 130 fire fighters, most of whom work full time in other jobs but are on call to the service. They are a highly trained professional group, involved in fire control and prevention. Engineers work continuously in the inspection of public buildings, such as dance halls, to ensure that fire regulations are implemented before the issuing of licences. Fire officers monitor fire-fighting equipment and appliances, and organise the

Staff outside Crossmolina's new branch library – Maureen Gallagher (left) and Margaret Staunton

continuous training of all personnel. The Fire Service is located throughout the county at 12 stations, as well as locally based hose-and-ladder service points. The headquarters of the Fire Service were opened in Castlebar in 1992 and also serve as a retained station for the town.

Mayo County Library Service

The Mayo County Library Service was established in 1925, three years after the first County Library scheme was introduced in Donegal. The library service was funded initially by a three-year grant provided by the Carnegie Library Endowment Fund. Ms. Bridget Redmond became Mayo's first County Librarian in November 1925 and was confirmed in her permanent appointment in 1928, when the County Council adopted the library service on a permanent basis. Funds remained limited and this was a constant problem for public library services nationally until the 1970s.

Mayo County Library's greatest challenge came in the years 1931 to 1932, when controversy over the appointment of Ms. Redmond's successor, Ms. Letitia Dunbar-Harrison, resulted in the suspension of Mayo County Council's Elected Members and a campaign of clerical opposition to her appointment. Ostensibly, this opposition was due to the fact that Ms. Dunbar-Harrison was not fluent in Irish. Resentment on the part of some Councillors to the Local Appointments Commission was also a factor. Ms. Dunbar-Harrison was a member of the minority Church of Ireland and her appointment to a post which would involve the selection of materials for the library service was regarded as unacceptable at the time. The campaign forced the closure of almost all library service points in the county, with the aim of making the Librarian's position untenable. Ms. Dunbar-Harrison departed for a post in the Department of Defence in 1932 and her successor, Ms. Ronaldson, was appointed later that year.

Mayo County Council was committed to a programme of library development and was one of the first counties to construct a purpose-built headquarters for the county library and a town branch in 1942 at Mountain View, Castlebar. Further developments continued with the opening of a series of full-time branch libraries – at Ballina in 1972 and Westport in 1975. Since the 1990s, new library facilities have been provided for all part-time branches throughout the county. Part-time branches opened in Ballyhaunis in 1972, while the former Church of Ireland buildings in Claremorris and Ballinrobe were converted to branch libraries in 1984 and 1996, respectively. Kiltimagh branch library opened in 1990, Belmullet branch library in 1994, Foxford branch library in 1996, followed by Swinford and Crossmolina branches in 1998, Clare Island in 2000 and Louisburgh in 2001. A highlight of this period of development was the opening of the Central Library in Castlebar in May 1990 by the then Minister of the Environment, Padraig Flynn, TD, a native of the town. This building has provided award-winning accommodation not only for the town branch of the library, but also for local studies and an exhibition centre for the county.

Pat Kilbane, Chairman of Mayo County Council, Des Mahon, Mayo County Manager, and Austin Vaughan, County Librarian, with members of the Council and public at the launch of Microsoft Libraries On-Line Project in Castlebar Library in 1997

In conjunction with the development of local branches, Mayo County Library has always been committed to serving all communities throughout the county. In the early years of the library service, hundreds of small collections were deposited in national schools and parish centres, in an attempt to reach the more isolated communities. These 'deposit libraries' were replaced in the early 1970s when mobile library services were introduced – first for the schools in 1972 as part of a nationwide programme of development, with assistance from the Department of Education, and then for the general public in 1975 to provide a lending, reference and local history service at a number of collection points in rural Mayo.

The Mission Statement of Mayo County Library, adopted in 1996, commits the organisation to 'providing and promoting a resource for information, education, recreation and culture' to the people of Mayo. Along with continuous expansion of book stock, recent developments include the introduction of Internet access to all library branches during the period 1997-2000, as well as the hosting of a range of programmes that promote reading, cultural and recreational activities for all ages and interest groups. In addition, through its publications programme and picture library, Mayo County Library promotes and makes accessible the rich heritage, culture and literature of the county.

Chapter 8

Sport

The history of sport in Mayo is both part of, and formed by, an evolving social environment, particularly in the last 100 years. Changes in education, income and lifestyle in Mayo have helped mould the developing structure of sporting activities. This ongoing dynamic will help to shape the health and fitness of future generations. Recently, the Irish Sports Council, in partnership with other public bodies, both statutory and voluntary, has taken an important initiative in this area – the establishment of county-based Sports Officers. The broad aim of this project is the promotion of sports activities on a county-wide basis.

Gaelic Athletic Association

The Gaelic Athletic Association (GAA) – An Cumann Luthchleas Gael – was established in 1884 as part of a wider cultural nationalist movement prevalent in Ireland in the closing decades of the 19th century. At a time of general growth in spectator sports, the GAA organised amateur team games of Gaelic football, hurling, camogie and rounders, initially on a club basis and later at both county and provincial level.

Two Mayo men, P.W. Nally (1856-91) of Balla and Michael Davitt (1846-1906) of Straide, played major roles in the founding of the GAA. P.W. Nally was born in Rockstown House, Balla, in 1856. A prominent athlete, he became involved with the Irish Republican Brotherhood (IRB) and was the Connaught representative on its Supreme Council. He organised athletic sports events in Mayo in 1879 and is acknowledged as being a major influence behind the establishment of the GAA. In March 1884, he was sentenced to ten years' penal servitude for conspiracy and died in prison in 1891, two weeks short of his release date. In 1900, a memorial to P.W. Nally was unveiled in Balla and in 1953 the Nally Stand at Croke Park in Dublin, the Gaelic games national stadium, was dedicated in his honour.

Michael Davitt (1846-1906), founder of the Land League, was one of the initial patrons of the GAA and later provided the finance for a tour of the USA by GAA athletes in 1888. He is buried in his birthplace of Straide, where a memorial museum was opened in 1984. The local football team, the Moy Davitts, is named in his honour.

Castlebar Sports Day, c. 1900

*(Above) Michael Davitt, founder of the
Land League and supporter of the Gaelic
Athletic Association*

*(Above right) The Ballina Stephenites
reached the finals of the All-Ireland
Championship on 17 March 1999*

The Mayo County Board of the GAA was formed in 1888 and the Connacht Council established in 1902. The Council's first President was Westport-man Joseph MacBride, a brother of Republican activist Major John MacBride (1865-1916). The Castlebar Mitchels, established in 1885, was the first GAA club in Mayo. Having won two senior football championships before the turn of the century, the club fell into decline for almost 30 years. Revived in the late 1930s, it acquired McHale Park, now one of the top grounds in the country with an all-seater capacity of almost 30,000. Over the years, the Mitchels have produced many great players, most notably All-Ireland Senior Winners Josie Munnelly, Henry Kenny, Patsy Flannery, Mick Flanagan, Éamon Mongey and Joe Langan.

The Ballina Stephenites, founded in 1886, was the first Mayo club to win the Croke Cup Final – the nearest equivalent to the current All-Ireland Championship – defeating Kerry, Kildare and Waterford in 1907, 1908 and 1909. At that time, clubs played for the county championship and the winner represented their county in the provincial games, from which they qualified for the Croke Cup. In recent years, Mayo clubs that have contested the All-Ireland Championship Final include Garrymore (1982), Castlebar Mitchels (1994), Knockmore (1997), Ballina Stephenites (1999) and Crossmolina, who captured the title in 2001.

The Green above the Red

The National League and the All-Ireland Championship, both played at various levels, are the two main GAA competitions. In the League, all 32 counties are divided into various divisions and each county team plays each of the other teams in its own division. The top teams in each division play off against each other to win the League. Traditionally in the All-Ireland Championship, county teams competed on a knockout basis

Some surviving members of the winning Mayo 1936 All-Ireland football team, photographed in 1963 – the football from the historic game is on permanent display in Claremorris Public Library

within each province, with the provincial winners contesting the All-Ireland semi-finals. Since 2001, modifications to this system were introduced that allowed beaten teams to re-enter the championship at various stages in an open draw 'All-Ireland Qualifier' series.

Between 1929 and 1939, Mayo won six successive National League titles and eight Connaught Senior titles. The county team had previously reached the All-Ireland finals in 1916, 1921, 1925 and 1932. In 1925, Mayo thought that they had won their first All-Ireland Senior title, but it was taken away in unusual circumstances. The Connaught championship had not taken place by the time the All-Ireland Final was due to be played in September that year. Mayo was nominated from the province to play against Wexford in the semi-final, whom they defeated. The GAA Central Council declared the other two semi-finalists, Kerry and Cavan, illegal and so Mayo was considered the All-Ireland champions. However, Galway later beat Mayo in the Connaught Final and the Central Council declared Galway as the All-Ireland champions for 1925.

Mayo won the Junior All-Ireland Final in 1933 for the first time and again in 1950. The Minor team won the All-Ireland Final in 1935. But it was the 1936 victory by the Senior team – trained and prepared by Dick Hearns, the boxing champion from Ballina – that was the first major event in Mayo football history. Mayo defeated Laois by 4-11 to 0-5 in a one-sided final.

Mayo had an outstanding team in the early 1950s, winning two All-Irelands back to back in 1950 and 1951. Two members of that team – Seán Flanagan (left corner back and Captain) and Tom Langan (full forward) – were chosen as members of the GAA Football Team of the Twentieth Century. Dr. Pádraig Carney, a member of the Mayo All-Ireland winning team of 1950 and 1951, was elected to the GAA Hall of Fame in 2001 and had

(Top) Stamp commemorating Seán Flanagan (1922-93), a member of the GAA Football Team of the Twentieth Century

(Centre) Stamp commemorating Tom Langan, a member of the GAA Football Team of the Twentieth Century

(Above) Stamp commemorating Dr. Pádraig Carney, elected to the GAA Hall of Fame in 2001

(Above right) The 1950 Mayo football team – winners of the All-Ireland Senior Championship

a stamp issued in his honour. In 1950, the county beat Louth 2-5 to 1-6 in a game in which Seán Flanagan, Éamon Mongey and John Forde starred. In 1951, the score was 2-8 to 0-9 for Mayo, with Meath being easily beaten in front of 78,201 spectators.

The 1960s and '70s were fallow years for the Senior county footballers, with the notable exception of a National League title in 1970. Mayo's hunger for glory was reawakened with their 1989 visit to Croke Park to play Cork in the All-Ireland Final. Mayo took the lead within a few minutes of the start of the game. The match was a tremendous display of skill and stamina, with Willie Joe Padden demonstrating his high fielding throughout the game. A goal in the early minutes of the second half from substitute Anthony Finnerty emphasized the team's determination to bring the Sam Maguire trophy across the Shannon. But the Corkmen were not to be beaten and the final score was Cork 0-17 to Mayo 1-11.

The 1990s will be remembered as the decade when the Men's Senior footballers *almost* won the All-Ireland Final on three separate occasions. Mayo reached the 1996 All-Ireland Final after defeating Kerry, the Munster champions. The team was managed by army officer John Maughan, himself a former Mayo footballer, whose career had been cut short because of injury. In the final against Meath, the green and reds were leading by six points at one stage in the match, but the game ended in a draw. The replay is remembered for the flare-up which resulted in the referee sending off Liam McHale, one of Mayo's key players, and Colm Coyle, Meath's right half back. The Mayo team rallied, but ten minutes from the final whistle Meath's Tommy Dowd scored a goal, giving 'the Royals' a one-point lead. Mayo's James Horan managed to level, but Meath answered with another point and 'Sam' was theirs. Final score: Meath 2-9, Mayo 1-11.

In 1997, Mayo again reached the All-Ireland Final in Croke Park, playing against Kerry. Mayo reduced Kerry's lead of seven points at one stage in the second half to a lead of only one point. But the might of

President Mary Robinson greets her fellow-countymen when the Mayo team competed in the All-Ireland Final in 1996

Mayo scores against Meath in the All-Ireland Final in 1996

Diane O'Hora, Captain of the Mayo Ladies' football team, holds aloft the Brendan Martin Cup after winning the All-Ireland Ladies' Senior Final in 1999

Mayo's Orla Cosby, under pressure during the All-Ireland Ladies' Senior Final in 1999

Kerry's Maurice Fitzgerald could not be contained and once again victory slipped from Mayo's grasp. Final score: Kerry 0-13; Mayo 1-7.

Mayo's hunger for a Senior All-Ireland title was at last satisfied when Mayo's Ladies' football team won the All-Ireland Ladies' Senior Final in October 1999 and again in 2000. The Captain, Diane O'Hora, accepted the Brendan Martin Cup on behalf of the team. Managed by John Mullin from Kilmaine, the Mayo team showed a spirited determination and confidence to successfully defeat their Waterford opponents by 0-12 to 0-8 in 1999 and by 3-6 to 0-14 in 2000. The team won the All-Ireland title again in 2002, beating Monaghan by 0-12 to 1-8.

Johnny Carey – 1971
All-Ireland All-Star

Joe McGrath – 1979
All-Ireland All-Star

Dermot Flanagan – 1985 & 1989
All-Ireland All-Star

Willie Joe Padden – 1985 & 1989
All-Ireland All-Star

Kevin McStay – 1985
All-Ireland All-Star

Gabriel Irwin – 1989
All-Ireland All-Star

Jimmy Browne – 1989
All-Ireland All-Star

Noel Durkin – 1989
All-Ireland All-Star

T.J. Kilgallon – 1992
All-Ireland All-Star

Kevin O'Neill – 1993
All-Ireland All-Star

Ken Mortimer – 1996
All-Ireland All-Star

Pat Holmes – 1996
All-Ireland All-Star

James Nallen – 1996
All-Ireland All-Star

Liam McHale – 1996
All-Ireland All-Star

James Horan – 1996 & 1999
All-Ireland All-Star

Pat Fallon – 1996
All-Ireland All-Star

*Dr. Mick Loftus of Crossmolina,
inaugurated as 28th President of
the GAA in 1985*

All-Ireland All-Star Awards 1971 – 1999

1971	Johnny Carey	1992	T.J. Kilgallon
1979	Joe McGrath	1993	Kevin O'Neill
1985	Dermot Flanagan	1996	Ken Mortimer
	Willie Joe Padden		Pat Holmes
	Kevin McStay		James Nallen
1989	Gabriel Irwin		Liam McHale
	Jimmy Browne		James Horan
	Willie Joe Padden		Pat Fallon
	Noel Durkin	1999	James Horan
	Dermot Flanagan		

Despite the disappointment of not winning the Sam Maguire Cup since 1951, many players who donned the red and green jersey over the years have been honoured with GAA All-Star Awards. Mayo's wealth of talent has been frequently recognised and acknowledged at national level.

Dr. Mick Loftus, a Crossmolina GP, was inaugurated as the 28th President of the GAA in 1985, two years after serving as Mayo's Person of the Year. Dr. Loftus first played Gaelic football for his local club, Deel Rovers, in Crossmolina and played at minor, junior and senior county level. He was a panel member of Mayo's 1950 and 1951 All-Ireland winning side and captained the Mayo Junior All-Ireland winning team in 1957.

Dr. Loftus retired from his red and green jersey to take on the onerous task of referee at Connaught and All-Ireland Finals levels. He contributed to the GAA as Chairperson of the National Referees' Committee and the Rules Revision Group, and as President of the Connacht Council of the GAA. As President of the GAA, Dr. Loftus created an indelible impression nationally, especially in his foresight in recognising the need for a complete revision of the organisation's administrative structure and a review of the promotion of the game. He has pleaded for unity and pride throughout the GAA and encouraged youth participation in Gaelic sports and in the organisation. He is also a champion of the movement to separate any association between Gaelic games and alcohol, and is vehemently opposed to the GAA's acceptance of sponsorship from alcohol companies.

Final of the 1901 Connaught Handball Tournament, played in the Foxford handball alley

Handball

The ancient Irish game of handball is among the oldest game played with a ball. The revival in handball at the end of the 19th century and beginning of the 20th saw three-walled handball alleys or courts built in many parishes. Handball was a social outlet for the players and spectators alike and was very popular throughout Mayo, notably in Charlestown, Cong, Hollymount, Killala, Kiltimagh, Newport and Swinford. Among the many Mayo champions was the great Dr. Jack Henry who hailed from Charlestown. He won the University College Dublin Championship in 1927. In recent years, Peter Carter from Killawalla, former Secretary of the Mayo Handball Board and Connacht Council of the GAA, was appointed President of the Irish Handball Council. From the 1980s, the game of handball transferred to indoor courts and many of the outdoor courts were demolished or let fall into ruin. Today, they remain as memorials to the sport and entertainment they provided for many decades. These old handball alleys are among Ireland's most distinctive architectural features and are in need of careful preservation.

The Foxford handball alley, built by the Sisters of Charity, was the site of the Handball Tournament of Connaught in 1901. The winner received a prize of a silver trophy valued at £20, presented by Robert McBride, a Belfast soap manufacturer, and a suit of Foxford tweed from the Providence Woollen Mills (also established by the Sisters of Charity). The tournament commenced on 10 June 1901, with teams from Swinford, Westport, Kiltimagh, Ballyvary, Pontoon, Ballina, Foxford, Castlerea, Castlebar and Balla. The final took place on 30 June, when Swinford were the reported victors. Controversy ensued and the tournament was replayed in June 1902, when Westport were declared the winners.

(Above) Members of the 1959 Mayo Camogie team, competitors in the All-Ireland Final that year, photographed in Killawalla in June 1997 with Joe McDonagh, President of the GAA

(Right) Recipients of the Mayo Hurling Awards, 2001:
(Front row, left to right) P.J. McGrath, Chairperson of Mayo GAA County Board; Martin Linnane, Winner of Lifetime Award for Services to Mayo Hurling; and Paddy Barrett, Senior Player of the Year.
(Back row, left to right) John Duffy, Under-21 Player of the Year; Philip Kelly, Managing Director of Desktop Solutions (sponsor); Jason Powers, Minor Player of the Year; and Keith Higgins, Under-16 Player of the Year.

Camogie

Camogie, played by women with a stick and ball, is equivalent to the ancient game of hurling played by men. Camogie was not a popular game when it started, but received a great boost in 1928 when it was included in the Tailteann Games, Inter-county Championships begun in 1932. Camogie became popular in Mayo during the 1950s and '60s, and teams included those in Manulla, Mulranny, Ballina, Ballintubber, Newport, Westport and Hollymount. Later, teams were formed in Achill Island, Breaffy, Ardnaree and Tooreen.

Seaghan Ó Dubhthaigh (Seán O'Duffy) was born in 1886 in Kinuary, Killawalla, near Westport, where his father was stationed in the Royal Irish Constabulary barracks. A prominent trade unionist who fought in 1916, Seán was one of the founders of Cumann Camogaiochata na nGael (The Camogie Association) and the sport's ultimate prize, the Seaghan Ó Dubhthaigh Cup, is named after him. In June 1997, a plaque was unveiled in Killawalla in his honour and members of the 1959 Mayo Camogie team, who were finalists in the All-Ireland Championship that year, gathered to pay tribute to his memory.

Hurling

While Mayo is chiefly associated with football, the county also has a proud hurling tradition, with a number of athletes playing both hurling and football. Hurling clubs were established throughout Mayo during the 1930s and '40s at Belmullet, Swinford, Westport, Castlebar, Claremorris and Ballina. But it was the village of Tooreen that became associated with Mayo hurling for many decades. Tooreen Hurling Club was established in 1957 and 26 members enrolled at its first meeting. Sunday after Sunday, training took place on the mossy grounds of Michael Tuohy's turlough field and by 1966 the club won its first Senior title against Cong. Interest in hurling has persisted in Tooreen and new clubs at Ballyhaunis, Ballina and Westport have also emerged. The Mayo Hurling Board continues to develop the sport by increasing children's participation through primary school competitions and the improvement of coaching provision and club structures.

Athletics

Born in Kiltimagh, Seán 'Baller' Lavan (1898-1973) was a superb athlete with tremendous natural ability in many different sports. Among his achievements was the initiation of the 'hand to toe' technique or 'solo run', which is today such an integral part of Gaelic football. Between 1918 and 1924, Lavan played Gaelic football for Kiltimagh and for Mayo. He won every athletic competition in Ireland in the 220 and 440 yard races (200 m and 400 m), played rugby on occasion and boxed when at college. In 1924, Lavan represented Ireland in the Paris Olympics on the first Irish national team since independence. He competed in the 400 yards (365 m) event, reaching the semi-finals. Four years later, he captained the Irish team in the Amsterdam Olympics and later acted as the Irish team's medical officer in the Helsinki Olympics.

Besides his sporting pursuits, Lavan had first trained as a national school teacher and later studied medicine in University College Dublin. He subsequently lectured there in anatomy and also worked for a while as a police surgeon. During his sporting career Lavan earned over 120 medals, which were exhibited in his native Kiltimagh in 1997.

Bohola-born Olympic champion, Martin Joseph Sheridan (1881-1918) was one of the most outstanding athletes of his time, winning more Olympic medals than any other Irish athlete. He retired from athletics in 1911, having established 16 new world records and winning nine Olympic medals – five gold, three silver and one bronze – at St. Louis (1904), Athens (1906) and London (1908).

Having emigrated to New York at the age of 19, Sheridan set his first world record in athletics when he was 20 with a discus throw of 120 feet 7¼ inches. He subsequently won the American All Round Athletic Championships three times between 1905 and 1909. Although an all-round athlete, his main expertise was in pole vaulting, discus throwing, the long jump and the high jump.

On a visit to Bohola in August 1908, Sheridan visited his family home where his brother Joe and his wife, Kitty, lived. She was an assistant teacher in Carragowan school, which Martin himself had attended, and was a sister of the renowned Republican and statesman Michael Collins (1890-1922). It was during this visit that Sheridan created yet another world record, this time by throwing a 7 lb weight a distance of 99 feet 10 inches, which was 2 feet 7 inches more than the previous world record. A memorial to Martin Sheridan was unveiled at Bohola in July 1966 by Gene

Seán 'Baller' Lavan of Kiltimagh, c. 1924 – one of Mayo's most accomplished sportsmen and an Olympic athlete

Martin Sheridan of Bohola, Olympic athletics champion, drawn by Robert Edgren in 1907

Anne Lennon and Josephine Macken, two of Mayo's leading athletes in recent years

Tunney, Junior, son of the Irish-American World Heavyweight Boxing champion, and Bohola-born Paul O'Dwyer, then Mayor of New York.

Interest in athletics in Mayo has grown significantly in recent decades. Many athletic clubs have sprung up and older clubs have been regenerated. The Claremorris Athletic Club was founded in the 1960s, with success coming quickly for many club members on the national scene. In the early 1990s, the club achieved major successes in track and field events. Ballina Athletic Club, which had been dormant for some years, was revived in the 1960s with Fr. Michael Flynn as chairperson. Ballina athletes have had many notable achievements over the years. For example, Deirdre Gallagher competed in the Olympic Games in Atlanta in 1996 and Pádraig Howard participated in the Special Olympics in North Carolina in 1999, where he won a gold medal in the shot putt. The Castlebar Athletic Club was founded in 1972 and has also enjoyed recent successes.

The Mayo Athletic Club, catering for junior and senior athletes within the county, was re-formed in the late 1980s. Brenda Murphy was the first female athlete to join the club and she had wonderful success in the Belfast Marathon. Other successes by athletes such as Anne Lennon, Josephine Macken and Frances Lally soon followed. Paddy Murray dominated the road race scene and Paddy Kearney brought great honour to the club for his numerous sprint titles. Eugene McTigue had huge success at national level in both the 56 lb (25.4 kg) and shot events.

The Special Olympics World Summer Games are held every four years with the aim of providing athletic competition in a variety of Olympic sports for intellectually challenged participants. In June 1999, 7,000 athletes from 150 countries participated in the Special Olympics, hosted in North Carolina, USA. Six athletes from Mayo brought back two gold

Members of the Western Care team who competed at the Special Olympics World Games in June 1999

medals, one silver and four bronzes, as well as ribbons for two fourths, one first and two sixths, in equestrian, bowling, basketball, swimming and athletic events. It was a success-story made possible by the hard work of the athletes and their coaches at home in Mayo. Fiona Hughes (Hollymount) received fourth place in both her equestrian events (the trail ride and equitation). Agnes McGee (Westport) participated with her unified partner, Colette McTigue, in the bowling event and achieved third place in the World Doubles and third place in a team event, receiving two Bronze medals. Agnes Melvin (Ballina) achieved the highest individual score on her team in the basketball event, winning an Olympic Gold medal. Caitriona Ryan (Easkey), participating in the 25 metre freestyle and 25 metre backstroke events, won both an Olympic Gold and a Silver medal. Pádraig Howard (Ballina) won the first Gold medal for Ireland in the shot putt and also received a fifth place in the athletics events of the 100 metre and 200 metre races.

Soccer

It is generally accepted that British sailors and soldiers introduced the game of association football or soccer to Mayo during the early 1800s. The game developed a small following, but remained largely a street game because of a lack of pitches. Initially, teams were concentrated in the garrison towns of Westport and Castlebar. Westport Town Club was formed in 1910, while Castlebar Celtic was officially formed in 1928, having already been in existence for some years. The Dooniver Swift team emerged in Achill in the 1940s and Swinford Club was founded in the early '50s. Westport United, with its distinctive red and black colours, was

Members of the British Police force soccer team, at the old entrance to Westport House, c. 1920

1980's Girl Soccer champions from Ballyhaunis

officially established in 1952. The Mayo Association Football League also emerged in the 1950s, despite the financial austerity of the period. The lack of money led to difficulties in providing transport to matches, thus making it hard for clubs to develop.

In recent years, television has expanded interest in the game of soccer among girls as well as boys. The abolition in 1969 of the GAA Rule 27, or 'the Ban' on members playing sports other than Gaelic games, has meant that soccer is increasingly played in schools at all levels and players no longer have to choose between it and Gaelic football.

In July 1996, Pat Quigley was inaugurated as the first Mayo-born President of the Football Association of Ireland (FAI). A native of Ballyheane, Quigley began his soccer days with the Road Rangers from the McHale Road area of Castlebar, who later amalgamated with Castlebar Celtic. His commitment and dedication soon saw him progress to being a delegate to the Connaught Football Association and later he was appointed to the FAI Board of Management. Subsequently, he became President of the FAI Youths' Council and in 1996 was elected President of the FAI – both a personal triumph and an honour for Co. Mayo. As President, representing the association both at home and abroad, Quigley fulfilled a demanding role, as well as constantly seeking improved facilities and opportunities for soccer enthusiasts throughout Ireland.

Mayo's silver Gill Cup, no longer played for, is preserved for posterity by the Mayo Association Football League. Frank Gill of Rosbeg, Westport, one of the pioneers of Mayo soccer, donated the Gill Cup to the Connaught Football Association in the 1920s. It was the prestigious trophy for the South Western League for many years. From 1954 until 1982, the Gill Cup was presented to the winners of Division One of the Mayo League. After the introduction of the Premier Division, in the 1979-80 season, the former Division One became the second division and from 1982 until 1998 second division teams played for the Gill Cup. More recently, other cups have been donated for soccer leagues. The Tom Kelly Cup was donated in 1999 for the new Super League, established to encourage the development and maintenance of good soccer facilities.

The Mayo League itself has top-class facilities at Milebush near Castlebar, which is being developed as a Regional Coaching Centre of Excellence.

(Above) Pat Quigley, first Mayo-born President of the Football Association of Ireland

(Above left) Kevin Moran Soccer School, playing on Castlebar's Mall in August 2000

Tennis

Tennis was a popular recreational game among the gentry in the early 20th century. By the late 1940s, lawn tennis became popular in Westport in the area known locally as The Paddock. In 1950, Fr. Canney, a curate in Westport and an avid tennis fan, initiated a new tennis court project. A site on the Newport Road was deemed suitable and transformed into a tennis court with clubhouse facilities. Today, Westport Tennis Club is a major club and, along with that in Castlebar, has been enhanced in recent years with the provision of floodlighting on the courts. Interest in the game has increased over the years and club membership is growing.

Castlebar Tennis Club was founded in the 1930s at what was then the outskirts of the town. In the 1950s, a new club pavilion was built under the chairmanship of Canon Willie Walsh, who was later succeeded by Fr. Charlie O'Malley. Judge John Garavan has been a great influence in the club's development, variously fulfilling the roles of long-time chairman, president and trustee over the years. The club has grown from strength to strength, producing recent champion players such as Conor McHale, Under-12 champion in 1999, and Warren Atkins, Under-14 champion in 2001. The sport has also grown in popularity throughout the county, with courts in Claremorris, Ballina, Ballyhaunis, Balla and elsewhere.

Tennis players of the early 1900s in Westport, where the sport first became popular in Mayo

(Above) Photographed by Judge John Garavan in 1949, a group of tennis players pose outside the original Castlebar Tennis Club pavilion – (from left to right) Malachy Glynn, Eve Egan, Charles Garavan, Brendan Ryan, Joan Hanly and Angela McDonnell

(Left) Adrian Sheerin of Swinford, National Senior Boxing Champion of 1997-98

Boxing

Amateur boxing has been a popular sport in Mayo for decades and has produced many champions over the years. Among the earliest was Ballina-born Garda Dick Hearns, five times the Irish Cruiser Champion, who fought throughout Europe and the USA. He won his first national senior title in 1933 and successfully defended it until his retirement in 1939 following an injury. After the disruption of World War II, the 1950s became a great era for Mayo boxing, drawing large crowds to tournaments. Tom McHugh, a former Castlebar boxer, returned from England and revitalised Castlebar Boxing Club. The club ran the hugely successful Connaught Championships in Castlebar each year between 1952 and 1958. Seán Horkan won the first National Championship for Castlebar in 1957, winning the Junior Light Heavy title.

Westport's Peter Mullen was the amateur Irish Heavyweight Champion from 1971 to 1973 and again in 1975. He represented Ireland against the USA in 1977, when he was defeated by Larry Holmes, later World Heavyweight Champion. Swinford's Adrian Sheerin became the National Senior Boxing Champion of 1997-98. The clubs in Ballina, Ballyhaunis, Belmullet, Claremorris, Castlebar, Killala, Geesala and Westport have also produced fine boxers. Paul Quinn from the Ardnaree Club in Ballina is one of the most successful young boxers in the county today. Peter Forde of Ballinrobe won the All-Ireland Junior boxing title in the 1980s. Besides his boxing abilities, Forde was also a great football player and captained the Mayo Gaelic Football team in 1992; he was a selector for the team from 1996-98.

Peter Forde of Ballinrobe, Mayo footballer and All-Ireland Junior Boxing Champion in the 1980s as well as selector and captain of the Mayo Gaelic Football team in the 1990s

James J. Corbett, World Heavyweight Champion 1892-97, with his wife, visiting Mayo in 1894

Two world heavyweight boxing champions – James J. Corbett and Gene Tunney – had Mayo connections. James J. Corbett (1866-1933) was the American boxer known as 'Gentleman Jim'. His father, Patrick Corbett, had emigrated from Ballycusheen, near Ballinrobe, to the USA in 1854. Corbett defeated fellow Irish-American, John L. Sullivan, in the World Heavyweight Championship in 1892, the first championship to be fought with gloves and governed by the Marquess of Queensberry Rules. He retained his heavyweight title until 1897, when he was defeated by Bob Fitzsimmons. Corbett was the first boxer whose life story was told on the silver screen, with actor Errol Flynn portraying him in the 1942 film *Gentleman Jim*.

In 1894, James J. Corbett returned to his ancestral Mayo. Among the highlights of his visit were the boxing demonstrations he gave in Ballinrobe Town Hall. Special trains were engaged to bring hundreds of supporters to the performance. The proceeds from the event's entrance fees were donated for the upkeep of Partry Church, where Corbett's uncle, the Reverend James Corbett, was parish priest at the time, as well as an active member of the Mayo Land League. Corbett also donated a stained-glass window to the church.

Gene Tunney, Junior (2nd from right), son of the World Heavyweight Boxing champion, with Bohola-born Paul O'Dwyer (2nd from left), then Mayor of New York, at the unveiling in July 1966 of the memorial to Martin Sheridan, another son of Bohola and world Olympic athlete; Andy Sheridan (left) is Martin's brother

Gene Tunney (1897-1978) was the son of two emigrants from Westport and Kiltimagh. He was born in New York City in 1897 and became World Heavyweight Boxing champion in 1926 when he defeated Jack Dempsey. He repeated his performance in Chicago a year later and retired in 1928 after successfully defending his title against New Zealander Tom Heaney. Tunney later pursued a successful business career and wrote his autobiography *Arms for Living*. Gene Tunney, Junior, attended the unveiling of the memorial to Bohola-born Olympic athlete Martin Sheridan in July 1966.

Rugby football

In 1885, a rugby club from Castlebar was represented at the establishment of the Connaught Rugby Branch in Dublin. However, the Castlebar club played a minor role during the formative years of the Connaught branch and only formally affiliated in 1934. In the 1930s, Castlebar, Ballina, Westport and Ballinrobe comprised the Connaught Junior League. Westport won back-to-back Connaught Junior Cups in 1930 and 1931. J. McNally's mesmerizing try and classic performance was decisive in the team's 9-5 victory over Athenry in 1931. The team went on to compete in a League and Cup double in 1955, defeating the Sparks (Electricity Supply Board) by 27-12 in the League. Westport captured their fourth League title as recently as 1998, with an 18-7 victory over Tuam.

(Above) Ciaran Fitzgerald of Ballina, former Captain of the Irish rugby team, Captain of the British and Irish Lions team in 1983 and Captain of the Irish Triple Crown team in 1985

(Right) Ballina Rugby team, winners of the Connaught Senior Cup in 1979: (Back row, left to right) Oliver Bourke (Coach), Pat Buckley, Eugene Cawley, Walter Doherty, Eddie O'Connor, Gerry O'Donnell, Liam O'Neill and Michael Rowe. (Front row, left to right) Séamus O'Dowd, Michael Begley, the late Aubrey Bourke, the late Seán Murphy, Charlie Mullaney, Niall Dodd and J.P. Leonard. (Front, on ground) Niall Brennan and Tommie Cooke. Missing from the photograph is John Byrne.

Mayo has been represented in the All-Ireland League since its inception in the mid-1990s. Talented young men, such as Gavin Duffy and Ger Brady, both from Ballina, and James Gill from Westport represented Ireland at underage level and their performances promise a bright future for rugby in Mayo.

Ballina has been a major rugby force since the 1940s, winning their first Connaught Junior Club title in 1948, defeating Ballinasloe 10-3 in the final. They repeated this achievement on four further occasions, most recently in 1985. Ballina has also made history by winning five Connaught Junior Leagues in a row during the period 1981-85.

At senior level, too, Ballina proved itself a formidable rugby team. They were crowned Connaught Senior League Champions in 1929. The coveted Connaught Senior Cup came to Mayo for the first time in 1951 when, inspired by Ivan Heffernan, Ballina overcame Corinthians 6-3. Ballina celebrated their golden jubilee in 1979 with their second Connaught Senior Cup success, when they beat Athlone by 10-6. The president of the Ballina Rugby Club on this famous day was the late 'Mr. Rugby', Seán Murphy. Niall Brennan scored the winning try in injury time, while the other points came from the boot of Charlie Mullaney. The team was captained by the late Aubrey Bourke and coached by his brother, Oliver, both brothers of the former President of Ireland, Mary Robinson. Oliver Bourke has coached many rugby players, including Ollie Campbell who captained the Irish Triple Crown team in the 1980s.

Castlebar qualified for their first Connaught Junior Cup Final in 1996, but Monivea (Galway) proved too strong and the game ended in a 23-9

Westport Rugby Club, four times winners of the League title, photographed in 1998

defeat. Castlebar became the fifth Mayo team to contest a Junior Cup Final, following in the footsteps of Westport, Ballina, Ballinrobe and Crossmolina (who affiliated to the Connaught Branch in 1960 and were led to a Junior Cup Final in 1962 by the Irish rugby legend, Tony Browne).

Mayo's fifth club, Ballyhaunis, was established in the 1976-77 season. New initiatives continue to develop the sport of rugby in the county, although it is still in the shadow of both Gaelic football and soccer.

Basketball

Twenty years ago, basketball was confined to the towns of Ballina, Castlebar and Ballinrobe. In recent years, however, the growth of the sport has been phenomenal. There are now also basketball League clubs in Ballycastle, Charlestown and Crossmolina, with Juvenile Leagues from Under-10 to 18 years. There are three Mayo men's teams (Ballina Longnecks, Team Lundy from Ballina and Team Westro from Castlebar) and one women's team (Castlebar Rockets) competing in the National Division One Leagues. School teams have been established throughout the county and St. Gerald's, Castlebar, succeeded in winning the All-Ireland Under-16 title in 2000, while St. Muredach's, Ballina, won the All-Ireland Under-19 title in 2002.

The recent development of basketball in Ballina is attributed to the initiative of Dubliner Danny Thompson who lived in the town and helped to develop and promote the sport. The Ballina Longnecks – fortified by the natural talent of the three McHale brothers (Anthony, Liam and Seán)

(Above) Liam McHale of the Ballina Longnecks (then Chambourcy Ireland), winners of the ICS Cup Basketball Final in 1996

(Above right) 'Live' chess game performed on The Mall during the 1969 Chess Week festival in Castlebar, organised by local enthusiast Michael Egan

and the relentless energy and speed of Diora Marsh, originally from Ohio, USA – became one of the most successful clubs in Ireland during the 1980s and '90s. The Ballina team, formerly known as Team Connacht Gold in 1991 and as Chambourcy Ireland in 1996, captured the ICS Cup National title in both years.

Chess

In August 1969, a week-long festival of chess took place in Castlebar. As part of the festivities, a 'live' chess game was performed on The Mall, the first time such a spectacle had been performed in Ireland. An international chess tournament was also organised for the event at the Royal Ballroom for a prize fund of £250, which attracted competitors from New Zealand, Germany, Denmark, England and elsewhere in Ireland, stimulating great interest in the game.

Cycling

Cycling became a popular sport at the end of the 19th century. Clubs were set up throughout the county and racing became fashionable among those who could afford the relatively expensive bicycles. Besides participating in racing tournaments, cyclists also travelled in groups to visit beauty spots. For example, the Westport Cycle Club organised a bicycle

(Above) The Westport and Castlebar Cycle Clubs' tournament of about 1900 from Westport to Letterfrack in Co. Galway, as captured by Wynne's Photographic Studio

(Far left) Stopover in Westport during the Rás Tailteann in 1970, when the overall winner was Russia's Alexander Gysiatnikov, seen here (right) with Paddy Shanley, the only local man who could speak Russian

(Left) David O'Loughlin from Cong, one of the most promising young cyclists in Ireland today

tournament to Letterfrack in Co. Galway in about 1900 and were joined by the Castlebar 'Wheelers' Club. The Castlebar men started their cycle at 7.30am and reached Westport in less than an hour. At 9.20am, the start was made from Westport to Letterfrack, where the small army of 'wheelmen' arrived at 2.30pm, having covered a distance of some 51 km (32 ml). Wynne's Photographic Studio captured the occasion on camera and in true entrepreneurial style encouraged the cyclists to buy copies of the picture as a memento.

The Rás Tailteann, recently renamed the FBD Milk Race, was established in 1953. There are eight stages in the race and it presents the ultimate test in speed, stamina and endurance under Ireland's climatic and geographical conditions. In the 1970 race, the late Paddy Shanley, the only Westport person who could speak Russian, read an address of

The 18-hole championship golf links at Carne, near Belmullet – a challenging seaside course, laid out in 1925

welcome to the members of the Russian team when they stopped over in the town during the Rás Tailteann. That year, Russia's Alexander Gysiatnikov was the overall winner. In the 1975 race, Ireland's Stephen Roche, now a renowned world cyclist, wore the Yellow Jersey on arrival in Westport for the stopover.

Golf

Golf, unknown in Mayo until the late 1890s, was initially a game solely for people of means. It is now a popular leisure and competitive sport, enjoyed at many excellent golf courses throughout Co. Mayo, including those at Achill, Ballina, Westport, Belmullet, Ballyhaunis, Castlebar, Claremorris, Ballinrobe, Swinford, Balla, Mulranny and Kilmeena.

Westport Golf Club, one of Mayo's 18-hole championship courses, was founded in 1908 and affiliated to the Golfing Union of Ireland in 1927. It offers a challenging course, which includes a feisty 15th hole involving a drive over an inlet of Clew Bay. The Westport Golf Club is often used for the Irish Close Championships, the last one being held there in 1997. The Smurfit Irish PGA Championship became the latest prestigious golfing event to be hosted by Westport in April 2002. Balla's 18-hole par-3 course is open all year round. Gerard (Gar) Golden from Westport held the position of President of the Golfing Union of Ireland in 1990. The first Castlebar golf course was established near the Moneen roundabout in 1905, but was relocated to Drumminrachaill five years later, in 1910, and became known as Hawthorn Lodge. Many notable golfers have played at Castlebar Golf Club, including Christy O'Connor, who gave lessons there in 1952, and Philomena Garvey, British Open Champion, who also played there in 1956.

Belmullet's 18-hole championship golf course, located at Carne, was laid

Spectators at a Ballina race meeting at Mount Falcon, c. 1900

out in 1925 and is owned by the local community group of Turasóireacht Iorras Teo. The links were developed across wild, tumultuous, roller-coaster sand dunes, against a backdrop of dramatic land and seascapes, and magnificent unrestricted vistas. Carne Golf Club has hosted a Pro-Am, an established event on the PGA calendar, since 1999.

Horse racing

Horse racing and leisure horse riding have a long history in Mayo. Augustus Moore (1817-45), third son of George Moore (1770-1840) of Moore Hall, was killed while riding 'Mickey Free' at the Grand National steeplechase on the Liverpool course in 1845. His brother, George Henry Moore (1810-70) – Member of Parliament for Mayo and father of the famous Mayo author, George Augustus Moore (1852-1933) – was also a famous steeplechaser in his youth. Race meetings were important occasions in the social and sporting calendar, made more popular in the late 19th century with the arrival of the railway, which brought huge crowds to race meetings throughout the county.

The grounds of the current Ballinrobe Race Course were acquired in 1920 from the Creagh Estate and the first meetings commenced soon afterwards. Race-goers gathered in the viewing stalls, erected in 1927 to provide a good

Cameron Hanley of Claremorris, international show jumper, on 'Ballaseyr Twilight' at the Essex Horse Show in 2000

vantage point from which to watch the races' progress. Amidst great excitement, the animals arrived in special trains fitted with horse boxes the day before the event until the Ballinrobe line closed in the 1960s.

Ballina race meetings were generally held in May between 1832 and 1927 on the property of the Knox family at Mount Falcon. In later years, the races were held at Gurteen Race Course, which, with its grandstand, attracted a large attendance. Bookmakers came early to put up their box stands beside the viewing stalls so as to be situated prominently and within easy reach of the punters.

Show jumping

While show jumping has always been a minority sport in Mayo, it has experienced phenomenal growth in recent years. The county now boasts a number of talented senior and junior riders, competing regularly at both national and international level. Notable among this ever-growing band of successful showjumpers is Cameron Hanley from Claremorris who, among his numerous international successes, won the prestigious King George V Cup at Hickstead in 2000 (the first time Ireland has done so since 1937). Hanley's international show jumping career began in 1989 when he competed against 13 nations to win an individual European

silver medal on an unusually young six-year-old pony called 'Kilclooney'. As anchor man of the Irish team, Hanley jumped three clear rounds, helping to assure Ireland of a team Bronze medal in the jump-off. Successes followed in the senior competitions and Young Rider Qualifiers at the Royal Dublin Society (RDS) in the early 1990s and as winner of the Swiss Young Rider Championships on 'Rocky Jackson' in 1993. Hanley had a remarkable year in 2000. In February, he came third in the Zurich Grand Prix, the world's largest indoor international show jumping competition. In May, he joined Ballaseyr Stables and was on the winning Nations Cup teams in June at Drammen (Norway), Helsinki (Finland), Falsterbro (Sweden) and Hickstead (England), where he also won the King George V Cup and the qualifying competition in July. In August, he won the Grand Prix at the Horse Show in Dublin's RDS and, to finish the year, he won the Grand Prix in November at the Millstreet Indoor International Horse Show.

Another great success in the show jumping world is Crossmolina-rider Damian Gardiner, now based in the USA and competing on the American circuit. He achieved the ultimate accolade in being selected to represent his country as a member of the Irish team in the 1996 Atlanta Olympics.

At 'Young Rider' level, the success achieved by some of the younger Mayo showjumpers is a positive indicator of the continuing growth and prosperity of the sport in the county. Samantha Duffy of Knockmore and Carl Hanley of Claremorris represented Ireland at the European Championships in Hungary in 2000 and produced exemplary performances. The selection of these Mayo showjumpers as members of the National European Showjumping Team is evidence of the limitless horizons to which young Mayo riders can now aspire.

The waters off Achill offer sports enthusiasts excellent conditions for surf-boarding, kayaking and surf-skiing

Water sports

Mayo's exposed western shoreline is excellent for wind surfing, canoeing and sailing, and has always attracted athletes to the coast. One of Ireland's leading water activity centres, UISCE, is located at Elly Bay, off the Mullet Peninsula. Also on the Mullet, to the west of Barr na Trá, lies Poll a Tómais, where the Sea Diving and Cultural Centre (Cuam na Farraige) is located.

The Achill Outdoor Education Centre blends into the panoramic setting of Keel Beach and Slievemore Mountain on Achill Island. Established by the Mayo Vocational Education Committee in 1972, it was the first such centre to be established in Ireland and has become successful both as a recreational and educational facility. Its resident instructors have expertise in a variety of sports, including canoeing, kayaking, orienteering, mountaineering, wind surfing and rock climbing.

Yawls, traditional working boats used for fishing and transporting turf and seaweed, now participate in an annual sailing competition off Achill Island. The Achill yawl, smaller than a hooker and larger than a currach, is a good sea-going vessel, whose origins remain obscure. The double-end design of the boat allows the stern to cut the water and give continued control to the helmsperson. In the early years of the 20th century, yawls began to be used for competitive sailing and since the 1960s the yawl races were again revived. In recent years, the races are organised by the local sailing club, Cumann Bádoirí Acla, and have become an annual summer event, in which modified yawls and the Achill transom stern boats also participate.

Whether for pleasure or competition, sailing in Mayo's western waters is a regular sight in the summer months

(Above) Mayo Cricket Club playing in July 2000 on Castlebar's historic Mall, former cricket pitch of the Lucans

(Above left) The Mayo Ladies' Darts team, competing in the 2001 INDO tournament in Daly's Hotel, Castlebar

Cricket

Cricket has a long, although largely unrecorded, history in Mayo. Castlebar's Mall was used by the Earls of Lucan as their private cricket pitch. The sport was introduced to the town in the early 19th century by soldiers billeted at the barracks, who formed a cricket club that regularly played against the barracks in Athlone.

In recent years, two cricket teams have been established in Mayo. Paul Large, son of the famous professional footballer, Frank Large, was among those who re-established the Mayo Cricket Club in Castlebar. The first game took place on 9 August 1998 on The Mall, where the team continues to play friendly matches. The club has played in the Dick O'Neill Cup and has the unusual achievement, as a Connaught team, of winning the Leinster Minor Cup in August 1999. A second cricket club has been established in Ballyhaunis, drawing its membership initially from the local Pakistani community.

Darts

The Mayo Ladies' Darts team competed in the Irish National Darts Organisation (INDO) Inter-counties Competition held in Limerick in February 2001. Youth and men's teams also compete in the INDO annual competitions.

The Mayo Darts Organisation is actively involved in promoting darts at all levels and is affiliated to INDO, the governing body of darts in Ireland. The sport is very popular throughout the county and many leagues and competitions are organised during the winter months, often in public houses.

Chapter 9

Education

Ireland's early Christian monasteries were seats of learning and education. Those in Mayo were no exception. The *Annals of Multifarnham* are said to have been compiled in the 13th century by Stephen d'Exeter at the Dominican Friary in Straide. Three centuries later, Grace O'Malley or Granuaile (c. 1530-1603) was educated by the monks at Murrisk Abbey. Mayo Abbey features among the famous educational centres: founded at the end of the 7th century, it attracted large numbers of students from abroad, as well as the sons of Irish chieftains. The Venerable Bede (673-735), writing from England, records that many English went for instruction to Mayo Abbey, including Alfred the Great, King of Northumbria. Alcuin, a Saxon monk living in the 8th century and advisor to the Emperor Charlemagne, also praised Mayo Abbey and the knowledge that emanated from there:

> To the beloved fathers in Christ of the Church of Mayo, Alcuin, a humble deacon, sends his greetings . . . a great light of knowledge was spread from you to various parts of our country. . .

During the reigns of Henry VIII (1509-1547) and his daughter Elizabeth I (1558-1603), the dissolution of the monasteries began the destruction of these centres of learning, a process that continued with Oliver Cromwell's military campaigns of the mid-17th century. The Tudor conquest and the resulting decline of the Gaelic chieftains dealt a mortal blow to the traditional patronage of the Gaelic Bardic schools. The consolidation of the Protestant Ascendancy after 1691 also had a negative impact on the provision of popular education. This was because an insecure establishment feared the political union of the Catholic masses with the Jacobite cause and introduced measures to disenfranchise the majority of the population politically, economically and socially. The infamous Penal or Anti-Popery Laws of the early 18th century affected the legal right of Catholics to avail themselves of education and further diminished the role of the Church in the provision of education for almost a century. The unofficial fee-based schools used at that time by Catholics were generally

Children performing in a school concert in Bofeenaun National School

In Penal times, schooling took place in private houses, like this one near Bellacorrick on the Mullet Peninsula which was used for many years as a 'hedge school' and replaced in 1892 by a government-funded national school

organised in the pupils' or schoolmaster's home and became known as 'hedge schools'. Several families would join together to raise money to engage a schoolmaster, who would then reside temporarily with each family. After Catholic emancipation in 1829, many of the Masters of the former hedge schools were absorbed into the national school system, introduced in 1831. Thereafter the education system placed increasing emphasis on a written, centrally devised curriculum, taught in a classroom setting. But the traditional apprenticeship of skills necessary for survival in a rural society continued to relatively modern times.

In the 18th century, formal schools were established in Mayo, including the Charter Schools at Manulla and Ballinrobe, noted by Dr. Richard Pococke (1704-65), Church of Ireland Bishop of Ossory, during his tour of Mayo in 1752. Founded after 1733, these schools were established for the education and conversion of the Catholic poor. Schools were also established for evangelical and proselytising purposes, and were often controversial. In the 19th century, the Irish Church Mission Society supported schools in Dugort on Achill Island and in Tourmakeady.

In the 1830s, Bishop Thomas Plunkett became a tenant in Tourmakeady on the Lynch-Blosse Estate. He eventually rented over 162 hectares (400 acres) and purchased this property in the post-Famine Encumbered Estates Court. He erected two schools on his property, which he placed under the Irish Church Mission Society. He allegedly threatened the eviction of any parents who refused to send their children to these Protestant schools. Fr. Pat Lavelle, originally from Murrisk, campaigned against Bishop Plunkett. The Franciscan Brothers opened a school in Tourmakeady in opposition to the Mission schools, which eventually closed when the Plunkett Estate was sold in 1863.

The Irish Church Mission Society opened the first school in Achill at Dugort in 1834 and enrolled 43 students that year. According to the *Achill Missionary Herald and Western Witness*, the Society's own newspaper, by the following year there were four Mission schools with a total of 430 students in attendance. Then in 1835, Archbishop John MacHale (1791-1881), Archbishop of Tuam, who was staunchly opposed to what he saw as the proselytising activities of the Mission Society, established four Catholic schools on the island. The competition between the two sides continued and by 1870 there were 16 schools on Achill Island, serving a population of just under 5,000 people.

Under the national education system, established in 1831, the Board of Education supplied funds towards building schools and employing teachers who met its criteria. However, these schools were opposed by members of *all* churches because of their non-denominational status, permitting no religious instruction or display of religious objects. Others opposed the new schools as being colonialist on the basis that neither Irish history nor the Irish language were taught.

Archbishop John MacHale was a leading critic of the national education system and was strongly opposed to allowing these new schools to be established in his archdiocese of Tuam. Instead, Dr. MacHale actively sought religious men and women to provide education for his congregation and brought the Sisters of Mercy, Franciscan Brothers and Christian Brothers to Mayo. The Marists, nuns and brothers, De La Salle Brothers, St. Louis Sisters and Jesus and Mary Sisters were among the other orders that taught within the county. Archbishop McEvilly, MacHale's successor, took a different attitude and brought many schools in the diocese into the national education system. After the establishment of the Irish Free State in 1922, the curriculum and management of primary schools gradually evolved. The vast majority of children now receive their primary education in the State-aided national school system, whereby each school is run by its own board of management but receives most of its funding from the State. By the end of the 19th century, there were some 400 national schools in Co. Mayo, catering for a population of approximately 30,000 pupils. By the end of the 20th century, there were less than 200 national schools in the county, serving approximately 14,500 pupils – a reflection of the dramatic population decline in Mayo over a century.

Rural schools built in the late 19th and early 20th centuries usually

BALLINA
Boarding & Day School,
FOR GENERAL EDUCATION.

Rev. Jas. R. Huston, A.B.
PRINCIPAL.

Terms for Boarders—30—35—or 40 guineas per annum—according to the age—class—objects of instructions &c., of the pupil.

For day pupils—4—5—or 6 guineas, according to circumstances.

THERE are three examinations held in the year—one at Easter, in the Holy Scriptures—one at Mid-Summer, and at Christmas, in Greek and Roman Classics, English, French, the Practice and Theory of Arithmetic, Euclid, Logic, use of the Globes, Composition, Corporial expression and Oratory, &c.

There will be no winter vacation this year.

Nov. 10, 1832.

Advertisements for private schools appeared regularly in newspapers during the 19th century, such as this one in the 'Ballina Imperial' in November 1832

Students outside Shrule National School in the early 20th century

Miss Kitty Walsh and her pupils assembled outside Cloughbrack National School, Boofeenaun, in 1953. This school, built in 1935, is now a private dwelling.

St. Muredach's College, Ballina,
founded in 1906

employed two teachers. These lay schools did not have the resources that the religious orders expended on their premises for the relative luxuries of heating, toilets and maintenance. The sole source of heat in rural schools came from an open turf fire and it was the teacher's first job of the day to light it. The turf was provided by the families of the pupils – two sods a day or the financial equivalent from those without access to a bog. More often than not, the greater part of the day would be over before the children at the back of the classroom felt the warmth of the fire. The core of the curriculum was 'the three Rs' – reading, writing (of English) and arithmetic – and catechetics.

Today, many of these rural schools have been converted to private dwellings or community halls. Others have been demolished or stand derelict. The old buildings were gradually replaced from the 1950s with more modern ones and frequently by schools centralised in towns and villages. The distinctive Board of Works' design for standard school buildings consisted of single-storey, two-classroom blocks, larger in scale than local houses. The name of the school and date of its foundation were usually placed in cut lettering on a stone plaque mounted on the school wall.

Secondary education became available in Mayo from the end of the 19th century, but remained inaccessible for most children. The Intermediate Education Act of 1878 established a Board to conduct written examinations and distribute grants to those schools whose pupils successfully passed the Intermediate Examination. The Technical Instruction Acts of 1891 and 1899 initiated technical and commercial training programmes, some of them grant-aided by the Congested Districts Board, established in 1891 to initiate long-term improvements in the West. The newly established Irish Free State enacted the Intermediate Education (Amendment) Act of 1924 to make financial assistance available to schools through capitation grants for each 'recognised' pupil and a partial payment towards teachers' salaries.

The Sisters of Charity in Foxford, the St. Louis Sisters in Kiltimagh and the Sisters of Mercy in Louisburgh were among those who received

Fr. Browne's 1938 photograph, called 'Scholars' Van', shows children being 'bused to school' in a horse-drawn covered wagon

financial aid for technical instruction, including lace-making classes and agricultural instruction. The Vocational Education Act of 1930 updated the provision of vocational and technical education for the needs of the 20th century by devising a new curriculum and opening co-educational schools. The first vocational schools in Mayo were opened in 1933 in Ballina and Castlebar, followed by further schools in Westport, Belmullet and Achill by the end of the 1930s. A network of vocational schools was gradually established throughout the county. In the 1970s, some were replaced by community schools, which combined vocational and academic education.

Dr. Conmy, Bishop of Killala, founded St. Muredach's College, Ballina, in 1906. It was built at a cost of £11,000 and replaced the Seminary College in Ardnaree, founded in 1851 but which had inadequate facilities. The new college was financed until 1967 by private fees – £3 a year for day pupils and £30 a year for boarders – and provided a liberal education for a growing student population. By the end of the 20th century, student numbers had grown to over 500.

The advent of free second-level education in 1967 and the provision of school transport dramatically increased the numbers participating in post-primary education in Mayo. The State allocated grants to

Boys coming home from school at Dooagh on Achill Island in 1948. Throughout Mayo, the demands of the farm often meant that school was not attended regularly. Children were needed to turn turf or help with cultivation and harvesting. Until free secondary schooling was introduced in the 1960s, this level of education was not accessible to most people.

In 1974, these children from Ballycroy were travelling to school on horseback and donkey

schools undertaking not to charge students' fees. By the end of the 20th century, over 2,000 students sat the Leaving Certificate examination in one year in the county.

Before the introduction of State-sponsored school transport, isolated schemes operated that were usually locally organised and funded. Fr. Browne, SJ, took a series of photographs near Nephin Mountain in the late 1930s, showing boys and girls from Errew and the surrounding area travelling to Crossmolina National School after their local school was closed. For many years, Anthony Mulhern was employed to bring them in his horse-drawn covered wagon, which was replaced in 1948 by a motor van driven by Jim Hiney.

Historically, third-level education, supported by public funds, had been available to a very small number of Mayo people. In 1910, Mayo County Council struck a rate of ½d in the £, to provide scholarships to University College, Galway. Later, the Council also played an important

The provision of free transport in 1967 greatly increased the numbers of children attending secondary schools in the county

Castlebar campus of the Galway – Mayo Institute of Technology (GMIT), opened in 1994

role in enabling participation in third-level education through the administration of the higher education grant scheme.

Third-level education is available within the county since the early 1990s. Through the campaigning of the Mayo Regional Technical College's Action Group, funding was secured for the opening of a Castlebar campus of the Regional Technical College (RTC) Galway in 1994, sited in the fine cut-stone building that was formerly St. Mary's Psychiatric Hospital. The Galway RTC had been established since 1972 and was constituted as an autonomous institute of higher education in 1993. The entire institution was officially renamed the Galway – Mayo Institute of Technology (GMIT) in 1998 to incorporate the Castlebar campus into the title. When it first opened, the Castlebar campus offered three vocationally oriented certificate courses in Business, Construction and Computing to just over 100 students. Within six years, the numbers attending GMIT had increased to over 700 full-time and 800 part-time students, with some 40% coming from Co. Mayo and a further 20% from neighbouring Co. Galway. The National Council of Education Awards initially validated the courses, but GMIT now has self-validating status from the Higher Education and Training Awards Council (HETAC) in respect of all National Certificate and National Diploma Awards.

Sisters of Mercy

The first convent of the Sisters of Mercy in the Archdiocese of Tuam opened in Westport in 1842. It was founded by Sister Mary Paul Cullen of the Mercy Convent in Co. Carlow, a sister of Cardinal Paul Cullen who had sought reforms in the national education system. Lord Sligo of Westport House, the local landlord, had donated a site to the nuns for

First-year students of the Sacred Heart School, Westport, in 2001

Class of 1957-58 at the Sacred Heart School, Westport

their new convent, called Mount St. Mary's, as well as a site for their new school building. In 1904, the Sisters used part of a legacy to purchase the Clendining Building in Westport's Mill Street, where they established a School of Rural Science. In 1925, they opened a secondary school for girls, the Sacred Heart School, in a building purchased from the County Sheriff.

In 1853, on the feast of St. Angela, a group of five Sisters of Mercy arrived in Castlebar at the invitation of Archbishop John MacHale. With the help of Frederick Cavendish, a local social reformer and newspaper proprietor, they obtained a house on the edge of the Earl of Lucan's property, commonly known as Rock House. They established a national school for the children of the poor in converted out-buildings at the back of the house. A new primary school, St. Angela's, was officially opened in 1897 (replaced by a new school building in 1964). They also established a private fee-paying school in Grove House on Charles Street. A new secondary school, St. Joseph's, was opened in 1918. By 1924, the Sisters had purchased part of the Lucan Estate, including the lodge and grounds of 37 hectares (92 acres). The lodge was converted into St. Joseph's Secondary School, which catered for boarders up to 1978, but is now a day school.

Some of the Sisters of Mercy moved from Westport in 1853 to found a new convent at Ballinrobe. This was followed by the opening of convents at Clonbur and Lecanvey, near Westport. The Sisters were extremely active in the educational field, opening a primary school in Ballinrobe in 1890 (replaced by a modern building in 1971) and taking charge of Lecanvey National School between 1925 and 1986. By 1902, they had established a number of schools for technical instruction at Ballinrobe Convent, offering laundry and cookery demonstrations, as well as classes in needlework, sprigging and embroidery. The Christian Brothers catered

for boys' education in the area from 1876 until 1990. Dr. Noel Browne, a former pupil, records memories of his days at the Christian Brothers' school (CBS) in Ballinrobe in his autobiography *Against the Tide*.

Members of the Sisters of Mercy order from Sligo founded Ballina Convent in 1851, which became fully independent of Sligo in 1854. The Sisters assumed responsibility for the girls' national school and were soon providing education for both boys and girls in Ballina. Some of the nuns from Ballina Convent transferred to Belmullet in 1894 to take charge of the workhouse and its school there, and later opened a second-level school in the area.

Bishop Durkin authorised the foundation of convents by the Sisters of Mercy at Swinford in the Diocese of Achonry and a convent was built in 1855. A girls' primary school opened in Swinford in 1856 and was recognised by the Commissioners of National Education in 1857. The Schools' Inspector's Report of 1863-64 declared the school to be the best in the district for the care of infants. In 1905, a new national school was opened in Swinford and served for 60 years, until it was replaced by another school built on a site provided by the Sisters. In 1990, the girls' national school was amalgamated with the boys' school, founded previously by the Marist Brothers.

In 1906, the Sisters of Mercy in Swinford opened St. Mary's Secondary School, the first second-level school for girls. The fee per term was set at £1. In 1916, they were grant-aided to open a school of Rural Domestic Economy in Swinford's Brabazon Park, which continued until 1974. A purpose-built secondary school was opened in 1970. Second-level education was not available to boys until after World War II, when St. Patrick's College was opened, staffed by diocesan priests and lay staff.

(Top) Staff and pupils assembled at St. Mary's National School, Swinford, founded by the Sisters of Mercy in 1905

(Above) Pupils of the Mercy Convent, St. Angela's, Castlebar, at break outside the school

Students of the Intermediate Certificate class at Swinford Secondary School

In 1985, St. Mary's and St. Patrick's amalgamated to form a new school called Meán Scoil Muire agus Pádraig. In 1993, the vocational school also joined the amalgamation.

In 1877, the Sisters of Mercy came from Tuam to Claremorris and moved into Claremount House, now known as Mount St. Michael. This was a fine Georgian house, once the residence of Denis Browne, brother of the first Marquis of Sligo. The property had been secured for the nuns by Fr. Richard MacHale, parish priest in Claremorris and a nephew of Archbishop John MacHale of Tuam. The Sisters quickly established a primary and secondary school in Claremorris during 1878, although it was not until 1941 that the first Leaving Certificate class graduated. The financial pressures on the Sisters, from the expense of organising these schools, was relieved in 1882 when the primary school was placed under the Board of National Education. In the same year, the Sisters opened the nucleus of what was to become St. Joseph's Rural Home Economics College, in the old coach house of Claremont House. By 1900, a residential course in aspects of home and farm management was organised there, which continued up until 1984.

The education of boys in Claremorris is catered for at St. Colman's College, established in 1945 under the patronage of the Archbishop of Tuam and named after the patron saint of the parish. Fr. John Colleran became the first Rector of the College, located in an old house at Castlegar, and 64 students were accepted in its opening year. The school remained fee-paying until the introduction of free education in 1967, when the college witnessed a great increase in numbers – from less than 200 pupils to over 400. Like other schools in Mayo, St. Colman's has seen many changes in education since its establishment. The increased numbers of students from the 1970s was mirrored by an increased choice

Fifth-year students of St. Colman's College, 1994-95

of subjects in the curriculum. Woodwork, building construction, metalwork, art and music were among the new subjects added to those already taught. In 1985, the local vocational school closed and its pupils were transferred – the boys to St. Colman's and the girls to the local Mercy Convent. Today, changes are a constant feature of school life – sports facilities have expanded greatly, computers and new technologies are normal features in all classrooms, a Parents' Council participates in the development of the school, and the curriculum is continually changing and evolving.

The first co-educational secondary school in Ireland opened in Louisburgh in 1920, a few years after the Sisters of Mercy arrived from Tuam. Louisburgh's Sancta Maria College was opened decades before secondary education was generally available elsewhere in the county and years before the concept of co-education became popular in Ireland. Without government subsidies, the Louisburgh school was initially fee-paying but, like so many other second-level schools, was able to abolish fees in the late 1960s. In 1986, a new school building replaced the original 1920s structure.

St. Louis Sisters

The St. Louis Order arrived in Kiltimagh in September 1897. The Sisters were invited from their convent in Monaghan town by the Reverend Denis O'Hara (1850-1922), parish priest of Kiltimagh since 1888, as part of his efforts to bring education and prosperity to the area. Fr. Denis had travelled to Monaghan to ask the nuns to establish a convent in Kiltimagh; his initial request was refused, but he boldly declared he was not leaving until they conceded. A year after their arrival, the nuns had

Middle-grade class at the St. Louis Convent, Kiltimagh

organised a school for infants, followed by the first boarding school for girls to open in the Diocese of Achonry. Carrie Doran, daughter of Sir Henry Doran, an inspector with the Congested Districts Board, was the first pupil to be enrolled in the St. Louis Boarding School. The school offered instruction in religion and other subjects, including English, French, Latin, German, Italian, music (piano, harp, violin and guitar), singing, drawing, painting, dancing, plain and fancy needlework, and domestic economy. In 1903, the Sisters opened St. Aidan's National School, which was to amalgamate with the local boys' school in 1988.

Changes took place in the St. Louis Convent school in the 1970s: boarders were phased out, the school became co-educational and was fully incorporated with the previously separate Commercial School. In 1993, a new secondary school, St. Louis Community School, came into being with the amalgamation of the St. Louis Secondary School and the vocational school of Coláiste Raifteirí, which had opened in 1963.

In 1918, the St. Louis Sisters of Kiltimagh acquired the Lynch-Blosse Estate in Balla. They established a school there that placed strong emphasis on the arts and Irish language. The Balla School was planned as a junior department of their Kiltimagh secondary school. In the late 1970s, the Sisters transferred the school land and property to the Community Board of Management to manage the newly constituted

Aerial view of Gortnor Abbey, outside Crossmolina

Two Sisters of the Convent of Jesus and Mary, Gortnor Abbey, pictured in 1938

Balla Co-Educational Community Secondary School, opened with the support of the Department of Education.

Besides academic education, the St. Louis Sisters recognised the need to provide a practical education to women, to offer them the means of earning an income. In 1898, they opened a technical school in Kiltimagh. Within a year, 200 females attended classes in dressmaking, laundry, dairy management, poultry, bee-keeping, cookery and lace work. In 1899, the Kiltimagh Lace School won its first prize for *guipure* and *appliqué* lace at the Royal Dublin Society Show. The purchase of lace by Lady Cadogan, wife of Ireland's Lord Lieutenant, on that occasion was seen as a great boost to the newly established Lace School.

Jesus and Mary Order

The Jesus and Mary Order of Nuns first founded a house at Errew near Crossmolina in 1912. Later, in 1916, they moved to Gortnor Abbey, where the nuns occupied a house originally built by the Ormsby family at the end of the 18th century and which had been the Lough Conn Hotel prior to their arrival. The Sisters taught in the girls' primary school in Crossmolina and in 1919 opened the girls' secondary school at Gortnor Abbey (which became co-educational in 1973).

(Above) Sisters of Charity girls' school in Foxford in about 1910

(Above right) Sketch from The Graphic newspaper of July 1905, showing one of the Sisters of Charity teaching spinning to pupils in Foxford

Franciscan Brothers photographed at Errew monastery near Crossmolina, c. 1900

Sisters of Charity

In 1891, the Sisters of Charity were invited to Foxford by the Bishop of Achonry. The nuns undertook the formal education of children and also taught the technical arts of spinning and weaving. They established the Providence Woollen Mills, which has become world-renowned for the quality of its wool fabrics and plaid blankets. They took over the existing girls' primary school in Foxford and transferred it to new premises – a former cornhouse on the banks of the River Moy. They built a new school in 1907, to which a 'secondary top' (schooling as far as Intermediate Certificate) was added in 1955. A new secondary school was opened in 1961.

Boys' education in Foxford originally took place in a schoolmaster's house in Irishtown, on the edge of the town. This system was replaced in 1882, when a national school was opened on the site of the former church (demolished in 1879). Lay teachers taught there, except for a short period between 1924 and 1932 when the Franciscan Brothers operated the school. In the 1980s, the boys' and girls' national schools amalgamated and a new school opened in 1991, to accommodate the growing numbers of pupils.

The original building of St. Patrick's Boys National School, seen here in c. 1900, was destroyed by fire in 1956

Students of Coláiste Chonnacht in Tourmakeady, founded in 1905

Christian Brothers

The Christian Brothers started to cater for boys' education in Westport in 1865 and have been providing education at primary and secondary levels since then. Over the years, they expanded and increased their facilities. In 1996, due to a decline in vocations, a lay principal was appointed to Coláiste Ris in Westport. The Christian Brothers finally left Westport in 2002 after a period of some 137 years. In Ballinrobe, the Christian Brothers looked after boys' education from 1876 until 1990. Dr. Noel Browne, a former pupil, records memories of his days at this CBS school in his autobiography *Against the Tide*.

Franciscans and De La Salle

The Franciscan Brothers came to Errew in 1839 and opened a monastery and primary school on land provided by Mayo-born James Hardiman (1782-1855), author and first librarian of Galway University. The monastery became a centre for training of teachers and monks, who founded monasteries elsewhere in Connaught.

The De La Salle Brothers arrived in Castlebar in 1888 to teach at the newly opened St. Patrick's primary school. The school was totally destroyed by fire in 1956 and the new St. Patrick's National School dates from 1961. The building known today as the Parochial Centre stands on the site of the original school. The De La Salle Brothers also taught at St. Gerard's Secondary College, which opened in 1908 and moved to a new building in 1971.

Oideachas trí Gaeilge – Education through Irish

The first Irish language college in Mayo, Coláiste Chonnacht, was founded by Conradh na Gaeilge in Tuar Mhic Éadaigh or Tourmakeady in 1905. Conradh withdrew its support for the college when the Catholic Church opposed its selection of a Mr. Henry, a graduate of Trinity College Dublin, to replace Michael Walsh, the first headmaster. The college continued and many notable people attended it, including Sinéad Bean de Valera, author and wife of President Éamon de Valera, and the notable Republican Seán Ryan. Pádraic Pearse, editor of *An Claidheamh Soluis* and signatory of the 1916 Proclamation, was an examiner for the college and the Galway poet Pádraic Ó Conaire was one of its teachers.

After 1922, the Department of Education established special Preparatory Teacher-Training Schools in an effort to revitalise the Irish language. Tuar Mhic Éadaigh was chosen as one of the Irish-speaking districts suitable for such a centre. Established in 1931, the school continued until the 1950s under the management of the Sisters of Mercy, when it became a Class A boarding school run by the nuns. In 1961, it became a day school for girls, then a co-educational secondary school from September 1987, and finally passed into local community ownership in 1992.

New developments

Attendance at full-time education has become compulsory for all children between 6 and 16 years, although most begin school in the September following their fourth birthday. The revised primary school curriculum, launched in 1999, encourages a rich variety of approaches to teaching and learning, and includes language, mathematics, social, environmental and

(Above left) Pupils of St. Angela's National School in Castlebar during 2001

(Above centre) Mary Bourke, the 'Lollipop Lady', busy helping Swinford's school children safely across the road

(Above right) Children at play in the Social Services Pre-School in Castlebar

Students receiving certificates at
St. Catherine's Training Centre, Ballina

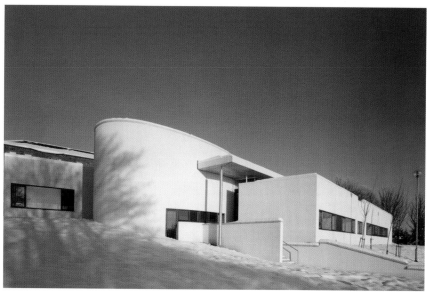

The award-winning, purpose-built
Mayo Education Support Centre in
Castlebar

scientific education, arts, and physical, social and health education. The second-level education sector consists of secondary, vocational, community and comprehensive schools, organised in a 3-year junior cycle followed by a 2- or 3-year senior cycle, aimed at preparing students for adult life.

Relatives and child-minders have traditionally played a significant role in the care and education of pre-school children. Regulated childcare facilities and services registered with the Western Health Board have grown within Mayo in recent decades. Increased participation of women in the labour force is one of the factors in the increased demand for childcare services.

Among the many new pre-schools, catering for children aged between 3 and 5 years, that have opened in Mayo are two in Castlebar and Ballyhaunis with the specific purpose of fostering the education needs of

'Arts in Schools Project' – one of the many programmes run by the Arts Office of Mayo County Council

the travelling community. Other educational centres catering for the travelling community include St. Catherine's Training Centre in Ballina, which was established to encourage students to continue their education. It offers a wide range of educational and training experiences, including sports, arts and personal development.

Mayo Education Support Centre (Ionad Oideachais Mhaigh Eo) in Castlebar is part of the national network of 20 full-time centres established to support educational innovation and to deliver training for those within the educational community. The centre, now operating from purpose-built offices with a full-time staff, provides in-service training, co-ordinates teacher support groups and offers a resource library and administrative support for the wider school community.

The Arts Office of Mayo County Council undertakes numerous initiatives designed to promote the arts and has been proactive in supporting creative activity in schools. The Arts Office sponsors a number of programmes in schools, including residencies by well-known writers and artists who work directly with pupils to develop their creative skills. The Mayo Arts Squad is another project sponsored by the Arts Office, aimed at providing hands-on creative experiences to pupils throughout the county, such as workshops in music, dance and the visual arts. The Arts Office's programmes concentrate on literature, drama and sculpture. However, Mayo's musical tradition is not neglected. A number of events are organised to showcase the county's vibrant musical scene and develop talent.

Chapter 10

Music

Traditional music is thriving in Mayo today, a testimony to its vibrant character in a county where tunes have been recorded since the 18th century. The harp was the dominant musical instrument in early Ireland, eventually becoming the emblem for the country. Two of Mayo's better known harpists were Foxford-native Charles Fanning (b. 1736) and Hugh Higgins (b. 1837) from Tirawley. Fanning was a prizewinner at the 1792 Belfast Harp Festival, organised by folklore collector Edward Bunting to record and revive traditional harp music. Higgins became blind at a young age and survived as a wandering musician. In both aspects, he followed in the footsteps of a master – Turlough O'Carolan (1670-1738), the renowned Bardic poet-composer from Nobber, Co. Meath, who has become synonymous with the harp throughout Ireland. Carolan was blinded by smallpox at the age of 18 and led a nomadic life as an itinerant harper, visiting and playing music for his patrons around the country. His Mayo patrons included the Dillons and Beytaghs of Mannin House in Achadh Mór, the Brabazons of Swinford, the Burkes of Castlebar, Colonel Manus O'Donel of Newport, the Brownes of Westport and Mrs. Garvey of Murrisk. He composed several tunes in their honour, including *Seóirse Brabazon*, which was recorded by The Chieftains in 1969, and *Thomas Burke*, recorded by Gráinne Yeats in 1992. In fact, two Mayo O'Carolan tunes – *Fanny Dillon* and *James Beytagh*, composed at Mannin – were published in the very first book of 'traditional' ancient Irish music by John and William Neale in Dublin in 1724.

Among native Mayo poets and musicians who wrote in the Bardic tradition were Riocard Bairéad (1739-1819), Antoine Ó Raifteirí (1779-1835) and Tomás Ó Caiside (c. 1705-75), an Augustinian friar of Ballyhaunis, known as *An Caisideach Bán*. Riocard Bairéad was from Belmullet and became known as the Bard of Erris. A hedge schoolmaster with a natural talent for verse, he composed satirical ballads and songs in Irish, reminiscent of the ancient bards. His works were written during a period of great decline in Gaelic civilisation when the Bardic poets were almost eclipsed. Antoine Ó Raifteirí, perhaps Mayo's most famous poet,

Matt Molloy of The Chieftains, playing outside his well-known public house in Westport

ANTHONY RAFFERTY IRISH
MINSTREL DIED OCT. 1835 ÆT. 51.

The last of the Gaelic bards—
Antoine Ó Raifteirí (1779-1835)
from Killeadan

was born in Killeaden, near Kiltimagh. He was the son of a weaver and,
like Carolan and other harpists, lost his sight in childhood. Although
Ó Raifteirí played the fiddle, he is best known for his songs and poems,
following in the tradition of travelling musicians seeking the support of
patrons. His poems were later collected by Douglas Hyde (1860-1949) and
Lady Gregory (1852-1932) at the turn of the century. They also collected
the memories of the old people who remembered the poet. Ó Raifteirí's
poetry provides a modern example of Bardic-style praise-poetry and a
contemporary record of Irish political and social history.

The accordion and fiddle have been the most common musical
instruments in Mayo for the last one hundred years. The concertina or
melodeon (a single row accordion) became extremely popular all over the
county for house dances in the late 19th and early 20th centuries. It is
notable that the first recording of traditional music on accordion was
made by John Heburn of Breaffy, Castlebar, and the USA. Pockets of
melodeon-style accordion still flourish near Crossmolina and in the
Knock – Achadh Mór area. Nigel Davey of Carracastle and David
Munnelly of Belmullet are two of the leading young exponents of the
accordion at present.

Three fiddle players are particularly associated with the composition
of tunes in the traditional idiom. John McGrath of Erris (1900-59) spent
most of his life in the USA and has dozens of tunes attributed to him,

many of which are still widely played, including *The Providence* or *Rossport Reel* and *Séan Sa Cheo*, which takes its name from the mountain in McGrath's native Ros Dubhach. His nephew, Vincent McGrath, keeps up the tradition and has also released a CD of his own compositions. Brendan Tonra of Gowel, Charlestown, another exile in the USA, has also composed and published scores of popular melodies. Martin Ruane of Aghaward, Foxford, was another composer of complex and beautiful tunes (so far unpublished). At present, tunes for the fiddle are being composed by artists such as Emer Mayock, Joe Byrne, Vereena Cummins, David Munnelly, Pádraic O'Láimhin, Séamas Heneghan and Paddy Mills.

Ballina Brass Band, c. 1900, with a 'Who fears to speak of '98?' banner

Music and dancing were the main form of social life and each townland generally had its own céilí house. Fiddlers, pipers and accordion players provided the music for dancing jigs, reels and polkas. Not all music-loving houses owned musical instruments and lilting or 'mouth music' was found throughout the county. After World War II, there was a decrease in house dances due in part to the increased enforcement of the Dance Halls Act, 1935, but the strength of the tradition ensured the music's survival.

Fife and drum, or flute bands became a common sight in Mayo from the late 19th century, notably at Land League and Temperance rallies. Most parishes in Mayo, particularly in the east of the county, had at least one flute band. Mayo bands included the Knock Fife Band, Kilmovee Fife

Foxford Céilí Band

Kilaturley Fife and Flute band

Balla Pipe Band, July 1972

and Drum Band, Killasser Marching Band and bands from Bohola, Charlestown, Foxford, Bonniconlon, Carracastle and Lacken, as well as the more recently formed Raifteirí Pipe Band from Kiltimagh. Some parishes had two and even three such bands. For example, there were bands in Glann, Kilmovee and Kilkelly in Kilmovee parish and in Doocastle, Carracastle and Rooskey in Carracastle parish. The Carracastle band was formed at the end of the 19th century and became known as the United Irish League Band, with the motto 'United we stand, Divided we fall'; it continues to perform on special occasions to this day. The Balla Pipe Band was founded in the early 1930s by Tommy Joe McWalter and was known locally as the LDF Band (Local Defence Force), later reformed as the St. Cronan's Pipe Band. The band has won many awards and was chosen to welcome US President Reagan on his visit to Ashford Castle in 1984 and also to lead the 1991 St. Patrick's Day Parade down New York's

Fifth Avenue. The Midfield Pipe Band, the Keel Pipe Band and the Dooagh Pipe Band continue Mayo's piping tradition today.

There has been an extensive piping tradition throughout Mayo since the 1700s. The Wallace brothers of Erris, Michael and Frank, born in the 1800s, were noted pipers and were described by the great piper Dinny Delaney as being the best pipers he had ever heard. Thomas 'Piper' Killeen (1828-1906) of Ballyglass, Claremorris, a noted piper in mid-Mayo, is reputed to have composed some famous tunes, including *The Lark in the Morning*, and played regularly for the Brownes of Claremont, the Blakes of Towerhill and the Moores of Moore Hall. Michael Carney (b. 1868) of Irishtown in south Mayo was also an outstanding piper; his solo recordings on cylinder, and later on 78 vinyl, with James Morrison are exceptional. Three generations of pipers of the Carney family are said to have played on the platform at the first Davitt Land League meeting in Irishtown in 1879. Carney later emigrated to the USA, where he taught pipes and became a pipe-maker. Another Mayoman, Kevin Hennelly of Castlebar, became one of the most renowned pipe-makers in Chicago after emigrating there. Edward Mullaney (b. 1885) of Kiltimagh and Chicago was another outstanding emigrant piper who made a number of recordings. His cousin, Jim Shannon of Kiltimagh and the USA, is a fine piper today and has also recorded extensively. The piping tradition continues in Mayo with such musicians as Joseph O'Grady, Ciarán Ó Máille, Vinnie Kilduff, Pádraic Langan, Pádraic Lavin, Emer Mayock and Eamon Walsh.

Piper Killeen of Carrahall, near Ballyglass, Claremorris

Ballad singing has a long tradition in Mayo, as is evident from Patrick Tunney's (1887-1951) collection *Songs and Ballads from the Vales of Mayo*. Several of Tunney's songs are still popular, such as *Flowery Sweet Mayo*. The ballad boom of the 1960s was preceded by the celebrated folk singer Delia Murphy (1902-71), who brought an essential element of traditional music to her singing. She grew up in Mount Jennings House, Hollymount – 'a big house' purchased by her father after making his fortune in the gold mines of North America. Delia acquired her love of traditional ballads from her firm friend Tom Maughan, the 'tinker's son', who taught her ballads as they walked to school together. Indeed, it was from him she learned *If I were a Blackbird*, which she was later to make famous all over Ireland. Delia became one of the most requested singers on Radio Éireann, with such songs as *The Spinning Wheel*, *Three Lovely Lassies from Bannion* and *The Moonshiner*.

In 1925, Delia married Dr. Tom Kiernan, who was shortly afterwards appointed Ireland's High Commissioner in London. During their married life, they lived in several countries including Australia, Germany, Canada and the USA. While Dr. Kiernan worked as a career diplomat, Delia combined her part-time singing career and family life with her role as hostess, often using her voice to entertain government ministers, churchmen, statesmen and literary figures throughout the world. She was a natural performer who developed an immediate rapport with her

*Musicans playing on Swinford's Main
Street during the Fleadh Ceoil of 1961*

audiences and made a great impact on the Irish entertainment scene. Many generations were raised listening to her singing and she did much to revive a love of Irish folk songs.

Traditional music has not remained static and modern instruments, such as guitars and bouzoukis, today accompany the traditional instruments of the uilleann (elbow) pipes, flute, tin whistle, fiddle and accordion. In 1950, Comhaltas Ceoltóirí Éireann was founded to promote Irish traditional music in all its forms. Two of its founding members were Séamus Ó Dubhthaigh from Achadh Mór and Manus O'Donnell from Achill. The Fleadh Ceoil, an All-Ireland three-day festival of Irish music, is held annually in different host towns throughout the country. The Fleadh was held in Mayo on three occasions – in Swinford in 1961 and in Ballina in 1997 and 1998.

An event held to celebrate 5,000 years of rural settlement, culture and heritage in Mayo had an extraordinary effect on the popularity of Irish music and dance throughout the world. The multi-media event *Spirit of Mayo* was a major part of the 1993 year-long festival *Mayo 5000*. Irish dancing champions Michael Flatley, Jean Butler and Colin Dunne performed in the dance section of the *Spirit of Mayo* show. Subsequently, producers John McColgan and Moya Doherty chose Flatley and Butler (whose parents hailed from Knock and Ballyhaunis) to feature in the intermission act for the 1994 Eurovision Song Contest, being hosted by Ireland that year. The spectacular seven-minute dance segment, entitled *Riverdance*, electrified the audience not only in Dublin's Point Theatre but also on television screens throughout the world. The performance ignited a new phenomenon and changed the face of Irish dancing forever. From an idea first expressed in *Spirit of Mayo* emerged *Riverdance – The Show,* which has inspired multi-million dollar Irish dance stage shows, including *Lord of the Dance, Dancing on Dangerous Ground* and *Feet of Flames.*

Limerick-man Bill Whelan composed the music, the *Millennium Suite,* for the *Spirit of Mayo* show, while Paddy Glacken, who has connections with north Mayo, hosted the traditional music segment. Anúna, the national professional Choral Group, worked with Mayo Choirs who performed in the show. Grainne Hambly, from Claremorris, one of the most promising young harpists in Ireland today, performed in the *Millennium Suite* as a member of the National Folk Orchestra. She released her first solo harp album in 1999, entitled *Between the Showers,* and included traditional dance music as well as three pieces by Carolan. When Maire Bhreathnach decided to leave *Riverdance,* Eileen Ivers, whose parents came from Mayo, was then chosen as fiddle player.

The village of Straide boasts the musical success of three members of the Smyth family – Cora, Breda and Seán, all of whom are medical doctors. After playing in the *Millennium Suite,* Cora Smyth was the solo fiddle accompanist to Brendan Graham's 1996 Eurovision song *The Voice,* performed by Eimear Quinn, which won the contest for Ireland that year. Together with her sister Breda, Cora starred in *The Lord of the Dance* stage show. Breda released her first album in 2002. Their brother, Seán Smyth, is an All-Ireland champion on both fiddle and whistle, with a magnificent flowing style. He released his first solo album, *The Blue Fiddle,* in 1993 and in 1997 was instrumental in forming the acclaimed quintet called Lúnasa.

Many talented traditional musicians have emerged in Mayo in recent decades. Among them is uilleann-piper and whistle-player Vinnie Kilduff, a native of Knock. A music performer and producer, Vinnie has played with U2 on their album *October,* as well as with a number of other well-known bands including In Tua Nua, General Humbert (of which Mary Black was also a member), the Rocking Chairs (who had the hit *Stuck in the Driving Rain*), the Waterboys and Clannad.

A major force in traditional music, Martin Donoghue (1923-89), from Ballindine, was taught to play the melodeon from an early age by his mother. A founder member of the Disabled Drivers Association of Ireland, Martin was an accomplished musician, composer and member of the céilí band An Tostal. He was also a talented teacher and the current healthy state of traditional music in Mayo can, in part, be attributed to him. His pupils include such notable musicians as Séamus Egan and Emer Mayock. Séamus Egan is a founding member of the acclaimed Irish-American band Solas. He also wrote the score for the 1995 hit movie *The Brothers McMullen* and, more recently, composed the music for *Dancing on Dangerous Ground,* starring Jean Butler, formerly of *Riverdance.* Flautist and piper Emer Mayock from Ross West, outside Castlebar, has released a number of solo albums and recorded with the Afro-Celt Sound System.

David Munnelly, composer and accordion-player from Belmullet, has achieved prominence in recent years. Performing with the finest musicians in traditional music, including Dé Danann and Sharon Shannon, he has also recorded with The Chieftains. His first solo album, *Swing*, featured Sharon Shannon, tenor-saxophonist Richie Buckley and fellow-Dé Danann member Andrew Murray. Munnelly also played on the sound track of the film *The Mammy*.

From Lacken in north Mayo, a brother and sister team form part of the talented group of traditional musicians known as Osna. Pádraic and Treasa Lavin play the uilleann pipes and low tin whistle, respectively. Other members of the group are Daraigh O'Reilly (vocals) and Johnny Towey (accordion). Osna have built a solid reputation with their tight, well-balanced sound.

The group Céide is comprised of five accomplished musicians – Foxford's Tom Doherty on accordion, melodeon and snare drum, John McHugh on fiddle, Kevin Doherty on double bass, Brian Lennon on flute and whistles, and Declan Asken on guitar and vocals. The group first started to play together at a regular Sunday evening session in Chieftain-member Matt Molloy's pub in Westport. They play both traditional and contemporary songs and arrangements, and launched their debut album, *Like a Wild Thing*, in 2001, the title track of which was written by Westport singer-songwriter Tony Reidy.

The county town, Castlebar, is home of the renowned singer-songwriter John Hoban. John plays the fiddle, guitar, mondocello, banjo and harmonica. He has performed on Sharon Shannon's album *The Diamond Mountain Sessions* and accompanied Steve Earle and Jackson Browne, as well as releasing a number of solo albums.

The interest among young people in traditional music is due, in large part, to the many excellent music teachers throughout the county. Their role in ensuring the future of the tradition cannot be overemphasized. Among them was the late Martin Donoghue from Ballindine (*see above*), whose pupils – including his daughter Bernie Geraghty, Tom Doherty from Foxford, and the brothers John and Noel Kilkenny from Castlebar – all became music teachers themselves. Other notable Mayo teachers are Walter McEvilly from Ballintubber, Rob Thornborough from Swinford, John Hoban from Castlebar, Peter Neary from Bofield and Mary Finn who taught in the Westport and Louisburgh areas.

Joe Byrne, a flautist from Achadh Mór, has provided a major service in chronicling and preserving a record of Mayo's traditional musicians, music and song through Dreolín Community Arts publications, which are a treasure trove of information on flute, whistle, box-playing, fiddler music and singers from East Mayo. Joe is also a broadcaster and hosts a music show on the local radio station, Mid-West Radio, offering a lively and informative guide to Mayo's songs and music.

Dance bands and country music

In the 1930s and '40s, while Delia Murphy was leading the revival of interest in folk songs, dance halls began appearing all over the county. Touring dance bands, such as the Stephen Garvey Orchestra (Castlebar), Tony Chambers Band (Newport), Brose Walsh Orchestra (Belcarra) and Jack Ruane Band (Ballina), enjoyed many years on the dance hall circuit, drawing huge crowds week after week. Many of the early halls had no mains electricity or public address systems, and so car batteries had to be used by the bands for amplification. After a little over an hour, the batteries belonging to the band's cars would be used up and the batteries of car-owners attending the dance were then called upon to keep the music going until 2 or 3 in the morning.

Stephen Garvey (1902-62), born in Castlebar's Castle Street, came to prominence when he was chosen to lead the first dance orchestra on Radio Éireann. In 1926, he formed the Stephen Garvey Orchestra and toured extensively throughout Ireland and Britain. The 1930s was the 'big band era' and Garvey was the king of music in Mayo. The members of the band changed over the years, at one time including Val Doonican. Garvey's interest in music extended to the production of Gilbert and Sullivan operas. He also produced *Little Red Riding Hood*, the first musical pantomime staged in the Town Hall, Castlebar, in February 1922. He retired in 1956, after 40 years in show business, and later died in the USA. His final wish was fulfilled when he was re-interred in Castlebar in 1996. Castlebar Urban

Musicians (left to right) Brian Scahill, John Kilkenny, Joe Skelton, François Rossi and Rosaleen Ward – playing in a music session in a Castlebar pub

La Salle, winners of the Castlear International Song Contest, which ran from 1967 to 1988

District Council unveiled a plaque to his memory in 1978 at his former home in Castle Street.

The legendary Tony Chambers (1922-2001), a native of Newport, performed in every hall in Mayo during his 60 years on the dance band circuit. His career began in 1937 when he joined a local céilí band. Two years later, he joined the Twilight Serenaders and then, in December 1948, formed the Tony Chambers Band, in which he played both fiddle and saxophone. The Glenn Miller composition *In the Mood* became the band's signature tune. In 1969, the Tony Chambers Band gave the inaugural performance at the Starlight Ballroom in Westport. In recognition of his musical contribution, Tony was acknowledged with a Hall of Fame Entertainment Award in 1980 by *The Connaught Telegraph*. He was chosen as the dance band leader in the joint RTE/BBC film adaption of William Trevor's famous novel *Ballroom of Romance*, filmed on location in Ballycroy in 1982. He also provided the musical accompaniment for Mary Black on her albums *Tired and Emotional* and *Love me or Leave me*.

The illustrious career of Brose Martin Walsh (1920-95) spanned 57 years in the world of dance band music. A native of Belcarra, outside Castlebar, Brose first played the button accordion at the local dance hall in French Hill. He was a gifted musician on both accordion and saxophone, as well as being an accomplished singer. He formed his own orchestra during the difficult years of the 1940s and recruited musicians from around the country. The popular instrumental hit *Zambezi* became synonymous with the Brose Walsh Orchestra. From the early 1960s, the band had an annual engagement in the Ierne Ballroom in Dublin on the eve of the All-Ireland Football Final. Renamed the Rockaways, the band recorded numerous tapes and CDs.

In tandem with the dance and showband scene, country music has enjoyed phenomenal popularity in Mayo, especially since the 1960s. The first superstars of country music – Jim Reeves, George Jones, Johnny Cash, Charley Pride, Merle Haggard, Buck Owens and Slim Whitman – were made popular on the airwaves of international pirate radio stations. Soon the big Irish showbands of the era began to feature more and more country in their programmes and 'country and western', as it was better known then, quickly became the music of the people. Tom Dunphy from Waterford, co-lead singer of the famous Royal Showband, was among the early pioneers, along with Shay Hutchinson of the Melody Aces.

The Smokey Mountain Ramblers were perhaps the first truly authentic 'all country' band in Ireland, enjoying great popularity in Mayo. Brian Coll from Omagh, who fronted the Plattermen and later his own band, the Buckaroos, carved out a special niche and was another of the leading pioneers of country. Without doubt, the singer and band that won the most plaudits and commanded the most loyalty among country followers in Mayo was Big Tom McBride and the Mainliners. Songwriter Johnny McCauley from Derry captured the essence of the era with his plaintive lyrics of childhood memories and longing for home. Among his best-known compositions are *Four Country Roads, I'll Settle for the Shores of Ireland* and *Cottage on the borderline of Galway and Mayo*.

Week after week throughout the 1960s, '70s and '80s, country singers rolled into the dance halls of Mayo – from Toreen to Pontoon, from 'The Beaten Path' near Claremorris to 'The Travellers' Friend' in Castlebar. Big Tom, Ray Lynam, Gene Stuart, Roly Daniels, Brendan Shine, Brian Coll, John Glenn, the Cotton Mill Boys, Margo O'Donnell, Phil Begley, Susan McCann, Larry Cunningham, Johnny McEvoy – these were just a few of the big names on the country scene to play the Mayo ballroom circuit in those years. A new batch of singers arrived in the mid- and late '80s with the advent of local 'pirate' stations, including Daniel O'Donnell, Mick Flavin, Declan Nerney, John Hogan and Paddy O'Brien.

Mayo's best-known country performer is, perhaps, Frank McCaffrey from Westport, the only artist from Mayo contracted to the prominent London-based Ritz Records Company. Involved in the country scene since the 1970s, Frank, together with Kieran Murphy from Ballinrobe, was a member of Margo's band for some years. He later fronted the Country Folk and other bands before going solo in the '80s. Today, he is in constant demand, still touring the English and Irish circuits.

Kevin Prendergast from Ballyhaunis has been popular since his first performances on the Radio Éireann music programme *Ceili House* in the 1960s. Kevin, who is based in Manchester but spends a few months of the year touring Ireland, has sold many thousands of albums since the mid-1980s. He has also performed on a number of occasions at shows in the USA.

All over Mayo today, there are local groups and singers who make a regular living from the country and Irish scene. Several of them have recorded their own CDs and albums, and have secured extensive exposure on local radio stations, which have played a major role in nurturing the

Frank McCaffrey is one of Mayo's best-loved country performers

ÉIRE 30 Margaret Burke-Sheridan 1889-1958
1989

Stamp, designed by Karl Uhlemann, issued in 1989 for the centenary of the birth of the famous soprano, Margaret Burke Sheridan – featuring a portrait of the singer by Gaetano de Gennaro, with a scene from La Bohème in the background

deep-rooted love of country music in the western region. The daily country music programmes of Mid-West Radio attract a considerable listenership, not only in Mayo but also in the neighbouring counties. Community Radio Castlebar also features a number of regular weekly country shows.

Country and traditional Irish music have a huge cross-over audience and many musicians are equally at home in either genre. Many country singers have taken on board some of the old Irish ballads, such as *The Boys from the County Mayo, The Rose of Mooncoin* and *The Homes of Donegal*, and made them an integral part of their repertoire. Country songs seem to resonate in a deeper way in areas where there is a tradition of emigration, finding fertile ground in Mayo by seemingly tapping into the folk memories of those emigrants who may have left the land behind but never forgot it. The music continues to play a major social role, retaining a special emotional attachment both for emigrants and for those living in Mayo.

Opera and Classical Music

Opera and classical music command a small, but nonetheless enthusiastic audience in Mayo and a number of talented singers and composers have emerged from within the county. Margaret Burke Sheridan (1889-1958) remains the best-known opera singer from Mayo. Born in Castlebar in 1889, the youngest of five surviving children of local postmaster John Burke Sheridan and his wife Ellen Cooley, Margaret came to be regarded as one of the greatest sopranos of all time. She captivated audiences in the leading opera houses of Europe, notably Milan's La Scala, Rome's Teatro Reale, Naples' San Carlo and London's Covent Garden.

Margaret was orphaned at the age of 11 and sent to boarding school in the Dominican Convent in Eccles Street, Dublin (also attended by Delia Murphy). She later attended the Royal Academy of Music in London and studied under Martini and Emma Corelli in Rome. In 1918, she made her operatic debut as Mimi in Puccini's *La Bohème* at La Constanzia in Rome. The following year, she made her Covent Garden debut as Cio-Cio-San, the lead role in *Madame Butterfly*. Puccini first heard Margaret sing in Milan in 1919, when she was again performing the lead role in his *Madame Butterfly*. He subsequently coached her for the lead in his *Manon Lescaut*, perhaps her most famous part. Burke Sheridan continued to charm audiences for many years with outstanding performances in operas by Puccini, Mascagni and Respighi, among others. When she died in Dublin in 1958, Seán T. O'Kelly, President of Ireland, recalled that when he 'first met the girl from Mayo who was to become, and for many years to remain, one of Italy's most admired, most beloved prima donnas . . . she was young and full of gaiety and charm, sparkling, radiant and devoted to her act'. John Feeney, who was born in Swinford in 1903 was one of the most popular Irish-American tenors of the twentieth century. A plaque now marks his birthplace in the town.

Patrick Cassidy (1956-), born in Claremorris, is one of Ireland's most important composers of classical music. His compositions have been described as following the Hiberno-Baroque tradition, frequently drawing

'A rave' in a Castlebar nightclub

on Irish legends and epic poetry, and reflecting a fusion of Irish themes with formal classical European forms. In this, he follows in the style of the famous composer Seán O'Riada. Cassidy's first album, *Cruit* in 1989, was an arrangement of 17th and 18th-century melodies for harp played by a Baroque ensemble. His composition *The Children of Lir* was released in 1993 and his new orchestration of *Deirdre of the Sorrows* in 1998. Cassidy has also written music for the feature film *Broken Harvest* and his 'A Famine Remembrance Symphony' in Neo-Classical style was a specially commissioned work to commemorate the 150th anniversary of the Great Famine.

Rock, pop, blues and folk

Like most Irish counties, Mayo has seen a proliferation of rock bands and singer-songwriters in the 1980s and '90s. To respond to the needs of these artists, a seminar, the first of its kind, on 'Careers in Music' was organised by Mayo County Council in September 2001. The event culminated in a 'showcase' concert, featuring some of the better known acts emerging from the area – the Dennis McCalmont Band, Definitely Blue, and Reverie.

The Dennis McCalmont Band are a five-piece 'funky-folky pop-rock combo', as their publicity material states, centred around the song-writing nucleus of Derry-born McCalmont. He released an album of original songs in 1998 entitled *The Language of My Soul.* The band released its first single, *Songs of Perfection,* in 2001 and toured nationwide, getting favourable reviews in the national and regional press. The band is currently planning another album and touring locally.

From Westport, Definitely Blue are purveyors of heavy rock with a strong pop sensibility. Their hook-laden and riff-heavy brand of melodic rock has seen them reach the threshold of big things here at home, with the release of their single *Summer's Gone*. Getting rave reviews for their demo tape in *Hot Press* and recording a session for the Dave Fanning Show on Radio 2FM have brought them to the forefront of the new wave of rock bands in the country.

The technological revolution in music has not bypassed Mayo, with the county's most recent chart success coming in the form of two remix versions of classic Irish songs. *The Lonesome Boatman*, and even more successfully *The Fields of Athenry*, have been chart hits for Castlebar's Cox's Crew. Centred around the studio expertise of disc jockey Johnny Oosten and sound engineer Ronan Courell, both tracks were rejuvenated and went down a storm with dance-techno fans. The presence of the state-of-the-art recording studio Westlink in Castlebar is an asset to the music industry of the county. In terms of venues, the Travellers' Friend Hotel is on the circuit for major touring DJs and celebrities, including Boy George who compèred a disco there in 2002.

Castlebar is also famous for its annual Blues Festival, held on the June Bank Holiday weekend each year. Attracting some of the biggest names in blues music, the festival has established itself as 'a must' for fans. The 2002 programme included Irish blues singer Mary Coughlan and legendary guitarist Jeff Lang.

Other festivals in the county include the Féile Iorras International Folk Arts Festival, taking place in Belmullet every July. The festival has grown from humble origins to its present status as one of the finest folk festivals in all of Ireland. Featuring a mix of international and Irish folk artists, it has hosted since its inception in 1996 such luminaries as Andy Irvine, Seán Keane, the Sawdoctors, Sharon Shannon, Don Baker, Ronnie Drew and Eleanor Shanley, as well as a plethora of groups from South America, Europe and Africa. Other important festivals include Scoil Acla, an annual festival of Irish music in Achill, Féile Chois Chuain in Louisburgh, and Ceol na Locha in Tourmakeady, all of which make important contributions to Mayo's music scene.

The pop world has not been untouched by the hand of Mayo either. Pop Svengali-figure Louis Walsh, a native of Kiltimagh, has risen to the top of the pop industry through perseverance and a keen eye for young talent. Having successfully managed the careers of the likes of Eurovision-winners Johnny Logan and Linda Martin, Louis then turned his eye to 'manufactured' boybands, after having seen the meteoric rise of the English group Take That. The result was the creation of Boyzone, who went on to achieve massive success worldwide. Louis followed this with another spectacular boyband – Westlife. He also promoted Samantha Mumba and Ireland's *Pop Idol* TV show-winners Six. He took over as manager of Scottish '60s singer Lulu and oversaw her come-back during the 1990s.

Mayo's new generation of musicians represents an impressive array of talent in various genres, encompassing traditional, blues, jazz, rock and classical music. All this talent is fuelled and influenced by many earlier generations of Mayo musicians, but given new expression and impetus by the artistry of a new generation. Mayo's proud musical tradition deserves fuller study. In the meantime, a select discography of traditional music recordings of the county is provided on the following pages.

Discography of Mayo's Traditional Musicians and Performers

Compiled by **Joe Byrne, Achadh Mór**

Fiddle

Duffy, Johnny (Charlestown) and Healy, Tommie (flute, Curry), *Memories of Sligo* (Ossian, OSS 46).

Fidiléirí: 22 Mayo Fiddlers (double cassette and book, Dreolín 005/006).

Henry, Johnny (Doocastle), *O'Riada Collection*.

Henry, Johnny (Doocastle), *The Coleman Archive, Vol. 1* (CD CC5).

Hoban, John (fiddle and banjo, Castlebar), *Sruthán* (CMCD 003).

McGreevy, Jimmy (Mayo and USA), *McGreevy and Cooley* (cassette, GTD 1021).

Smyth, Seán (Straide), *The Blue Fiddle* (Lun. CD 060).

Tonra, Brendan (Gowel, Charlestown), *The Music of Brendan Tonra* (cassette and book of original fiddle tunes).

Song

A Bar of a Song, including Séamas O'Dubhthaigh (Achadh Mór), Cómhaltas Ceoltóirí Éireann (cassette).

Amhrán ar an Sean Nós (Ó Dhún a nGall, Muigh Eo, etc.), including Tomás O'Domhnaill (Oileán Acla) and Pádraic Ó Maolruaidh (Tuar Mhic Éadaigh) (CD and book, RTE).

Cantan agus Cotillion: Songs and Music of Nan Morrsi (compilation), performed by various Mayo artists (Foxford, Dreolín 006).

Fadgin, Johnny (Westport), *Sticks for the Reek* (cassette).

Gallagher, Mickey (Attymass), *Songs and Stories* (CD and book, Dreolín 012).

Glór Mhaigh Eo (compilation), including Tomás Ó Máille (Tuar Mhic Éadaigh), Pádraic Ó Maolruaidh (Tuar Mhic Éadaigh), Cáit Nic Suibhne (Acaill), Donncha Ó Gallchóbhair (Acaill), Micheál Ó Seighin (Ros Dubhach), Micheál Ó Conghaíle and Fiachra O'Mungain (Iorras), (CIC.D 125).

Hoban, John (Castlebar), *John Hoban* (CD).

Keating, Charlie (Westport), *When the weakest are maltreated* (Idle Wall, CD single)

Lavelle, Mick (Westport), *The Lotto Man* (cassette).

Mac Dhonnagáin, Tadgh (Achadh Mór), *Solas Gorm* (original songs, Gael Linn vinyl and cassette).

Mac Dhonnagáin, Tadgh (Achadh Mór), *Bliain na Amhrán* (12 songs for children).

Mac Dhonnagáin, Tadgh (Achadh Mór), *Raiftéirí San underground* (original songs, CC. CD 094).

McHale, Tom (Bangor), *Songs from Erris* (00A GV102801).

Ó Maolruaidh, Pádraic (Tuar Mhic Éadaigh), *Songs and Seanchas* (CD and book, Dreolín 015, May 2002).

O'Toole, Johnny (Louisburgh), *From the Heart* (CD).

Reidy, Tony (Aughagower), *Will you ever get sense?* (cassette).

Reidy, Tony (Aughagower), *Bertra Beach* (original songs).

Reidy, Tony (Aughagower), *The Coldest Day in Winter* (original songs, TR CD 01).

Songs of Past and People, I (1994), Songs and singers from East Mayo (cassette and book, Dreolín 001).

Songs of Past and People, II (1995), Songs and singers from East Mayo (double cassette and book, Dreolín 005/006).

Flute/Whistle

Doyle, Tom (flute, Bohola) and Cashin, Michael (flute, Leitrim), *Fluters of Old Erin* (cassette, Viva Voce 002; original Victor Chicage 1928).

Egan, Séamas, (Foxford and Philadelphia) *When Juniper Sleeps* (Shanachie 79097).

Fíf agus Fideóg, 24 fluters and whistlers of East Mayo (double cassette and book, Dreolín 0010/0011).

Gavin, Michael (flute, Ballina), *Flags of Dublin* (vinyl).

Henry, Kevin (Doocastle), *One's Own Place*, including Johnny, Verona and Maggie Henry (CD, Bogfire 2001).

Kilduff, Vinnie (whistle, Knock), *The Boys from the Blue Hill* (Mulligan Lun. CD 050).

Mayock, Emer ((flute, Castlebar), *Merry Bits of Timber* (CD).

Mayock, Emer (flute, Castlebar), *Playground* (Is Mise 001).

Ryan, Thomas Bernard and Ryan, Mick Joe (Doocastle), *The Coleman Archive, Vol. 1* (CD CC5).

Sherlock, Roger (flute, Doocastle), *Bringing it all back home*, compilation CD (BBC, Z CD 844).

Sherlock, Roger, Maguire, Seán and Ryan, Mick Joe (Doocastle), *O'Riada Collection* (Outlet, vinyl).

Sherlock, Roger (solo flute), (vinyl, London).

Smyth, Breda (whistle, Straide), *Basil and Thyme* (JHRCD 001).

Harp/Mandolin/Guitar/Banjo

Belfast Harp Orchestra, *Carillon*, including Gráinne and Róisín Hambly (BHO 005).

Belfast Harp Orchestra, *Feasting with Carolan*, Clarshere, including Gráinne Hambly (BHO 006).

Egan, Séamus (banjo/flute), *A week in January* (CD and cassette, Shanachie 65005).

Gaughan, Dick (Mayo and Glasgow), *Coppers and Brass*, Irish and Scots dance music on guitar (cassette, OSS 41).

Hambly, Gráinne (harp, Claremorris), *Between the Showers* (Shamrock 1050-2).

Hambly, Gráinne (harp, Claremorris), *Ceol na Meala* (cassette).

Kelly, Laoise (harp, Westport), *Just Harp* (LK 001).

Kilkelly, Frank (guitar, Castlebar), *Accompanying Irish music on guitar* (CD and book, DMP CD 2001).

Kilkelly, Frank (guitar, Castlebar), *New Celtic Mandolin* (CDA CS 035).

Kilkenny, Noel (banjo, Castlebar) and Baynes, Mick (guitar, Castlebar), *First Take* (CD).

O'Regan, Brendan (mandolin/banjo), *A Change in the Weather* (Mulligan CLUN 056).

Scahill, Brian (banjo, Mayo Abbey), *Banjo* (CD).

Accordion

Boscaí Singil (1994), Ten single row and melodeon-style accordionists from East Mayo (Dreolín 002).

Cleary, Johnny (Claremorris), *Live Sessions* (GTD).

Cleary, Johnny (Claremorris), *Trad Music on Accordion* (GTD C110).

Davey, Nigel (Carracastle), *Brí* (CD).

Davey, Nigel (Carracastle), *The Accordion Sounds* (cassette).

Friel, Pat (Westport) and Grealis, Liam (fiddle, Louisburgh), *Humours of Westport* (CD and cassette, GTD C056).

Gannon, Fr. Peter, *The Musical Priest*, with Mary Friel on piano (cassette).

Geraghty, Bernie (Ballindine) and O'Brien, Monica (Kiltimagh), *Tongs by the Fire* (cassette, GTD HC091).

Heneghan, Séamus (Louisburgh), *Caught in the Surf*, including Heneghan family (CD, Surf 01).

McGrath, Vincent (Ros Dubhach), *Ó Cheartlár mo Chroí* (CD, original tunes, Rin na Rón).

Munnelly, David (Belmullet), *Swing* (DDCD 002).

O'Mongain, Séamus, O'Mongain, Fiachra (Dubh Thuama) and Cummins, Vereena (Ballina), *From East to West: Live Sessions* (CD).

Staunton, Mary (Tuar Mhic Éadaigh), *Bright Early Mornings*, (CD, accordion and songs, FMCD 001).

Triad, *Three from Trad*, including David Munnelly (Belmullet) on accordion.

Group music/Compilation

Achadh Mór/Knock Leeds Tour Group 1990, *Caise Cheoil* (cassette, Dreolín).

Beginish I, including Noel O'Grady, (bouzouki, Swinford), (CD, Inis 001).

Beginish II: Stormy Weather (CD, Inis 002).

Bofield Céilí Band, *100 years a growing* (CD and book, HB 0022).

Bofield Céilí Band, *From Bofield to Battery* (plus video, group music and solos, 2001).

Cáirde Crann Mór (music), including Carmel McGlynn, Jas Sheridan, Louise McEvaddy, Gráinne Kyne, Colette and Bernadette O'Loughlin, and John Donnellan (all Ballinrobe/Mayo Abbey).

Calua, *Bóthar gan briseadh*, including Pádraig Ó Broin (guitar, Castlebar).

Castlebar Live and Alive, compilation with various Mayo performers (CD, 1999-2000).

Céide, *Like a Wild Thing*, Westport-based group including John McHugh and Tommie and Kevin Doherty (CD, 2001).

Céilí Band (Westport), *Heather Breeze* (CD).

Celtic Airs and Ballads, including Michael Henry (Tuairín), 13 songs, compilation (BE JOCD).

Ceol Tigh Neachtain, including Seán, Breda and Cora Smyth, and Brendan O'Regan (CD).

Ceoltóirí Iorrais Part I, 20 musicians/singers (cassette, Erris).

Cobblestone Sessions, including Peter Gallagher (accordion, Bangor) and Michael and Peter O'Grady (fiddle and flute, Kilmovee), (Cob 001).

Egan, Séamus and Egan Family, *Séamus Egan* (Shanachie).

Fonnchaoi, with Vereena Cummins (accordion, Ballina), Julie Langan (fiddle, Newport) and Pádraig Ó Broin (guitar, Castlebar), (VJCD 001).

General Humbert I, Castlebar group with John Donegan, Shay Kavanagh, Ruairí Somers, Frank O'Reilly, Vinnie Kilduff and Mary Black (Gael Linn).

General Humbert II, Castlebar group with John Donegan, Shay Kavanagh, Ruairí Somers, Frank O'Reilly, Vinnie Kilduff and Mary Black (Gael Linn, CEFC 095).

Gráda, *Endeavour*, including Anne Marie O'Malley (lead singer, Crossmolina).

Hoban, John and friends, *Up Mayo* (and live music from Matt Molloy's), (CD, 1997).

Island Singers and Musicians, *A Taste of Clare Island* (Clare MC 001).

Lán Dóchais, compilation with various Mayo performers (no label).

Live from Lenehans, with Joe Carey (accordion), Paddy Mills (fiddle) and Pat Egan (guitar).

Lúnasa, *The Merry Sisters of Fate* (GLCD 1213).

Lúnasa, *Live*, led by Seán Smyth (fiddle, Straide), (Compass, B00005LN2I).

Lúnasa, *Otherworld* (GLCD 1200).

McHugh Family (Bekan), *Live in Connemara* (MCQ 002).

Meelick Foróige, *A Touch of Youth* (cassette, Perfect Leisure).

Music at Matt Molloy's, including Pádraic Morell, Peter Gallagher, Michael Conboy, Jimmy Murphy, Olcan Masterson, Seán, Cora and Breda Smyth, John and Kevin McHugh, Noel O'Grady, John Joe Geraghty, Liam Grealis, Pat Friel and Mick Lavelle (Real World, CDR W26).

Music in Exile, *Celebration of Cómhaltas in Leeds*, including John Ferguson, Pat McNicholas, Gaughans, Ruanes and Tommy McLoughlin (WES 20).

Musical Trip to the Coleman Country, including Mick McDermott (fiddle, Kilmovee) and Maria Lynn McHugh (piano, Foxford), (CD CCOOZ).

Osna, with Pádraic and Treasa Lavin (pipes and whistle, Lacken), Dara O'Reilly (guitar, Ballina) and John Towey (accordion, Kilmovee), *Osna* (CN CD 1002).

O'Toole, Patrick and friends, *Lovely Isle: Clare Island* (cassette).

Ragus, including Feargal O'Murchu (accordion/vocals, Moygownagh), (Gael Linn, RAG CD 002).

Solas, T*he Edge of Silence* (Shanachie 78046).

Solas, *The Hour before Dawn* (CD P113).

Solas, *Sunny Spells and Scattered Showers* (Shanachie 78010).

Sound of Sliabh Félim, *Dream of Eibhle*, including Paul Smyth (flute, Cill Moibhi).

Swallows Tail Céilí Band, *Hell for Leather*, including John McHugh (Foxford) and Michael Hurley (Achadh Mór).

The Fairy Dance, Celtic Collection, including Michael Henry, (Tuairín).

Westport Whispers, including Michael Duffy (songs/guitar), Jennie Kilroy (accordion/vocals) and Joanne Keegan (whistle/vocals).

Chapter 11

Commerce and Employment

T raditionally, Mayo was a rural society where the material needs of the people were generally met locally. Hand-crafted goods made from local resources, augmented by trading along the west coast, supplied the needs of the farming community. Turners, potters, coopers, wheelwrights, blacksmiths, cobblers, tailors and tinsmiths were among the diverse range of artisans operating throughout the county. Examples of their crafts can be seen today in the National Museum of Country Life at Turlough, near Castlebar.

A range of industries took root in the county's towns during the 19th century, largely based around the processing of agricultural products. Pre-Famine industries in Ballina included an extensive tobacco and snuff manufactory, an important bacon-curing factory, large ale and porter breweries, and extensive oatmeal and flour mills. The flour mills, brewery and tan yard in the south Mayo town of Ballinrobe were also significant. *The Connaught Telegraph* printers, established in 1828, is one of the oldest industries in the county's capital of Castlebar; other industries in the town included a brewery and tannery, soap and candle-making factories, snuff and tobacco manufactories, and a brick-making plant.

The coming of the railway in the late 19th century facilitated the importation of mass-produced materials into the county. Factory-produced footwear and clothing offered an alternative to locally produced materials and heralded a change in consumer purchasing patterns.

The Congested Districts Board, established in 1891, was a government-sponsored initiative to develop the economy of the West. It remained in operation until 1922 and promoted the development of the western regions in a variety of important and imaginative ways. It financed employment on public works, provided grants for technical education and for the establishment of new factories, such as the Providence Woollen Mills at Foxford.

Pat Lavelle, Castlebar's last saddler who worked in Castle Street

*Swinford Convent Laundry,
c. 1920 – a typical religious
enterprise of the period*

The national economic strategy of the Irish Free State protected native industries, replacing imported goods with locally manufactured products. This policy helped in the establishment of a number of Westport-based industries, including the Westport Irish Sewing Cotton Company, the Clog Factory, the Reliable Shoe Company, Westport Handkerchiefs and the Westport Clothing Company. The Bacon Company was established in Claremorris and Western Hats opened in Castlebar in 1939.

In the 1950s, the national economic strategy changed from import substitution to export-led industrialisation. A major component of this strategy was to attract multinational industry to Ireland. Incentives, including grant-aid and tax concessions for corporate profits, induced industrialists to locate in Mayo. The Local Government (Planning and Development) Act of 1963 placed local authorities to the fore in the development of their areas, with responsibility to encourage industrial and commercial development. The economic upturn in the 1960s and Ireland's membership of the EEC in 1973 provided further catalysts for industrial development. The Industrial Development Authority (IDA), founded in 1949, became an autonomous State-sponsored organisation in 1970, with responsibility to foster enterprise and development. The IDA's development plan for the West included the provision of advance factory buildings at strategic locations such as Westport, Kiltimagh, Claremorris, Charlestown, Keel, Louisburgh and Castlebar.

Mayo became a site for multinational industries in the healthcare sector, as well as synthetic manufacturing facilities. Westport Textiles opened in the early 1960s and the Chicago-based Travenol Company (now called Baxter Healthcare) opened in Castlebar in 1971, with satellite plants at Belmullet and Swinford. In 1974 the Asahi Group, one of the largest chemical companies in

Japan, selected Killala as the location for its acrylic fibre and spinning plant; the operation continued until 1999. Hollister Overseas came to Ballina in 1974, providing 400 jobs in the manufacture of healthcare products. Allergan Pharmaceuticals, a major North American company, opened in Westport in 1976. In the early 1980s, Halal Meat Packers opened in Ballyhaunis (the plant is now operated by Glanbia). By the mid-1980s, multinational companies were providing approximately 2,500 jobs throughout the county.

These industries were seen as a means of rapid industrial development – enhancing technical and managerial skills within the workforce and offering an opportunity for indigenous companies to provide support and sub-supply services. Sub-supplier companies established for the healthcare, engineering and electronic sectors include injection moulding, precision engineering, steel products, blow-moulding bottles and gamma sterilisation.

Industrial growth within the county has been aided by the continuing development of infrastructure, local energy supply and the establishment of the Mayo County Enterprise Board in 1993. The Board has the primary objective of supporting enterprise and an 'enterprise culture' within the county. The development of Mayo as a tourist destination has also helped to generate local employment.

The county's industrial base continues to expand with the establishment of local micro-industries, as well as investment by multinationals. Two US companies established plants in Mayo during 2000: Ballina Beverages (Coca Cola) set up one of the most modern plants of its kind in the world, while Delta Dental, a health insurance company, located initially in Claremorris due to Mayo's modern telecommunications network, which offers services for voice, data and image transmission, as well as ISDN capabilities.

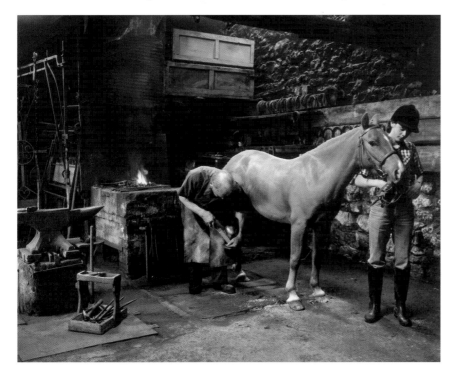

Paddy McDonagh from Shrule, one of the last working blacksmiths in south Mayo

Crafts and trades

Wheelwrights, blacksmiths and saddlers were in high demand throughout the county up to the mid-20th century because horses and donkeys were still used for transport and farm work. Blacksmiths' forges were always located near water and were bustling places where news and ideas were exchanged, particularly in the spring and summer months. Blacksmiths acted as farriers and shod the wheels of horse-drawn vehicles with iron bands. They also made and repaired agricultural tools (such as scythes and sickles for grain-cutting and loys and slanes for turf-cutting), as well as 'pointing' harrows and, in more recent times, repairing mowing machines.

The growth in the number of motor cars and tractors heralded the demise of forges throughout the county. Some blacksmiths diversified into welding and mechanical work, but the craft gradually declined. Recently, there has been a renewal of interest in blacksmithing and successful courses have been run throughout the county to revive the craft.

The craft of producing custom-made shoes and boots by cobblers or

Tom McHugh, shoemaker, at work in his busy Castlebar shop

Vigilant law enforcement, as photographed in Erris in 1885, discouraged the practice of illegal distillation of poitín or whiskey

shoemakers survived well into the 20th century in the towns of Mayo. A shoemaker would measure the foot of his customer and create a last, or replica of the foot, around which new shoes were made. The last was kept for the next time the customer wanted a new pair of shoes. The trade was badly affected by the importation of machine-made footwear from England in the second half of the 19th century. Today, although the craft is changed, shoemakers still conduct a busy trade in repairing shoes and other leather items, such as handbags and belts.

Not all industry was legal. Illicit whiskey or poitín distillation was common in Mayo, particularly in the 19th century. The ingredients, consisting of oats or barley or sometimes potatoes, were heated to boiling point in a still of copper or tin; the steam was then passed through a tin worm that stretched from the head of the still through a vessel full of cold water. As the steam passed through the 'worm' or coil, it was cooled by the water and condensed into liquid, which was collected drop by drop in a vessel at the end of the still. Poitín-making continued unabated, even up to modern times, in remote parts of Mayo where it proved difficult for the Revenue Police or Gardaí to find and destroy the stills.

Maritime trade

Transport and trade by sea have always been important in a maritime county such as Mayo. The extent of trading off the western coast is recalled today through tales of Grace O'Malley, the 16th-century Pirate Queen. At the end of the 18th century, Captain George O'Malley, like his illustrious namesake, acquired a reputation as a successful smuggler around Clew Bay. The development of land-based transport, combined with the introduction of the Coast Guard in 1822 (for the

The once-bustling port of Westport Quay, as depicted by James Arthur O'Connor (1792-1841) in one of a series of 16 paintings of Westport House and environs

collection of excise duty and suppression of trade in smuggled goods), heralded the demise of Mayo's sea-borne illicit trading.

Westport Quay was a busy port on the west coast, particularly in the early 19th century. Against the backdrop of Croagh Patrick and Clew Bay, horse-drawn carts transported goods to and from steamers. Flour and general cargo were accommodated in the steamer sheds and warehouses along the waterfront. Cattle drovers brought the livestock to the port by foot and later by train after Westport was linked to Castlebar by rail in 1866. There were regular sailings to transport goods, livestock and people between Westport, Liverpool and Glasgow. However, the port was in decline by the mid-20th century, caused partly by the Economic War between Ireland and Great Britain and also as a result of World War II.

Ballina, located at the mouth of the River Moy, developed as a merchant town and a commercial port, aided by the building of The Quay in 1836. The 1837 *Topographical Dictionary of Ireland* records Ballina as a sea port, market and post town. Writing in 1853, Sir John Forbes refers to the large export of corn and salmon to Liverpool from Ballina and the importation of Indian corn. In 1860, the Moy Harbour Commissioners were established by an Act of Parliament to administer

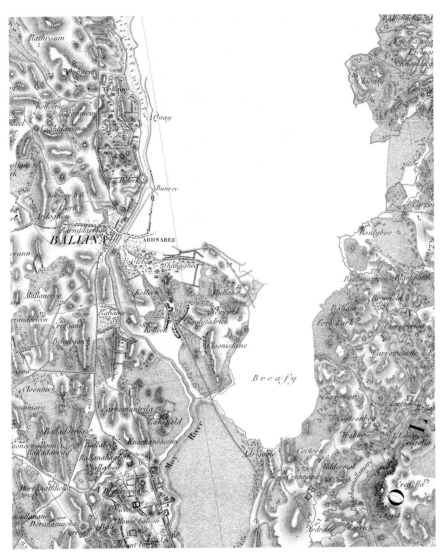

Bald's 'Maritime County of Mayo', completed in 1817, shows the strategic location of Ballina

the port. Ballina became a significant centre for the importation of timber, coffee and tea, sugar, tobacco, coal, fruit, iron, cement and furniture. Exports included pigs, cattle, sheep, potatoes, barley, oats, salmon, seaweed and fertiliser. The collapse in the export of livestock as a result of World War II contributed to the eventual decline of the port.

A passenger service operated from Ballina to Great Britain and North America for over a hundred years, from 1850. In that year, at the height of the Great Famine, over 200 passengers sailed from Ballina to Canada. The passenger service was later operated by the Limerick Steamship Agency, which ceased local operation in the late 1960s. The Quay closed for regular trading in 1983, but was later reopened in 1985 on a limited scale. Business now consists mainly of pleasure boats and a number of large commercial vessels.

There has always been excellent sea fishing off the west coast of Mayo, where the catch includes mackerel, haddock and herring. Fish

Aerial view of Killala Harbour, showing the modern fish-processing factory

was solely for home consumption until after the development of fish-curing skills and adequate transport to distant markets. A Scotsman, Alexander Hector, was among the first to establish a fishing business in Mayo on Achill Island in 1856, when 100 people were employed processing salmon and basking shark. In modern times, fish-processing plants have operated at Ballina, Doohoma, Killala and Newport.

Fishing boosted the local economy in many parts of Mayo, such as Achill. Paul Henry lived on the island between 1910 and 1919, and recorded many scenes of daily life, including his painting of 'Launching the currach'. The currach was an ideal craft for fishing since it was light, without a sail, easily manoeuvred in the water by oars and required no harbour, being lifted ashore on the men's shoulders after a day's work. It was also, however, a dangerous vessel since it offered no protection against strong winds and was witness to many tragedies over the years.

Fallmore, Blacksod and the islanders of Inishkea have traditionally fished for lobster, using pots made out of twisted heather roots. The lobster season began in April and most of the catch was exported to England. Today, lobster fishing continues off the coast of Mayo, with

most of the catch being exported live to Spain. Oyster fishing has also provided an important source of income for a number of part-time fishermen in the waters off Achill, Belmullet and Clew Bay. In 1995, the Belmullet and Achill areas produced 39 tonnes of oysters; in the same year, the Clew Bay area produced 110 tonnes. By 1998, however, dwindling stocks allowed only a total catch of 12 tonnes. Fortunately, by 2000, Blacksod Bay had recovered and was producing 53 tonnes of oysters, while Clew Bay alone produced 14 tonnes.

Whales were killed for processing by commercial whaling stations off the west coast of Mayo until the early 20th century. The species hunted were mostly fin whales, but also sei, sperm, blue and humpback. The products produced included lighting oil, low-quality soap, crayons, candles and ingredients for use in explosives, medicines and varnishes. Whalebone was used in corsets, bristle brushes, fabric stiffener, bone meal and cattle food. The Inishkea whaling station operated from 1907 until 1913 at Rusheen under the management of a Norwegian company, run by Captain Bruun. In 1910, Bruun established another station at Blacksod Bay, but operations were suspended there during World War I. Whaling

Paul Henry's painting 'Launching the currach', inspired by his stay on Achill Island

(Above) Freshly landed lobsters at Killgalligan in Erris

(Above right) The whaling station at Elly Bay on the Mullet Peninsula was one of a number of such stations operating along the Mayo coast in the early 20th century

Village of Keel, Achill, c. 1900 – home to a small fishing community

recommenced in 1920 under a new enterprise called the Northern Seas Company, but closed permanently in 1923. The life of the Mayo men and Norwegians at the whaling stations is documented in Robert W. Paul's 1908 film *Whaling Ashore and Afloat* and in James Fairley's 1981 book *Irish Whales and Whaling*.

Legal tender and banking

Only in relatively modern times did Mayo transfer from the barter system of exchange to an almost wholly cash-based economy. Barter of goods and services persisted, particularly among the farming community, long after legal tender became widespread. The seasonal nature of farm work and perishable farm produce encouraged a communal approach, with farmers forming a *meitheal* or work group to assist each other with harvesting and other busy seasonal tasks. Eggs, potatoes and corn, for example, were bartered with shops for tea, sugar, tobacco and meal. Cash required for paying the rent and shop bills was usually earned from seasonal work, illicit whiskey-making, and home spinning or weaving, as well as by remittances from relations abroad.

A number of important hoards of medieval coins have been found in Co. Mayo, including those at Kilmaine, Blacksod and Gortnaheltia, near Newport. These hoards may have been either deliberately deposited (as in Gortnaheltia) or simply lost. Coins penetrated the Gaelic society in the area now known as Mayo before the arrival of the Normans. The Kilmaine hoard, discovered in 1946, is comprised of 280 short-cross pennies of the type issued between 1180 and 1247, including English coins from the reigns of Henry II, Richard I and Henry III, and Irish coins from the reign of King John. The hoard of coins found at Blacksod in 1939 were minted in the late 13th and early 14th centuries in Ireland and included an Irish penny of Edward I. Coins found at Gortnaheltia in 1945 included a shilling of James I issued in 1623-24, a sixpence of Elizabeth I dated between 1594 and 1596, two shilling coins of Charles I, and two Spanish 'cobs' (irregular pieces of precious metal struck into gold and silver coins by the Spanish in South America). Fishing fleets from Spain trading in the medieval period brought Spanish coinage into circulation in Mayo where, by the second half of the 17th century, the Spanish *real* was made legal tender.

George Clendining (1770-1843) of Glebe House, Mill Street in Westport, was the second son of the Reverend Alexander Clendining. George established a merchant banking business and acted as banker for wealthy families in the area, such as the Brownes of Westport House. In 1826, he was appointed as agent for the Bank of Ireland and established one of the earliest branches of that bank outside Dublin. He was honoured in 1845, shortly after his death, by the erection of a significant monument in the centre of Westport's Octagon – his statue stood atop the tall Doric column until its removal in the 1940s and was later replaced by a statue of St. Patrick in 1990.

Banking in Mayo generally followed seasonal patterns, reflecting the agricultural base of the county. Formal banking facilities appeared in the 18th century with the establishment of small private banks, which were later absorbed into or merged to form Allied Irish Bank and the Bank of Ireland. Banks were usually housed in classical-style buildings, with interiors suggesting an aura of formality and propriety. As banks expanded and became popular, so too did their style of décor and

(Top) Specimen penny from the Kilmaine hoard, discovered in 1946

(Centre) A coin from the Blacksod hoard, discovered in 1939

(Bottom) Coin from the Gortnaheltia hoard, found in 1945, which consisted of 17th-century coins that had remained in circulation until the great recoinage of 1696

(Top) Interior of the Bank of Ireland, on the corner of Castlebar's Mall, in the 1930s

(Above) Front of a £1 note, issued by the Ballina branch of the Provincial Bank of Ireland in 1856, complete with the symbols of Britannia and Hibernia, the Order of the Garter surrounding Queen Victoria and the bank manager's signature

(Above right) An imposing monument to George Clendining, one of Mayo's earliest bankers, was erected in Westport's Octagon in 1845

architecture. The banks also brought diversity to the towns in which they were located through their staff, who were regularly transferred between branches and brought with them increased movement of goods and ideas.

Individual banks, such as the Provincial Bank, issued their own bank notes until the Banking Commission centralised the practice, shortly before World War II. Consolidated bank notes were issued nationally for an interim period. These notes had a common design, which was overprinted by individual banks. The £50 consolidated bank note, designed by E.L. Lawrenson, included an image of Croagh Patrick on its reverse side.

Agricultural-based industry

Milling was one of the first agricultural-based industries in Mayo. From early times, saddle querns and later stone querns were used to grind corn for local consumption. In the medieval period, small water-powered mills, with either horizontal or vertical wheels, were introduced to provide for commercial milling. Besides food production, mills were also used for other applications, including stone cutting, threshing, sawing, pumping and the manufacture of textiles, paper and agricultural tools.

The ruins of mills, such as Murphy's Flour Mills in Ballina and Pollexfens Mills in Westport, are found throughout the county. The Ballina mill operated between 1936 and 1963 on the site of an earlier 18th-century mill to which the Murphys added a purpose-built, five-storey, steel-framed mill building, later demolished in 1985. The original 18th-century mill used two sets of mill stones driven by turbines to grind oatmeal. The new 20th-century building housed the most modern machinery of its day and was powered by the River Moy. Flour under the brands of 'Moy Rose', 'Irish Glory' and 'Irish Maid Flour' were produced for export by Murphy's, using both local and imported grain.

The Mill in Ballinrobe, as depicted by James Arthur O'Connor – one of a series of four paintings of the town

Murphy's Flour Mills, built in 1935 at the Ridge Pool, Ballina, operated until 1963 and was demolished in 1985

Ranks of Limerick supplied flour all over Mayo from its store at Westport Quay and assisted the establishment of small commercial bakeries throughout the county. Many eventually amalgamated into a few large operations. Duffy's, Gavin's, Irish Pride, Moran's and O'Hara's are among Mayo's best-known bakeries.

The Castlebar Bacon Factory was built on a site originally owned by the local landlord, Lord Lucan. It provided the sole income for generations of Castlebar families over a 70-year period, from 1917 to 1986. There were many divisions within the factory, including the

Staff of Castlebar's Bacon Factory, photographed in 1986

slaughterhouse, ham section, canning section and sausage department where, for many years, the sausages were 'linked' by hand. In the early years, products were ferried from the factory to the railway station by horse-drawn carts, later to be replaced by lorries. During 'The Emergency' (1939-1945) when petrol was scarce, factory goods continued to be distributed by lorry, driven on charcoal gas produced in the factory.

Textiles

Self-sufficiency in making fabric and clothes was the norm in Mayo up until recent times. The available materials and colour agents influenced local fabrics and styles, which took on regional variations. Arthur Young (1741-1820), the English agriculturist and writer, noted on his visit to Mayo in 1776 that spinning was universal. Riocard Bairéad, 'The Bard of Erris', in his 18th-century satirical poem *Eoghan Coir*, alludes to the importance of home-made cloth or frieze for the tenant farmer. The poem is about the avaricious Owen Conway, land agent for the local Erris landlord, who obtained the rent by any means including taking the cloth from the loom.

He was pleasant in collecting the rent
A month or two until the cow was sold at the fair
Or the piece of cloth in the loom
Was readily agreed to.

Ba soirbh ag togail an chios e
Is ba bheag aige mi no dho
No go ndioltai an bho ar an aonach
No an giota bhi ins an tseol.

Since World War II, clothes are typically shop-bought, manufactured across the globe and influenced by international fashion trends. But in the past, most people in Mayo wore home-spun clothes – coarse woollen yarn for the women and frieze for the men. The playwright John Millington Synge (1871-1909), travelling in Erris in 1905, was informed that most women spun their own wool in that area. After spinning, the wool was woven by a weaver for three pence a yard if it was a single weave and for sixpence a yard if it was double woven. Synge was told by a woman in Erris that 'The women in this place have little time to be spinning, but the women back on the mountain mix colours through their wool till you'd never ask to take your eyes from it. They do be throwing in a bit of stone colour, and a bit of red madder, and a bit of crimson, and a bit of stone colour again'.

The novelist George Augustus Moore (1852-1933) in his book *Hail and Fairwell*, recalling life at Moore Hall in Claremorris, notes how men and women's fashions changed at the end of the 19th century. The young men who were employed as labourers on the estate wore corduroy trousers and frieze coats, while the old men were still in knee breeches and tall hats. Of the women, he said red petticoats hung to their knees and they wore a printed handkerchief around their heads.

Flax has been grown, spun and woven into linen cloth from ancient times. But from the 1720s, a number of factors influenced the growth of

A series of sketches on 'The Mayo Peasantry', published in the Illustrated London News of November 1880, showed a Mayo farmer (above) and a Mayo girl spinning in her home (above left)

*William Hincks' engraving of 1783
illustrates the winding, warping and
weaving stages in the preparation of linen*

the linen industry in Mayo. Sir Arthur Wellesley, Chief Secretary for Ireland during 1807-08, encouraged the expansion of flax-growing throughout the country to satisfy the demand for sail cloth during the Napoleonic War. Landlords shrewdly supported Mayo's linen industry, recognising that it would enable small tenant farmers to generate more income from their land and thus allow them to pay higher rents. Newport on the Medlycott Estate and Manulla on the Browne Estate were developed in part to support the linen industry. Lord Lucan and the Marquis of Sligo built fine stone buildings, called Linen Halls, in Castlebar and Westport to attract drapers to their linen markets. Markets also developed in Claremorris, Newport and Ballina for the sale of yarn, in both brown and bleached states, to Belfast, Dublin and Cork.

In 1776, Arthur Young reported that 200 looms were employed in Castlebar and the surrounding area, and that 300 pieces of linen were sold in a week. Large quantities of yarn were exported from the town. The weavers were housed in Tucker Street and New Antrim Street, adjoining the newly built Linen Hall, which became the heart of Castlebar's linen industry. The cloth produced in the region was graded, auctioned and baled for transport, its sale bringing a stable income to the town and surrounding countryside.

In the late 18th century, weavers and other textile workers came to Mayo from Ulster, where the linen industry was flourishing and had established an international reputation. These migrant workers brought new skills and expertise to Mayo's linen trade. The trickle of weavers into the county turned into a flood after the Battle of the Diamond in 1795, when an estimated 4,000 refugees came to Mayo, a significant population movement at the time. The names of many of the migrants have been preserved for posterity in the records of landlords, such as those on the Marquis of Sligo's estate.

The Linen Hall, Castlebar, was built in the 1790s by Lord Lucan and is used today as a theatre and arts centre

The 'Linen Stream' sculpture by Michael Burke, sited at the roundabout into Castlebar from Westport, resembles the rough weave of linen and is symbolic of the importance that the linen industry once had in Castlebar

The linen trade in Mayo was in decline from the mid-19th century. In 1834 while visiting Westport, Henry D. Inglis noted that only 100 pieces of linen cloth were sold on a market day compared to 900 pieces sold at the market eight years earlier. The production of flax and its weaving into linen declined largely as a result of the introduction of large-scale, factory-based spinning and weaving in Ulster. Flax continued to be grown on a small scale in Mayo in support of the Ulster industry. Gilmartin's Store in Ardnaree, Ballina, for example, exported flax from Mayo up until the 1950s.

The woollen industry, with an even older history than linen, received a boost when the Congested Districts Board assisted the introduction of fly-shuttle looms in the 1890s. The Board also supported the establishment of lace schools and the Irish Lace Depot and Irish Industries

St. Colman's Knitting Factory on Achill Island, c. 1900

Women weavers at the Providence Woollen Mills in Foxford, photographed in the 1920s kneeling for the Angelus

Association aided the distribution of their goods during this period. In addition, the Board established a crochet school at Pullathomas, where local girls were induced by payment to attend classes. Within a few years, these girls were making dresses that were exported to Paris and the crochet classes spread to other locations in Erris, including Belmullet, Bangor and Glenamoy.

Mother Morrogh-Bernard (Mother Arsenius) of the Sisters of Charity founded a convent in Foxford in 1891 and a year later established the Providence Woollen Mills, known locally as the Foxford Woollen Mills. The factory consisted of an elegant timber-clad structure, with light segmental roofs built out across the River Moy. Over 200 people were employed there in the 1930s and working conditions were described as among the best of the period. The novelist George A. Bermingham (a pen name of Canon James Owen Hannay) reputedly satirised Mother Arsenius and her work in *Hyacinth*, published in 1906, which caused a local controversy.

The fleece was prepared and all the processing involved in producing the finished woollen tweeds and blankets was carried out on site at Foxford Woollen Mills. The wool from local sheep, known as 'mountainy wool', was used to produce the coarse tweeds. As the factory's products diversified, higher quality wool was imported from Australia for finer materials. Mother Arsenius organised a three-day Connaught Industrial Exhibition at Foxford in 1895. The exhibition promoted the Mills and other local products through technical exhibitions and prizes for

The Connaught Industrial Exhibition at Foxford in 1895 promoted local products and crafts

excellence in hand-knitting, spinning, weaving, needlework, basketwork, carpentry and quality farm produce.

At the beginning of the 20th century, Scottish designer Thomas Turnbull arrived at Foxford Woollen Mills. He was the first to introduce colour to the factory's products. New designs in colourful tweeds and plaid-patterned rugs were added to the production of white bainín wool fabrics and white blankets. Foxford's diverse produce of flannels, frieze, kerseys, tweeds, clerical clothes, shawls and plaid blankets became known at trade exhibitions throughout Ireland and England, winning acclaim for their quality and design.

The Foxford Woollen Mills went into receivership in 1987 and was taken over by a wholly owned Irish company, which rationalised the working of the factory and accelerated the automation of the production process. The Mills now specialise in the weaving and finishing of quality wool products. Despite the competition from duvets and new synthetic materials, Foxford woollen blankets and rugs continue to be market leaders worldwide today, along with tweeds, mohairs and lambs' wool products.

Factory production of textiles grew from the 19th century and gradually replaced the cottage industry. From that time, many emigrants from Mayo got work in textile industries in Great Britain in areas such as Lancashire. Modern textile and clothing assembly factories opened in the 20th century, included the Asahi Plant in Killala, Rowear in Ballina, Kennedy's Knitwear in Charlestown, the Hat Factory in Castlebar, and Farrah (later TJT) in Kiltimagh and Ballyhaunis. Today, Mayo's long

Today, Foxford Woollen Mills combines new products and designs with traditional woollen blankets and rugs

tradition of textile production continues in the Knitwear Factory in Tourmakeady, the locally owned Portwest factory in Westport and the Foxford Woollen Mills.

Western Hats, known locally as the Hat Factory, operated in Castlebar between 1939 and 1981 on a 9-acre site in what was then known as 'Alice Quinn's field', on the outskirts of Castlebar. It was among the largest employers in Mayo, with over 150 staff. When the factory was built, just before World War II, it was one of the most modern in the country. Built almost entirely of concrete and constructed to allow in plenty of natural light, it was worked by steam power and was well ventilated. The chimney tower of the factory became a landmark for the town between the 1940s and 1980s.

A Belgian group, with a similar industry on the continent, developed the Castlebar factory under the management of Franz Schmolka, a native of Prague and one of the few members of the Jewish community living in the town at the time. The first members of staff were sent to Belgium for technical training in various manufacturing processes, but their time there was cut short by World War II, which also caused problems for the supply of building materials for the factory. Nonetheless, the factory went into full operation by the end of 1941.

Felt hoods for the millinery trade and fine hats, including the Stetson brand, were made at Western Hats and sold both nationally and internationally. The challenges of changing fashion saw the company diversifying into the production of men's tweed caps and hats in the 1960s. The factory changed hands in the 1970s and continued in production until 1981. Then it was sold to the Rehabilitation Institute (now the National Training and Development Institute), which moved

production to a green field site in Breaffy Road, Castlebar, where it continues in operation today.

Another textile industry that brought welcome employment to an area and built on local skills (in this case, needlework) was the soft-toy dolls factory in Elly Bay on the Mullet Peninsula. It was one of a group throughout Ireland that collectively manufactured the largest number of soft toys in the country before global influences eclipsed this industry in the 1970s. The soft-toy factory was later replaced by a children's clothes factory and subsequently by the Belmullet-based American Warner Company, makers of high-quality undergarments, which closed in 2000.

From the 1930s, government policy supported the establishment of textile production on a satellite basis in Gaeltacht areas to help preserve the Irish language by the creation of locally based employment. A number

(Top) Western Hats, whose staff are pictured here in the 1950s, was one of the largest employers in the county at that time

(Above left) 'Forming Department' at Western Hats in Castlebar in the 1950s

(Above right) Photographed in the Dye House of Western Hats in the 1950s (from left to right) John Eddie McEllin, E. Schmolka, Arthur Campbell, Mr. Polesi, Jack Kestrus and Fred Schmolka, the first manager of the 'Hat Factory'

Mary Hughes (left) and Rose Nealon, employees of the soft-toy dolls factory in Elly Bay, photographed by Fr. Browne in the late 1930s

The hand-flat machine, as used in the Belmullet Knitwear factory in 1938, is still part of the process in such factories today

of small factories were consolidated to form the Gaeltarra Éireann Knitwear factory in Tourmakeady in 1969. Producing tweeds and woollen garments, the Belmullet Knitwear factory and the Tourmakeady factory were both successful enterprises that drew on the traditional skills of Mayo's cottage industries. The opening of such factories was a significant development, enabling the producers to compete within the increasingly mechanised textile industry. The work processes at the Belmullet factory included knitting and cutting out the shapes of jumpers, which were then linked and finished. Employees were responsible for packaging their work into small parcels, ready for quality inspection and eventual export.

Powering industry

Gas works in Mayo's major towns supplied the power for public lighting long before electricity was introduced throughout the county. The gas works in Westport, for example, was not closed until 1940. In 1938, Seán Lemass, then Minister for Industry and Commerce, prepared a plan for peat-fired electricity generation in Ireland. Subsequently, Bord na Mona began development of 6,000 acres of bog at Oweninny in Erris. The bog was prepared for large-scale mechanical harvesting for the planned new electricity power station at Bellacorrick, near Bangor Erris. By 1962, the bog had been drained, new railway lines laid and roads constructed. Production began officially in May 1963, with all milled peat being supplied to the Bellacorrick Electricity Supply Station, which was later connected to the national grid. In the power station, the heat generated by burning turf in the furnace transforms water in the boilers into steam; this turns the turbine blades attached to a shaft, which drives the generator. A cooling tower, with a diameter of over 60 m (200 ft) at the base and a height of 90 m (296 ft) above ground, is required to cool the steam, which is pumped back into the boilers for reuse.

The development of Oweninny bog and the Bellacorrick power station led to a great reduction in emigration from Erris. Previously, people from this part of Mayo had migrated to work in Bord na Mona's bogs supplying fuel for the first peat-fuelled power station at Clonsast, near Portarlington in Co. Laois. They were later able to return to work in their own county at Bellacorrick.

Bellacorrick is the site of a new type of energy production since 1992

(Above) Employees of Mayo County Council, laying water pipes and electricity lines between islands in Clew Bay

(Above left) The cooling tower at Bellacorrick Electricity Supply Station became operational in 1963 and is due to cease production in 2004

Wind farms, a more recent method of energy production in Ireland, are now a familiar sight in Mayo

when the Department of Energy, in conjunction with Bord na Mona and the ESB, established a wind farm there. The 21 wind turbines, installed by the Danish company Nordtank, take advantage of the prevailing south-north-west winds to turn the turbines' blades. The blades turn when the winds reach 16 km (10 ml) per hour and cut out when they reach 90 km (56 ml) per hour, so as to protect the turbines. The Bellacorrick wind farm produces a combined output of 6.5 MW, enough for about 4,500 households, which feed through underground cable into the ESB grid.

Remotely controlled windmills have become a feature in many parts of Mayo. In 2000, five windmills were constructed in Burren outside Castlebar with the capacity to produce enough electricity for between 400 and 500 households. Constructing the massive windmills was a major feat, requiring the use of a 60-tonne crane to erect the huge 15 m (49ft) long blades.

In 2000, Enterprise Ireland discovered natural gas off the west coast of Mayo in the Corrib Gas Field, with prospects that an oil find would follow. The company's intention was to pipe the gas ashore at Ballinaboy, Erris, giving rise to an expected 1,000 short-term jobs in construction of

Scale model of the proposed gas terminal site at Ballinaboy in Erris

Aerial view of the Ballina Beverages Plant – one of the most modern plants of its kind in the world

the terminal and 50 specialist permanent jobs. At the time of the discovery, there was much controversy and debate about the impact of the gas find on Mayo. Some argued that it represented a great opportunity, while others claimed that it posed a threat to the local environment without enhancing local power supplies.

Modern work and industry

The proportion of farmers in the working population has remained relatively high at the start of the 21st century, at approximately a quarter of the labour force. For many generations, the decline in numbers employed in agriculture and the lack of alternative jobs contributed to emigration from the county. In more recent years, emigration has declined while employment has grown in the manufacturing, services and administrative areas.

The end of the 20th century saw a noticeable change in the labour market in the county as a result of strategic efforts to attract industrial investment, improve the infrastructure and enhance the skills base of the workforce. Multinational industries provided increased employment in

Aileen O'Connell, Assistant Chief Fire Officer at Castlebar Fire Station

the manufacturing sector, which was augmented by locally owned companies and service industries. The Galway – Mayo Institute of Technology (GMIT) in Castlebar has raised the level of educational attainment and added to the skills base available in the county. The challenge of providing good infrastructure to attract industry is being met by substantial improvements in road, rail and airport facilities.

In the 1970s, major US corporations established subsidiary manufacturing operations at various locations throughout Mayo. Hollister Overseas located at Ballina to manufacture disposable products for the healthcare industry. The plant began recruiting in 1975 and was considered a model of its kind in terms of excellent working conditions. Allergan, an international eye and skin care company, opened its plant at Westport in 1977. Baxter manufactures innovative healthcare products used in hospitals, blood banks and kidney dialysis centres throughout the world. It became one of the largest industrial employers in the west of Ireland in the early 1970s and has centres at Castlebar and Swinford.

Since 1973, women working in the public service were no longer required to resign from their jobs upon marriage. The 1977 Employment Equality Act introduced further changes, which facilitated the participation of women in employment. Women could no longer be treated differently on grounds of sex or marital status. As a result, women gained access to previously perceived non-traditional employment and craft apprenticeships. In subsequent years, there was a substantial rise in female participation in all sectors of paid employment. Between 1991 and 1996, participation of women in the Mayo labour force rose from 30% to 36%, adding to the pool of talented labour available within the county.

Aileen O'Connell, Assistant Chief Fire Officer, employed by Mayo County Council, was among those women who successfully broke the mould of perceived gender roles within the paid workforce. She was the third woman to join the Mayo Fire Service, following Mary O'Brien and Marie Melia, the latter subsequently becoming the first female Chief Fire Officer in Ireland for Wexford County Council.

Tourism

Tourism in Mayo began to be important in the 19th century. Westport led the way and was one of the first towns to be serviced by the Bianconi Tourist Car Service. The first commercial hotel in Connaught, Robinson's Hotel (now the Railway Hotel), opened in 1790 in the town. In the early 1800s, the first Marquis of Sligo installed warm water baths at Westport Quay and made the town a resort for bathers. Steamship excursions and other attractions operated for visitors to the area.

Visitors continue to be attracted to Mayo for many reasons, not least because of the unspoilt scenery of the county, its blue-flag beaches and other natural features. Other visitor attractions include pilgrimage, angling, sport, adventure holidays, health and heritage tourism. Many communities throughout Mayo have been sustained by tourism, creating

(Above) CBE Software, Claremorris, received the 1998 Mayo Company of the Year Award, sponsored by the Mayo County Enterprise Board

(Left) Mayo Crystal is one of the county's many new thriving locally owned industries

jobs and fostering local pride in the county's cultural and natural heritage. Mayo County Council, in partnership with local communities, has been to the fore in developing visitor facilities, partly financed by European Union Structural Funds.

Tourism has grown steadily in recent years, aided by the availability of quality accommodation and museum attractions such as Ballintubber Abbey, the Céide Fields Visitors' Centre, Foxford Woollen Mills, Knock Folk Museum, the National Museum of Country Life and more than a dozen other community-based museums. In 1998, Lough Lannagh Holiday Village – a tourism development consisting of self-catering cottages, guesthouse/ hostel, conference room, leisure centre and caravan park – opened in Castlebar with funding from Mayo County Council, Castlebar Town Council and Bord Fáilte. Westport Leisure Park, which was developed by the Urban District Council, opened in 1999 and includes a swimming pool, health spa, fitness suite and auditorium. In 1999, an estimated 300,000 overseas visitors came to Mayo, generating €166 million in revenue for the county.

In 1991, Mayo County Council bought the 19th-century Turlough Park House, designed in Gothic Revival style by the Cork architect Sir Thomas Newenham Deane. A new, four-storey exhibition centre was built in the grounds of Turlough Park and opened in 2001 as home to the National Museum of Country Life, housing the Folklife Collection of the National Museum of Ireland. This is the National Museum's first Division to be located outside Dublin. The National Museum of Country Life displays objects collected from all over the country reflecting aspects of rural life between 1850 and 1950. The exhibits interpret and cover the themes of agriculture, clothing, furniture, trades and crafts, transport and religion.

Mayo County Council established the much-acclaimed Tír Sáile, or

Ramblers crossing the old bridge at Burren during the Castlebar Four-day Walk Festival in 2000

Sculpture Trail, in north Mayo in 1993. The project was initially proposed by artist Marian O'Donnell at a symposium devoted to the Céide Fields' discovery. It evolved to explore ideas of settlement, folklore and mythology, and resulted in the creation of 15 site-specific sculptures (made from a specified and limited range of organic materials) – from the Moy Estuary to the Mullet Peninsula on the north Mayo coastline. The sculptures were put in place during 1993 as part of that year's celebrations to mark 5,000 years of Mayo's rural civilisation.

Mayo – offering deep sea fishing, lake angling, coarse and salmon angling – has gained the reputation of being an angler's paradise. In 1892, W.H. Maxwell wrote of the inducements for anglers to fish the county's lakes and rivers: 'The streams are plentifully stocked with trout, and the rivers, which communicate with the sea, have a good supply of salmon . . . in those noble and expansive sheets of water, Lough Conn, Lough Mask and Lough Corrib, the largest and finest specimens of fish are easily obtained.'

The Moy, straddling the Mayo – Sligo border, is one of the most important river systems for angling in Ireland. It is most famous as a salmon river, with impressive numbers of fish landed each year. The Moy estuary comprises a large area of tidal waters to the north of Ballina, where local knowledge of the drifts and tidal conditions is crucial for good angling results. Sea trout are found in the estuary and further upstream. The Moy

'Tearmon na Gaoithe' by sculptor Alan Counihan is located at Benwee, Kilcummin Head. Part of the Tír Sáile or Sculpture Trail of north Mayo, the sculpture is made of sandstone slabs and evokes both meditation and sanctuary, recalling the monastic tradition along Ireland's western seaboard.

The National Museum of Country Life in Turlough Park, opened in 2001

Fishery in Ballina, which is just over 2.5 km (1.5 ml) long and divided into eight beats, is one of the most famous salmon angling areas in Europe. In 1776, Arthur Young described the fishery as one of the 'most considerable in the kingdom'. The main Moy channel – from Ballina through Foxford to Cloongullaun Bridge near Swinford – is mainly in private ownership or managed under licence by angling clubs or associations. In the year 2000, just under 10,000 salmon licences were issued by the North-Western Regional Fisheries Board, which includes north Mayo. Of these licences, nearly 80% were sold to visiting anglers, with the majority coming from Northern Ireland and Great Britain. Among the thousands of anglers who regularly visit the area is former Irish soccer team manager Jack Charlton.

The tributaries and loughs of the Moy system are home to rich stocks of both salmon and trout. The Pollagh, Glore and Trimogue are all tributaries of the Gwestion River, itself a tributary of the Moy, between Swinford and Bohola. The Pollagh is a limestone-based river, containing both grilse and brown trout. The Glore is a fast-flowing river with brown trout, averaging about 1 kg (0.5 lb). The Trimogue also has trout up to 1.6 kg (0.75 lb), but is in need of development. In the east Mayo area, around Kiltimagh, Knock and Manulla, the small loughs contain perch, pike, rudd and tench.

North Mayo has good angling potential for salmon, sea trout and other species. Among the best rivers for salmon is the Palmerstown River on the western side of Killala Bay. The Ballinaglen River, which flows into the sea

*The basement of the 'Ice House',
Ballina – former home of the Little
family – was once used to store salmon
in the days before artificial refrigeration*

*Young Mayo anglers, delighted
with their catch*

(Above) Successful day's catch off the Mayo coast

(Above left) Over 30 species of fish can be caught in the waters off Mayo, making them a sea-angler's paradise

at Ballycastle Bay, has late runs of salmon and trout. The Glenamoy River, famous for its stock of salmon and sea trout, enters the sea at an inlet of Broad Haven Bay and, along with the Owenmore, is among the most important angling rivers in north Mayo after the Moy. The Owenmore, formed by the confluence of the Oweninny and Altnabrocky rivers, flows through Bangor village and is noted for its salmon and sea trout fishing, as is the Owenduff River, which rises in the Nephin Beg mountain range.

In south Mayo, the Erriff and Delphi Salmon Fisheries are among the best in the region. Other important rivers in south Mayo include the Carrowniskey, which flows into the sea to the south of Louisburgh, and the Bunowen, which flows through Louisburgh into Clew Bay. The Cong River, which enters Lough Corrib at Ashford Castle, contains a good run of spring salmon (with the best fishing in April), while grilse are caught later in the season. Good stocks of large brown trout are also found in this river. The Clare River, which rises to the north of Ballyhaunis and flows south into Lough Corrib, is home to brown trout, spring salmon and grilse. The Robe, a significant wild brown trout river, flows through Ballinrobe into Lough Mask.

Good angling is also found on many of Mayo's lakes, the most important of which are Loughs Conn and Cullin, drained by the Moy. The peak fishing season is at the end of May. Loughs Carra and Mask also provide good brown trout fishing. Lough Mask is well known for its large ferrox trout, which often weigh in excess of 22 kg (10 lb).

Sea angling, either shore- or boat-based, is also popular off the coast of Mayo, where over 30 species of fish can be caught. Indeed, angling journalist David Houghton has said, 'Think of a fish and it can probably be caught off Belmullet'. The four main centres for sea angling are Achill Island, Blacksod, Clew Bay and Killala Bay, each of which hosts its own sea-angling festival in the towns of Achill, Belmullet, Newport and Killala, respectively.

Select Bibliography

Aalen, F.H.A., Whelan, K. and Stout, M. (Eds.), *Atlas of Rural Irish Landscape*. Cork University Press, Cork, 1997.

Akenson, Donald Harmon, *The Irish Education Experiment: The National System of Education in the 19th Century*. Routledge & Kegan, London, 1970.

Ashworth, John Hervey, *The Saxon in Ireland or the Rambles of an Englishman in Search of a Settlement in the West of Ireland*. John Murray, London, 1851.

Baker, Joe, *My Stand for Freedom: Autobiography of an Irish Republican Soldier*. Westport Historical Society, Westport, 1988.

Barrow, John, *A Tour Round Ireland: Through the Sea Coast Counties in the Autumn of 1835*. John Murray, London, 1836.

Bennett, William, *Narrative of a Recent Journey of Six Weeks in Ireland, in Connection with the Subject of Supplying Small Seed to Some of the Remoter Districts: with Current Observations on the Depressed Circumstances of the People, and the Means Presented for the Permanent Improvement of their Social Condition*. J. Curry, London, 1847.

Berleth, Richard, *The Twilight Lords*. Allen Lane, London, 1979.

Bethu Phátraic: The Tripartite Life of Patrick, edited and translated by Kathleen Mulchrone. Royal Irish Academy, Dublin, 1939.

Bingham-Daly, Theresa, *The Mayo Binghams*. The Pentland Press, Edinburgh, 1997.

Böll, Heinrich, *Irish Journal* (translated from German by Leila Vennewitz). McGraw Hill, London, 1967.

Boylan, Henry, *A Dictionary of Irish Biography*. Gill & Macmillan, Dublin, 1978.

Brabazon, Wallop, *The Deep Sea and Coast Fisheries of Ireland, with Suggestions for the Working of a Fishing Company*. James McGlashan, Dublin, 1848.

Browne, Denis, *Westport House and the Brownes*. Moorland, Ashbourne, 1981.

Browne, Noel, *Against the Tide*. Gill & Macmillan, Dublin, 1986.

Browne, Patrick, *Flowers of Mayo*. Éamon de Búrca, Dublin, 1996.

Burke, Eamonn, *Burke, Bourke and De Burgh, People and Places* (Revised Edition). Edmund Burke, Dublin, 1995.

Byrne, Art and McMahon, Seán, *Faces of the West, 1875-1925. A Record of Life in the West of Ireland*. Appletree Press, Belfast, 1976.

Cabot, David, *The New Naturalist: Ireland*. Harper Collins, London, 1999.

Carlyle, Thomas, *Reminiscences of my Irish Journey in 1849*. Sampson Low, London, 1882.

Caird, James, *The Plantation Scheme or the West of Ireland as a Field for Investment*. William Blackwood & Sons, London, 1850.

Chambers, Anne, *La Sheridan: Adorable Diva. Margaret Burke Sheridan, Irish Prima-Donna, 1889-1958*. Wolfhound Press, Dublin, 1989.

Chambers, Anne, *Chieftain to Knight: Tibbot-ne-Long Bourke, 1567-1629*. Wolfhound Press, Dublin, 1983.

Chambers, Anne, *Granuaile: The Life and Times of Grace O'Malley, 1530-1603*. Wolfhound Press, Dublin, 1979.

Comer, Michael, *The Burma Road: Claremorris to Collooney Railway*. Swinford Historical Society, Swinford, 1996.

Connolly, S.J. (Ed.), *The Oxford Companion to Irish History*. Oxford University Press, Oxford, 1998.

Coogan, Tim Pat and Morrisson, George, *The Irish Civil War*. Weidenfeld & Nicholson, London, 1998.

Cooney, Gabriel, *Landscapes of Neolithic Ireland*. Routledge, London, 1999.

Costello, Nuala, *John MacHale, Archbishop of Tuam*. Talbot Press, Dublin, 1939.

Coulter, Henry, *The West of Ireland: Its Existing Condition and Prospects*. Hodges & Smith, Dublin, 1862.

Curwen, J.C., *Observations on the State of Ireland, Principally Directed to its Agriculture and Rural Population in a Series of Letters, Written on a Tour through that Country*. Baldwin, Craddock & Joy, London, 1818.

Davitt, Michael, *The Fall of Feudalism in Ireland or the Story of the Land League Revolution*. Harper & Brothers, London, 1904.

De Búrca, Marcus, *The GAA: A History*. Cumann Lúthchleas Gael, Dublin, 1980.

De Búrca, Seán, *The Irish of Tourmakeady, Co. Mayo: A Phonemic Study*. Dublin Institute for Advanced Studies, Dublin, 1958.

De Latocnaye, *A Frenchman's Walk through Ireland, 1796-7*. Blackstaff Press, Belfast, 1984.

De Paor, Liam, *Saint Patrick's World: The Christian Culture of Ireland's Apostolic Age*. Four Courts Press, Dublin, 1993.

De Valera, Rúaidhrí and O'Nualláin, Seán, *Survey of Megalithic Tombs of Ireland. Vol. II: County Mayo*. Stationery Office, Dublin, 1964.

Doorways to the Past: A Social Atlas, Charlestown, Bellaghy and District. Charlestown/Bellaghy & Districts Heritage Society, Charlestown, 1997.

Dun, Finlay, *Landlords and Tenants in Ireland*. Longmans, Green & Co, London, 1881.

Dunlevy, Mairead, *Dress in Ireland*. B.T. Batsford, London, 1989.

English, Richard, *Ernie O'Malley: IRA intellectual*. Oxford University Press, Oxford, 1999.

Fairley, James, *Irish Whales and Whaling*. Blackstaff Press, Belfast, 1981.

Fallon, Niall, *The Armada in Ireland*. George Phillip, London, 1978.

Faulkner, Thomas Patrick, *The Career of George Robert Fitzgerald, Better Known as Fitzgerald the Fire-Eater, in the West of Ireland*. Sealy, Bryers & Walker, Dublin, 1893.

Finlay, Fergus, *Mary Robinson: A President with a Purpose*. O'Brien Press, Dublin, 1990.

Finlay, T.A., *The Story of an Irish Industry: Foxford and the Providence Woollen Mills*. Fallon & Co, Dublin, 1932.

Flanagan, Thomas, *The Year of the French*. Macmillan, London, 1979.

Fletcher, George, *Connaught*. Cambridge University Press, Cambridge, 1922.

Forbes, John, *Memorandums of a Tour in Ireland*. Smith, Elder & Co, London, 1853.

Freeman, Martin A. (Trans.), *The Compossicion Booke of Conought*. Stationery Office, Dublin, 1936.

Gillespie, Raymond and Moran, Gerard (Eds.), *A Various Country: Essays in Mayo History, 1500-1900*. Foilseacháin Náisiúnta Teoranta, Westport, 1987.

Goodbody, Rob, *A Suitable Channel: Quaker Relief in the Great Famine*. Pale Publishing, Bray, 1995.

Greer, James, *The Windings of the Moy with Skreen and Tireragh*. Alex Thom & Co, Dublin, 1924.

Grimble, Augustus, *The Salmon Rivers of Ireland*. Kegan, Paul, Trench, Trubner & Co, London, 1913.

Grose, Francis, *The Antiquities of Ireland*, 2 volumes (facsimile of 1791 edition). Wellbrook Press, Kilkenny, 1982.

Gwynn, Aubrey and Hadcock, R., *Medieval Religious Houses of Ireland*. Irish Academic Press, Dublin, 1970.

Hamrock, Ivor, *The Famine in Mayo, 1845-1850: A Portrait from Contemporary Sources*. Comhairle Chontae Mhaigh Eo (Mayo County Council), Castlebar, 1998.

Harbison, Peter, *Pilgrimage in Ireland: The Monuments and the People*. Barrie & Jenkins, London, 1991.

Harbison, Peter, *Guide to National and Historic Monuments of Ireland*. Gill & Macmillan, Dublin, 1988.

Harbison, Peter, *Pre-Christian Ireland: From the First Settlers to the Early Celts*. Thames and Hudson, London, 1988.

Harbison, Peter, Potterton, Homan and Sheehy, Jeanne, *Irish Art and Architecture from Prehistory to the Present*. Thames and Hudson, London, 1978.

Healy, John, *No One Shouted Stop* (formerly *Death of an Irish Town*). House of Healy, Achill, 1988.

Healy, John, *Nineteen Acres*. Kennys, Galway, 1978.

Healy, John, *Death of an Irish Town*. Mercier Press, Cork, 1968.

Henry, Paul, *An Irish Portrait: The Autobiography of Paul Henry* (with a Foreword by Seán Ó Faoláin). B.T. Batsford, London, 1988.

Hickson, Mary, *Ireland in the Seventeenth Century or the Irish Massacres of*

1641-1642, their Causes and Results, Vols. I and II. Longmans, Green & Co, London, 1884.

Higgins, John, *Kiltimagh Renewal: Best Practice in Community Enterprise.* Oak Tree Press, Dublin, 1996.

Hill, Judith, *Irish Public Sculpture: A History.* Four Courts Press, Dublin, 1998.

Hone, Joseph, *The Moores of Moore Hall.* Carra Historical Society, London, 1939.

Hone, Joseph, *The Life of George Moore.* Victor Gollancz, London, 1936.

Howard, John Eliot, *'The Island of Saints' or Ireland in 1855.* Seeleys, London, 1855.

Hughes, Harry, *Croagh Patrick (Cruach Phadraig - The Reek): An Ancient Mountain Pilgrimage.* Harry Hughes, Westport, 1991.

Hutchinson, John, *James Arthur O'Connor.* National Gallery of Ireland, Dublin, 1985.

Hyde, Douglas, *Songs ascribed to Raftery (Abhráin atá Leagtha ar an Reachtúire).* Irish University Press, Shannon, 1903.

Inglis, Henry D., *A Journey Throughout Ireland During the Spring, Summer and Autumn of 1834, Vols. I and II.* Whittaker, London, 1835.

Jackson, Rev. J., *The Basking Shark. How it is Caught by Net on Achill Island, Co. Mayo, Ireland.* Galway (no publisher details available).

Jordan, Donald E., *Land and Popular Politics in Ireland: County Mayo from the Plantation to the Land War.* Cambridge University Press, Cambridge, 1994.

Keane, Maureen, *Ishbel: Lady Aberdeen in Ireland.* Colourpoint Books, Newtownards, 1999.

Kelly, Tom, *Boots, Rules and Fantasy Free: A History of Mayo Football.* Association Football League, Castlebar, 1996.

Kiltimagh Historical Society, *Seán Thomas Lavan 1898-1973: Teacher, Surgeon, Footballer, Olympic Athlete.* Kiltimagh Historical Society, Kiltimagh, 1996.

Kingston, Bob, *Achill Island: The Deserted Village at Slievemore.* Kingston, Achill, 1990.

Knight, Patrick, *Erris in the Irish Highlands and the Atlantic Railway.* Martin Keane & Son, Dublin, 1836.

Lalor, Brian, *The Irish Round Tower.* Collins Press, Cork, 1999.

Langan-Egan, Maureen, *Women in Mayo 1821-1851: A Historical Perspective.* University College, Galway, 1986 (thesis submitted).

Lavelle, Rev. Patrick, *The Irish Landlord since the Revolution.* W.B. Kelly, Dublin, 1870.

Lavelle, Thomas, 'The County of Mayo' in *The Oxford Book of English Verse*, A.T. Quiller-Couch (Ed.). Clarendon Press, Oxford, 1919.

Leavy, Una and Leavy, Lorcan, *Wildflowers of Clooncouse, Co. Mayo: Wildlife's Salute to the New Millennium.* Charlestown, 1999 (self-published).

Lewis, Samuel, *A Topographical Dictionary of Ireland Comprising of the Several Counties, Cities, Corporate, Market, and Post Towns, Parishes and Villages, with Historical and Statistical Descriptions, Vols. I and II.* S. Lewis & Co, London, 1837.

Life and Times of George Robert Fitzgerald Commonly Called Fighting Fitzgerald. James McGlashan, Dublin, 1852.

Lindsay, Patrick J., *Memories*. Blackwater Press, Dublin, 1992.

Litton, Helen, *The Irish Famine: An Illustrated History*. Wolfhound Press, Dublin, 1994.

Lohan, Rena, *Guide to the Archives of the Office of Public Works*. Stationery Press, Dublin, 1994.

Lynd, Robert, *Rambles in Ireland*. Mills & Boon, London, 1918.

MacCarron, Donal, *Wings Over Ireland: The Story of the Irish Air Corps*. Midland Publishing Ltd, Leicester, 1996.

MacDonnell, Eneas, *The Hermit of Glenconella*. G. Cowie, London, 1820.

MacEoin, Uinseann, *Survivors*. Argenta, Dublin, 1980.

Mangan, James Clarence, 'Farewell to Patrick Sarsfield' in *Anthology of Irish Verse*, Pádraic Colum (Ed.). Boni & Liveright, New York, 1922.

Mangan, James Clarence, 'A vision of Connaught in the thirteenth century' in *The poetry and song of Ireland*, John Boyle O'Reilly (Ed.). Home University League, New York, 1898.

Maxwell, W.H., *Wild Sports of the West: Interspersed with Legendary Tales and Local Sketches*. Phoenix Publishing Company, Dublin, 1832.

Mayo County Council, *Comhairle Chontae Mhaigh Eo: A Commemorative Guide*. Comhairle Chontae Mhaigh Eo (Mayo County Council), Castlebar, l989.

McCalmont, Rose E., *Memoirs of the Binghams*. Spottiswoode & Co, London, 1915.

McDermott, Joe, *Public Spirited People, Mayo County Council 1899-1999*. Comhairle Chontae Mhaigh Eo (Mayo County Council), Castlebar, 1999.

McDermott, Joe, *St. Mary's Hospital, Castlebar: Serving Mayo Mental Health from 1866*. Western Health Board, Castlebar, 1999.

McDermott, Joe and Chapman, Robert, *County Mayo, Bealach Béal Easa – The Foxford Way*. Comhairle Chontae Mhaigh Eo (Mayo County Council), Castlebar, 1995.

McDermott, Joe and Chapman, Robert, *County Mayo, The Western Way – Slí an Iarthair*. Comhairle Chontae Mhaigh Eo (Mayo County Council), Castlebar, 1993.

McDermott, Joe and Chapman, Robert, *County Mayo, The Bangor Trail*. Comhairle Chontae Mhaigh Eo (Mayo County Council), Castlebar, 1992.

McDonald, Theresa, *Achill Island [Archaeology - History - Folklore]*. IAS Publications, Tullamore, 1997.

McNally, Kenneth, *The Islands of Ireland*. B.T. Batsford, London, 1978.

McNally, Kenneth, *The Sun-Fish Hunt*. Blackstaff Press, Belfast, 1976.

McNally, Kenneth, *Achill*. David & Charles, Newton Abbot, 1973.

McParlan, James, *A Statistical Survey of the County of Mayo*. The Dublin Society, Dublin, 1802.

Micks, William L., *An Account of the Constitution, Administration and Dissolution of the Congested Districts Board for Ireland from 1891 to 1923*. Eason & Son, Dublin, 1925.

Moody, T.W., *Davitt and Irish Revolution: 1846-82*. Clarendon Press, Oxford, 1981.

Moore, George Augustus, *The Lake*. William Heinemann, London, 1905.

Moore, George Augustus, *Hail & Farewell*. William Heinemann, London, 1925. Originally published in 3 volumes, as *Ave* (1911), *Salve* (1912) and *Vale* (1914).

Moore, Maurice George, *An Irish Gentleman: George Henry Moore*. T. Werner Laurie Ltd, London, 1913.

Morahan, Leo, *Croagh Patrick, Co. Mayo: Archaeology, Landscape and People*. Croagh Patrick Archaeology Society, Westport, 2001.

Moran, Gerard, *Radical Irish Priests, 1660-1970*. Four Courts Press, Dublin, 1998.

Moran, Gerard, *A Radical Priest in Mayo. Fr. Patrick Lavelle: The Rise and Fall of an Irish Nationalist, 1825-86*. Four Courts Press, Dublin, 1994.

Morrissey, James, *On the Verge of Want: A Unique Insight to Living Conditions along Ireland's Western Seaboard in the Late 19th Century*. Crannóg Books, Dublin, 2001.

Mulloy, Bridie, *Itchy Feet and Thirsty Work: A Guide to the History and Folklore of Ballinrobe*. Lough Carra and Lough Mask Tourist Development Association, Ballinrobe, 1990.

Myers, Michael, *Wanderings in Ireland*. Knickerbocker Press, London, 1908.

Myler, Patrick, *Gentleman Jim Corbett: The Truth Behind a Boxing Legend*. Robson Books, London, 1998.

Newman, Edward, *Notes on Natural History, More Especially Ferns*. John Van Voorst, London, 1840.

Ní Cheanainn, Áine, *The Heritage of Mayo*. The Western People, Ballina, 1982.

Nicholson, Asenath, *Lights and Shades of Ireland: Annals of the Famine of 1847, 1848 and 1849*. E. French, New York, 1851.

Nolan, Rita, *Within the Mullet*. Belmullet, 1997 (self-published).

Nolan, William, *Tracing the Past: Source for Local Studies in the Republic of Ireland*. Geography Publications, Dublin, 1982.

Noone, Rev. Seán, *Where the Sun Sets: Ballycroy, Belmullet, Kilcommon, & Kiltane, County Mayo*. Erris Publications, Naas, 1991.

Ó Baoighill, Pádraig, *Nally as Maigh Eo*. Coiscéim, Dublin, 1998.

Ó Brádaigh, Ruairí, *Dílseacht: The Story of Comdt. Gen. Tom Maguire and the Second (All-Ireland) Dáil*. Irish Freedom Press, Dublin, 1997.

O'Brien, Mrs. William, *My Irish Friends*. Burns, Oates & Washbourne, Dublin, 1937.

O'Brien, Mrs. William, *Under Croagh Patrick*. John Long, London, 1904.

Ó Caiside, Tomás, *An Caisideach Bán: The Songs and Adventures of Tomás Ó Caiside*, translated from Irish by Adrian Kenny. Greensprint, Ballyhaunis, 1993.

Ó Cuimin, Pádraig, *The Baronial Lines of the Midland Great Western Railway: The Loughrea and Attymon Light Railway, the Ballinrobe and Claremorris Light Railway*. Transport Research Association, Dublin, 1972.

O'Donovan, John (Ed.), *Letters Relating to the Antiquities of the County of*

Mayo (Ordnance Survey Letters), Vols. I and II (mimeographical edition). Bray, 1929.

O'Donnell, Peadar, *The Bothy Fire and All That: With a Reprint of Article on Arranmore Disaster from the 'Irish Press'*. Irish People Publications, Dublin, 1937.

O'Dwyer, Paul, *Counsel for the Defense*. Simon & Schuster, New York, 1979.

O'Flaherty, Roderick, *A Chorographical Description of West or h-Iar Connaught, written in 1684*. Irish Archaeological Society, Dublin, reprinted 1846.

O'Flaherty, Roderick, *Ogygia*. W. M'Kenzie, Dublin, 1793.

Ó Floinn, Críostóir, *Blind Raftery: Selected Poems*. Clo-Lar Chonnachta, Indreabhán, Galway, 1998.

Ó Gadhra, Nollaig, *Civil War in Connacht, 1922-1923*. Mercier Press, Cork, 1999.

O'Hara, Bernard, *The Archaeological Heritage of Kilasser, Co. Mayo*. Research and Development Unit, Regional Technical College, Galway, 1991.

O'Hara, Bernard, *Michael Davitt Remembered*. Michael Davitt National Memorial Association, Straide, 1984.

O'Hara, Bernard (Ed.), *Mayo: Aspects of its heritage*. Archaeological, Historical and Folklore Society, Regional Technical College, Galway, 1982.

Ó hUiginn, Ruairí, *The Year of the French: Songs of 1798*. Ciaráin MacColuain, Dublin, 1983.

O'Keefe, Daniel, *The Story of Knock*. Mercier Press, Cork, 1949.

O'Malley, Ernie, *Raids and Rallies*. Anvil Books, Dublin, 1982.

O'Malley, Ernie, *The Singing Flame*. Anvil Books, Dublin, 1978.

O'Malley, Ernie, *On Another Man's Wound*. Anvil Books, Dublin, 1936.

Ó Moráin, Pádraig, *An tAthair Mánus MacSuibhne: Sagart ó Mhaigh Eo in Éirí Amach 1798* ('Father Manus Sweeney: A Mayo Priest in the Rebellion of 1798'), edited and translated by Sheila Mulloy. Westport Historical Society, Westport, 1999.

O'Sullivan, William (Ed.), *The Strafford Inquisition of County Mayo*. Stationery Office, Dublin, 1958.

Otway, Caesar, *Sketches in Erris and Tyrawly*. William Curry, Dublin, 1841.

Otway, Caesar, *A Tour in Connaught, Comprising Sketches of Clonmacnoise, Joyce Country and Achill*. William Curry, Dublin, 1839.

Padden, Bridie, *History of Attymass*. Attymass, 2000 (self-published).

Pakenham, Thomas, *The Year of Liberty: The Story of the Great Irish Rebellion of 1798*. Hodder & Stoughton, London, 1969.

Parliamentary Gazetteer of Ireland, *Adapted to the New Poor-Law, Franchise, Municipal and Ecclesiastical Arrangements, and Compiled with a Special Reference to the Lies of the Railroad and Land Communications Existing in 1843-44 and Presenting the Results in Detail, of the Census of 1841 compared with that of 1831* (3 volumes). A. Fullarton & Co, Dublin, 1844-46.

Parnell, Anna, *The Tale of a Great Sham*, edited and with an introduction by Dana Hearne. Arlen House, Dublin, 1986.

Patrick the Pilgrim Apostle of Ireland: St Patrick's Confessio and Epistola, edited and translated by Máire B. de Paor. Veritas, Dublin, 1998.

Petty, Sir William, *Hibernia Delineatio: Atlas of Ireland, 1685*. Frank Graham, Newcastle-upon-Tyne, reprinted 1968.

Pococke, Richard, *Pococke's Tour in Ireland in 1752*, edited and with an introduction and notes by George T. Stokes. Irish Academic Press, Dublin, 1891.

Poirteir, Cathal, *Famine Echoes*. Gill & Macmillan, Dublin, 1995.

Praeger, Robert Lloyd, *The Way that I Went: An Irishman in Ireland*. Collins, Cork, reprinted 1997.

Praeger, Robert Lloyd, *The Botanist in Ireland*. Hodges Figgis, Dublin, 1934.

Praeger, Robert Lloyd, *A Tourist's Flora of the West of Ireland*. Hodges, Figgis & Co, Dublin, 1909.

Quinn, J.F., *History of Mayo* (5 volumes). Brendan Quinn, Ballina, 1993 (Vols. 1 and 2), 1996 (Vol. 3), 2000 (Vol. 4), 2002 (Vol. 5).

Redmond, D.B., OSA, *The Augustinian Abbey of St. Mary the Virgin, Ballyhaunis, 1348-1948: An Historical Sketch*. Good Counsel Press, Dublin, 1948.

Reilly, Terry, *Dear Old Ballina*. The Western People, Ballina, 1993.

Reilly, Terry, *The Goal of Victory – History of Ballina Stephenites (1886-1986)*. The Western People, Ballina, 1986.

Reilly, Terry and Neill, Ivan, *The Green above the Red: A Compilation of Mayo's Greatest Football Triumphs*. The Western People, Ballina, 1985.

Seddall, Henry, *Edward Nangle: The Apostle of Achill, a memoir and a history*. Hatchards, London, 1884.

Shand, Alexander Innes, *Letters from the West of Ireland, 1884*. William Blackwood & Sons, Edinburgh, 1885.

Shepherd, Ernie, *The Midland Great Western Railway of Ireland: An Illustrated History*. Midland Publishing Ltd, Leicester, 1994.

Sheridan Memorial Community Centre, *The Martin Sheridan Story*. Bohola, 1998.

Simington, Robert C., *The Transplantation to Connacht, 1654-58*. Irish Manuscripts Commission, Shannon, 1970.

Simington, Robert C., *Books of Survey and Distribution being Abstracts of Various Surveys and Instruments of Title, 1636-1703. Vol. II: County of Mayo*. Stationery Office, Dublin, 1956.

Solan, Betty and Sobolewski, Peter (Eds.), *Kiltimagh: Our Life and Times*. Kiltimagh Historical Society, Kiltimagh, 1996.

Somerville-Large, Peter, *Ireland's Islands: Landscape, Life and Legends*. Gill & Macmillan, Dublin, 1999.

Stock, Joseph, *A Narrative of What Passed at Killala, in the County of Mayo, and the Parts Adjacent, During the French Invasion in the Summer of 1798*. R.E. Mercier, London, 1800.

Stone, J. Harris, *Connemara and the Neighbouring Spots of Beauty and Interest*. Health Resort Publishing Company, London, 1906.

Swords, Liam, *A Hidden Church: The Diocese of Achonry 1698-1818*. Columba Press, Dublin, 1997.

Synge, John Millington, *In Wicklow, West Kerry and Connemara: With drawings by Jack B. Yeats,* Articles reprinted from *The Manchester Guardia*n and *The Shanachie.* Maunsel, Dublin, 1911.

Taylor, George and Skinner, Andrew, *Maps of the Roads of Ireland* (facsimile of the second edition, 1783). Irish University Press, Shannon, reprinted 1969.

Thackeray, William M., *The Irish Sketch Book: 1842.* Chapman & Hall, London, 1843.

Timony, Michael (Ed.), *Red Brian Carabine's Prophesy and other Interesting Historical Matters, Part 1.* M.H. Gill & Son, Dublin, 1906.

Tuke, James Hack, *Irish Distress and its Remedies: A visit to Donegal and Connaught in the Spring of 1880.* Ridgway, London, 1880.

Tunney, Gene, *Arms for Living.* Wilfred Funk, New York, 1941.

Viney, Michael, *Another Life.* The Irish Times, Dublin, 1979.

Wadell, John, *The Prehistoric Archaeology of Ireland.* Galway University Press, Galway, 1998.

Waldron, Jarlath, *Maamtrasna: The Murders and the Mystery.* Edmund Burke, Dublin, 1992.

Waldron, Kieran, *Sancta Maria College, Louisburgh: The Story of Ireland's First Catholic Co-Educational Secondary School.* Louisburgh, 1986.

Weld, Charles Richard, *Vacations in Ireland.* Longman, Brown, Green, Longmans & Roberts, London, 1857.

White, T.H., *The Godstone and the Blackymor.* Jonathan Cape, London, 1959.

Wilde, Sir William Robert, *Wilde's Loch Corrib, its Shores and Islands with Notices of Lough Measga,* Fourth edition abridged and edited by Colin O'Lochlainn. Three Candles, Dublin, 1955.

Williams, Jeremy, *A Companion Guide to Architecture in Ireland, 1837-1921.* Irish Academic Press, Dublin, 1994.

Yeats, William Butler, *Cathleen Ní Houlihan.* A.H. Bullen, London, 1902.

Yeats, William Butler, 'Easter 1916' in *Michael Robartes and the dancer.* Cuala Press, Dublin, 1920.

Young, Arthur, *A Tour in Ireland: With General Observations on the Present State of that Kingdom made in the Years 1776, 1777 and 1778,* Constantina Maxwell (Ed.). Cambridge University Press, Cambridge, 1925.

Picture Credits

The following abbreviations are used for the most frequently mentioned picture sources: **CUCAP** = Cambridge University Collection Air Photographs; **D** = Dúchas; **MCC** = Mayo County Council; **MCL** = Mayo County Library; **MN** = Mayo Naturally; **NGI** = National Gallery of Ireland; **NLI** = National Library of Ireland; **NMI** = National Museum of Ireland; **RIA** = Royal Irish Academy; **RTE** = Radió Telefís Éireann; **TCD** = Trinity College, Dublin; **UM** = Ulster Museum; **WPC** = Wynne Private Collection, Castlebar.

Where there are several pictures on a page, the following abbreviations, or combinations of, are used to denote position: **L** = left; **M** = middle; **R** = right; **T** = top; **TL** = top left; **TM** = top middle; **TR** = top right; **B** = bottom; **BL** = bottom left; **BR** = bottom right.

Chapter 1: A People and a Place

Frontispiece (foldout map) = MN; **p. 3**: T = MCL, Map Collection, B = MCC; **p. 4**: T = NLI, Charles R. Browne Collection, B = NLI, Prints and Drawings, R. 22,147; **p. 5** = Angela Campbell; **p. 7** = Liam Lyons; **p. 8** = Liam Lyons; **p. 9** = UM, 'The Road to the West' by John Luke, © Neville McKee; **p. 10** = CUCAP, ASY 21; **p. 11** = MCL, Map Collection; **p. 12**: T = Wendy Walsh, B = Wendy Walsh; **p. 13**: T = Wendy Walsh, B = Angela Campbell; **p. 14**: T = Liam Lyons, B = Angela Campbell; **p. 15** = Liam Lyons; **p. 16**: T = MCC, Architects' Department, B = Liam Lyons; **p. 17** = Liam Lyons; **p. 18** = Angela Campbell; **p. 19** = NGI, 20,438; **p. 20**: T = Liam Lyons, M = Liam Lyons, B = Liam Lyons; **p. 21** = Liam Lyons; **p. 22**: L = Simon Berrow, R = Jeremy Stafford-Deitsch; **p. 23**: T = MCL, Map Collection, B = Liam Lyons; **p. 24**: T = Bord Fáilte, M74/35, M = MCC, Architects' Department, B = MCC, Architects' Department; **p. 25** = Brian Holmes; **p. 26** = Liam Lyons; **p. 27** = Liam Lyons; **p. 28** = MCL, Map Collection; **p. 29** = Tom Campbell; **p. 30**: T = Angela Campbell, B = Lorcan Leavy; **p. 31** = Angela Campbell.

Chapter 2: People and Politics

Frontispiece = Department of Foreign Affairs; **p. 34**: T = Dúchas, M = Noel O'Neill, B = Dúchas; **p. 35**: T = NMI, B = Dúchas; **p. 36**: T = Dúchas, M = NMI, B = M.E. Robinson, University of Manchester; **p. 37**: T = Gerry Walsh, B = Dúchas; **p. 38** = UM, 'The Children of Lir' by Wilhelmina Geddes, © Mrs. J. Kerr, London; **p. 39** = MCC, Architects' Department; **p. 40** = Chris Corlett; **p. 41**: TL = Dúchas, TM = Michael Murphy, TR = Michael Murphy, B = Liam Lyons; **p. 42**: T = TCD, Board of Trustees, Ms. 1440; **p. 43** = Dúchas; **p. 44** = Dúchas; **p. 46**: T = NLI, R. 14,189, B = NGI, 11,037; **p. 47** = MCL, Map Collection (courtesy of De Burca Rare Books); **p. 48** = TCD, Board of Trustees, Ms. 1440; **p. 49**: T = Coiste an Asgard, B = RIA; **p. 50**: T = Bord Fáilte, M52/61, B = NGI, 3830, © Michael Yeats; **p. 51** = Angela Campbell; **p. 52** = NGI, 249 (after Samuel Cooper); **p. 53** = MCL, Map Collection (from *Hibernia Delineatio*, 1685); **p. 54**: TL = NLI, TR = NGI, 4010, M = NLI, B = NLI; **p. 55** = NGI, 1772; **p. 56** = Bord Fáilte, M46/57; **p. 57**: L = RTE Library, R = Bord Fáilte, M5/48; **p. 58**: L = Angela Campbell, R = WPC, © Gary Wynne; **p. 59**: T = NLI, Prints and Drawings (from John Barrow, *A Tour around Ireland*, London, 1836), M = Liam Lyons; **p. 60**: T = Angela Campbell, B = MCL, Photograph Collection; **p. 61** = Angela Campbell; **p. 62** = Angela Campbell; **p. 63** = Maps reproduced from the Ordnance Survey of Ireland material, © Government of Ireland, Permit No. MP004200; **p. 64** = MCL, Newspaper Collection; **p. 65**: T = Kiltimagh Museum, M = MCL, Newspaper Collection, B = MCL, Newspaper Collection; **p. 66** = MCL, Newspaper Collection; **p. 67**: T = WPC, © Gary Wynne, B = NLI, MS Collection; **p. 68**: T = NLI, Prints and Drawings, B = NLI; **p. 69** = WPC, © Gary Wynne; **p. 70**: T = J.J. Leonard, © Anthony Leonard, Ballisodare, Co. Sligo, B = Clew Bay Heritage Centre; **p. 71** = Kilmainham Gaol and Museum; **p. 72** = WPC, © Gary Wynne; **p. 73**: T = Tricia Forde, © Knock Folk Museum, B = WPC, © Gary Wynne; **p. 74** = Edward Weston, courtesy of Collection Center for Creative Photography, University of Arizona, © 1981 Arizona Board of Regents; **p. 75** = J.J. Leonard, © Anthony Leonard, Ballisodare, Co. Sligo; **p. 76**: T = J.J. Leonard, © Anthony Leonard, Ballisodare, Co. Sligo, M = Liam Lyons, B = Willie Sammon; **p. 77** = NLI, Ms. 11,122; **p. 78** = J.J. Leonard, © Anthony Leonard, Ballisodare, Co. Sligo; **p. 79** = Richard Gillespie; **p. 80**: L = Garda Museum and Staines Family, R = MCC, Architects' Department; **p. 82** = Fr. Browne, SJ, Collection; **p. 83** = Liam Lyons; **p. 84** = Tom Campbell; **p. 89** = Liam Lyons; **p. 90** = University College, Galway; **p. 91** = MCC.

Chapter 3: Religion and Pilgrimage

Frontispiece = Angela Campbell; **p. 94** = Angela Campbell; **p. 96** = Liam Lyons; **p. 97** = CUCAP, AVM 83; **p. 98**: L = Angela Campbell, R = Dúchas; **p. 99**: T = Gerry Bracken, B = Angela Campbell; **p. 100**: T = Tricia Forde, BL = Tricia Forde, BR = Angela Campbell; **p. 101**: L = Dúchas, TR = Dúchas, BR = Dúchas;

p. 102 = Angela Campbell; **p. 103**: T = NMI, B = Dúchas; **p. 104**: T = Dúchas, B = MCL, Postcard Collection ('Cong' by Mason Photography, Dublin); **p. 105**: L = Angela Campbell, R = Dúchas; **p. 106** = Edwin Smith; **p. 107** = Dúchas; **p. 108** = Dúchas; **p. 109** = Angela Campbell; **p. 110**: T = NMI, B = Micheál Murphy; **p. 111**: L = NLI, Prints and Drawings, TA1496, R = Liam Lyons; **p. 112**: TL = Angela Campbell; BL = NLI, MS Collection, D3236, R = NLI, MS Collection, D3236; **p. 113**: L = NLI, Charles R. Browne Collection, R. 27,604, R = NMI, Folklife Collection; **p. 114**: L = MCL, Newspaper Collection, R = Angela Campbell; **p. 115**: L = NLI, Lawrence Collection, R = WPC, © Gary Wynne; **p. 116** = NLI, Prints and Drawings, 1493TA; **p. 117**: L = WPC, © Gary Wynne, TR = Liam Lyons, BR = NLI, Lawrence Collection, 6033; **p. 118**: L = Angela Campbell, R = Angela Campbell; **p. 119** = NGI, 10,050 (mezzotint after Hugh Douglas Hamilton); **p. 120**: TL = Fr. Browne, SJ, Collection, TR = WPC, © Gary Wynne, B = Angela Campbell; **p. 121**: T = Foxford Resources, B = Angela Campbell; **p. 122** = Knock Shrine; **p. 123** = WPC, © Gary Wynne; **p. 124**: T = Tom Campbell, B = Tom Campbell; **p. 125**: T = Bord Fáilte, RL1/66, B = Bord Fáilte, RL19/56; **p. 126** = Gerry Bracken; **p. 127**: T = WPC, © Gary Wynne, B = Gerry Walsh.

Chapter 4: Landed Gentry

Frontispiece = Angela Campbell; **p. 130** = Westport House Estate; **p. 132**: L = NGI, 10,177 (mezzotint possibly by John Opie or W. Whiston Barney), R = Liam Lyons; **p. 133** = Bord Fáilte, M77/52; **p. 134**: L = Liam Lyons, R = Bord Fáilte, M4/63; **p. 135** = Bord Fáilte, M35/62; **p. 136** = NGI, 873; **p. 137** = Angela Campbell; **p. 138**: TL = Bord Fáilte, M46/57, TR = WPC, © Gary Wynne, B = WPC, © Gary Wynne; **p. 139** = Angela Campbell; **p. 140** (all photographs) = NMI, © Royal Ontario Museum Collection; **p. 142** = Richard Green Galleries, London; **p. 143** = WPC, © Gary Wynne; **p. 144** = WPC, © Gary Wynne; **p. 145** = MN; **p. 146**: T = NLI, Lawrence Collection, B = Martin McGarrigle; **p. 147**: L = WPC, © Gary Wynne, TR = Liam Lyons, BR = NLI, Lawrence Collection.

Chapter 5: Farming the Land

Frontispiece = Angela Campbell; **p. 150** = Fr. Browne, SJ, Collection; **p. 151** = MCL, Postcard Collection; **p. 152** = An Post; **p. 153** = Leo Morahan; **p. 154** = Angela Campbell; **p. 155** = Gerry Bracken; **p. 156** = NLI, R. 27,254 (from John Eliot Howard, *'The Island of Saints or Ireland in 1855'*, London, 1855); **p. 157** = CUCAP, ALO 13; **p. 158**: L = Bord Fáilte, M114/48, R = NLI, R. 6064; **p. 159**: L = MCL, Newspaper Collection, R =NMI; **p. 160** = WPC, © Gary Wynne; **p. 161** = NLI, Charles R. Browne Collection, R. 27,596; **p. 162** = NLI, Prints and Drawings; **p. 163**: T = WPC, © Gary Wynne, B = NLI, Prints and Drawings;

p. 164 = J.J. Leonard, © Anthony Leonard, Ballisodare, Co. Sligo; **p. 165** = CUCAP, ALN 78; **p. 166**: T = Fr. Browne, SJ, Collection, B = Angela Campbell; **p. 167** = Limerick Art Gallery; **p. 168** = NGI; **p. 169** = An Post; **p. 170**: TL = Bord Fáilte, M1/48, TR = NLI, R. 27,607, B = WPC, © Gary Wynne; **p. 171**: L = MN, R = Angela Campbell; **p. 172**: L = Bord Fáilte, TY81, R = Fr. Browne, SJ, Collection; **p. 173** = WPC, © Gary Wynne; **p. 174**: T = Tricia Forde, B = MCL, Newspaper Collection; **p. 175**: L = Fr. Browne, SJ, Collection, R = Angela Campbell; **p. 176** = NGI, 4082; **p. 177** = Fr. Browne, SJ, Collection; **p. 178**: TL = Martin McGarrigle, TR = Tom Campbell, B = Bord Fáilte, TY194; **p. 179** = J.J. Leonard, © Anthony Leonard, Ballisodare, Co. Sligo; **p. 180**: L = Angela Campbell, R = NMI; **p. 181** = Angela Campbell.

Chapter 6: Transport and Communications

Frontispiece = NLI; **p. 184** = Angela Campbell; **p. 185** = George Taylor and Andrew Skinner (from *Maps of the roads of Ireland*, London, 1778); **p. 186**: L = Yutta Kirrkamm (artist), R = NLI, R. 27,606; **p. 187** = J.J. Leonard, © Anthony Leonard, Ballisodare, Co. Sligo; **p. 188**: TL = NLI, Prints and Drawings (from John Barrow, *A Tour around Ireland*, London, 1836), TR = MCL, Photograph Collection, B = Mark Adams, Sotheby's, London, © Michael Yeats; **p. 189** = WPC, © Gary Wynne; **p. 190**: T = WPC, © Gary Wynne, B = John D. Clark; **p. 191**: L = Bord Fáilte, M1/46, R = Tom Campbell; **p. 192**: TL = John D. Clark, BL = John D. Clark, R = Martin McGarrigle; **p. 193**: T = Liam Lyons, B = NGI, 20,435 (steel engraving by W.H. Bartlett/H. Advard); **p. 194**: T = Eamon De Burca, Postcard Collection, B = Fr. Browne, SJ, Collection; **p. 195**: L = John D. Clark, R = Liam Lyons; **p. 196**: TL = Fr. Browne, SJ, Collection, TR = Fr. Browne, SJ, Collection, B = NLI, Lawrence Collection; **p. 197** = Angela Campbell; **p. 198** = NLI, Lawrence Collection, R. 11,049; **p. 199** = NLI, Imperial 3369; **p. 200** = NLI, Lawrence Collection; **p. 201**: L = Angela Campbell, TR = NLI, Lawrence Collection, 3367, BR = Tricia Forde, © Knock Folk Museum; **p. 202**: T = WPC, © Gary Wynne, B = WPC, © Gary Wynne; **p. 203**: TL = Liam Lyons, TR = Tom Campbell, B = Liam Lyons; **p. 204** = NLI, Prints and Drawings, R. 14,381 (lithograph by A. Fussel); **p. 205** = NLI, Charles R. Browne Collection, R. 27,608; **p. 206**: TL = Joe Mellett, TR = Tom Campbell, B = National Archives, Board of Works Collection; **p. 207**: L = National Archives, Board of Works Collection, R = Mike Walsh, Dangan More, Ballyvary and Texas, USA; **p. 208**: T = Fr. Browne, SJ, Collection, B = Joe Mellett; **p. 209**: TL = Richard Gillespie, TM = Western People, TR = Mayo News, B = Cathal Henry.

Chapter 7: Towns and Services

Frontispiece = Angela Campbell; **p. 212** = George Taylor and Andrew Skinner (from *Maps of the roads of Ireland*, London, 1778); **p. 213** = NLI, Lawrence Collection, 4237; **p. 214**: TL = MCC, Architects' Department, TR = NLI, Lawrence Collection, 1993, B = MN; **p. 215** = NLI, Lawrence Collection, 7404; **p. 216**: T = WPC, © Gary Wynne, B = NLI, Lawrence Collection, 7314; **p. 217** = Martin Waters; **p. 218**: L = MCL, Photograph Collection, R = Martin McGarrigle; **p. 219** = WPC, © Gary Wynne; **p. 220**: T = WPC, © Gary Wynne, B = WPC, © Gary Wynne; **p. 221** = Liam Lyons; **p. 222**: T = NLI, Lawrence Collection, B = NLI, Lawrence Collection; **p. 223** = NLI, Lawrence Collection; **p. 224**: L = NLI, Lawrence Collection, R = NLI, Lawrence Collection; **p. 225** = Joe Mellett; **p. 226** = Joe Mellett, Postcard Collection; **p. 227** = MCL, Map Collection; **p. 228**: T = NLI, Lawrence Collection, B = MCL, Postcard Collection; **p. 229** = WPC, © Gary Wynne; **p. 231**: T = Liam Lyons, B = Fr. Browne, SJ, Collection; **p. 232** = Fr. Browne, SJ, Collection; **p. 233**: T = Fr. Browne, SJ, Collection, B = Liam Lyons; **p. 234**: L = MCC, R = Kiltimagh Museum; **p. 235** = MCL, Map Collection (from Patrick C.E. Knight, *Erris in the Irish Highlands*, Dublin, 1836); **p. 236** = MCC, Architects' Department; **p. 237**: T = WPC, © Gary Wynne, B = Charlestown/Bellaghy and Districts Heritage Society; **p. 238**: T = Liam Lyons, B = Liam Lyons; **p. 240** = Bord Fáilte, RL20/78; **p. 241**: T = Angela Campbell, B = Angela Campbell; **p. 242** = NGI, 3829, © Michael Yeats; **p. 243**: TL = Cathal Henry, TR = Cathal Henry, B = MCC, Architects' Department; **p. 244** = Angela Campbell; **p. 245**: T = WPC, © Gary Wynne, B = WPC, © Gary Wynne; **p. 246**: T = MCC, B = MCC; **p. 247**: T = Liam Lyons, B = MCC; **p. 248** = Eamon O'Boyle; **p. 249** = Frank Dolan.

Chapter 8: Sport

Frontispiece = WPC, © Gary Wynne; **p. 252**: L = MCL, Photograph Collection, R = Western People; **p. 253** = Liam Lyons; **p. 254**: L = An Post, R = MCL, Photograph Collection; **p. 255**: T = Tommy Eibrand, Connaught Telegraph, B = Western People; **p. 256**: T = Western People, B = Western People; **p. 257**: All photographs from Sportsfile, *except* Johnny Carey/Courtesy Carey Family, Joe McGrath/Courtesy Joe McGrath, Willie Joe Padden/Courtesy Padden Family, Jimmy Browne/Courtesy Browne Family, Kevin O'Neill/Courtesy Kevin O'Neill, Pat Fallon/Courtesy Pat Fallon; **p. 258** = Sportsfile; **p. 259** = WPC, © Gary Wynne; **p. 260**: L = Frank Dolan, R = Frank Dolan; **p. 261** = Kiltimagh Museum; **p. 262**: T = Frank Dolan, B = Connaught Telegraph; **p. 263** = Angela Campbell; **p. 264**: T = WPC, © Gary Wynne, B = Connaught Telegraph; **p. 265**: L = Martin McGarrigle, R = Connaught Telegraph; **p. 266** = WPC, © Gary Wynne; **p. 267**: L = Sportsfile, R = Judge John Garavan; **p. 268**: L = Sportsfile, R = WPC, © Gary Wynne; **p. 269** = Liam Lyons; **p. 270**: L = Sportsfile, R = Pat Buckley; **p. 271** = Mayo News Archive; **p. 272**: L = Keith Heneghan, Phocus Photography, R = Liam Lyons; **p. 273**: T = WPC, © Gary Wynne, BL = Liam Lyons, BR = Henry Wills; **p. 274** = MN; **p. 275** = WPC, © Gary Wynne; **p. 276** = Andrew Parkes;

Chapter 9: Education

Chapter 10: Music

Chapter 11: Commerce and Employment

Index